Multiple Award
Schedule Contracting

Multiple Award Schedule Contracting

John W. Chierichella &
Jonathan S. Aronie

To order additional copies of this book, contact:
Xlibris Corporation
1-888-7-XLIBRIS
www.Xlibris.com
Orders@Xlibris.com
24538

DEDICATION

To my Mom and Dad, for the irreplaceable gift of
a happy childhood. To my wife, Shannon,
because . . . . And to my children—Amy, Becky,
Michael, Robert, John and Ruth Anne—who
make my world a beautiful place.

—John W. Chierichella

To Liza, for putting up with too many dinners
alone over the course of this project. This book
could not have been written without your support
and encouragement. And to Jaclyn and Alexis,
proof that I took at least some time off from
writing. I love you all with all my heart.

—Jonathan S. Aronie

FOREWORD

The GSA Multiple Award Schedule Program has evolved over the years from a modest experiment in leveraging the Government's enormous, aggregate purchasing power in the market for commercial products into a procurement vehicle of choice for a multiplicity of goods and services that is administered by a contracting organization that takes a backseat to no one in the federal system. The Program today facilitates the purchase of more than $30 billion in commercial items for virtually all federal agencies. It brings together more than 16,000 contractors, ranging in size from the very large to the very small, covering all socio-economic categories, offering more than 10 million different commercial products and services.

While the MAS Program has faced its share of issues and criticisms over the years, its importance to the federal acquisition community has been demonstrated by its incredible growth, and by the enthusiasm with which buyers and sellers alike have embraced the Program, all without any requirement to use it. This is a testament to the incredible value that it delivers in the marketplace. Notwithstanding OIG reports taking agencies to task for misusing the MAS Program in a manner that avoided competition, GAO reports criticizing MAS contracting officers for failing to achieve fair and reasonable pricing, and Defense Department directives reining in the use of the MAS Program by DOD purchasing activities, the Program has proven to be resilient, flexible and extremely effective.

Its success can be linked to a number of factors. Foremost is the fact that the Program works. It saves federal agencies significant energy, time and money, enabling them to focus on their core missions. Without the MAS Program, federal agencies would need many more contracting officers, would need to invest much more time without significant return on that investment, and would unnecessarily duplicate trivial tasks hundreds of thousands of times per year. The MAS also benefits contractors by transforming traditional Government procurements into something more akin to commercial procurements, and reduces the overhead necessary to provide their products and services to the federal government. And tied into the GSA credit card program, the combination of both innovations has saved billions of dollars in administrative costs per year for federal agencies.

But the success of the MAS Program is not tied only to its ability to save the Government and contractors time and money. The Program is successful also because a number of extremely bright and energetic people have dedicated themselves to making it that way. People like Bill Gormley and Carolyn Alston, early architects of the MAS Program; John Chierichella and Jonathan Aronie, Government contracts legal experts and the co-authors of this book; Ed Naro and Mary Jane Sweeney, industry leaders who helped blaze the MAS trail for others; Roy Chisholm, Robin Bourne and Deborah Lague, champions of the highly successful IT portion of the MAS Program doing their part from within GSA, all are due significant credit for transforming the Program into what it is today.

For three years, I too had the honor of playing a first hand role in the continuing development of the MAS Program. Following my service in the United States Air Force, I joined GSA as the Assistant Commissioner for Commercial Acquisition of the Federal Supply Service. In this capacity, I oversaw the entire MAS Program, in addition to GSA's Government-Wide Acquisition Contracts (GWACs) and its government-wide charge card program. I am proud to say that, under my leadership, the

MAS Program continued to grow and to mature, nearly doubling in sales and number of vendors.

It's recent growth, however, has not been free from pain. During the 2003-2005 timeframe, the utility of the MAS Program has been questioned by some within the Government, most specifically from within the Department of Defense. At the same time, a few high profile allegations of Program misuse have been lodged against procuring agencies and contractors alike, which have prompted Congress and others to take a close, hard look at the MAS Program.

In response to this high level attention, GSA did three things. First, in coordination with DOD, GSA implemented its "Get It Right" campaign. Designed primarily better to educate users and contractors regarding the rules of the MAS Program, the Get It Right campaign involved enhanced training for purchasers, enhanced oversight by auditors, and better guidance for contractors. Second, under the watchful eye of Congress, GSA effected a wholesale restructuring of the Federal Supply Service and its sister service, the Federal Technology Service, into the Federal Acquisition Service. (I discuss this in greater detail later in this book.) Third, GSA initiated an effort to expand the post-award audit rights of the Office of Inspector General.

While all three "innovations" purportedly were intended to secure the future of the MAS Program, their success obviously will be measured only with time.

As it has many times in the past, the MAS Program again stands at a crossroads. Down one path lies continued growth of a healthy and successful Program enhanced by a constructive criticism that values the achievements of the Program and seeks to preserve and enhance its value. Down the other lies the prospect of "reform" that could strip the Program of the widespread utility that has made it such a favorite on both sides of the procurement equation. The struggle of acquisition reform versus overly intrusive oversight lives on, but it is my hope (and my expectation) that Government and industry together will opt for continued growth. Again, time will tell.

In the mean time, contractors must live in the "what is," not the "what may be" state. Unfortunately, the "what is" is not always clear. And as GSA struggles to educate its own people, contractors are often left to figure things out for themselves. Enter this handy book—often referred to as THE roadmap to the MAS Program.

While the GSA publishes several worthwhile guides that provide a useful overview of the MAS Program, I am aware of no guide with the breadth, depth, and practical information of this one. Indeed, in all candor, Multiple Award Schedule Contracting is one of the first books that I read upon joining FSS, and I referred to it regularly throughout my tenure. Since leaving GSA, I have been personally involved in putting together the Second Edition of the book. This book brings together the expertise, experience, and best practices of the country's leading experts from industry, from the Government Contracts bar, and from inside Government. It is truly an indispensable resource.

Whether you are a seasoned veteran or a newcomer to the MAS Program, you will find something in this book for you. So while you may not be of the mind to curl up with a blanket in front of a fire and read the following 600+ pages while sipping a steaming cup of hot chocolate (or even something more bracing), I do recommend that you keep it within arm's reach of your desk. If you are involved in any way with the MAS Program, you will find yourself reaching for it more often than you might think.

Neal Fox
Neal Fox Consulting
Former Assistant Commissioner for Commercial Acquisition,
GSA Federal Supply Service
Washington, DC
December 2005

CONTENTS

QUESTIONS AND COMMENTS

In all projects, there comes a time when one has to stop gathering information and start turning that information into something concrete. In Government contracts, this point in time typically is referred to as the "design freeze." As we knew would be the case, the "design freeze" for this project came about while much information still could be gathered—and much text still could be written. As a concession to the shortness of life, however, we have settled our editorial pens and will save, as Paul Harvey would say, "the rest of the story" for a third edition.

If you are interested in helping us craft the third edition of this book, please forward your comments and suggestions to the address set forth below. (You also can use the address to send us your criticisms and complaints should you have any.) While we do not promise to respond to all letters personally, we will use the letters to determine what new issues should be addressed (or simply expanded upon) in a third edition of this book.

John W. Chierichella or Jonathan S. Aronie

Sheppard, Mullin, Richter & Hampton
1300 I Street, N.W.; Suite 1100
Washington, DC 20005

202-218-0000
jchierichella@sheppardmullin.com or
jaronie@sheppardmullin.com

Additionally, for more information regarding the MAS Program—and for important announcements regarding the contents of this book—log on to our web site at *http://www.schedulecontracts.com.*

NOTICES

- This book provides a general overview of the Multiple Award Schedule Program administered by the General Services Administration. While many of the problems that contractors face are shared by other contractors, every problem also is necessarily unique. Thus, this book should not be used as a substitute for qualified legal advice. Indeed, this book is not intended to, and does not, provide legal advice.
- The views presented in this book are those of the individual contributors. They do not necessarily represent the views of Sheppard, Mullin, Richter & Hampton or its clients. Likewise, the views presented in this book by Government officials do not necessarily represent the views of their respective agencies.
- Due to the constantly changing nature of Government contracting, the information in this book may have changed subsequent to the submission of the manuscript to the publisher in December 2005. Additionally, due to publication deadline constraints, information in the first edition of this book may have changed yet may not have been updated for this edition. Before taking action based upon the information contained herein, readers are strongly encouraged to seek qualified legal advice to ensure the continued accuracy of the subject material.

- The logos and emblems displayed on the cover of this book are the property of, and are used with the permission of, the respective agencies. The use of such logos and emblems shall not suggest approval, sponsorship, endorsement, or any other opinion (positive or negative) regarding this book or its content. Neither the Department of the Navy nor any other component of the Department of Defense has approved, endorsed, or authorized this product.

ABOUT THE AUTHORS

John W. Chierichella is a litigation partner resident in Sheppard, Mullin, Richter & Hampton's Washington, DC office with over 30 years of Government contracts experience. Mr. Chierichella has a broad range of experience in Government contract matters, including GSA Multiple Award Schedule contracting, *qui tam* and other False Claims Act litigation, related internal audits and investigations, prime contractor subcontractor disputes, teaming agreements, claims and appeals, cost recovery issues, foreign military sales, bid protests, and suspension and debarment. He has written numerous articles and lectured extensively on various subjects relating to the federal procurement process, including GSA Multiple Schedule Contracting, false claims, independent research and development, teaming agreements, foreign procurement and foreign ownership, state and local procurement, and the product liability problems of Government contractors. He writes a monthly column for the *Washington Business Journal* on Government Contracting.

Before he entered private practice, Mr. Chierichella served as attorney/advisor to the Secretary, Office of the General Counsel, Department of the Air Force, in the area of procurement law (1973-75). He received his J.D. in 1972 from Columbia Law School, where he was a James Kent Scholar, a Harlan Fiske Stone Scholar, and a member of the *Administrative Board of the Law*

Review; he received his A.B. in 1969 from Cornell University. He is admitted to the bar in the District of Columbia, California, and New York.

Mr. Chierichella has been recognized by the *Legal Times* and *Chambers* as a "leading lawyer" in the area of Government Contracts.

Jonathan S. Aronie also is a partner in the Washington, D.C. office of Sheppard, Mullin, Richter & Hampton. Since graduating from law school in 1993, Mr. Aronie has counseled and represented a diverse collection of large and small clients. His professional experience includes federal procurement counseling and litigation (including extensive work in the area of GSA Multiple Award Schedule contracting); bid protests (classified and unclassified); claim identification, analysis, and resolution; counseling in the areas of defective pricing, export compliance, and commercial item acquisitions; internal audits, reviews, and investigations; and litigation involving the *qui tam* provisions of the False Claims Act. He speaks and writes regularly on the MAS Program, teaches an "Advanced Issues in GSA Schedule Contracting" course for Federal Publications, Inc., and writes a monthly column for *Federal Computer Week* focusing on the federal procurement process.

Mr. Aronie received his J.D. from the Duke University School of Law in 1993 and his B.A. with honors in political science from Brandeis University in 1990. He has been in private practice since his judicial clerkship with the Honorable Patricia A. Wynn, District of Columbia Superior Court in 1993.

Both Mr. Chierichella and Mr. Aronie are cleared at the highest levels and frequently counsel clients in areas relating to national security.

ABOUT THE CONTRIBUTORS

Larry Allen manages and directs the operations of the Coalition for Government Procurement and brings to that post a strong background in Government relations. Mr. Allen's previous positions include Assistant Director of Government Affairs for the National Association of State Universities and Land-Grant Colleges as well as Legislative Assistant to Congressman Alex McMillan of North Carolina, where he covered the Government Operations, Armed Services, and Foreign Affairs Committees. Mr. Allen received his B.A. in Political Science from Emory University and did post-graduate work at American University.

John T. Boese is co-chair of the litigation department in the Washington, DC office of Fried, Frank, Harris, Shriver & Jacobson. Mr. Boese joined the firm in 1977 after five years with the Department of Justice. Mr. Boese concentrates his practice on civil, criminal, and debarment and exclusion cases arising from federal fraud investigations and the development of corporate compliance programs. Mr. Boese is nationally recognized for his knowledge about the Civil False Claims Act and *qui tam* actions. His book, *Civil False Claims and Qui Tam Actions*, originally published in 1993 and updated semiannually, is the leading treatise on this subject and is routinely cited as authority by federal district and appellate courts, as well as by practitioners and academics. He has litigated *qui tam* actions involving many diverse industries, including Government contracts, healthcare, oil and gas, textile imports, insurance, and nuclear energy. Prior to joining Fried Frank, Mr. Boese was a trial attorney with the Civil Division of the U.S. Department of Justice. He received his B.S. from Washington University in 1969 and, in 1972, his J.D., *magna cum laude*, from St. Louis University Law School, where he served as an associate editor of the *Law Journal*.

John Cornell is an attorney with the General Services Administration Office of General Counsel. From 1990 through January 2001, he was head of the litigation group for the GSA Federal Technology Service and Federal Supply Service. He is presently providing legal services to the General Services Administration Chief Information Officer, the Office of Government wide Policy, the Federal Technology Service Office of Information Security, and the ACES program. Mr. Cornell is a 1979 graduate of Michigan State University and a 1983 graduate of the Thomas M. Cooley School of Law. Mr. Cornell actively supports the summer programs of Brighton Woods Girl Scout Day Camp and is a Den Leader in Cub Scout Pack 419.

Cynthia B. Curling is the Electronic Resources Librarian in the Washington, DC office of Fried Frank Harris Shriver & Jacobson and has over ten years of experience working in law libraries. She writes a monthly column, Notes from the Technology Trenches, for the Law Librarian's Resource Exchange (*http://www.LLRX.com*) on legal research, research training, and legal information technology. An occasional contributor to other publications covering information research, she has also spoken at several conferences concerning Internet resources and legal research. She leads the Legal Research Training Focus Group of the Law Librarians' Society of the District of Columbia.

Neal Fox is a consultant to industry on government procurement. He is the former GSA Assistant Commissioner for Commercial Acquisition, Federal Supply Service, serving in that position through July 2005. In this role he managed the GSA Schedules program, the government-wide acquisition contracts (GWACs), the government-wide SmartPay credit card program. He is also a retired Air Force Colonel who spent most of his career in procurement, where he developed, produced and deployed a variety of major systems. His last Air Force assignment was as Director, Information Technology, where he provided the entire Air Force with commercial IT products and services. Mr. Fox has a B.A in Economics from Grove City College, Pennsylvania, and Master of Business Administration and Management from the University of Wyoming. He is also a graduate of the Defense Systems Management College.

William ("Bill") Gormley joined the Washington Management Group in 2000 as Senior Vice President in charge of consulting operations. With extensive experience reengineering the GSA Multiple Award Schedule Program, and as the catalyst for moving the Federal Government to commercial acquisition practices, he is recognized by Government and industry for his enthusiasm, innovation, and professionalism. While serving as Assistant Commissioner for the Office of Acquisition, Federal Supply Service, GSA, he received both the Presidential Rank Award for Meritorious Executives and the Vice President's "Hammer Award" for changes to the Federal Supply Schedule Program. Mr. Gormley is an alumnus of the University of Maryland and a Certified Public Purchasing Official of the National Institute for Government Purchasing, and he has done post-graduate work at Penn State University.

Deborah Lague is the ITAS Division Director with GSA's Federal Supply Service, Information Technology Acquisition Center. Ms. Lague has 12 years experience working with contractors and federal purchasers, negotiating offers, and educating the public generally regarding the benefits of the Multiple Award Schedule Program. She also has played a significant role in the development of the IT Schedule solicitation. Ms. Lague is a graduate of George Mason University.

James J. McCullough is a litigation partner resident in the Washington, DC office of Fried, Frank, Harris, Shriver & Jacobson. Mr. McCullough concentrates his practice on Government contracts law and litigation. His practice includes pre-award litigation and counseling on contract formation issues, post-award disputes and litigation, and representation of Government contractors in various enforcement proceedings, including voluntary disclosure and suspension and debarment matters. Prior to joining Fried Frank, Mr. McCullough served as a trial attorney and assistant to the general counsel in the Office of the General Counsel of the Navy (1976-1979). Mr. McCullough received his J.D. from the University of Virginia School of Law in 1976 and his B.A., *cum laude*, from Villanova University in 1969. He is admitted to the bar in the District of Columbia and Virginia.

Deneen J. Melander is a litigation partner resident in the Washington, DC office of Fried, Frank, Harris, Shriver & Jacobson, where she concentrates on Government contracts law and litigation. In addition to representing clients in bid protests before the United States Government Accountability Office, the United States Court of Federal Claims, and United States district courts, Ms. Melander provides counseling and assistance to clients on contract formation and performance issues, subcontract administration, criminal and civil fraud investigations and litigation, and compliance issues. She writes and lectures regularly on procurement-related topics.

Douglas B. Parker, of Parker, Chaney & Anderson, has over thirty years of experience in Government marketing and relations and is recognized by industry and Government as an expert in his profession. He has represented many corporations and groups to State and Federal Governments. Among them are International Utilities, Pan American World Airways, Mid American Corporation, the Minority Business Development Association, Consolidated Freightways, and Westinghouse Electric Corporation. Mr. Parker has mounted many successful marketing and lobbying campaigns during his career, including Dade County Rapid Transit, Social Security Administration information retrieval, rail and air price supports, road use tax rollbacks, GSA's attempt to scale back the use of Multiple Award Schedules, and GSA's adoption of a broad-based contract for systems furniture and adoption of the "modular" furniture concept. Well versed in marketing and sales, Mr. Parker is very knowledgeable in regulatory procedures, contracting, and procurement law and policy.

Anne B. Perry is a litigation partner in the Washington, DC office of Sheppard, Mullin, Richter & Hampton, concentrating in the area of Government Contracts, on which she has lectured and written extensively. Her broad experience in Government Contracts includes, bid protests before the U.S. Government Accountability Office, and the United States Court of Federal Claims, complex litigation in connection with the False Claims Act, claims litigation before boards of contract appeals, and counseling and litigation in the areas of technical data, appropriations, suspension/debarment, and more. Prior to moving into private practice, Ms. Perry served as a hearing officer for the United States Government Accountability Office (GAO) deciding bid protest cases.

G. Diane Sandford is the Library Director in the Washington, DC office of Fried, Frank, Harris, Shriver and Jacobson, with more than twenty-five years of experience on Capitol Hill and in private law firms. Her background includes extensive Government contracts research in both the FAR and its predecessors as well as the compilation of government contracts legislative histories. She is an experienced writer and editor on legal and administrative issues.

Murray Schooner is the Director of the Supplier Diversity Program for Unisys Corporation. He was formerly Director of Procurement for Unisys Government Systems and has been involved in the corporate small business program and small and minority business legislation since 1979. Mr. Schooner serves on the Board of Directors of the National Minority Supplier Development Council, the Virginia Regional Minority Supplier Development Council, and the Try Us Directory Publications. He is currently the National Co-Chairman of TRIAD, the small business advisory panel to the industry. Mr. Schooner graduated from Boston University with a degree in Business Administration in 1958. He served twenty-one years in the Army and retired as a Lieutenant Colonel. Mr. Schooner received a Masters Degree in Procurement and Contracting from George Washington University. Mr. Schooner and Unisys have been honored with dozens of awards for their work with women and minority-owned businesses.

Mary Jane Sweeney is a Director of Contracts and Pricing at Northrop Grumman. With over twenty years of experience in federal IT contracting, Ms. Sweeney has dealt with all elements of Multiple Award Schedule contracting. Additionally, she has extensive experience handling issues relating to state and local government contracts, commercial contracts, and commercial subcontracts. She actively participates in several IT industry coalitions, including the Coalition for Government Procurement. Ms. Sweeney received her B.S. from the University of Maryland.

Richard J. Wall, CPA, Ernst & Young LLP, is a partner in the Government Contract Services practice of Ernst & Young, operating out of Washington, DC. Mr. Wall is a former U.S. Air Force contracting official who held positions as the Chief of Pricing for the Air Force Systems Command, Air Force representative to the DoD CAS Working Group, and Chairman of the DoD Contract Finance Committee. While at Ernst & Young, he has undertaken a highly visible role in the Government's commercial pricing reforms, such as those adopted under FASA, FARA, and the MAS Improvement Project. He has authored numerous articles on commercial pricing and twice testified on private industry's behalf at hearings sponsored by the Government. Mr. Wall was a principal architect of the Government Electronics and Information

Technology Association petition in 1999 to the Office of Federal Procurement Policy regarding GSA's pricing policies and audit rights on MAS contracts. He is widely recognized for his extensive expertise and experience in MAS contract pricing and has been involved in dozens of voluntary disclosures over pricing matters with the GSA, VA, and DOJ.

John Walsh is an audit manager for the General Services Administration, Office of Inspector General. He has worked for the GSA OIG for the past fourteen years. Mr. Walsh received a B.A. in Accounting from Loras College in Dubuque, Iowa in 1986 and passed the Certified Public Accountant exam in 1987. Currently, Mr. Walsh is a licensed CPA in the state of Missouri.

ACKNOWLEDGEMENTS

This book truly is the product of a collaborative effort. Consequently, there are many people deserving of our heartfelt thanks. In no particular order, we thank the following friends and colleagues: **Mary Jane Sweeney** of Northrop Grumman, whose detailed review of our draft manuscript provided us with unmatched insight into several aspects of the MAS Program; **Alexander Minard**, whose pen and ink drawings enliven several of the pages of this book; **Joseph Pantella**, whose early involvement in this project proved especially helpful; **Beth C. McClain**, whose knowledge of the False Claims Act proved tremendously valuable; **Neal Fox**, former deputy commissioner of the Federal Supply Service, **Robin Bourne** of the GSA FSS IT Acquisition Center, **Skip Duncan** and **Arthur Hackney** of the GSA Furniture Center, **Shaloy Castle Higgens** and **Carole Bastole** of the General Products Center, and **Deborah Harms** of the Facilities and Maintenance Acquisition Center, all of whom provided an essential governmental perspective on the content of this book; **Sabrina Snell** and **Lynn Cartwright**, our student interns for the first edition of this book, whose assistance in putting the finishing touches on the manuscript proved invaluable; and, last, but not least, the management of **Sheppard, Mullin, Richter & Hampton**, whose support allowed this project to succeed.

We also offer our sincere appreciation to those experts who have contributed chapters or subchapters to this book, including our colleague **Anne B. Perry**, whose knowledge of the bid protest process is second to none; **John T. Boese, James J. McCullough, Deneen J. Melander, G. Diane Sandford**, and **Cynthia B. Curling** of Fried, Frank, Harris, Shriver & Jacobson, with whom we have had the pleasure of working for many years; **Richard J. Wall** of Ernst & Young, who also provided significant substantive comments throughout the drafting process; **Larry Allen** of the Coalition for Government Procurement; **William Gormley** of the Washington Management Group; **Deborah Lague** of the GSA FSS IT Acquisition Center; **Douglas B. Parker** of Parker, Anderson, & Chaney; **John Walsh** of the GSA Office of Inspector General; **John Cornell** of the GSA Office of General Counsel; and **Murray Schooner** of Unisys Corporation.

And, finally, a very special thanks goes to **Mary Ferguson**, our former secretary of many years, who tirelessly typed (and retyped) and read (and reread) our manuscript and, without whom, this book never would have found its way to the publisher; to **John Sedlak**, whose ability to make sense out of more than 1,000 endnotes was truly a remarkable feat; to **Lorie Grotos**, who carried the laborious research oar throughout the initial phases of this project; and to **Andrea Rainey** who entered this project late in the game, but who greatly contributed to the final product. Thank you, **Mary, John, Lorie**, and **Andrea**, for your energy, your dedication, and, especially, your patience.

PREFACE

The General Service Administration's Multiple Award Schedule ("MAS") Program has experienced tremendous growth over the past eight years, and all signals indicate that this growth will continue into the future as the Government strives to make Government contracting a more "user-friendly" experience.

Currently, GSA administers approximately 8,000 Schedule contracts (held by approximately 3,000 companies), covering more than 4 million different commercial supplies and services. In FY 2003 alone, the United States purchased more than $27 billion worth of supplies and services through the MAS Program—a $6.3 billion increase from 2002. Gone are the days when Government contracting was a sales avenue open only to the corporate giants of the world. We now operate in an environment where the smallest company has access to the federal marketplace and where a "mom and pop" operation can play in the same ballgame as the Fortune 500.

These changes, however, come with a cost. Government contracting sets traps for the unwary. In 1998, a Department of Justice ("DOJ") press release announced that, in just three years, the Government had recovered $1 billion in False Claim Act awards and settlements against federal contractors. In November 2003, DOJ posted its recovery at $2.1 billion for that year alone. MAS vendors represent a growing percentage of these recoveries.

In fairness, much of this litigation is spawned by the absence of meaningful guidance from the Government. While the MAS Program has been in existence since the 1950s, vendors (and their attorneys) frequently must grope for solutions with little to guide them beyond the missteps of those who came before. While much has been written (and even more has been spoken) about the intricacies of the MAS Program, so far nothing exists that attempts to synthesize the limited and often contradictory guidance that does exist.

Against this background, we offer this book as a roadmap for those who would venture into the world of MAS contracting, as well as for the attorneys who guide them. It is designed, however, as a useful resource for a much wider audience. We wrote this book with the following readers in mind:

- Managers responsible for deciding whether or not to pursue a MAS contract
- Company staff tasked with administering the MAS contract from day to day
- Compliance officers charged with ensuring adherence to all terms and conditions
- Government contracting officers responsible for planning, negotiating, and administering MAS contracts
- Government buyers responsible for procuring the goods and services that enable our country to function, and
- Last, but not least, attorneys—be they advising, negotiating, or defending

We have included in this book material that, we hope, will be as useful to the experienced as it will be to the novice. While this book may not contain all the answers to all the questions asked by all people, it should provide a useful starting place to find the answers—whether the question involves identifying, responding to, or preventing problems.

In drafting this book, we tried to be conscious of the tension that exists between comprehensiveness and user-friendliness. We consciously adopted a middle approach.

With respect to comprehensiveness, we have attempted to address, in some way, the complete range of issues that Schedule vendors and their attorneys typically face. Beginning with

Chapter I, which provides a historical overview of the MAS Program, this book responds to the following questions:

- Should a vendor go on Schedule?
- How does a vendor get on Schedule?
- What does a vendor do once it is on Schedule?
- How does a vendor stay on Schedule?
- What does a vendor do if it finds itself in noncompliance with the terms and conditions of the Schedule?
- Where does a vendor (or its attorney) go to find more information?

We have sought to provide comprehensive—and practical—answers to these (and many other) questions relating to the MAS Program. Additionally, while the case law dealing with MAS contracts is anything but abundant, we have included detailed discussions of all the major cases affecting the MAS Program. Likewise, we have included detailed discussions of all major relevant statutes and regulations, including the Competition in Contracting Act, the Trade Agreements Act, and the Service Contract Act, among others.

With respect to user-friendliness, we have incorporated into this book several features intended to make the material accessible to as wide a range of readers as possible. First and foremost, we have written this book in plain English—something of which, according to Richard Wydick, lawyers often are incapable.[*] We avoid legalese whenever possible, we define terms

---

[*] In his excellent book entitled Plain English for Lawyers, Richard Wydick writes that "[w]e lawyers cannot write plain English. We use eight words to say what could be said in two. We use arcane phrases to express commonplace ideas. Seeking to be precise, we become redundant. Seeking to be cautious, we become verbose. Our sentences twist on, phrase within clause within clause, glazing the eyes and numbing the minds of our readers." Richard C. Wydick, PLAIN ENGLISH FOR LAWYERS 3 (2d ed. 1985). We have endeavored to take Mr. Wydick's message to heart.

of art, and we provide illustrations and examples whenever doing so will help eliminate confusion. Additionally, we have incorporated several special features into this book that we believe further contribute to its user-friendliness:

- Several of the book's chapters include *Advice from the Trenches,* written by individuals experienced on both sides of the MAS Program. These short features provide an inside look at various elements of the MAS Program through veteran eyes.
- Throughout the book, we have referenced useful web sites. Whenever possible, we have provided Internet addresses for readers seeking additional information.
- At the conclusion of the book, we have included a lengthy *Vendor Resource Guide.* This guide—which will be accessible electronically at *http://www.schedule contracts.com*— provides important telephone numbers, consultant information, Internet resources, a helpful bibliography, free e-mail services, and much more.

Additionally, this book includes a comprehensive index that will help you find what you are seeking by topic, term, contract provision, or case name.

These various features, however, would be of little value if they were not built upon a foundation of experience and expertise. The team we have put together to help us write this book delivers that capability:

- Former FSS Assistant Commissioner William ("Bill") Gormley, who currently serves as Senior Vice President of the Washington Management Group, and Larry Allen, Executive Vice President of the Coalition for Government Procurement, provided their expertise in the areas of contract negotiation and contract administration.
- Richard J. Wall of Ernst & Young contributed his storehouse of knowledge relating to MAS pricing.

- John T. Boese, author of the foremost treatise on the False Claims Act, drafted the chapter relating to the False Claims Act's application to the MAS Program.
- James J. McCullough and Deneen J. Melander contributed their years of combined experience in the bid protest arena to the chapter entitled Multiple Award Schedule Protests.
- Annd B. Perry, our partner at Sheppard, Mullin, Richter & Hampton, supplemented the MAS Protest chapter with practical advice derived from her 15+ years as a bid protest expert, first with the GAO as a hearing officer and now with Sheppard Mullin as a partner in the firm's Government Contracts practice group.
- Douglas B. Parker, a partner in Parker, Chaney & Anderson, contributed sections relating to selling and marketing under a MAS contract.

In addition to these primary teammates, as noted above, we also have incorporated the thoughts and opinions of a series of individuals and organizations that work day in and day out with the Government. The organizations from which these contributions have been drawn include Northrop Grumman, Gateway, 3M, CACI, and a number of Government entities. If the quality of this book reflects the quality of this team, we will have generated a tremendously useful product.

Whether you are a vendor, a consultant, a lawyer, or a Government official, there are many different ways to use this book. *First*, this book can be read from start to finish as a primer on the MAS Program—a "welcoming kit," if you will. We recommend this approach to anyone who is new to the MAS Program, whether or not you are new to Government contracting generally. *Second*, this book can be used as a reference guide as questions or problems arise. Just flip through the table of contents or index until you find what you are looking for. *Third*, this book can be used as a critical resource should you (or your client) ever find yourself on the receiving end of a federal audit or investigation. Whatever approach you take, we think that you will find that there is something in here for you.

* * *

As far as we know, this is the only comprehensive treatment of the MAS Program. The MAS Program—like federal procurement law generally—changes rapidly. In the race to keep pace with these changes, we hope only to give our readers a little head start. The rest is up to you.

John W. Chierichella
Jonathan S. Aronie
December 2005
Washington, DC

I.

INTRODUCTION TO MULTIPLE AWARD SCHEDULE CONTRACTING

"You've got to be very careful if you don't know where you're going, because you might not get there."

-Yogi Berra

A. *The MAS Program—What Is It?*

W hen people think of Government contracts, they typically think of items such as aircraft, missiles, and satellites. While these high profile military staples may receive the lion's share of the press time, the Government purchases far more of the other kinds of staples than it does military hardware. Just like any other business, the Government needs staples—and paper, pencils, and paperclips—and it uses a lot more of them than any other business.

In the past, the Government procured commercial items in the same way that it procured military hardware. If it wanted to buy pencils, for example, it would have to plan an acquisition, hold a competition, conduct a source selection evaluation, make a selection decision, and award a contract. Needless to say, over time, as the Government's purchasing needs continued to grow, this acquisition process proved overwhelmingly time-consuming and expensive. Enter the General Services Administration ("GSA").

In the 1950s, the GSA proposed a solution to the Government's purchasing problems—the Federal Supply Schedule Program, also called the Multiple Award Schedule ("MAS") Program. The Federal Acquisition Regulation ("FAR") describes the Federal Supply Schedule Program as follows:

> The Federal Supply Schedule program, pursuant to 41 U.S.C. 259(b)(3)(A), provides Federal agencies with a simplified process of acquiring commonly used supplies and services in varying quantities while obtaining volume discounts. Indefinite-delivery contracts (including requirements contracts) are awarded using competitive procedures to commercial firms. The firms provide supplies and services at stated prices for given periods of time, for delivery within a stated geographic area such as the 48 contiguous states, the District of Columbia, Alaska, Hawaii, and overseas.[1]

Eventually funded through a 1 percent (now ¾ percent) "industrial funding fee" paid to GSA by the agencies that purchase supplies and services through the Program,[2] the MAS Program soon became the Federal Government's commercial item supermarket. Since its creation, the MAS Program has grown tremendously, impelled in no small part by the Government's movement toward purchasing commercial supplies and services instead of Government-unique supplies and services whenever possible. Equally responsible for the growth of the MAS Program, however, is the fact that the Program provides the Government with a simple, cost-effective means of acquiring commercial supplies and services.

GSA touts the MAS Program as providing ordering agencies with the flexibility to select the best value item that meets their needs at the lowest overall cost. Once GSA issues a MAS contract, the buying agencies order directly from the vendor. The agency is relieved of the requirements of developing a statement of work (except when ordering professional services), issuing a Request for Proposals, and conducting a competition, as well as much of the administrative work associated with those requirements. A study conducted by the GSA Federal Supply Service concluded that it takes a Schedule purchaser an average of:

- 49 days to establish a blanket purchase agreement ("BPA")[3] under a GSA schedule;
- 15 days to issue an order under a Schedule contract; and
- 13 days to issue an order under a Schedule contract where a BPA has already been established.[4]

These figures compare to an average of 268 days to put a contract in place by the Federal Government as a whole. (In contrast, the average time for the private sector to put a contract in place is 77 days.[5]) Thus, the MAS Program translates into significant savings for customer agencies in terms of resources and costs.[6]

Through the MAS Program, as outlined in FAR 38.101, GSA awards commercial vendors indefinite-delivery/indefinite-quantity contracts to provide commercial supplies and services to the Federal Government and other authorized users. For any given item, GSA awards *multiple* contracts, hence the term "Multiple Award Schedule." GSA's Information Technology Schedule, for example, includes more than 3,000 different contracts, many of which offer similar products to the Government. Indeed, recently, GSA announced that it would award multiple contracts for identical items as long as the contracting officer determines that the prices are fair and reasonable.[7]

As of September 2005, GSA administered more than 40 Schedules.[8] New Schedules are added routinely. There are Schedules for household and office appliances (Schedule 41 I), for lighting fixtures and lamps (Schedule 62 I), for professional engineering services (Schedule 871), and the list goes on and on. Within each Schedule, supplies and services are categorized by Special Item Numbers. Vendors may join the MAS Program to sell a single item under a single Schedule or multiple items under multiple Schedules as long as GSA determines that the vendor is responsible and the products it offers are priced reasonably.

B. *Interaction Between Purchasers And Sellers*

Once a vendor is awarded a Schedule contract, any "authorized purchaser" may purchase supplies and services from that vendor, for the most part, without additional competition. Because MAS contracts are awarded through "full and open competition," individual purchasers under the MAS Program do not need to undertake additional effort to meet the requirements of the Competition in Contracting Act of 1984 ("CICA").[9] Agencies must, however, comply with certain basic requirements set forth at FAR Part 8.[10]

Notwithstanding the easing of many competitive requirements, however, the procedures for MAS contracting do *not* allow for ad hoc sole source awards.[11] Indeed, several recent court decisions have emphasized the need for agencies to review at least three Schedule price lists (or GSA *Advantage!*) prior to issuing an order to a particular vendor.[12] While agencies may impose some restrictive conditions on their Schedule procurement requirements, they may do so only to the extent necessary to meet their requirements. Restrictions that are imposed but are not necessary to meet the agencies' requirements and that result in a *de facto* sole source will not be allowed.[13]

Once a selection is made, Schedule purchasers issue purchase orders *directly to the vendor*. Notably, the award of a MAS contract does not guarantee sales though the MAS Program (except a $2,500 minimum requirement placed on each contract by GSA to ensure that the contract between it and each vendor meets the "peppercorn" test of consideration and therefore will be binding).[14] Thus, a MAS contract has been described as a "hunting license." A MAS contract simply provides an efficient vehicle for the vendor to approach agencies that might be interested in its supplies and services. While GSA administers each Schedule contract, each ordering agency handles the administration of the delivery orders it issues under the contract.

C. *Who Enters Into MAS Contracts?*

The Federal Government is a huge source of potential business. GSA reports sales through the MAS Program of more than $30 billion annually.[15] While a MAS contract does not guarantee that a vendor will hit a home run every time at bat, it does provide a ticket to the game. For an aggressive vendor that understands the risks inherent in the MAS Program—and takes efforts to mitigate those risks—the potential rewards are significant.

The MAS Program, however, is not for everyone. Indeed, many vendors may be precluded from obtaining a MAS contract for any number of reasons, discussed below.

1. Volume Requirements

GSA requires that at least $25,000 worth of orders be made against a MAS contract each year.[16] If the $25,000 threshold is not met, GSA may not exercise an option or renew the contract. Likewise, GSA has been known to cancel contracts that repeatedly fail to meet this threshold.

2. Product Requirements

The supplies and services offered under the MAS Program must be "commercial." [17] That is to say, they must meet the definition of a "commercial item" set forth at FAR 2.1.[18] In this regard, FAR 2.101 provides that a "commercial item" is

    a. Any item, other than real property, that is of a type customarily used by the general public or by non-governmental entities for purposes other than governmental purposes, and—

        (1) Has been sold, leased, or licensed to the general public; or

        (2) Has been offered for sale, lease, or license to the general public.

Under this definition, a product need not actually have been sold to the general public as long as it has been "offered" to the general public.

Items that are not yet available in the commercial marketplace, but that will be available in time to meet the Government's requirements, constitute commercial items under FAR 2.101. Additionally, commercial items may be modified at the request of the Government (as long as the modification is considered "minor") and still qualify as a "commercial item" under the FAR.[19]

The term "commercial item" also includes commercial services offered in support of a commercial product (*i.e.*, ancillary services) where the source of the services offers such services to the general public and the Federal Government contemporaneously and under similar terms and conditions.[20]

Finally, the term "commercial item" encompasses commercial services that are of a type offered and sold competitively in substantial quantities in the commercial marketplace, the prices of which are based on established catalog or market prices for specific tasks performed under standard commercial terms and conditions.[21] Notably, the FAR specifically excludes from the definition of commercial item stand-alone services based on hourly rates without an established catalog[22] or market price[23] for a specific service performed.[24]

3. Vendor Requirements

Prior to awarding any Schedule contract, GSA makes an affirmative determination regarding the vendor's "responsibility." This determination involves an assessment of a number of factors, including whether the vendor:

- Has adequate financial resources to perform the contract,
- Is able to comply with the required or proposed delivery or performance schedule,
- Has a "satisfactory performance record,"
- Has a "satisfactory record of integrity and business ethics,"
- Possesses the skills and abilities necessary to perform the contract,
- Possesses the facilities and equipment necessary to perform the contract, and
- Is otherwise qualified and eligible to receive an award.[25]

The foregoing factors encompass an assessment of whether the vendor ever has been suspended or debarred from doing business with the Federal Government. Indeed, vendors are required to certify whether they are suspended or debarred or whether they have been suspended or debarred within the three years prior to submission of their proposal.[26] If a vendor answers in the affirmative on the certification, it is required to provide additional information to the contracting officer.[27] Prior to awarding a contract to such a vendor, the awarding contracting officer must notify the agency official responsible for initiating the suspension or debarment action.[28] Failure to execute this certification may result in a determination of nonresponsibility.[29]

As the factors set forth at FAR Subpart 9.1 suggest, however, a responsibility determination involves far more than an assessment of whether the vendor ever has been suspended or debarred. While this always has been the case, the FAR Council recently attempted dramatically to expand the scope of the responsibility determination that GSA must make before awarding a MAS contract.

Specifically, on December 20, 2000, the FAR Council issued a final rule clarifying what constitutes a "satisfactory record of integrity and business ethics" in making vendor responsibility determinations under FAR Part 9.[30] The new rule requires contracting officers to consider a vendor's past compliance with a variety of procurement and non-procurement related laws and permits contracting officers to base a finding of nonresponsibility on the vendor's failure to comply with any of the laws in question.[31] Vendors and some Government agencies strongly opposed these regulations, arguing that they amount to an attempt to "blacklist" vendors based simply on accusations, without regard to the truth of the allegations, the seriousness of the alleged wrongdoing, or the penalties that already may have been incurred for violation of non-procurement laws.[32]

The final contractor responsibility regulations became effective on January 19, 2001 and adopted a majority of the changes initially included in the June 2000 revised draft regulations and incorporated certain additional changes in response to comments received after the revised draft regulations were issued. On April 3, 2001, however, the newly issued rule was stayed for a period of 270 days or until a finalization of the rule is issued, whichever is earlier. The stay was issued in response to the outcry by both industry and Government personnel against the rule as issued.[33] In issuing the stay, the FAR Council cited insufficient time allowed for industry compliance and the possibility of abuse and lack of training for contracting personnel. As of the submission of this manuscript to the publisher, a revised final rule still had not been issued.[34]

D. _Who Purchases From MAS Contracts?_

The MAS Program is open to all executive branch agencies, independent federal agencies, military branches, mixed ownership

Government corporations, and a host of other entities, including the following:

- Government contractors may purchase supplies and services through the MAS Program as long as they have been authorized to do so, in writing, by a federal agency and comply with certain requirements;[35]
- Certain non-federal firefighting organizations may purchase wildfire suppression equipment and supplies through the MAS Program;[36]
- Tribes and tribal organizations are eligible under section 102(13) of Public Law No. 103-413 (the Indian Self-Determination Act Amendments of 1994) when carrying out a contract grant or cooperative agreement under the Indian Self-Determination and Education Assistance Act and when deemed an executive agency for purposes of subsection 201(a) of the Property Act;
- Certain educational institutions, such as Howard University, Gallaudet University, the National Technical Institute for the Deaf, and the American Printing House for the Blind;
- Insular governments, such as the governments of American Samoa, Guam, the Northern Mariana Islands, and the Virgin Islands;
- Entities organized under the Foreign Assistance Act (includes the Red Cross and Presidential authorization of friendly countries and international organizations);
- Non-appropriated fund activities, such as military commissaries (as long as not used for resale); and
- State and local governments engaged in counter-drug activities under the "1122 program."[37]

A detailed list of authorized purchasers is set forth in Appendix III.[38]

In the past, each Schedule identified the executive agencies that were required to use it as a *mandatory* source of supply. An agency listed as a mandatory user had a legal obligation to ascertain whether its requirements could be met by a product or service on the Schedule before soliciting other sources. If the items on the Schedule met the agency's minimum needs, the agency was required to purchase from that Schedule.[39]

Effective for solicitations issued after January 13, 1994 (including Department of Veterans Affairs ("VA") solicitations), mandatory use of most MAS contracts was eliminated.[40] While the concept of "mandatory users" is no longer important, the FAR does establish a priority list for the use of Government supply sources to satisfy an agency's requirements. For example, when procuring services, federal agencies must look to the following sources in the order shown:[41]

- Services available from the Committee for Purchase from People Who Are Blind or Severely Disabled.[42]
- Mandatory Federal Supply Schedules.
- Optional use Federal Supply Schedules.
- Federal Prison Industries, Inc. or commercial sources.

When procuring supplies,[43] agencies must look to these sources in the order shown:

- Agency inventories.
- Excess agency inventories.
- Federal Prison Industries, Inc.
- Products available from the Committee for Purchase from People Who Are Blind or Severely Disabled.[44]
- Wholesale supply sources, such as stock programs of the GSA,[45] the Defense Logistics Agency,[46] the VA,[47] and military inventory control points.
- Mandatory Federal Supply Schedules.
- Optional use Federal Supply Schedules.
- Commercial sources.

* * *

In May 2003, the MAS Program was expanded well beyond its traditional federal user-base to encompass states and localities purchasing information technology products and/or services.[48] Under GSA's "Cooperative Purchasing" program, states and localities now have access to MAS offerings—and prices—available through GSA Schedule 70 (the IT Schedule) contract and through Corporate Schedule contracts containing IT products and services.[49] Vendors take advantage of this program by entering into a bilateral modification with GSA.

The Cooperative Purchasing rules authorize states and local governments (including cities, towns, counties, educational agencies, housing authorities, and tribal governments) to purchase goods and services under the IT Schedule only. Considering that the annual value of the state and local IT marketplace is estimated to be in the neighborhood of $40 billion annually, it is expected that this change will expand dramatically the potential customer base for IT Schedule contractors. In the first two months of the cooperative purchasing program alone, GSA reported $7.5 million in state and local purchases.

Once a MAS Contract has been modified to permit cooperative purchasing, vendors may treat state and local purchasers, for the most part, just like federal purchasers. The following aspects of the program, however, should be kept in mind.

- The program works by transforming each purchase order between a vendor and a state or local buyer into a new contract (to which the United States is *not* a party) every time the vendor voluntarily accepts an order from a state or locality. This new contract then incorporates all of the terms of the Schedule contract except, among a few other provisions, the Disputes Clause. Disputes under the Cooperative Purchasing program between a state or local purchaser and a vendor are resolved by whatever federal *or state* court has jurisdiction over the parties, "applying Federal procurement law . . . ."[50] Thus, in addition to the GSA Board of Contract Appeals, MAS contractors need to be aware that they may be subject to interpretative decisions from a wide variety of state and local courts that may be called upon to interpret the FAR and the GSAR.

- While GSA is not a party to the contract between the vendor and the purchaser, purchasers may not incorporate into their contract any clauses that conflict with the clauses of the MAS Contract. This is a change from the language of the original regulation, which prohibited states and localities from adding *any* terms or conditions at all to the contracts.[51] Nonetheless, the prohibition could create a significant obstacle for states that have laws requiring that certain clauses be incorporated into all state contracts. Presumably, the ordering activity in such a situation would have to choose between finding a way to avoid the application of its state law or foregoing the GSA Schedule as a viable procurement vehicle.

- States and localities are not permitted to place orders through blanket purchase agreements (BPAs) that pre-dated the modification of the MAS Contract to permit cooperative purchasing unless the state or local entity previously was identified as a user of the BPA. The interim rule makes clear, however, that states and localities are allowed to establish their own BPAs under appropriate circumstances.[52]

- Sales to states and localities through the cooperative purchasing program are subject to the Industrial Funding Fee ("IFF") and vendors must include such sales in their quarterly IFF reports.

- It is unclear whether sales to state and local entities at non-standard prices will trigger the Price Reductions Clause. Notwithstanding GSA's intent to put states and localities in the same (or similar) position as federal purchasers, the standard Price Reductions Clause was not modified to exclude state and local buys, as a matter of course, from the category of customers to which discrepant sales will trigger the Clause. Thus, the Clause continues to provide that "There shall be no price reduction for sales . . . to Federal agencies."[53] The Clause does *not* say that there shall be no price reduction for sales to authorized Schedule purchasers. While entities purchasing through the Cooperative Purchasing program should be exempt from the Price Reductions Clause as a matter of sound policy and common sense, until the issue is clarified, vendors would be wise to raise and attempt to resolve the issue with their GSA contracting officer before executing the cooperative purchasing modification. Moreover, even if the issue is formally resolved with GSA, vendors must take care to avoid parallel independent obligations under some specially crafted state or local contract provision.

Many commentators (and contractors) believe that the implementation of cooperative purchasing is long overdue. They tend to agree generally that it is good policy to permit states and localities to take advantage of the Federal Government's negotiating power and to provide contractors access to the massive state and local IT marketplace without requiring them to submit to 50 different procurement regimes. At this time, however, the program covers only IT products and services. An expansion of the program to cover non-IT items would require congressional action.[54]

While Cooperative Purchasing offers an excellent opportunity for vendors, potential offerors also should keep in mind that at least eleven states now have *qui tam* (*i.e.*, whistleblower) laws that provide for treble damages and significant penalties for fraud. Thus, a healthy degree of caution is warranted before signing up to this program. Participation in the cooperative purchasing program is completely voluntary.[55]

* * *

The MAS Program is the procurement vehicle of choice for many Government buyers. It is open to most Government agencies; it is easy to use; it significantly reduces the administrative burdens of traditional Government procurements; and it has grown so much over the past few years that, currently, almost every major purveyor of commercial supplies and services holds one or more Schedule contracts.[56] From the vendor's viewpoint, the MAS Program provides excellent revenue-generating opportunities without many of the burdens of traditional Government contracts.

To better understand the nature of the MAS Program, however, it is useful to understand its origins. Chapter II offers such a historical overview.

Advice From The Trenches

Neal Fox, Neal Fox Consulting
Former Assistant Commissioner for
Commercial Acquisition, GSA FSS

For the vendor that wants to sell commercial products or services to the federal government, a GSA Schedule contract is a must. Government agencies find that the Schedules introduce them to a wide variety of vendors, allow them to procure commercial products and services with minimal effort, and generally make the procurement process faster and easier. As you likely know if you have made it to this point in this book, GSA has been given special authority to run the Schedules program and, in doing so, to streamline the procurement of commercial items. Its success in performing this mission has led to a reliance by government agencies on the GSA Schedules as the procurement vehicle of choice for the purchase of commercial products and services.

GSA, however, has changed over the years, and so has the way vendors interface with that organization. 2005 marked a period of particular change, with the wholesale reorganization of the Federal Supply Service (FSS) and the Federal Technology Service (FTS) into a new organization called the Federal Acquisition Service (FAS). (A third GSA service, the Public Building Service (PBS), was not affected by this reorganization.) Since companies that deal with GSA may be affected by this significant organizational shift—and since I was involved in implementing at least the first stages of this shift—let me explore some of the reasons for the reorganization, and offer some suggestions on how to deal with the new FAS.

The combination of FSS and FTS actually began in 2003, when responsibility for GSA's government-wide acquisition contracts (GWACs), such as Millenia and ANSWER, was transferred from FTS to FSS. While FTS continued to perform assisted services functions, that is continued to place task orders through a variety of GSA procurement vehicles on behalf of its customers, this transfer of responsibility placed responsibility for all Information Technology (IT) contracting in the hands of FSS. Only direct telecom contracting remained with FTS.

Coincident to the transfer, FTS experienced the beginning of a series of embarrassing revelations concerning allegedly inappropriate task order contracting, use of improper procedures, and unauthorized extensions of expired funds. The result of these revelations was a loss of confidence in FTS's capabilities, and an erosion in the FTS customer base. The revelations also hurt FSS's business volume on its GWAC contracts _and_ the IT Schedule, since FTS had been placing significant task orders on behalf of its customer agencies through those vehicles.

The combination of the public spotlight on FTS coupled with increasing customer complaints concerning a lack of service at that organization exacerbated the level of competition already occurring between FTS and FSS. In the shadow of all these events, pressure from the Office of Management and Budget and from Capitol Hill led to a decision to combine the two organizations into one service. Enter FAS.

Although the impetus to combine the services derived from several sources, the overwhelming momentum clearly grew out of a shared desire to stop the competition between the two organizations, which competition was interfering with both organizations' ability to serve their customers. Testimony from GSA before the House Government Reform Committee in 2004 illustrates the point: "A key question to ask is whether customers are confused by the various offerings of FTS and FSS or uncertain regarding which organization to turn to when in need of procurement assistance. Next, we would suggest reducing the overlap and duplication of contract offerings currently available."

So now that the landscape has changed, how do companies that want to sell through GSA's various procurement programs work with the new FAS? It is a complicated answer with several sub-parts. If your company deals only with the Public Building Service, however, nothing has changed for you. Congratulations.

On the other hand, if your company holds a GSA Schedule or a GWAC, or participates in GSA's Global Supply or SmartPay credit card programs, or if your company is highly dependant on GSA assisted services, there are a few things you should know.

The FAS organization changes the nature of and inter-relationship between GSA's (i) contracting and (ii) assisted procurement services. Previously, the two functions were separated within GSA, with FTS performing assisted services for customer agencies and FSS performing direct contracting. In FAS, however, the two are combined, and this has complicated the contracting side of the equation.

The good news is that, if your company has only one or two GSA Schedules or GWACs, and generally only interfaces with its GSA contracting officer for routine matters, then life did not change much for you. GSA did not significantly disrupt operations at the contracting officer level, which means that the interface between a vendor and its contracting officer will remain (for good or for bad) as it has in the past.

But for companies with a large number of Schedules, with contracts that rely heavily on GSA assisted services, or with other needs for higher level interaction with GSA officials, life just got harder. With the Schedules split among various business lines, vendors with many Schedule contracts now must interface with more than one part of GSA in order to have issues redressed and problems solved. This change, while not insurmountable, necessarily will complicate some vendor's relationships with GSA.

All in all, though, even with the birth of FAS and the confusion that birth has caused, vendors will find that dealing with GSA is well worth the investment. Through its many programs, GSA provides the opportunity to reach a broader range of federal customers than otherwise would be possible. That does not mean that every GSA vendor will be successful, or even that every vendor should sell through the GSA Schedule. But it does mean that the GSA Schedules program still is one of the best procurement vehicles around, and a vendor looking to increase its footprint in the federal marketplace would be remiss if it did not at least consider the opportunities available through the program.

Notes:

[1] FAR 38.101(a).
[2] The industrial funding fee is incorporated into the price of supplies and services sold on Schedule. As discussed *infra* in Chapter XIV, if the vendor does not plan for this fee in pricing the supplies and services it sells under the MAS Program, the fee will be paid from what otherwise would have been the vendor's profit.
[3] Blanket purchase agreements are described *infra* in Chapter XV.
[4] *See Impact of FAR 8.4 Comparison Analysis of Customer Elapsed-Time Savings* (1998), *at http://www.fss.gsa.gov/schedules/far-84impact.cfm.*
[5] *Id.* at 5.
[6] It also has been noted, however, that the MAS Program—like other streamlined contracting vehicles—translates into a tendency on the part of agencies inappropriately to avoid competition. For an excellent discussion on this topic, *see* The Nash & Cibinic Report, ¶ 60, Vol. 11, No. 11 (Nov. 1997); *id.* ¶ 3, Vol. 12, No. 1 (Jan. 1998). *See also* The Nash & Cibinic Report, ¶ 11, Vol. 15, No. 2 (Feb. 2001), discussing the issuance of a GAO report (*Contract Management: Not Following Procedures Undermines Best Pricing Under GSA's Schedule*, Comp. Gen. Rep. GAO-01-125 (Nov. 2000)), that concluded that Government purchasers were using the MAS Program without obtaining the necessary competition.
[7] Multiple Award Schedule Process, Section B: Variable Contracts, *at http://www.fss.gsa.gov/vendorguide/section-b.cfm.*
[8] *See http://www.gsaelibrary.gsa.gov/elib/Schedules.jsp* for a complete listing of Schedule contracts. The number of Schedules has decreased

over the years due to GSA's attempt to render the MAS Program more efficient by consolidating multiple Schedules.

9 Pub. L. No. 98-369, § 2711, 98 Stat. 1175 (codified as amended at 41 U.S.C. § 253).

10 *See United Communications Sys., Inc.,* B-279383, June 2, 1998, 98-1 CPD ¶ 148 (Under FAR 8.404(a), an agency may place an order under the MAS Program without seeking further competition or synopsize the requirement if the agency follows the procedures of FAR 8.404.); *National Office Sys., Inc.,* B-274785, Jan. 6, 1997, 97-1 CPD ¶ 12 (When agency requirements are satisfied through the use of the MAS Program, an agency is not required to seek further competition, synopsize the requirement, make a separate determination of fair and reasonable pricing, or consider small business set-asides. The agency is required to reasonably ensure that a selection represents the best value and meets the agency's needs at the lowest overall cost by considering reasonably available information about products offered under MAS contracts. This standard can be satisfied by reviewing GSA *Advantage!*, GSA's on-line purchasing web site.); *CPAD Technologies, Inc.,* B-278582.2, Feb. 19, 1998, 98-1 CPD ¶ 55 (Protest challenging agency's placement of an order against a MAS contract at a price higher than that offered by protester is denied where record reflects that the agency reasonably concluded that the ordered product was the lowest priced Schedule product that met the agency's needs.). *See also Amdahl Corp.,* B-281255, Dec. 28, 1998, 98-2 CPD ¶ 161, at 3 ("Under the [MAS] . . . program, agencies are not required to request proposals or to conduct a competition before using their business judgment in determining whether ordering supplies or services from a [MAS] . . . vendor represent[s] the best value and meet[s] the agency's needs at the lowest overall cost.").

11 *See* Chapter XV (Order Fulfillment) for a discussion of sole source awards.

12 DOD imposes additional competition requirements in the context of the procurement of service through the GSA Schedule. *See* Section 803 of the National Defense Authorization Act for Fiscal Year 2002; *see also* DFARS 208.404-70; 70 Fed. Reg. 32280 (June 2, 2005)

(Proposed Rule: "Defense Acquisition Regulation Supplement; Competition Requirements for Federal Supply Schedules and Multiple Award Contracts").

13 *See Hoechst Marion Roussel, Inc.*, B-279073, May 4, 1998, 98-1 CPD ¶ 127 (CICA requires that restrictive conditions or provisions will be allowed only to the extent necessary to satisfy the needs of the agency or as authorized by law. Here, the RFP reflected an intent by the Department of Veterans Affairs to modify the contract on a sole source basis after award. Such a modification would be tantamount to an improper sole source award.).

14 The term "peppercorn" refers to the contracts law concept that something as trifling in value as a peppercorn can qualify as contractual "consideration" as long as it is bargained for. Over time, this became known as the "peppercorn theory of consideration." *See, e.g.,* E. Allan Farnsworth, Farnsworth on Contracts § 2.11 (2d ed. 1998). Until recently, the guaranteed minimum MAS contract value was set at $100. This "trifling" amount prompted some experts to question whether MAS awards actually were contracts. *See* The Nash & Cibinic Report, ¶ 60, Vol. 11, No. 11 (Nov. 1997), for an excellent discussion on this topic. It is unclear whether the increase in the minimum from $100 to $2,500 will quell such criticisms in the future.

15 As reported by the Online Schedule Sales Reporting System for Fiscal Year 2000, *at http://ssq.fss.gsa.gov/.*

16 FSS Clause I-FSS-639 (7/2000). The Federal Supply Service has supplemented the General Services Administration Acquisition Regulation ("GSAR," now the General Services Administration Acquisition Manual ("GSAM")) list of prescribed contract clauses with MAS-specific clauses. If applicable, these clauses will be included in the contract and designated by the "FSS" prefix. Hereinafter, such clauses will be cited by the FSS clause number.

17 GSAR 538.271(a).

18 Absence evidence to the contrary, the Government will presume commerciality. *See, e.g., Firearms Training Systems, Inc.*, B-292819.2 *et al.*, April 26, 2004 ("However, as the Air Force

argues, and we agree, absent a solicitation provision or some indication that the proposed items are not commercial, there is no requirement that an agency formally evaluate or document whether an offered item is a commercial item when using the commercial item procedures of FAR Part 12."). Also, a mere improvement to an existing product will not render that product non-commercial. *See, e.g., HK Sys.*, B-291647.6, 2003 CPD ¶ 159, Aug. 29, 2003.

[19] FAR 2.101.

[20] *Id.* (as revised by Final Rule, 66 Fed. Reg. 53,483-53,484 (Oct. 22, 2001) (to be codified at 48 C.F.R. pts. 2, 12, 46, and 52)).

[21] *Id.*

[22] The FAR defines "catalog price" as "a price included in a catalog, price list, schedule, or other form that is regularly maintained by the manufacturer or vendor, is either published or otherwise available for inspection by customers, and states prices at which sales are currently, or were last, made to a significant number of buyers constituting the general public." FAR 2.101.

[23] The FAR defines "market prices" as "current prices that are established in the course of ordinary trade between buyers and sellers free to bargain and that can be substantiated through competition or from sources independent of the offerors." *Id.*

[24] *Id.*

[25] FAR 9.104-1. Additionally, pursuant to FAR 52.219-9(h), the contracting officer will consider an offeror's prior compliance with subcontracting plans under previous contracts in determining the offeror's responsibility.

[26] FAR 52.209-5. *See infra* Chapter IX concerning certifications.

[27] FAR 9.408(a)(1).

[28] FAR 9.408(a)(2).

[29] FAR 9.408(b).

[30] 65 Fed. Reg. 80,256 (Dec. 20, 2000) (to be codified at 48 C.F.R. pts. 9, 14, 15, 31, and 52). This discussion is adapted from Fried Frank Government Contracts Alertä News Brief No. 00-12-3, *at http://www.ffhsj.com/govtcon/ffgalert/index.html.*

[31] *See* Fried Frank Government Contracts Alertä News Brief Nos. 99-6-6, 99-7-3, and 00-6-1.

[32] *See, e.g.*, William Matthews, *New Procurement Rule Draws Fire*, FEDERAL COMPUTER WEEK (Dec. 21, 2000), *available at http:// www.fcw.com/fcw/articles/2000/1218/web-rules-12-21-00.asp.*

[33] 66 Fed. Reg. 17,754 (Apr. 3, 2001) (to be codified at 48 C.F.R. pts. 9, 14, 15, 31, and 52).

[34] Vendors will be able to obtain information regarding the final rule by accessing the Fried Frank Government Contracts Alertä archives at *http://www.ffhsj.com/govtcon/ffgalert/index.html.*

[35] Under Section 201 of the Federal Property and Administrative Services Act of 1949, as amended, in order to promote greater economy and efficiency in Government procurement programs, contractors performing cost-reimbursement type contracts or other types of negotiated contracts may be authorized to use GSA sources of supply as long as the contractor is authorized in writing by the agency and the requirements of FAR Subpart 51.1 are satisfied. *See* GSA Order ADM 4800.2E, "Eligibility to Use GSA Sources of Supply and Services," at 7(d)(1) (Jan. 3, 2000), *available at http:/ /www.fss.gsa.gov/schedules/adm4800_2.cfm.*

[36] *Id.* at 7(d)(4).

[37] Section 1122 of the National Defense Authorization Act for FY 1994 vested state and local governments with the authority to purchase law enforcement equipment used for counter-drug activities through federal procurement channels. Pub. L. No. 103-160, § 1122(a)(1), 107 Stat. 1754 (codified at 10 U.S.C. § 381). As of the submission of this edition to the publisher, 44 states were participating in the 1122 program. Additional information regarding this program is available from the National Institute of Justice at http:// www.nlectc.org/equipment/1122.html.

[38] *See* GSA Order ADM 4800.2E, *supra* note 32. *See also* Section 201 of the Federal Property and Administrative Services Act of 1949, Ch. 288, § 201, 63 Stat. 378, 383 (codified as amended at 40 U.S.C. § 471 *et seq.*).

[39] *See The GSA Schedule*, FEDERAL PUBLICATION SEMINAR COURSE MANUAL 113 (Fed. Publ'ns Seminars LLC 2000).

[40] As of September 7, 2000, there were only three mandatory Schedules: the Customized Business Cards: JWOD Schedule

(effective 7/1/00); Airline City Pairs; and Express Domestic Small Package Delivery Service (FedEx). Note: Mandatory use of the FedEx contract is determined by agency agreement. As of the publication of this Edition, legislation was pending before the Senate that would require the Veterans Administration to purchase health care items through the Multiple Award Schedule. *See* H.R. 3645.

[41]   *See* FAR 8.002(a)(2).

[42]   *See* FAR 8.7.

[43]   *See* FAR 8.002(a)(1).

[44]   *See* FAR 8.7.

[45]   *See* 41 C.F.R. § 101-26.3.

[46]   *See id.* § 101-26.6.

[47]   *See id.* § 101-26.704.

[48]   68 Fed. Reg. 24372 (May 7, 2003) implementing Section 211 of E-Government Act of 2002. Cooperative Purchasing was implemented through an Interim Rule following a determination by GSA that "urgent and compelling reasons exist to promulgate this interim rule without prior opportunity for public comment." *Id.* at 24377.

[49]   68 Fed. Reg. 24372 (May 7, 2003).

[50]   48 C.F.R. 552.238-79 (May 2004).

[51]   Aronie, Jonathan S., "Cooperative Buying Overdue," FEDERAL COMPUTER WEEK (Feb. 24, 2003).

[52]   68 Fed. Reg. 24372, 24374 (May 7, 2003).

[53]   48 C.F.R. 552.238-75(d).

[54]   In response to a contractor comment regarding the narrowness of the program, the Cooperative Purchasing Interim Rule noted as follows: "Cooperative purchasing may only be conducted pursuant to statutory authorization. Section 211 of the e-Government Act of 2002 authorizes GSA to provide State and local government entities access to information technology products, services, and support equipment. Section 211 does not grant authority to GSA to broaden the scope of this rule to include products and services other than those specifically authorized by that Section." 68 Fed. Reg. 24372 (May 7, 2003).

55 Vendors wishing to end their participation in the cooperative purchasing program after electing to participate may do so by submitting a contract modification request to their GSA contracting officer.

56 This is not to say, of course, that the GSA Schedule Program is the appropriate procurement vehicle for all situations. *See, e.g.,* GSAOIG: Acquisition Rules must be followed even in crisis, gov't contractor, Vol. 47, No. 19, May 11, 2005 at ¶ 222, describing GSA Office of Inspector General criticism of a sole source order awarded to a Schedule contractor following the 2001 anthrax contamination of the Government's remote mail facilities. According to the OIG, the procureing agency failed to produce sufficient documentation, failed to include a ceiling price in a time and materials order, improperly included open market items, and made several other mistakes. The OIG concluded that a MAS Contract was "not an optimal choice for acquiring 'an emerging technology under unfolding, urgent conditions.'"

II.

HISTORICAL OVERVIEW

"Those who do not remember the past are condemned to repeat it."

-George Santayana

The MAS Program is a unique contracting vehicle for the Government that developed in response to the Government's need for such mundane articles as paper, pens, and desks. While the Program has evolved over the years, the goal of the Program has remained constant: to offer Government agencies an easier, less expensive, and quicker way to purchase the products that they require to operate. Like the Program itself, the scope of products offered under the Program has evolved as well. Over the years the Program has been expanded to include literally thousands of supplies *and services*. An understanding of the Program's roots and underlying policies will assist the vendor in understanding and complying with the unique requirements of the Program.

A. *The Beginning*

A form of the MAS Program has been in existence since 1910. Administered at that time by the General Supply Committee of the United States Treasury Department, the "General Schedule of Supplies," as it was called, was created to supply other Government agencies with supplies that were ready for immediate delivery.[57] In 1933, administration of the Program was transferred to Treasury's "Procurement Division," renamed the Bureau of Federal Supply in 1947.

In 1949, with the passage of the Federal Property and Administrative Services Act ("FPASA"),[58] Congress created the GSA "as a centralized Federal procurement and property management agency whose primary objective was to save taxpayers' money."[59] FPASA explicitly vests GSA with the authority (and responsibility) of prescribing "policies and methods of procurement" for most civilian agencies.[60] Following the creation of GSA, the Department of the Treasury transferred to it the authority for managing the General Schedule of Supplies.

In order to carry out its responsibilities for (i) facilitating the procurement, storage, and provision of supplies to federal agencies; (ii) regulating the supply functions for other agencies; and (iii) standardizing the Federal Government's purchase specifications, GSA created a new division, the Federal Supply Service.[61]

B. *1982 GSA Multiple Award Schedule Policy Statement*

From its inception through 1982, GSA administered the nation's civilian procurement activities without a clear directive (beyond the broad implementing language contained in the statute) regarding its mission and the means of pursuing its mission. Then, on November 5, 1982, GSA filled the gap with the issuance of its "Multiple Award Schedule Policy Statement"[62]— perhaps the most far-reaching GSA pronouncement to date. Effective for all solicitations issued on or after October 1, 1982, the MAS Policy Statement outlined the policies and procedures that would be followed by GSA when contracting for supplies or services through its MAS Program. To this day, many aspects of the 1982 MAS Policy Statement remain points of contention between industry and GSA.

The keystone of GSA's 1982 MAS Policy Statement was the stated requirement that GSA expected to receive most favored customer pricing from all vendors. In other words, if vendors wanted to participate in the MAS Program, they would have to show GSA that no other customers were getting a better deal.[63] Under the 1982 MAS Policy Statement, GSA sought a vendor's most favored discount other than that offered original equipment manufacturers ("OEMs") or dealers. This OEM/dealer caveat notwithstanding, GSA still required the submission of OEM/dealer data in order to assure itself that OEMs/dealers, in fact, were performing OEM/dealer functions as a predicate for disparate pricing treatment.[64] Unless vendors could demonstrate that there were substantial differences between the products or terms and conditions offered to OEMs or dealers, then the 1982 MAS Policy Statement allowed the Government to require cost or pricing data from OEMs and/or dealers.[65]

The 1982 MAS Policy Statement also compelled vendors to establish that the supplies and services they wanted to sell through the MAS Program were "commercial items." Unless such a showing could be made, the vendor was required to provide certified cost or pricing data under the Truth in Negotiations Act ("TINA")[66]—a requirement that brought with it a host of risks and penalties for noncompliance. In addition to the commercial item certification, the 1982 MAS Policy Statement required vendors to certify that their supplies and services were being sold in substantial quantities to the general public.[67]

To facilitate GSA's effort to obtain most favored customer pricing in those instances where a contract was exempt from the requirements of TINA, the 1982 MAS Policy Statement introduced the Discount Schedule and Marketing Data ("DSMD") form. The DSMD form, which GSA required to be submitted with every Schedule proposal, soon became the bane of every Schedule vendor's existence. The DSMD form required vendors to disclose all discounts to any of its commercial customers, including *ad hoc* and temporary discounts. And, as with TINA, the vendor had to certify that the data provided were current, accurate, and complete on the date on which the contract was signed.[68] Perhaps the most burdensome aspect of the DSMD form, however, was its complexity. In fact, in 1992, the United States Court of Appeals for the First Circuit, in the renowned *Data Translations* case, effectively prohibited GSA's continued use of DSMD forms, finding the forms "virtually unintelligible *if read literally.*"[69]

C. *Competition In Contracting Act Of 1984*

The Competition in Contracting Act ("CICA") was signed into law on July 18, 1984 by President Ronald Reagan.[70] As its name suggests, CICA was designed to increase competition in the awarding of Government contracts by severely restricting the use of other than competitive procedures in procurements. CICA modified the procurement standard from "free and full competition" to "full and open competition." Prior to the enactment of CICA, a contracting officer could limit distribution of solicitation information if adequate competition and fair and reasonable prices were obtained. "Full and open competition" requires that all potentially responsible vendors be permitted to receive or have access to solicitations involving competitive procurements.[71] When an agency fails to afford full and open competition, a protest might be in order.[72]

CICA marked the first statutory recognition of GSA's MAS Program. In defining authorized competitive procedures, CICA included the MAS Program as a procurement vehicle that potentially is "best suited to the circumstances of the contract action and consistent with the need to fulfill the Government's requirements efficiently."[73] Currently, the MAS Program satisfies the requirements of CICA as long as (a) participation in the Program is open to all responsible sources and (b) orders and contracts under such procedures result in the lowest overall cost alternative to meet the needs of the Government.

D. *The Multiple Award Schedule Improvement Project*

Throughout the late 1980s, criticism regarding the MAS Program escalated. In 1990, GSA responded with the initiation of its "Multiple Award Schedule Improvement Project."[74] Through the use of a number of different pilot programs, GSA attempted to reform the MAS Program. Not surprisingly, it began with a revised DSMD form in 1991. The modifications, however, were rejected both by Government purchasers and commercial vendors. GSA tried again in 1992, with no better success. Indeed, the 1990s witnessed a continual back-and-forth between GSA and industry over the DSMD form, the Price Reductions Clause, and the 1982 MAS Policy Statement generally. Finally, in 1996, GSA canceled the 1982 MAS Policy Statement and issued a revised MAS pricing policy.[75]

On August 21, 1997, this interim rule was adopted as final with changes.[76] One of the major changes was that the DSMD form was replaced by the Commercial Sales Practices Format ("CSP Format"). Although the CSP Format was not precisely that for which industry had lobbied, it was an improvement. For one, it substantially reduced the amount of information a vendor was required to submit to GSA. Rather than requiring information on all sales, the vendor was now required to report only those commercial customers that received a better price than that being offered the Government.[77]

Although industry regarded these changes as a minor step in the right direction, they were considerably less than anticipated. One of the major disappointments to industry, for example, was GSA's failure to adhere to the Federal Acquisition Reform Act of 1996,[78] also known as Clinger-Cohen, and to discontinue post-award audits. As a result, MAS contracts remained subject to post-award audits of pre-award information. Additionally, the Price Reductions Clause remained, and still remains, as a sore point for industry.

E. *The Federal Acquisition Streamlining Act*

In late 1994, Congress passed the Federal Acquisition Streamlining Act ("FASA"),[79] which had a significant impact on the MAS Program. For example, FASA eliminated a number of certification requirements from commercial item contracts, including the Walsh-Healy Act,[80] the prohibition against contingent fees in soliciting or securing a contract,[81] the Drug-Free Workplace Act,[82] and more.[83] Additionally, FASA brought with it a strict prohibition against requiring cost or pricing data in the acquisition of commercial items.[84]

On February 16, 1996, GSA issued an interim rule revising the General Services Administration Acquisition Regulation ("GSAR"), GSA's regulations that supplement the FAR, to implement those portions of FASA that deal with TINA and the acquisition of commercial items.[85] Effective March 4, 1996, these changes, among other things, canceled the 1982 MAS Policy Statement and replaced the DSMD form with the new CSP Format. The CSP Format is included in all MAS contracts today.

The interim rule also revised GSA's approach to evaluating MAS offers.[86] Although the new rule retains the principle that the Government will seek to obtain a vendor's best discount, the rule notes that the terms and conditions of commercial sales vary and that there may be legitimate reasons why the best discount cannot be achieved.[87] While this acknowledgement is not new, the interim rule, in theory at least, effected a shifting of the burden in this regard from the vendor to GSA. The interim rule required the contracting officer to compare the terms and conditions of the MAS solicitation with the terms and conditions of commercial agreements when establishing negotiation objectives and determining price reasonableness.[88] The interim rule further provided that a contracting officer may award a contract containing pricing that is less favorable than the best discount that the vendor extends to a given commercial customer, but only after making a written determination that (a) the prices offered to the Government are fair and reasonable even though comparable discounts were not negotiated and (b) the award of a contract is otherwise in the best interest of the Government.[89]

F. *The Federal Acquisition Reform Act*

In early 1996, Congress passed the Federal Acquisition Reform Act, commonly referred to as "Clinger-Cohen."[90] Clinger-Cohen continued the reforms to the procurement process that were begun by the passage of FASA. One major change resulting from the passage of Clinger-Cohen was the removal of the post-award defective pricing audit provisions for commercial items granted by FASA. This audit authority had authorized the examination of a vendor's books and records directly related to information other than cost or pricing data submitted by the vendor to support a determination of price reasonableness or cost realism.[91] This right was available to agency contracting officers for a period of two years after contract award.[92] Unfortunately, GSA has declined to follow Clinger-Cohen's direction in this regard and audits remain a feature of MAS contracts. (*See* Chapter XXII for a discussion of GSA Office of Inspector General audits.)

Additionally, Clinger-Cohen also exempted commercial items from compliance with Cost Accounting Standards and revised the exemption for compliance with TINA from that of an "established catalog or market price" to that of "commercial item."[93] Clinger-Cohen also limited the contracting officer's right to request information other than cost or pricing data[94] and established a trial program using simplified procedures for acquisitions over $100,000 but less than $5 million until January 1, 2000.[95]

G. *Is The MAS Program Legal?*

Because MAS contracts are unfunded "standing contracts," questions have arisen regarding their validity. For the most part, these questions were put to rest in 1983 by the Comptroller General of the United States.

In *GSA—Multiple Award Schedule Multiyear Contracting,*[96] the Comptroller General, acting through the Government Accountability Office ("GAO"), was faced with the following two questions regarding multiyear MAS contracts:

1. Do MAS contracts violate 31 U.S.C. §§ 1341 and 1502, which make it illegal to commit Government funds to future unfunded obligations?
2. Do MAS contracts violate 41 U.S.C. § 11, which prohibits Government purchases in the absence of adequate appropriations?

The GAO concluded that MAS contracts do not violate any of these statutory provisions. Reasoning that the mere signing of the MAS contract did not result in a commitment to pay funds, no obligation of funds actually occurred in advance of an appropriation. The GAO also considered the question from the perspective of whether there could be a violation subsequent to contract award—*i.e.*, at the time of order placement. Concluding that the funds actually expended would come out of appropriations for the fiscal year in which the given products were ordered, the GAO again found no violation.

This determination, of course, does not address the legality of GSA's refusal to adopt, for the MAS Program, the full panoply of reforms mandated by FASA.

Notes:

[57] *See The GSA Multiple Award Schedule Program: Current Issues and Future Trends,* 1994 A.B.A. SEC. PUB. L., COM. PRODS. & SERVS. COMM. REP., Tab G, at 2.

[58] Ch. 288, § 302, 63 Stat. 393 (codified as amended at 41 U.S.C. § 252 *et seq.*).

[59] *See* GSA 1999 ANNUAL REPORT 21, *available at http://www.gsa.gov/attachments/GSA_PUBLICATIONS/extpub/99arp01.pdf.*

[60] 40 U.S.C. § 481(a)(1).

[61] *See* National Archives, *at http://www.nara.gov/guide/rg137.html.*

[62] 47 Fed. Reg. 50,242 (Nov. 5, 1982) (to be codified at 41 C.F.R. Chapter 5). (NOTE: Older citations have been superseded and have been cited for historical purposes only.)

[63] *Id.* at 50,243.

[64] *Id.* at 50,248.

[65] *Id.* at 50,245.

[66] Ch. 1041, 70A Stat. 130 (1962) (codified as amended at 10 U.S.C. §§ 2306, 2306a); Ch. 288, § 304C (1949) (codified as amended at 41 U.S.C. § 254(d)).

[67] 47 Fed. Reg. 50,242, 50,247 (Nov. 5, 1982) (to be codified at 41 C.F.R. Chapter 5).

[68] FSS Clause M-FSS-330 (1984).

[69] *See United States v. Data Translation, Inc.*, 984 F.2d 1256, 1260 (1st Cir. 1992) (emphasis in original).

[70] Pub. L. No. 98-369, § 2711, 98 Stat. 1175 (1984) (codified as amended at 41 U.S.C. § 253 (1984)).

[71] *See* FAR 6.101.

[72] *See, e.g., Packaging Corp. of Am.*, B-225823, July 20, 1987, 87-2 CPD ¶ 65 (Failure to send the Request for Proposals to incumbent contractor, one of only three possible suppliers of item solicited, improperly deprived contractor of opportunity to submit offer contrary to CICA.); *Qualimetrics, Inc.*, B-262057, Nov. 16, 1995, 95-2 CPD ¶ 228 (Agency's failure to provide solicitation to incumbent due to the solicitation being mailed to the wrong address, when agency had informed GSA of the contractor's new address, violated CICA.).

[73] *See* FAR 6.101(b); 41 U.S.C. § 253.

[74] 56 Fed. Reg. 56,956 (Nov. 7, 1991) (to be codified at 48 C.F.R. pts. 515 and 538).

[75] Interim Rule, 61 Fed. Reg. 6164 (Feb. 16, 1996) (to be codified at 48 C.F.R. pts. 501, 504, 507, 510, 511, 512, 514, 515, 538, 539, 543, 546, 552, and 570).

[76] 62 Fed. Reg. 44,518 (Aug. 21, 1997) (to be codified at 48 C.F.R. pts. 504, 507, 510, 511, 512, 514, 515, 538, 539, 543, 546, 552, and 570).

[77] *See infra* Chapter VII for a complete discussion of the CSP Format.

[78] Pub. L. No. 104-106, 1996 U.S.C.C.A.N. (110 Stat.) 642.

[79] Pub. L. No. 103-355, 1994 U.S.C.C.A.N. (108 Stat.) 3243.

[80] 41 U.S.C. § 43.

[81] 41 U.S.C. § 254(a); 10 U.S.C. § 2306(b).

[82] 41 U.S.C. § 701 *et seq.*

[83] *See* FAR 12.503.

[84] *See* 10 U.S.C. § 2306(a); 41 U.S.C. § 254(b); and FAR 15.403-1(c)(3).

[85] *See* 61 Fed. Reg. 6164 (Feb. 16, 1996) (to be codified at 48 C.F.R. pts. 501, 504, 507, 510, 511, 512, 514, 515, 538, 539, 543, 546, 552, and 570).

[86] *Id.* at 6169 (*see* GSAR 538.270).

[87] *Id.* (*see* GSAR 538.270(a)).

[88] *Id.* (*see* GSAR 538.270(d)).

[89] *Id.* (*see* GSAR 538.270(e)).

[90] Pub. L. No. 104-106 (1996), 1996 U.S.C.C.A.N. (110 Stat.) 642.

[91] Lynda Troutman O'Sullivan & Douglas E. Perry, *Commercial Item Acquisitions, in* BRIEFING PAPERS 3, No. 97-5 (Fed. Publ'ns Inc. Apr. 1997).

[92] *Id.*

[93] *Id.*

[94] *Id.*

[95] *Id.*

[96] B-199079, Dec. 23, 1983, 84-1 CPD ¶ 46.

III.

MULTIPLE AWARD SCHEDULE ESSENTIALS

"The gods have their own rules."
-Ovid, *Metamorphoses*

L   ike any Government contract, MAS contracts are subject to a maze of rules and regulations, noncompliance with which brings significant penalties. These rules and regulations include the explicit terms and conditions of each MAS contract, as well as a plethora of clauses incorporated into each contract by reference or by operation of law. This chapter identifies the primary sources of a vendor's obligations and the primary agencies charged with ensuring compliance with those obligations.

A. *What Rules Govern The MAS Program?*

1. The Terms Of The MAS Contract Itself

Like any party to a contract, Schedule vendors must comply with the terms and conditions of the contract itself. While these terms and conditions can vary from contract to contract in some respects, for the most part, they are a constant. FAR Part 12 identifies several clauses that a contracting officer must incorporate into each contract for commercial items.[97] It also identifies several clauses that *may* be incorporated into a contract. Notwithstanding the provisions of FAR Part 12, however, vendors are well advised to read the text of their contracts carefully as implementation of FAR Part 12 varies between and among contracting officers.

2. The Federal Acquisition Regulation

The FAR provides the source of most of the contract clauses that are incorporated into each Schedule contract prior to award. Specifically, vendors should become familiar with the following FAR provisions:

- FAR Part 8, "Required Sources of Supplies and Services," provides the regulations concerning the acquisition of supplies and services from or through Government supply sources. FAR 8.001 provides a listing of the required sources of supply, in descending order, which an agency must follow when acquiring supplies and services. Included in this list is the MAS Program. FAR Subpart 8.4 covers the MAS Program and provides a general description of the Program. FAR 8.404 contains the procedures that must be followed by agencies placing orders and provides direction regarding (i) inspection and acceptance of supplies or services, (ii) delinquent performance, and (iii) procedures for disputes and terminations for convenience or default.

- FAR Part 12, "Acquisition of Commercial Items," provides the procedures required for acquisition of commercial items. Because GSA is using the MAS Program to acquire commercial items, this section must be followed by all agencies. FAR 12.101 requires agencies to conduct market research to determine whether commercial items could meet their needs and, if applicable, whether they should satisfy their needs with commercial items. FAR

Subpart 12.3 provides the solicitation provisions and contract clauses to be used in commercial acquisitions. In addition, the laws and regulations applicable to commercial acquisitions and streamlined evaluation procedures are discussed in FAR Subparts 12.4, 12.5, and 12.6.

- FAR Part 15, "Contracting by Negotiation," establishes the required policies and procedures to be used for competitive and noncompetitive negotiated acquisitions. Because MAS contracts are negotiated procurements, these procedures must be followed. FAR Part 15 covers the topics of source selection processes and techniques, development and issuance of solicitations, source selection, pricing and pre-award/post-award mistakes, protests, and notifications.[98]

- FAR Part 38, "Federal Supply Schedule Contracting," prescribes the policies and procedures for contracting for supplies and services under the MAS Program, describes the Program, and provides GSA with the authorization to allow other agencies, such as the Department of Veterans Affairs, to award and publish Schedule contracts. FAR Part 38 also provides direction to agency contracting officers with the responsibility for awarding MAS contracts to make changes to Schedules.[99]

- FAR Part 52, "Solicitation Provisions and Contract Clauses," provides a matrix listing the FAR clauses and provisions applicable to each type of contract and provides instructions regarding the use and inclusion of these provisions and clauses. If a clause is incorporated by reference into a solicitation or contract, FAR Part 52 provides the full text of the provision. Solicitation/contract clauses should be reviewed and understood by a vendor prior to the submission of a bid.

Specific FAR clauses that are incorporated into every MAS contract are discussed in depth in Chapters XII and XIII.

3. The General Services Administration Manual

Like most federal agencies, GSA publishes a supplement to the FAR known as the General Services Administration Acquisition Manual, or "GSAM." The provisions and clauses set forth in the GSAM are known as the General Services Administration Acquisition Regulation, or "GSAR." The GSAM provides an additional source for vendor obligations that either add to or supplement the provisions of the FAR. Although the line between "clarification" and "contradiction" is often obscure, by law, the GSAR may not contradict the FAR.[100] The GSAM is available on-line at *http://www.arnet.gov/GSAM/gsam.html.*

4. GSA Policy Statements And Other Agency Guidance

In addition to the FAR and GSAR,[101] GSA, like other agencies, publishes internal guidance regarding the MAS Program. For example, GSA publishes Procurement Information Bulletins that provide detailed explanations of FAR and GSAR policies. GSA also publishes FSS Acquisition Letters that provide contracting officers with additional information and guidance on new clauses and their application.

B. *Oversight Of The MAS Program*

1. General Services Administration

GSA is the primary agency responsible for the issuance and administration of MAS contracts. (The VA plays this role with respect to Schedules relating to medical supplies and services through an official delegation from GSA.[102]) GSA functions not only as the MAS Program's contract administrator, but also as the Program's ultimate problem solver. Agencies and vendors alike look to GSA to resolve any number of problems that arise during the course of contract performance. The GAO has held that, ultimately, GSA is responsible for the resolution of legal issues that arise between vendors and purchasing agencies when such issues cannot be resolved at the agency level.[103]

GSA also functions as the MAS Program's primary rulemaker. Even the individual purchasing agencies must operate within the confines of the contractual agreement negotiated and administered by GSA. GSA ensures compliance with the numerous policies and procedures applicable to the MAS Program and develops new policies and procedures where necessary to improve the functioning of the Program.

Historically, GSA was divided into three primary divisions: the Federal Supply Service ("FSS"), the Federal Technology Service ("FTS"), and the Public Buildings Service ("PBS"). The FSS had been responsible for administering the MAS Program. The FTS procured and provided information technology and network services to Government agencies. The PBS served as the Federal Government's builder, developer, lessor, and manager of its portfolio of owned and leased property.

Along with the MAS Program, the FSS also oversaw the Stock Program and the Special Order Program. The Stock Program leverages purchasing power to provide more than 7,000 high demand items to agencies using a requisition system. Under the Special Order Program, the FSS provided a "buy on demand" commercial buying service to ordering activities.

In mid-2005, GSA announced that it would restructure the FSS and FTS into a new organization called the Federal Acquisition Service, or FAS. According to GSA, the FAS organization will have the following five program areas:

- Customer Accounts and Research—enables GSA to better understand customer requirements and become a strategic partner in helping agencies meet their acquisition needs.
- Acquisition Management—ensures that GSA's activities are fully compliant with federal laws, regulations and policies, and that operating practices are consistent across business lines and regions.

- Integrated Technology Services—groups together the GSA units that acquire information technology, telecommunications and professional services.
- General Supplies and Services—groups together the GSA units that acquire a broad range of commercial products and closely-related services, as well as some specialized logistics-based activities.
- Travel, Motor Vehicles and Card Services—groups together business lines which share commonalities that provide opportunities for synergy and scale.

As of the submission of this manuscript to the publisher, the details of this reorganization still were being worked out.

2. General Services Administration, Office Of Inspector General

While the GSA FSS administers Schedule contracts and ensures compliance on a day-to-day basis, the GSA Office of Inspector General ("OIG"), pursuant to its statutory responsibility "to prevent and detect fraud and abuse,"[104] is GSA's primary contractual watchdog. In this role, the OIG audits and investigates Schedule vendors pursuant to its statutory authority as well as pursuant to the terms of the MAS contract itself. GSAR 552.215-71 incorporated into every Schedule contract, provides as follows:

> The Contractor agrees that the Administrator of General Services or any duly authorized representative shall have access to and the right to examine any books, documents, papers and records of the Contractor involving transactions related to this contract for overbillings, billing errors, compliance with the Price Reduction clause and compliance with the Industrial Funding Fee clause of this contract. This authority shall expire 3 years after final

payment.[105] The basic contract and each option
shall be treated as separate contracts for purposes
of applying this clause.[106]

The Administrator of GSA considers the OIG to be its "duly
authorized representative" for the purposes of this clause.

The OIG reports administrative violations to the cognizant
contracting officers and suspected fraud to the Department of
Justice ("DOJ").[107] DOJ directives mandate a referral of civil
fraud cases by agencies to local Assistant United States Attorneys
when single damages are $1 million or less.[108] Additionally, the
OIG, where necessary, will refer matters to the GSA suspension
and debarment official.[109]

There is an argument that the OIG is legally prohibited from
performing *any* auditing function for GSA due to a statutory
prohibition against the OIG's assumption of the programmatic
functions of its agencies.[110] Moreover, while the GSA OIG has
played this role for some time, a second and distinct question
exists regarding the legality of the OIG's role in reviewing a
vendor's pre-award disclosures to GSA in the context of a post-
award audit. As previously discussed, Clinger-Cohen explicitly
precludes GSA from asserting post-award audit rights over
commercial item contracts.[111] There is, however, a fine line
between an OIG Price Reductions Clause audit and an OIG audit
of pre-award disclosures. In practice, the fact that the two audits
may require a review of the same documents leaves vendors little
room to argue that the OIG is acting beyond its authority. Neither
argument has suppressed to date the OIG's appetite to serve as
GSA's primary contract monitor.

For a more thorough discussion of the role of the OIG in
auditing Schedule contracts, *see* Chapter XXII.

3. Department Of Veterans Affairs

As noted above, GSA has delegated the authority to issue
MAS contracts for the procurement of medical supplies and

services (*e.g.*, drugs, medical equipment, medical services, etc.) to the VA. Under FAR 38.201, however, VA contracting officers must coordinate and obtain approval from the FSS prior to establishing new Schedules; discontinuing Schedules; changing the scope of agency or geographical coverage of existing Schedules; or adding, deleting, or revising the description of Special Item Numbers or national stock numbers. In all other aspects, the VA plays the same role with respect to medical supplies that GSA plays with respect to all other Schedules.

4. Department Of Justice

Although the DOJ is not involved in the day-to-day monitoring of a Schedule vendor's activities, GSA can—and does—refer matters of suspected fraud to the DOJ for investigation and, if necessary, prosecution. Indeed, in the six-month period ended March 31, 2001, the DOJ has been called to investigate more than fifty allegations of fraud relating to GSA contracts.[112]

Cases referred to DOJ typically find their way to its Civil Fraud Unit within the Civil Division's Commercial Litigation Branch. Additionally, GSA may refer instances of suspected fraud directly to the cognizant United States Attorney's Office, which may handle the matter with or without the assistance of "main" Justice.

Over the past few years, the DOJ has become more active in involving itself in suspected procurement fraud. In 2000, for example, the DOJ recovered more than $100 million from defense contractors alone.[113]

5. Government Accountability Office

The GAO monitors the MAS Program in two ways. First, the GAO has jurisdiction over bid protests, and this role is discussed in detail in Chapter X. Second, the GAO has authority to perform audits.[114] Specifically, the Schedule contract provides that the Comptroller General

> shall have access to and right to examine any of the Contractor's directly pertinent records involving transactions related to this contract.[115]

In actuality, this clause is based on statute, not contract.[116] Pursuant to this clause, Schedule vendors must make available for the GAO's examination contract-related "records, materials, and other evidence" for a period of three years (or a shorter period if explicitly provided by regulation) after final payment.[117] Although not explicitly stated in the new Schedule solicitations being issued by GSA, GAO's audit authority may even gain it access to a vendor's cost information.[118]

In practice, the Examination of Records by the Comptroller General Clause is infrequently invoked. The Government clearly favors the Examination of Records by GSA Clause.[119]

6. Department Of Labor

The Department of Labor ("DOL"), through its Office of Federal Contract Compliance Programs ("OFCCP"), ensures federal contractor compliance with federal labor laws. Vendors holding MAS contracts may be subject to audits performed by the OFCCP. One major area of concern for the OFCCP will be compliance with the Equal Employment Opportunity ("EEO") and affirmative action requirements.[120] Vendors with more than fifty employees and contracts valued at $50,000 or more will be required to develop written affirmative action programs for each of their establishments.[121] Other audits may be performed by DOL to ensure contractor compliance with the Service Contract Act, if applicable, and requirements regarding employment of veterans.

In addition, for contracts over $10 million, the contracting officer must request a pre-award audit of the vendor to ensure EEO compliance prior to award of the contract.[122] Vendors are required to allow the audit; the review of their affirmative action program and personnel, payroll, and other employment records; and the interview of their employees and officers.[123]

7. Small Business Administration

The Small Business Administration ("SBA") oversees a host of federal programs aimed at expanding the number of federal contracting opportunities available to small, minority, and women-owned businesses.[124] In the context of the MAS Program, the SBA plays two primary roles. The first relates to certain contracts that are "set aside" for small, minority, or women-owned businesses. The second relates to GSA's requirement that MAS vendors provide subcontracting opportunities to small, small disadvantaged, veteran-owned small, service disabled veteran-owned small, HUBZone, and women-owned small businesses to the maximum extent practicable.[125]

8. Whistleblowers

While clearly not an agency of the Federal Government, whistleblowers (called "relators" when the whistle they blow is attached to a complaint under the False Claims Act) can play a significant role in enforcing compliance with the terms and conditions of the MAS Program. Pursuant to the provisions of the False Claims Act,[126] ordinary citizens who are privy to fraud against the United States are encouraged to report such fraud to the DOJ in return for a percentage of any financial recovery that the Government receives. Thus, each and every one of a vendor's employees is a potential (and undisclosed) federal auditor in a very real sense. The False Claims Act—and what vendors can do to minimize the risks arising therefrom—is discussed in more detail in Chapter XXIII.

Notes:

[97]   GSAR 512.203 requires contracting officers to use the policies in FAR Part 12 and GSAR Part 512 in conjunction with the policies and procedures in FAR Part 38 and GSAR Part 538. GSAR 512.3

provides solicitation provisions and contract clauses for the acquisition of commercial items.

[98] FAR Part 15 does not govern competitive procurements *under* the MAS Program. *CourtSmart Digital Sys., Inc.* B-292995.2, B-292955.3, Feb. 13, 2004, 2004 CPP ¶ 79. But where an agency conducts such a procurement, the GAO will look to FAR Part 15 to assess the propriety of the agency's actions in the event of a bid protest. *Id.*

[99] FAR 38.201.

[100] FAR 1.304(b)(2).

[101] This book uses traditional "GSAR" (not "GSAM") citations when referring to GSA regulations. The term "GSAM" is used when referring to the GSA manual generally, which includes the GSAR.

[102] FAR 38.101(d).

[103] *See Digital Equip. Corp.*, GSBCA No. 9618 *et al.*, 90-2 BCA ¶ 22,808 (GSBCA held that contractor could consolidate all of its counterclaims with various agencies into claims against GSA as the oversight agency of MAS contracts. Contractor would not be forced to counterclaim in a piecemeal fashion.). A proposed rule affecting the handling of disputes, however, was issued on December 19, 2000. 65 Fed. Reg. 79,702 (Dec. 19, 2000) (to be codified at 48 C.F.R. pts. 8 and 51). Under the proposed rule, ordering contracting officers can resolve disputes involving performance under a Schedule order or transfer the dispute to the GSA Schedule contracting officer. If the dispute pertains to terms and conditions, then the ordering contracting officer is required to refer the dispute to the GSA Schedule contracting officer. Any appeals of final decisions could be appealable either to the board of contract appeals servicing the agency that issued the final decision or to the United States Court of Federal Claims.

[104] *See generally* Inspector General Act of 1978, Pub. L. No. 95-452, 92 Stat. 1101 (1978) (codified as amended at 5 U.S.C. app. 3, § 2).

[105] The Government Contracts Reference Book defines "final payment" as "[t]he last payment the Government makes on a contract when the parties believe all obligations under the contract have been closed out." Robert C. Nash, Steven L. Schooner, & Karen R.

O'Brien, GOVERNMENT CONTRACTS REFERENCE BOOK 247 (G.W. Press 2d ed. 1998).

[106] GSAR 552.215-71 (Aug. 1997). Under recently developed "evergreen contracts," the base and each option are five years each for a total of twenty years that a contract may be in place.

[107] OIGs are required by law expeditiously to report to the DOJ when, during the course of their duties, they come across "reasonable grounds to believe that there has been a violation of Federal Criminal law." 5 U.S.C. app. 3, § 4(d).

[108] 28 C.F.R. Part O, Subpart Y, App., Directive 14-95 (Apr. 6, 1995).

[109] See GSA OIG SEMIANNUAL REP. TO CONG. (Oct. 1, 1999-Mar. 31, 2000), at 35.

[110] See 5 U.S.C. app. 3, § 9(a)(2); National Defense Authorization Act for Fiscal Year 1996, Pub. L. No. 104-106, 1996 U.S.C.C.A.N. (110 Stat.) 186, 642. See also Truckers United For Safety v. Mead, 251 F.3d 183 (D.C. Cir. 2001) (noting that the IG Act specifically prohibits the OIG from assuming "program operating responsibilities"); Burlington N. R.R. Co. v. Office of Inspector General, 983 F.2d 631 (5th Cir. 1993) (refusing to enforce IG subpoena due to IG's lack of authority to engage in regulatory compliance investigations that are part of an agency's general functioning).

[111] Pub. L. No. 104-106, 1996 U.S.C.C.A.N. (110 Stat). 642; see H.R. CONF. REP. NO. 104-450, at 966 (1996), reprinted in 1996 U.S.C.C.A.N. 238, 451.

[112] GSA OIG SEMIANNUAL REP. TO CONG. (Oct. 1, 2000-Mar. 31, 2001), available at http://oig.gsa.gov/publications.html.

[113] DOJ Press Release, Justice Recovers Record $1.5 Billion in Fraud Payments, Highest Ever for One Year Period (Nov. 2, 2000), available at http://www.usdoj.gov/opa/pr/2000/November/641civ.htm.

[114] FAR 52.212-5.

[115] FAR 52.212-5(d)(1).

[116] 10 U.S.C. § 2313 et seq.

[117] See, e.g., GSA Information Technology Solicitation D.1(c)(3); see also 10 U.S.C. § 2313(i); 41 U.S.C. § 254d(1); supra note 92.

[118] *See, e.g., SmithKline Corp. v. Staats,* 668 F.2d 201 (3d Cir. 1981). *See also Bowsher v. Merck & Co.,* 460 U.S. 824 (1983). In *Bowsher,* the Supreme Court reviewed an examination of records clause substantially similar to FAR 52.215-5. The Court determined that the "directly pertinent" language permitted the Comptroller General to review the direct costs of a contractor's firm, fixed-price contracts, but not the indirect costs.

[119] GSAR 552.215-71 (Aug. 1997).

[120] Exec. Order No. 11,246, 30 Fed. Reg. 12,319 (Sept. 24, 1965), *reprinted as amended in* 41 C.F.R. § 60-1.1 (1978).

[121] *See* FAR 22.804-1.

[122] FAR 22.805(a).

[123] *See* 41 C.F.R. § 60-1.12, *supra* note 107.

[124] *See* Small Business Act of 1953, § 204, Ch. 282, Pub. L. No. 163, 67 Stat. 232 (1953) (codified as amended at 15 U.S.C. § 631 *et seq.*).

[125] The SBA utilizes "Commercial Marketing Representatives" to monitor prime contractor compliance with the requirements of their Subcontracting Plans. In a 2002 report, the GAO identified shortcomings in the manner in which the CMRs perform this task. Finding the role of the CMR to be "conflicted and in decline," GAO recommended that the SBA reevaluate the effectiveness of its monitoring methods. GAO-03-54 (November 2002).

[126] 31 U.S.C. §§ 3729-3733.

IV.

DECIDING WHETHER OR NOT TO GO "ON SCHEDULE"

"Next to knowing when to seize an opportunity, the most important thing in life is knowing when to forego an advantage."

-Benjamin Disraeli

A MAS contract is not for everyone. For all of its commercial trappings, it is *not* a commercial contract. It is a Government contract that brings with it a host of administrative terms and conditions, regulatory obligations, and statutory requirements. A contractor that is not capable—for whatever reason—of complying with those terms, conditions, obligations, and requirements has no business entering the business.

Unfortunately, many would-be MAS vendors look no further than the proposal requirements set forth in the solicitation and the revenue potential before deciding that the MAS Program is for them. This is a critical, shortsighted mistake since it is not difficult to secure a Schedule contract, but it can be very difficult to comply with one. Indeed, the process is a little like jumping out of a plane. Hitting the ground is the easy part; surviving is the greater challenge.

Thus, like the parachutist who checks his equipment before jumping, potential vendors must look beyond the proposal stage of the MAS Program before jumping headlong into the process. This chapter examines both the advantages of the jump as well as a few of the disadvantages that might counsel in favor of staying in the plane.

A. *Advantages*

1. Revenue

The U.S. Government is the largest single purchaser in the world, with an annual procurement budget of approximately $300 billion. [127] As such, it is one of the largest potential sources of revenue for any vendor in the world. Having a MAS contract provides easy access to this revenue by providing easy access to the federal agencies that spend the Government's money.

2. Access

Entry into the MAS Program provides the vendor with the ability to market its supplies and services to a vast number of authorized users. For the MAS vendor, identifying and targeting agencies for marketing efforts is relatively easy. On the agency side, MAS contracts offer a user-friendly procurement vehicle. Because of its many user-friendly features and the intense marketing efforts by GSA, there has been a dramatic upswing in the use of MAS contracts in the last few years.[128] Moreover, some agencies insist that their contractors hold MAS contracts and will not even consider supplies and services offered by contractors that do not hold a Schedule contract.[129] Non-Schedule contractors will have a difficult time marketing or selling their supplies and services to such agencies.

3. Approval

A MAS contract brings with it the Government's "stamp of approval" in that it signifies that GSA already has determined that the vendor is responsible and its prices are fair and reasonable. While Schedule vendors are prohibited from representing that the Government endorses any specific product or service,[130] Schedule vendors may bill themselves as approved GSA Schedule vendors and reap the rewards that that designation brings. In fact, GSA encourages Schedule vendors to identify themselves using the official GSA Schedule vendor logo.[131]

B. *Disadvantages*

All that glitters is not gold, however, and would-be Schedule vendors are well advised to consider the disadvantages of the MAS Program as well.

1. Government Audit Rights

One of the primary burdens of the MAS Program is the Government's extensive authority to audit a MAS vendor's books and records. The Government maintains this authority for up to three years after final payment under the contract.[132] While the Government takes advantage of this authority primarily to assess a vendor's compliance with the Price Reductions Clause and the contract's provisions relating to payment of the Industrial Funding Fee, in actuality, the Government can audit to assess compliance with any of the terms and conditions of the MAS contract. While industry has attempted on several occasions to have these audit burdens eliminated from the MAS Program, so far, such attempts have resulted in only modest success.

Generally speaking, audits are burdensome, time-consuming, and expensive. They are also unpredictable as they are performed by people with differing opinions as to what constitutes compliance. A clean audit, therefore, may generate a momentary sense of relief, but the reality is that a new auditor may have a substantially different opinion of the breadth and spirit of a vendor's compliance. Therefore, each audit must be viewed by a vendor as a potential minefield.

Recently, GSA has moved toward relying more heavily upon pre-award audits as opposed to post-award audits. This has not, however, done away with the willingness of the GSA's Office of Inspector General to perform post-award audits where necessary. Interestingly, GSA continues to maintain post-award audit rights contrary to the changes made by the passage of Clinger-Cohen as implemented in the FAR, which eliminated certain rights by the Government to audit information supplied by commercial vendors in lieu of certified cost or pricing data. GSA does so notwithstanding a Congressional letter dated September 18, 1996 to the Office of Management and Budget, clearly stating that GSA's plan to continue to permit post-award audits of certain commercial item contracts was inappropriate and contrary to Congress' clear intent. However, to industry's regret, these changes and directives went unheeded and post-award audit rights seem destined to remain a feature of MAS contracts indefinitely.

2. Record Keeping Requirements

Whatever records a commercial contractor maintains as a matter of course, it can rest assured that its record keeping burden will increase immediately upon award of a Schedule contract. The terms of a MAS contract make it clear that vendors must maintain, among other things, all records that reflect compliance with the Price Reductions Clause for a period of at least three years after final payment.[133] Due to the nature of the Price Reductions Clause, this record keeping requirement alone sweeps within its grasp documents relating to Government sales, commercial sales, discount policies, discount practices, and more. When one adds to this requirement the similar requirements imposed relative to the industrial funding fee, the subcontracting plan, and the other socio-economic clauses of the contract, the broadscale impact of this requirement starts to become clear.

While the record keeping requirement is significant for any vendor, it becomes even more difficult for a vendor with an aggressive and independent-minded sales force. Sales representatives are often, as a class, not overly fond of maintaining records. This attitude, however, can lead to significant problems for the vendor, which could face significant penalties for failure to comply with the terms of the MAS contract.

3. Reduced Sales Flexibility

Purely commercial vendors can sell their supplies and services at whatever price the market will bear. MAS vendors, however, operate within a different marketplace and, as a result, have to abide by a different set of rules. Some of these rules negatively affect a vendor's ability to sell products at whatever price it wishes. Most notable in this regard is the Price Reductions Clause. While the function and impact of the Price Reductions Clause is discussed in detail in Chapter XIV, suffice it here to say that the clause functions as a Most Favored Customer Clause, designed to ensure that the Government receives uniquely favorable pricing treatment not just when negotiating the MAS contract, but throughout the life of the contract. As a result, before granting a post-MAS award discount to a commercial customer, MAS vendors must ask themselves whether that discount will trigger the Price Reductions Clause and, thus, compel a corresponding discount to the Government from that point forward. While there are numerous legal ways to mitigate some of this burden (which will be discussed in Chapter XIV), there is no getting around the fact that, at some level, the award of a Schedule contract brings with it the loss of some sales flexibility.

As a result, MAS contracts often create a certain tension within a vendor between its Government sales division and its commercial sales division as to the prices that are linked for Price Reductions Clause purposes. The commercial sales division, for example, frequently is willing to offer significant discounts and/or concessions with a given customer in order to make a sale. While this may be a wise business decision, such discounts may have a direct financial impact on the Government sales division, depending on the way in which the vendor negotiated its Price Reductions Clause prior to contract award. The internal tension that often results is best dealt with at the corporate level and, as noted above, can be mitigated with careful advance planning.

In the end, the effect of the Price Reductions Clause upon a particular business is, in large measure, up to the vendor. It is important to realize that the Government is not obligated to help a vendor make a fair deal. The Government's job is to obtain the best deal for the Government. Vendors that enter into a MAS contract without advance planning will pay the price in the end.

4. Internal Costs

The maxim "it costs money to make money" is alive and well in the world of Government contracting. To succeed in the MAS Program, most vendors need to increase spending in the areas of training, contract administration, and compliance monitoring. Additionally, as noted above, the Program's record keeping requirements, the industrial funding fee, and the Price Reductions Clause each brings the potential for added vendor expenditures. A medium-sized commercial vendor that never has contracted with the Federal Government before should expect, for example, to expend funds for some or all of the following:

- Enhanced training program, including production of training materials focusing on the sometimes peculiar requirements of the MAS Program;
- Enhanced compliance activities, including perhaps the retention of a dedicated compliance officer;
- Additional record keeping facilities;
- Additional staff in the areas of sales, administration, and compliance; and
- Last, but not least, consultants and lawyers.

While the extent of such expenditures will vary from vendor to vendor and will depend greatly upon the vendor's pre-existing infrastructure, it would be foolhardy to think that the MAS Program is only about revenue.

5. Penalties

Perhaps the most significant "disadvantage" of the MAS Program is the severity of the penalties that may be imposed for noncompliance. These include, but are not limited to, the contractual repayment of funds under the Price Reductions Clause, contract termination, suspension or debarment from Government contracting, civil fines and penalties under the False Claims Act, and even criminal prosecution. What is worse, the complexity of many of the rules that govern the MAS Program almost guarantees something less than 100 percent compliance. This is not to say that participation in the MAS Program is not worth the risk, but only to highlight both the importance of understanding and mitigating the risk through careful planning and compliance monitoring.

C. *Questions To Ask Before Getting Involved*

Every vendor should ask itself the following questions before deciding to enter the world of MAS contracting:

- Do we have the personnel to administer a Government contract?
- Do we have the discipline to comply with the requirements of a Government contract?
- Is management willing to instill the necessary discipline in our staff?
- Are we willing to spend money at the outset to ensure compliance during performance?
- Are we willing to create the infrastructure necessary to ensure compliance?

If a vendor is comfortable with its answers to these questions, then the MAS Program may be a good source of additional revenue.

Notes:

[127] *See* Office of Advocacy, Small Business Administration, *The Small Business Economy: A Report to the President*, 36 (2004).

[128] Schedule sales as reported by the Federal Supply Service are as follows (in billions): FY95 - $1.1, FY96 - $3.6, FY97 - $5.9, FY98 - $8.4, FY99 - $11.6, and FY00 - $13.8. *See http://ssq.fss.gsa.gov/*.

[129] The GAO has upheld this and, in fact, has held that non-Schedule vendors do not have standing to challenge such a Schedule purchase. *See DSD Labs., Inc. v. United States*, 46 Fed. Cl. 467 (2000) (A contractor must be on Schedule to protest.); *Spacesaver Systems, Inc.*, B-284924 *et al.*, June 20, 2000, 2000 CPD ¶ 107 (Agency correctly eliminated protester as responsible bidder because it could not meet delivery requirements with a product that was on its MAS contract.); *Sales Resource Consultants, Inc.*, B-284943 *et al.*, June 9, 2000, 2000 CPD ¶ 102 (A vendor that does not have a MAS contract is not an "interested party" to challenge an agency's determination as to its minimum needs and its decision to conduct limited competition among MAS vendors for a particular brand of software. GAO held that "as a general rule, obtaining information from the [MAS] program and [MAS] vendors satisfies the agency's obligation to conduct procurement planning and market research."); *Draeger Safety, Inc.*, B-285366 *et al.*, Aug. 23, 2000, 2000 CPD ¶ 139 (Although the protester had equipment that could have competed with the selected vendors, because that equipment was not listed on its MAS contract, it could not be awarded a contract limited to MAS vendors.); and *L.A. Sys., Inc.*, B-276349, June 9, 1997, 97-1 CPD ¶ 206 (Protester was not prejudiced by agency's relaxation of its requirements because, although it offered compliant products, these products were not on its MAS contract list of offered products.).

[130] GSAR 552.203-71, Restriction on Advertising (Sept. 1999).

[131] *See http://www.fss.gsa.gov/partnership* for more information.

[132] GSAR 552.215-71 (Aug. 1997). *See supra* note 92.

[133] *See supra* note 92.

V.

PRE-PROPOSAL CONSIDERATIONS

"It is easier to resist at the beginning than at the end."

-Leonardo da Vinci

O nce a vendor makes the decision to pursue a Schedule contract, the work—in the words of the Carpenters— has "only just begun." This decision brings with it a lengthy list of questions that must be answered even before a proposal can be submitted to GSA. Should we pursue a contract independently or enlist a teammate? Should we sell our products and/or services directly or sell through a dealer? Should we offer our entire product line or only certain products? Should we submit our proposal in the name of our company or in the name of a subsidiary? Each of these questions, and more, must be answered before the proposal drafting process begins.

Additionally, to ensure compliance during contract performance, compliance must be a significant factor during the vendor's pre-award planning. A potential vendor must consider all aspects of compliance and consider the following questions: Do we have sufficient personnel? Do we have qualified personnel? Who will administer the resulting contract? Who will be responsible for compliance? Do we have the commitment of management to ensure contract compliance? Who will administer the subcontracting plan? Do we have an adequate training program? Do we need an ethics hotline? Where did we put our lawyer's telephone number? The list goes on.

This chapter discusses the issues upon which a vendor should focus prior to submitting a proposal to GSA.

A. *Personnel*

1. Retention Of A Qualified Contracts Manager

A critical element of a successful MAS experience is the retention of a competent and dedicated contracts manager. This individual should have substantial Government contracting experience, ideally in the MAS Program. (The National Contract Management Association web site at *http://www.ncmahq.org* provides an excellent forum for identifying such an individual.) Additionally, if possible, the contracts manager should be involved from the very beginning—even before the proposal drafting phase. Ideally, the contracts manager should be involved in structuring the company's approach to internal compliance, hiring and training personnel, and compiling (or drafting) any necessary policies and procedures.

Subsequently, the contracts manager should be involved in developing a negotiation strategy and negotiating the final contract with GSA. It is during this phase that GSA establishes the company's "Basis of Award" category of customers for purposes of enforcing the Price Reductions Clause. The contracts manager not only can have a tremendous impact in negotiating a workable Basis of Award, but also likely will have the best understanding of that with which the company can and cannot comply in practice. Indeed, the importance of involving someone with practical knowledge of the company's sales force (whether or not that person is the contracts manager) in the negotiation process cannot be overemphasized.

2. Identification Of A Dedicated Sales Team

Because the MAS contract brings with it a host of unique obligations that require training beyond that typically given to commercial sales representatives, MAS vendors frequently assemble a dedicated federal sales team to handle all sales that result from the MAS Program. Such a team must be well trained, adequately monitored, and properly incentivized; it must be aware of what products it can and cannot offer through the MAS Program;[134] it must understand what discounts it can and cannot give and under what circumstances; it must understand what it can and cannot say to Government customers; and it must understand that selling to the Government is not like selling to a commercial customer and that the failure to comply with the terms and conditions of the MAS Program can result in significant repercussions both for the vendor and, potentially, for the individual sales representatives.

3. Identification Of A Subcontracts Manager

Equally important to identifying and training the sales force is the selection of a subcontracts manager—at least for "large vendors."[135] The subcontracts manager will be responsible for all aspects of the vendor's small business subcontracting plan. A detailed explanation of the requirements of a subcontracting plan and program are addressed in Chapter XIII. The selection and training of a competent subcontracts manager are important factors in the successful execution of a MAS contract. Rest assured— the subcontracting program will be audited at one point or another.

4. Identification Of An Ethics/ Compliance Officer

The Government seeks to contract with ethical vendors. Many large Government vendors, for many different reasons, retain a dedicated ethics/compliance officer. While this position is not compelled by the terms and conditions of the MAS Program, assigning a trusted individual to this position brings with it several advantages, discussed at length in Chapter XX.

B. *Policies And Procedures*

The quantity and complexity of the rules and regulations pertaining to MAS vendors necessitate the creation of internal policies and procedures designed to ensure compliance with those rules and regulations. While the commercial nature of the MAS Program has eliminated many of the more burdensome requirements in this regard (for example, MAS vendors no longer need to employ Government-approved accounting systems, comply with the Cost Accounting Standards, or adhere to the Cost Principles), a Schedule vendor should not fall prey to the faulty belief that its standard commercial policies and procedures are adequate to ensure compliance with the terms of the MAS Program.[136]

Schedule vendors should review carefully the FAR, GSAM, and MAS contract clauses to ensure that all obligations flowing therefrom are covered. Clearly, this may require vendors to develop policies and procedures that are not required by their other contracts. Given the significant financial consequences for not complying with the requirements of the MAS Program, the front-end development of such policies and procedures is well worth the cost.

At a minimum, a MAS vendor will want to develop policies and procedures that relate to the following areas:

- The Price Reductions Clause and the Price Adjustment—Failure to Provide Accurate Information Clause,
- The industrial funding fee,
- The Buy American and Trade Agreements Acts,
- The subcontracting plan and all related FAR requirements,

- All socio-economic clauses, and
- All record keeping requirements.

The particular aspects of each of these areas are discussed in detail in Chapters XIII and XIV.

Additionally, vendors must understand that, by entering into the MAS Program, they are agreeing to abide by certain statutes that apply to Government contractors. For example, the following statutes are incorporated into every Schedule contract:

- 31 U.S.C. § 1352 prohibits vendors from using funds from a federal contract, grant, loan, or cooperative agreement to influence any officer or employee of the agency or employee or member of Congress in connection with the award of any federal contract, grant, loan, or cooperative agreement. Moreover, a vendor is required to disclose all lobbying activities and file a statement that it has not used any federal funds to influence or bribe employees or officials in connection with an award. (General lobbying activities are excepted from this prohibition.)
- 40 U.S.C. § 328 requires vendors to pay overtime for certain employees working in excess of a forty-hour workweek and to ensure that such employees are not working under unsafe conditions.[137] It is applicable to contracts of $100,000 or more,[138] and violations are misdemeanors and each offense carries a $1,000 fine and/or imprisonment of not more than six months.[139] All commercial contracts are subject to these requirements without reference to a contract clause or certification.[140]
- 41 U.S.C. §§ 51-58 prohibit kickbacks in any form in relation to any federal contract or subcontract.[141] Violations of this law result in penalties being imposed upon the individuals involved in the kickback scheme. Penalties are substantial and can include both criminal and civil action being taken against individuals.[142]

Vendors are required to develop and implement procedures to prevent and detect violations in its operations and direct business relationships.[143]

- 41 U.S.C § 265 and 10 U.S.C. § 2409[144] both prohibit employers from engaging in retaliatory acts against employees who have provided information regarding employer violations (whistleblowers). Such retaliatory acts include discharge, demotion, or other discriminatory acts. If an employee is retaliated against by an employer, the employee may file suit for recompense for the employer's actions. Remedies include reinstatement with back pay and attorneys' fees.
- 49 U.S.C. § 40118 requires that reimbursable travel required under a Government contract be accomplished using a domestic air carrier.
- 41 U.S.C. § 423 prohibits vendors from, among many other things, engaging in employment discussions with agency employees who are involved in contract award decisions.

Noncompliance with any of these statutes could lead to contract termination, significant monetary penalties, civil sanctions, or criminal prosecution by DOJ. Thus, vendors are advised to develop an understanding of what these statutes require *before* "signing on the dotted line."

* * *

It is essential to keep in mind that creating policies and procedures is worthless absent adherence to those policies and procedures. Indeed, noncompliance with one's own procedures can arguably be worse than the absence of such procedures because a vendor's failure to comply with its own policies and procedures can be used by the Government to infer a "knowing" violation of any number of rules and regulations, which, in the right or wrong circumstances, could effect a violation of the False

Claims Act. Thus, policies and procedures should be written in a way that ensures that they (1) satisfy the applicable legal requirements and (2) can and will be followed by vendor personnel.

C. *Contract Negotiation*

While most aspects of a Schedule contract are set by rules, regulations, and/or statutes, several aspects may be negotiated prior to award. Understanding and taking advantage of these negotiable aspects at the outset of a contract can pay huge dividends down the road.

During contract negotiation, the vendor and GSA negotiate the three most negotiable aspects of the MAS Program, all relating to the Price Reductions Clause: the Basis of Award category of customers, the discount relationship between the Government and the Basis of Award category of customers, and the maximum order threshold over which a discounted sale to a Basis of Award customer will not trigger the Price Reductions Clause. Each is discussed briefly in turn below. (Each also is discussed in greater detail in Chapters VI and VII, which focus on the preparation of the vendor's proposal.)

1. Basis Of Award

The Price Reductions Clause is designed to ensure that the Government receives the benefit of discounts granted to customers that fall within a certain "relevant category of customers," sometimes called the "Basis of Award" category of customers. The customer or customers that fall within this Basis of Award *is negotiable.* Vendors generally want to select a very narrow Basis of Award, while the Government seeks as broad a Basis of Award as possible so that virtually any discounted sale anywhere in the vendor's operations will entitle Schedule purchasers to comparable discounts. The reasons for this and the impact of a failure in this regard are discussed in detail in Chapter XIV.

2. Discount Relationship

The Government and the vendor negotiate a relationship between the discount Schedule purchasers receive and the discount the Basis of Award category of customers receives. When the Schedule vendor modifies this relationship by granting a Basis of Award category of customers a deeper discount (or better terms and conditions) or granting a Schedule purchaser a more shallow discount (or worse terms and conditions), the Price Reductions Clause may be triggered. This relationship *is negotiable* at the time of contract award and, under some circumstances, renegotiable during contract performance.

3. Maximum Order Threshold

The "maximum order threshold" serves two primary purposes.[145] First, when applied to a Government sale, it provides a dollar threshold over which (i) a Government purchaser is supposed to take additional steps to ensure competition and request an additional discount from the Schedule vendor[146] and (ii) the Schedule vendor has the option of declining the Government's order. Second, it provides a dollar threshold for non-Schedule sales over which a vendor may grant a deep discount without triggering the Price Reductions Clause as long as the contract is a firm, fixed-price definite-quantity contract with specified delivery.[147]

Notwithstanding the dual purposes of the maximum order threshold, vendors have a single goal in its negotiation. *Vendors want as low a maximum order threshold as possible.* A low maximum order threshold provides maximum flexibility when dealing with non-Government customers that fall within the company's Basis of Award category of customers. While a low maximum order threshold also will prompt additional discount requests from federal purchasers, in practice, federal purchasers request additional discounts anyway, and "requests" are not "requirements" that trigger mandatory contractual price reductions. Most vendors will see that a low maximum order threshold will have little negative consequence in this regard. Unfortunately, GSA recently has clamped down on its willingness to negotiate MOTs, and vendors very well could find themselves in the position of having to accept the MOT initially set forth in the solicitation.

D. *Disclosure Of Information*

The submission of a MAS proposal brings with it the obligation to submit to GSA a sizeable dossier supporting the proposal. Vendors must be aware that thoroughness and accuracy are essential in this context and that false statements can lead to severe penalties, including criminal penalties. Thus, the wisdom of taking early steps to ensure compliance in this regard cannot be overemphasized.

1. Required Submissions

The primary source of GSA's documentation requirements stems from the Government's goal of obtaining for itself "most favored customer" pricing.[148] Unlike in the commercial world, vendors must disclose to GSA documentation demonstrating whether GSA is receiving, in fact, most favored customer pricing. While technically "cost or pricing data" is not required to be provided, GSA will expect to see information regarding the vendor's Government *and* commercial sales, prices, discounts, pricing policies, and terms and conditions. Much of this information will be submitted along with the vendor's Commercial Sales Practices Format, discussed at length in Chapter VII. Furthermore, the vendor itself may have an incentive to provide GSA much of this information in order to convince GSA that certain commercial discounts should not be given to the Government due to disparate circumstances in the nature of the sales. In this context, GSA clearly places the burden on the vendor to support its contentions.

2. Getting Started

To ensure the submission of current, accurate, and complete data, vendors should do the following *before* submitting any information to GSA:

- Involve knowledgeable personnel—with firsthand knowledge of the data being gathered—in the data gathering effort.
- Charge one employee with primary responsibility for ensuring the completeness and accuracy of the data being gathered, and afford that employee the time and resources necessary to accomplish the task and the corporate authority to compel the cooperation of others.
- Employ a broader sweep than seems necessary to capture all potentially relevant data.
- Develop a document management system to maintain traceability between documents and their "owners."
- Mark all proprietary documents "proprietary."
- Within fourteen days of submission, update all data to ensure that it is still current, accurate, and complete.
- Keep a copy of all material ultimately provided to GSA.

While these efforts may not eliminate problems, they will mitigate the likelihood that problems will arise.

3. The Risks Of Noncompliance

The primary risks of noncompliance flow from the "Price Adjustment—Failure to Provide Accurate Information" Clause.[149] The Price Adjustment Clause provides that the contracting officer may reduce the price of a contract (or contract modification) if it is determined after award that the price negotiated by GSA was increased significantly because the vendor failed to:

- Provide information requested by the solicitation/contract or by the Government;

- Provide current, accurate, and complete information; or
- Disclose changes in its commercial price list(s), discounts, or discounting policies that occurred after the initial submission and prior to the completion of the negotiations.[150]

For purposes of the Price Adjustment Clause, the Government considers data current, accurate, and complete if it is current, accurate, and complete as of fourteen days prior to submission.

Should it be determined that the vendor failed to comply with the requirements of the Price Adjustment Clause, the vendor will be subject to a retroactive (*i.e.*, backward looking) "price adjustment." Additionally, the vendor will be required to pay simple interest computed from the date(s) of overpayment to the date the Government is repaid.[151] Beyond the repayment of funds, however, violation of the Price Adjustment Clause also can lead, depending on the attendant circumstances, to contract termination, suspension, debarment, or a referral to the DOJ for action under the False Claims Act.

E. *Record Keeping*

From the Government's point of view, MAS purchases are a godsend in terms of paperwork. Unlike traditional procurements, which typically generate a mountain of paper, including solicitations, Q&As, specifications, selection criteria, evaluation documentation, and more, MAS purchases typically require only a purchase order.[152] On some occasions, the contracting officer must prepare additional documentation, such as when purchasing professional services, purchasing in excess of the maximum order threshold, or entering into other than a firm, fixed-price purchase order; but, for the most part, a simple purchase order will suffice.

MAS vendors, on the other hand, do not have it so good. The record keeping requirements of the MAS Program are significant. Vendors are required to maintain documentation demonstrating compliance with the Price Reductions Clause (which, in practice, necessitates maintaining almost all documents reflecting both commercial and federal sales), the industrial funding fee (which covers all Schedule sales), and the subcontracting plan (which covers almost all subcontracts). Additionally, vendors must keep records relating to contract administration, including contract documents, modification documents, correspondence with Schedule purchasers, and correspondence with GSA.

Compounding the foregoing burden is the fact that, pursuant to the Examination of Records Clause incorporated into every Schedule contract, vendors must maintain such records for at least three years after final payment under the contract.

F. _Ethics And Compliance_

The primary reason to adopt a comprehensive ethics/compliance program is that it will help prevent problems before they arise, but it also will help mitigate the damage caused by compliance problems should they arise. For example, a suspension/debarment official always will look to see whether a company had a functioning ethics/compliance program in the context of a suspension/debarment proceeding. Likewise, the DOJ can look for a functioning ethics/compliance program in making its determination as to whether to support a False Claims Act case brought by a whistleblower. Accordingly, the manner in which a vendor deals with ethics and compliance is a subject that should be evaluated in great detail prior to proposal submission.

The components of an effective ethics program are discussed in Chapter XX.

G. _Training_

Like the existence of an ethics/compliance program, the creation of a training program is a task that should be initiated prior to proposal submission. The first step in attempting to achieve contract compliance is ensuring that the vendor's staff understands what it means to comply—and what it means not to comply. The second step is ensuring that the training program is comprehensive and that it covers both specific contract issues and general ethics issues. An effective training program should cover all levels of company staff, from the top down.

H. *Dealers And Resellers*

The matter of dealers and resellers arises in two circumstances. First, some non-Schedule manufacturers sell to the Government through dealers and resellers that hold Schedule contracts. In this context, it is important to understand that, while GSA approves of this practice, it will reach beyond the Schedule holders to the manufacturer in order to obtain performance guarantees (since the dealer/reseller itself does not control manufacturing and product support), manufacturer discounts, and sales and marketing data to use in the negotiation of the Schedule contract. When requested, the dealer or reseller must submit, prior to contract award, *either* (1) a letter of commitment from the manufacturer that will assure the reseller of a source of supply sufficient to satisfy the Government's requirements for the contract period or (2) evidence that the reseller will have an uninterrupted source of supply from which to satisfy the Government's requirements for the contract period.[153]

Second, on the flip side of the foregoing coin, some Schedule holders permit "participating dealers" to bill the Government and accept payment in the Schedule holder's name. Such an arrangement is appropriate where the "Contractor's Billing Responsibilities" Clause[154] is applicable to the contract. In such a situation, however, the Schedule holder must assure GSA that it has obtained a written agreement from each participating dealer that requires the dealer to:

- Comply with the contract's price-related terms and conditions;
- Maintain a sales reporting system that tracks (i) the date of sale, (ii) the agency to which the sale was made, (iii) the product/model sold, (iv) the quantity sold, (v) the price (including discounts), and (vi) "all other significant sales data";

- Consent to Government audit; and
- Place orders and accept payment in the name of the vendor, in care of the dealer.[155]

The vendor must certify that "all dealers participating in the performance of this contract have agreed that their performance will be in accordance with all terms and conditions regarding prices of the contract including the provisions listed above."[156]

Regardless of whether a Schedule holder is seeking to engage a participating dealer or a non-Schedule holder is seeking to take advantage of a dealer's Schedule contract, the importance of a carefully drafted, written agreement cannot be overstated.

I. *Teaming*

As more and more federal purchasers have looked to the MAS Program to fulfill their procurement needs over the years, the nature of MAS procurements has become more complex. No longer are Schedule purchasers looking only to buy pens, pencils, and paper. Now Schedule purchasers are looking to the MAS Program for everything from complicated engineering management services to complete information technology solutions. And, as the Government's procurement requests have become more complex, so too have vendors' solutions to meeting those requests. One outgrowth of this has been the rising number of vendors that have joined together as teammates to provide integrated solutions to Government needs. Unfortunately, as GSA itself admits, its guidance regarding the proper use of Contractor Team Arrangements has been far from adequate.[157]

1. Teaming Generally

Facilitating the growth of teaming is the fact that the MAS Program explicitly allows—and, indeed, encourages[158]—the formation of "Contractor Team Arrangements."[159] The regulations provide that "[a] teaming arrangement is a contractual arrangement between two or more vendors to cooperate in connection with a particular government contract or acquisition program."[160] Vendors may form a variety of team arrangements, as long as the resulting arrangement meets the definition at FAR 9.601, which defines a team arrangement as follows:

(a) Two or more companies form a partnership or joint venture to act as a potential prime contractor; or

(b) A potential prime contractor agrees with one or more other companies to have them act as its subcontractors under a specified Government contract or acquisition program.

According to the FAR, team arrangements "may be desirable from both a Government and industry standpoint in order to enable the companies involved to . . . complement each other's unique capabilities; and . . . [o]ffer the Government the best combination of performance, cost and delivery for the system or product being acquired."[161] Moreover, the FAR recognizes that "[c]ontractor team arrangements may be particularly appropriate in complex research and development acquisitions, but may be used in other appropriate acquisitions, including production."[162]

The most common types of arrangements are partnerships, joint ventures, and cooperative agreements.[163] Each type of team arrangement provides certain advantages depending upon a company's specific goal in forming the arrangement. In addition, depending upon the order or contract being pursued, the desirability of each type may vary and a vendor could form a partnership for one project but choose to enter into a cooperative agreement for another. The decision as to what type of arrangement, if any, best suits a company's particular needs will result in different legal obligations and rights.

Team arrangements may involve two companies or several companies. The teammates may be small or large or somewhere in between. The work may be split equally between the teammates or weighted more heavily upon one teammate. The team may be formed before or after acceptance of the Government's purchase order.[164] The only requirement in the MAS context is that each team member must possess a Schedule contract of its own.[165]

2. The Advantages And Disadvantages Of Teaming

From its side of the equation, GSA has identified a number of benefits that it sees in what it refers to as "Contractor Team Arrangements," or "CTA's." Some of them, along with our commentary, are set forth in bold face type below:

- Satisfies the customer with a single solution—By combining under the auspices of a single offer the products and services available from a variety of Schedule contracts, the team enhances the "one stop shopping" potential for the customer;
- Increases competitive edge—Presumably, "one stop shopping" simplifies the customer's administrative life, thereby increasing the attractiveness of the offer;
- Increases market share—Simplifying the customer's job enhances sales, which increases market share;
- Increases visibility—Because each member of the team has the opportunity to deal directly with the customer, those members with less of a contracting history with the customer will find themselves getting more "face time" with the customer;
- Focuses on core capabilities—If each member of the team concentrates on what it does best, then the overall quality of the offer is improved, thereby increasing competitiveness and, hopefully, market share (simple arithmetic tells us that five "10's" from five separate team members who concentrate on their specialties will outscore a single competitor that draws one or two "8's" when it tries to stretch its offer in areas where it is not particularly strong internally);

- Increases small business participation—This has long been an objective of prudently constructed teaming arrangements.[166]

On its web site, GSA goes on to identify a number of additional perceived benefits. Each of these, however, appears to be a but a variant of one or more of the benefits outlined above. For the sake of completeness, however, they are delineated below:

- Obtains complementary capabilities
- Integrates different skills
- Offers additional opportunities with customers
- Builds direct relationships with customers
- Maximizes use of one or more GSA Schedule solutions, and
- Shares risks and rewards*

Because team arrangements involve a temporary alliance between two or more potential competitors, it is important to recognize that the long—and short-term interests of the teammates may differ. It is precisely for this reason that a teaming agreement has been called an "alliance between . . . competitors."[167] And it is precisely for this reason that a vendor must carefully consider the advantages and disadvantages of teaming in advance.

Under the theory that the whole is greater than the sum of its parts, teaming allows vendors to pool resources to meet the Government's requirements that they would not be able to meet independently, thus opening up new contracting opportunities— and new sources of revenue—that otherwise would be unavailable. However, as suggested above, a teaming agreement is a double-edged sword:

> [T]eammates may not share the same objectives and, in all likelihood, will not have invested equally in the procurement. For example, one contractor may have teamed to secure a long-term

market niche, while the other teammate's purpose may be limited to one particular procurement.[168]

These divergent interests and objectives should be addressed in the negotiating process. To foster the adequate consideration of these issues, vendors should ask themselves the following questions *before* entering into a teaming agreement:

- What are our goals in teaming?
- Do we need a team arrangement?
- Whom do we want as a teammate?
- Will the team arrangement adversely affect our competitive position in the future?
- What advantages does my teammate bring to the team?[169]

Such questions can help shape the internal discussion that should precede the negotiation of any team arrangement.

3. Negotiating A Team Arrangement

Potential teammates typically form a formal team arrangement *prior to* submitting an offer, but this need not be the case. Indeed, FAR Part 9 explicitly provides that team arrangements may be formed later in the acquisition process, including after contract award. Each type of team arrangement—whether partnership, joint venture, or cooperative agreement—offers different advantages depending upon a company's specific goals and the nature of the contract being pursued. The decision as to what type of team arrangement, if any, best suits a vendor's needs involves consideration of multiple factors and, in most cases, should involve the company's legal counsel.

Regardless of the type of team arrangement, the resulting team can go about meeting the Government's requirements in different ways. *First*, each team member can focus upon meeting a different aspect of the Government's requirements. *Second*, the team can work together to offer the Government a "team solution" to meet the requirements. Whatever path the team takes, GSA will recognize the integrity and validity of team arrangements as long as the team arrangements are openly identified and the relationship between the teammates is disclosed in the offer (or, for arrangements entered into after submission of an offer, before the arrangement becomes effective).[170] GSA, in fact, "strongly recommends" that ordering agencies, in issuing their Requests for Proposals ("RFQs"), require contractors to identify the offer as that of a CTA, where that is the intent. Although there is no prescribed GSA form for the creation of a CTA, and while GSA will not formally approve or endorse a CTA, GSA is interested in knowing that the offer is being submitted pursuant to a CTA, who the members of the CTA are, what the GSA Schedule contract numbers are of the members, what work will be performed by what members using which labor categories at what prices, and which member will serve as the team leader.

In theory, teaming agreements are simple to effect. In practice, however, such agreements must be drafted with great care to avoid downstream problems. In this context, an effective team arrangement should address, at least, the following issues:

- **Information.** To the extent any teammate will have access to another teammate's proprietary material, the parties are well advised to sign a "proprietary information exchange agreement" prior to entering into the teaming agreement. The purpose of such an exchange agreement is to address, up front and in writing, the disclosure, dissemination, and control of proprietary information.[171]
- **Structure.** Team arrangements may take a number of different forms. The teaming agreement must address (i) the form of team the teammates have chosen, (ii) the specific role of each teammate, and (iii) the method of apportioning payment between or among the teammates.
- **Scope.** Because the goals of the team members may differ, it is important to set in writing the scope of the team

arrangement. In this context, the written teaming agreement should set forth (i) the purpose of the team arrangement, (ii) whether the teaming agreement is exclusive or whether team members can enter into unrelated team arrangements with other parties, and (iii) the nature of the activities to be undertaken by the team.

- **Duration.** Since team arrangements seldom last forever, a well-written teaming agreement will include provisions regarding the duration of the agreement. Since team arrangements are more likely to withstand antitrust challenges if they are not open-ended, "the teaming agreement should include a provision specifying that the agreement will expire at a certain specified time or upon the occurrence or nonoccurrence of certain events . . . ."[172]

Other issues to be considered in the drafting of the CTA include:

- Termination
- Representations and warrantees between and among team members
- Limitations on liability and indemnification between and among members
- Governing law
- Disputes procedures
- Force majeure
- Administrative issues, such as notices, changes, and assignments

Like any contract, a teaming agreement must be drafted with great care and must respond to the factual circumstances that are unique to each situation. Thus, while the foregoing elements provide a starting point, they are no substitute for the advice of counsel to ensure that the vendor is adequately protected.

4. Forming A Team

FAR 9.603 emphasizes that, although no special documentation requirements exist, teaming relationships must be disclosed to GSA *before* the vendor team arrangement becomes effective. To prevent any misunderstandings later between team members and/or customers, GSA advises its contracting officers to review carefully team arrangements before they become effective. At a minimum, GSA likely will review documentation relating to the constitution of the team, the products or services the team will offer, the role of each team member in offering those products or services, and, of course, the price and discount that the team is offering.

The members of the team should, of course, take care to ensure that no provision of the CTA is inconsistent with the terms of any member's individual Schedule contract. As between the individual contractor and the GSA, the terms of the contract negotiated between them will control over any inconsistent CTA provisions.

5. Administering A Team Solution

Each GSA team is comprised of one "team leader" and one or more additional "team members." The team leader serves as the prime contractor, yet each team member is required to abide by the terms and conditions of its own respective Schedule contract. Likewise, each team member is at risk in the event of any noncompliance on the part of the team.

The team leader, which deals directly with GSA, typically secures orders from Schedule purchasers and distributes those orders to team members as appropriate. Team members have the option of limiting or capping the percentage of orders for which they will be responsible.[173] To be effective, any caps must be stated in the team arrangement.[174] These caps may be set for a variety of reasons, including limitation of resources, availability of materials, and/or production capabilities. For example, a small business team member with limited capability may want to limit the percentage of orders for which it is responsible. If no limits are set, then the team members are responsible for responding to all orders that require their products or services.[175] If a team is selected by an agency, the agency has the option of setting caps on the percentage of orders for individual team members, even if the orders are placed under a blanket purchase agreement.[176] In this way, the agency retains control over the percentage of orders that may be placed under a team arrangement.[177]

All members of a team arrangement may market the team arrangement to potential federal customers.

Perhaps the most problematic aspect of a CTA relates to billing and payment. The problem lies not in the strict legal answer to the question of who may bill the customer for the work done under the CTA, but rather, in the disconnect that members will often see between that strict legal answer and customer preferences.

From a strict legal perspective, there should be no question with respect to how billing and payment should proceed. Because each member of the team will be performing under the terms and conditions of its own Schedule contract and, thus, has privity of contract with the Government, each member should bill for its own goods and services under its own GSA contract.

This requirement is unattractive to many buyers, who view the administrative convenience of a CTA as one of its major benefits and, therefore, balk at the need to process multiple payment requests for what they view as a unitary offering from the CTA. The rules in this regard, however, are quite unclear. While the team leader certainly can simplify the buyer's life on the billing end by "bundling" the members' invoices, the bundle must be sufficiently specific to permit the buyer to make separate payments to each member. Many argue, however, that the team leader cannot, consistent with the Assignment of Claims Act, submit one bill, accept payment on behalf of the team, and distribute the proceeds to the team members. GSA's **prior** guidance on this topic was as follows:

Many times, an agency will want to receive one invoice. In such cases, the team leader may submit a single invoice for all team members, provided that the invoice indicates each team member's GSA Schedule contract number, the applicable services/products provided and the corresponding dollar value attributable to that team member. In accordance with the Assignment of Claims Act (31 U.S.C. 3727), a contractor may only assign moneys due under a contract if the assignment is made to a bank, trust company, or other financing institution. Thus, in a CTA, although the team leader may submit a single invoice on behalf of all team members, each team member must be paid separately; the team leader cannot accept payment on behalf of the entire team. [178]

Notwithstanding this prior internal GSA guidance, CTA members often were faced with contracting officers who would remit payments to the team leader and leave it to the leader to serve as the clearinghouse for funds due the individual CTA members. In an effort to stave off such problems, GSA advised offerors specifically to address invoicing and payment in the CTA agreement that they will provide to the Government and to use the CTA terms and conditions (as well as the GSA guidance) to attempt to conform the buyers' payment practices to the legal requirements that apply to those practices.

Apparently as a concession to the needs of its customers, however, in late 2004, GSA modified its official guidance regarding payments under CTAs. Specifically, as of the publication of this edition of this book at least, GSA advises vendors and agencies as follows:

> The CTA document should designate who is responsible for invoicing and payment. While the team lead may submit an invoice on behalf of all

team members, GSA recommends that payment be made to each team member. GSA recognizes, however, that there may be instances where it is advantageous to craft the CTA document so that payment is made to the team lead who, in turn, pays each team member. Under such circumstances, the CTA document should clearly indicate that all team members agree to this payment arrangement. The CTA document should also acknowledge that any dispute involving the distribution of payment between the team lead and the team members will be resolved *by the team members*, without any involvement by the government.

GSA is in the process of developing a clause in which each team member agrees that payment will be made to the team lead, who will then distribute payment to each team member. The clause will also indicate that each team member agrees that, in the case of a dispute involving the distribution of payment between the team lead and the team members, the dispute will be resolved by the team, not the government.[179]

It is notable that the law regarding assignments did not change between GSA's initial guidance and its revised guidance. One is tempted to quip that the prior guidance has been "terminated for the convenience of the Government".

6. Teaming And The Industrial Funding Fee

Each Schedule team member is responsible for paying its respective share of the industrial funding fee ("IFF") for every

Schedule product or service provided under the team arrangement. For example, if Company X, which offers a product, and Company Y, which offers a service, form a team, each company is responsible for paying the IFF on its respective product or service. Therefore, each team member is responsible for tracking any product/service provided in effecting the team solution and remitting the appropriate IFF. There is often confusion regarding the IFF under a team arrangement. However, because each team member has a contract, each effort or product supplied should be traceable to a price reflected in the contract.

7. CTA's and Prime Contractor/ Subcontractor Arrangements Under the FAR Compared

As should be apparent from the foregoing discussion, CTA's differ in a number of respects from the types of teaming agreements more customarily encountered under FAR Part 9.6. This is because many of the more routine FAR teams are crafted to deal with idiosyncratic requirements that call for unique and technologically innovative mission needs of user agencies that are being advertised for the first time. By contrast, the Schedule Program creates an ongoing relationship between the Government and Schedule contractors to provide goods and services that are, by definition, commercial in nature. Each member of a CTA, thus, already has a contractual vehicle in place to provide directly to the buyers some portion of that which is being purchased. The CTA merely "packages" all of the different commercial goods and services that may be needed in a particular case in a convenient format.

GSA has summarized for contractors its views with respect to the differences between CTA's and more standard prime contractor/subcontractor teaming arrangements under the FAR, as follows:

Contractor Team Arrangement (CTA)	Prime Contractor/ Subcontractor Arrangement
Each team member holds a GSA Schedule contract.	Only prime contractor has a government contract.
Any team member may be designated the team leader. Team leader is only responsible for duties addressed in the CTA.	Prime contractor cannot delegate responsibility for performance to subcontractors.
Any team member can interact directly with the government.	Only prime contractor can interact with government.
Responsibility of each team member is described in the CTA.	Prime contractor is totally responsible for performance.
Each GSA Schedule contractor's prices have been determined fair and reasonable.	Prime contractor determines price reasonableness of its subcontractors.
Each contractor has privity of contract with the government.	Only prime contractor has privity of contract with the government.
Ordering agency is invoiced at each GSA Schedule contractor's prices.	Ordering agency is invoiced at the prime contractor's prices.
Total solutions can be put together quickly and easily.	

J. _Non-Legal Consultants_

Schedule vendors have numerous avenues from which to obtain assistance throughout the proposal preparation process. Many vendors, for example, have expertise within their own organizations of which they may be completely unaware. Additionally, both GSA and the Small Business Administration offer workshops focusing on proposal preparation, as well as web sites that provide a wealth of information. In the commercial marketplace, a number of non-legal consultants offer a wide range of solutions for interested vendors. The advantages of using such consultants, however, depend upon the vendors' unique circumstances, including the vendors' budgets.

Non-legal consultants can—and often do—play an important role in walking a vendor through the proposal preparation, contract negotiation, and contract administration phases of the MAS Program. Several non-legal consultants are quite well respected within GSA and do a great job helping vendors cut through governmental red tape. Vendors should be wary, however, that "several" does not mean "all." Vendors should be wary of consultants that promise unrealistic access to Government personnel or unrealistic processing times for Schedule proposals. If it sounds too good to be true, it probably is. While we offer no guarantee that any particular consultant will meet a vendor's needs in every circumstance, we have listed several with which we have had positive experiences in the past in Appendix I.

While non-legal consultants do provide a useful service, they are not suitable for all situations. For example, most are not lawyers and, thus, cannot offer legal advice. Likewise, because they are not lawyers, a vendor's conversations with consultants are not protected by the attorney-client privilege. While this may not pose a problem during the typical proposal planning meeting, it may pose a problem if the vendor wants to discuss its compliance with the terms and conditions of its MAS contract.

Notes:

[134] *Pyxis Corp.*, B-282469 *et al.*, July 15, 1999, 99-2 CPD ¶ 18 (Non-Schedule items over micro-purchase threshold must be acquired in accordance with applicable acquisition rules and regulations and cannot merely be added to Schedule orders.); and *Draeger Safety, Inc.*, B-285366 *et al.*, Aug. 23, 2000, 2000 CPD ¶ 139 (Citing *Pyxis*, agency could not purchase product because a conforming product was not on its Schedule contract.).

[135] All large businesses awarded a contract that exceeds $500,000 will be required to submit a Small Business Subcontracting Plan. GSAR 552.219-71 (Sept. 1999).

[136] When a vendor believes its existing policies and procedures are satisfactory, such policies and procedures may be disclosed to GSA during the negotiation phase in support of the reasonableness of the vendor's negotiation position.

[137] 40 U.S.C. §§ 328, 333.

[138] 40 U.S.C. § 329. While the statute is silent as to how one values a contract for purposes of this section, the value of a MAS contract likely is the estimated contract value including option periods. *Cf.* FAR 25.403 (setting forth method of valuing indefinite-delivery/indefinite-quantity contracts for purposes of the Trade Agreements Act).

[139] 40 U.S.C. § 332.

[140] *Id.* § 334.

[141] 41 U.S.C. § 53. *See infra* Chapter XIV for a detailed discussion of the Anti-Kickback Act.

[142] 41 U.S.C. §§ 54-55.

[143] *Id.* § 57.

[144] Both of these statutes concern reprisals against whistleblowers. However, 41 U.S.C. § 265 covers such actions in association with public contracts and 10 U.S.C. § 2409 covers such actions in association with Department of Defense contracts.

[145] The maximum order threshold, previously called the "maximum order limitation," had a different role earlier in the Program. Historically, the Government simply could not place any orders above the maximum order limitation.

[146] In January 2001, the GSA Office of Inspector General concluded that many Schedule purchasers failed to request additional discounts even though the value of the order was over the maximum order threshold. *See Limited Audit of Federal Supply Service's Contracting for Services Under Multiple Award Schedule Contracts*, Report No. A000897/F/3/V01002 (Jan. 9, 2001), *available at http://hydra.gsa.gov/staff/ig/A000897.doc.*

[147] GSAR 552.238-75 (Sept. 1999).

[148] For a more detailed discussion of the materials that must be submitted to GSA with a proposal, *see infra* Chapter VI.

[149] GSAR 552.215-72 (Aug. 1997). For convenience, we will refer to the clause as the "Price Adjustment Clause." *See infra* Chapter VI for a detailed discussion of the Price Adjustment Clause.

[150] GSAR 552.215-72(a).

[151] *Id.* at (c)(2).

152 Government buyers, of course, still must define their requirements. Additionally, further documentation may be required in some circumstances. FAR 8.405-7(a)("The ordering activity shall document . . . the circumstances and rationale for restricting consideration of Schedule contractors to fewer than that required in 8.405-1 or 8.405-2 . . . .").

153 *See, e.g.*, IT Solicitation Clause F.3 ("Dealers and Suppliers") (I-FCI-644) (Oct. 1988). Other solicitations likely will identify this clause as I-FSS-644.

154 G-FSS-913, Contractor's Billing Responsibilities (May 2000).

155 *Id.*

156 *Id.*

157 Statements made by GSA FSS personnel at the 2005 GSA Expo.

158 According to GSA, "Team Arrangements combined with the Federal Supply Schedule Program provide Federal customers a powerful commercial acquisition strategy." GSA Procurement Information Bulletin 98-7 (Apr. 13, 1998), at Insert 2.

159 FAR Subpart 9.6.

160 John Chierichella & Douglas Perry, *Negotiating Teaming Agreements*, ACQUISITION ISSUES, June 1991, at 1 [hereinafter "Chierichella & Perry"]. *See also* FAR 9.601.

161 FAR 9.602(a).

162 FAR 9.602(b).

163 FAR 9.601.

164 FAR 9.602(c).

165 The Contractor Guide, Section B: The Multiple Award Schedule Process, *available at http://www.fss.gsa.gov/vendorguide/.*

166 *See* U.S. General Services Administration, *Frequently Asked Questions: Contractor Team Arrangements.* http:www.gsa.gov/Portal/gsa/ep/contentView.do?faq=yes&pageTypeId=8199&contended=8124&contentType=GSA_OVERVIEW#2.

167 Chierichella & Perry, at 1.

168 *Id.* at 3

169 *Id.*

170 FAR 9.603.

[171] Chierichella & Perry, at 3.

[172] *Id.* at 9.

[173] *http://www.fss.gsa.gov/schedules/faqTeam.cfm.*

[174] *Id.*

[175] *Id.*

[176] Blanket purchase agreements are discussed more fully *infra* in Chapter XV.

[177] *http://www.ecamerica.com/elibrary/files/STAFAQ.PDF*

[178] *See* http://www.MARKETUS.COM/files/teamingdb.asp.

[179] GSA "Frequently Asked Question" regarding Contractor Team Arrangements.

VI.

PROPOSAL PREPARATION

"Well begun is half done."

-Aristotle

Once the decision is made to pursue a Schedule contract, a potential MAS vendor must prepare and submit a formal proposal to GSA. Before putting pen to paper, however, a vendor must perform a number of preliminary activities. For a vendor without prior proposal drafting experience, accomplishing these activities can seem daunting. This chapter describes, in general terms, how a vendor goes about obtaining the proper solicitation and preparing a proposal.

A. *Obtaining A Solicitation*

On October 1, 1999, in order to comply with the "full and open competition"[180] requirements of the Competition in Contracting Act ("CICA"), GSA began employing an electronic posting system as its preferred method of distributing synopses, solicitations, and other documents relating to the MAS Program. Offerors access the system, known as FedBizOpps, through the Internet at *http://www.eps.gov* or *http://www.fedbizopps.gov*. Since most Schedules have an "open solicitation," interested vendors can obtain a solicitation (and submit a proposal) at any time through this system.[181]

The FedBizOpps web site encompasses two basic sections: one for Government purchasers and one for vendors. Vendors simply go to the "Vendors" section to access a searchable, on-line database of open Government solicitations (including solicitations outside the MAS Program). Vendors also can sign up for GSA's "Acquisition Notification Service," through which they will receive electronic notices for a particular solicitation, notices from a particular agency, or all procurement notices issued by the United States Government.

For a vendor new to the world of MAS contracting, the FedBizOpps web site can be a bit intimidating. A vendor begins by determining its "North American Industry Classification System" ("NAICS")[182] for the product or service to be offered through the MAS Program. This information is necessary to enable vendors to identify the appropriate GSA Schedule solicitation that corresponds to the product or service to be offered. While this need to cross-reference the NAICS to GSA's Schedule solicitation seems like an unnecessary step in the proposal process, GSA's web site facilitates the process.

Because a vendor is limited in its ability to sell its products or services to GSA by the particular Schedule that it holds, identifying the proper Schedule is an important step in the proposal process.[183] To locate a specific solicitation, vendors should access the FedBizOpps web site and search for the applicable Schedule code or Group number.[184] For example, a vendor looking for the GSA solicitation covering "General Purpose Commercial Information Technology Equipment, Software and Services" (which happens to be Schedule Group 70) would enter the code "70" in the appropriate web site box. The FedBizOpps web site provides a link to a downloadable "vendors' manual" that includes step-by-step instructions for locating a particular solicitation.[185]

B. *Reviewing The Solicitation*

Like all solicitations—whether in the commercial or the Government context—the Schedule solicitation should be reviewed very carefully. Vendors that are new to the world of Government contracting should be especially careful in this regard, but veteran Government contractors should be cautious as well. Whether new to the MAS Program or not, vendors' legal counsel should be involved in the review process. Also, vendors should not hesitate to contact GSA with any questions regarding the solicitation prior to submitting a proposal. As noted above, GSA maintains a "help line" to assist vendors through the solicitation and proposal process.

Because solicitations are revised, or even rewritten, periodically, vendors currently holding MAS contracts also are cautioned to review the solicitations anew when submitting a new proposal. The rules, regulations, statutes, and terms and conditions that affect the MAS Program change frequently.

C. *Understanding The Proposal*

A proposal, sometimes called an offer, is "a response to a solicitation that, if accepted, would bind the offeror to perform the resultant contract."[186] Because a MAS contract is an indefinite-delivery/indefinite-quantity ("IDIQ") contract, GSA's acceptance of a vendor's proposal does not guarantee the vendor anything more than the Schedule minimum, typically $2,500 in sales.[187] GSA acceptance, however, immediately creates legal obligations with which the vendor must comply.

While a step-by-step proposal preparation tutorial is beyond the scope of this book, this subsection highlights several important elements of the proposal preparation process. As with most other aspects of the MAS Program, the proposal preparation phase is fraught with traps for the unwary. Consultation with a lawyer or consultant well versed in the MAS Program is *highly recommended.*[188]

In the context of the MAS Program, an offeror's proposal is made up of the following components.

- **A Standard Form 1449.** FAR 52.212 prescribes the format to be used for commercial item acquisitions—Standard Form ("SF") 1449. SF 1449 is almost always used as the cover for a vendor's response to a solicitation. It sets forth the information that the vendor must provide when submitting an offer. When an offer is accepted, SF 1449 is executed by both parties and becomes a part of the contract.
- **The Solicitation Itself.** The MAS solicitation and the numerous clauses included therein become a part of the contract upon contract award;[189] thus, the solicitation must be submitted as a part of a vendor's proposal.
- **A Commercial Price List.** Offerors must submit one copy of a dated commercial price list and two copies of a catalog containing the products proposed for inclusion in the MAS Program. (Dealers must submit information from the manufacturer.) In this context, GSA accepts published price lists, computer generated price lists, and even copies of internal unpublished price lists. In all cases, each offered product must be identified by Special Item Number ("SIN"). All products not being offered on Schedule must be identified as "excluded."
- **A Complete and Accurate Commercial Sales Practices Format (CSP Format).** The heart of a vendor's proposal is its CSP Format. This document will be discussed in detail below.
- **Past Performance Evaluation Report.** Many Schedule solicitations require vendors to submit a Past Performance Evaluation Report. This requirement once was limited to vendors offering professional services, but it now applies to most vendors offering products as well. Notably, a vendor must submit its request for a Past Performance Evaluation Report *prior* to the submission of the proposal

to GSA. A copy of the completed evaluation then is submitted to GSA with the offer.[190]

- **Other Data as Necessary.** Such data may include a letter of supply from the manufacturer of the products offered, if the offeror is a dealer, or documentation supporting any differences between the discount offered to the Government and the best discount available.[191] The scope of this requirement will depend upon the circumstances of each individual proposal.

In addition, a vendor must ensure that its proposal covers the following topics:

- It must designate one or more "authorized negotiators" with whom GSA will deal throughout the negotiation process as well as after award. These individuals must have the authority to bind the company. Care in selecting these individuals is paramount because many contracting officers refuse even to speak with any company individual who is not listed in the contract as an authorized negotiator.
- It must include contact information, including telephone numbers, mailing addresses, and e-mail addresses.
- It must present ordering information,[192] including whether the vendor will accept orders via facsimile and electronic transfer. In this context, if the vendor is willing to receive orders electronically, it must provide GSA with the name, address, and telephone number of the individual who can be contacted regarding the establishment of the computer Electronic Data Interchange interface. Similarly, if the vendor opts to receive orders by facsimile, then it must provide the name, facsimile number, and telephone number of the individual who will receive such orders. Finally, proposals also must identify the names, addresses, and telephone numbers of the individuals who will receive mail orders. Finally, if the vendor uses dealers, it must provide the names,

addresses, telephone and fax numbers of any dealers that may receive orders under the contract.

- It must identify where the contract will be performed and whether it will be performed at more than one site.

In addition to the foregoing substantive requirements, a MAS proposal, to be accepted by GSA, must meet a few procedural requirements as well: Proposals must be written in English, and dollar figures must be stated in U.S. currency. While not a requirement, GSA "encourages" vendors to submit proposals on double-sided, recycled paper.[193]

D. *Understanding The Commercial Sales Practices Format*

Perhaps the most important element of a vendor's MAS proposal is the "Commercial Sales Practices Format," or simply the "CSP Format." GSA employs the CSP Format, set forth at GSAR 515.408, to assure itself that it is receiving "most favored customer" status. It does this by using CSP Format disclosures as the foundation for contract negotiations. Thus, the data included in the CSP Format ultimately forms the foundation for the Basis of Award category of customers and discount structure negotiated between the vendor and GSA.

Compliance with the requirements of the CSP Format is essential for several reasons. First, a vendor's failure to provide current, accurate, and complete data can—and likely will—lead to stiff penalties pursuant to the contract's Price Adjustment Clause or, worse, the False Claims Act.[194] Second, a vendor's inattention to detail can lead to compliance problems down the road in the context of the Price Reductions Clause. Third, a vendor's failure to take advantage of the opportunities that the CSP Format offers can lead to costly missed opportunities during negotiation and contract performance. In short, although it may require a significant front-end effort, a vendor will be well served in making a corporate commitment to ensure accurate completion of this CSP Format.

The following example will illustrate this point. Assume Fullstaff Co., a large commercial contractor specializing in the production of flag poles, wants to obtain a Schedule contract. Assume that, during contract negotiation, Fullstaff does not include a certain category of customers (say local government) on its CSP Format because it believes that that category is "different" from the Government. Finally, assume that, based upon the information that Fullstaff did disclose to GSA, GSA negotiates a 25 percent discount for all Schedule purchases.

Now fast forward a year or two to Fullstaff's first GSA Office of Inspector General audit when GSA learns that, since contract award, Fullstaff has been granting local governments a 30 percent discount. Fullstaff will now find itself facing a Price Adjustment Clause claim, a Price Reductions Clause claim, and, perhaps, even a False Claims Act threat. This unfortunate turn of events could have been avoided had Fullstaff simply disclosed its local government pricing to GSA during contract negotiation and used its negotiating skills (or its consultants' negotiating skills) to convince GSA that, for whatever reason, the Federal Government should not be entitled to (and would not be extended) the same discount as local governments. Remember, vendors are not required to grant GSA their best pricing under all circumstances—only fair and reasonable pricing.[195]

This section discusses the history of the CSP Format. Chapter VII provides detailed information regarding preparing the CSP Format.

Back in the days when the MAS Program was a novel concept in Government contracting, GSA relied upon a document called the Discount Schedule and Marketing Data form ("DSMD form") to collect information from would-be Schedule vendors regarding their off-Schedule pricing and discount practices. The DSMD form is the precursor to the CSP Format.

The DSMD form required offerors to disclose, for the twelve-month period preceding the submission of the proposal, on a SIN-by-SIN basis, total annual sales to the Government, total annual sales to non-governmental customers at catalog prices (less published discounts), and total annual sales to non-governmental customers at other than catalog prices. The DSMD form also required offerors to identify the largest discount(s) given to any non-governmental customer during the past year. The advent of the DSMD form immediately caused confusion within the procurement industry. It was complex, poorly written, and internally inconsistent; and it presented great risk to vendors because it encompassed a provision that required offerors to certify that

> [a]ll of the data (including sales data) submitted with this offer are accurate, complete and current representations of actual transactions to the date when price negotiations are concluded.[196]

Notwithstanding the confusion inherent in the form, GSA relied upon this certification to ensure that it received an offeror's most favored pricing, going so far as to argue, successfully on at least one occasion, that a contractor violated its certification by not disclosing to GSA an unimplemented internal company decision to increase dealer discounts at some point in the future.[197]

In 1991, GSA embarked upon an effort to improve the MAS Program. This effort involved a reconsideration of the role the DSMD form played in contract negotiation. To facilitate this effort, GSA created a special task force to review the entire MAS Program. The task force's conclusions were published in the form of a proposed rule in late 1991.[198] The proposed rule, however, received as much criticism as the initial DSMD form and GSA headed back to the drawing board. Such review efforts were not limited to GSA. Congress very much was involved as well.[199]

In February 1992, GSA issued another revised temporary rule, known as "Pilot I."[200] Like the first proposed rule, Pilot I again revised the DSMD form. The revisions, however, were very limited. Only when an offeror was willing to certify that the Government was receiving its most favored customer pricing would any of the DSMD form's data requirements be reduced. Absent such a certification, the offeror would be required to comply with the data and documentation requirements encompassed by the initial DSMD form. GSA incorporated the Pilot I DSMD form into five solicitations as a test before concluding that it did not meet the needs of industry or the Government.

GSA issued two more proposed rules in 1993. The first, issued June 8, 1993, maintained the Pilot I revised DSMD form.[201] The second attempted to get at the problem by focusing on the terms of the Price Reductions Clause.[202] Neither proposal met with success, and the procurement community continued to complain about the excessive data required by the DSMD form.

Industry's complaint with the DSMD form centered primarily on the fact that the required data was not normally required in commercial transactions and that gathering such data was time-consuming, expensive, and, in some cases, impossible. Additionally, the DSMD form required disclosure of "concessions," which were defined very broadly. The breadth of this definition, for example, at least if read literally, forced offerors to track and disclose and value *any* promotional items given to any customer in order to determine whether this would result in a customer getting a better deal than that given to the Government.

The vendor also was required to identify and justify why any terms and conditions provided to commercial customers, which would result in a better price than that offered to the Government, should not be extended to the Government. Industry also continued to question the need for the Price Reductions Clause, an issue that continues to be debated today. (As is argued today, adherence to the requirements of the clause imposes an onerous burden on vendors. At the time, however, the Price Reductions Clause was triggered any time the vendor reduced its prices either to other customers *or to the Federal Government.* Changes have occurred that reduce the monitoring burdens somewhat (for example, discounts to the Federal Government no longer trigger the clause[203]) but not entirely. Thus, the Price Reductions Clause remains a bone of contention between GSA and industry.)

After years of confusion, the DSMD form finally was challenged in court in the early 1990s. In a case whose name soon became a catchphrase in the MAS contracting community, the United States Court of Appeals for the First Circuit struck down GSA's reliance on the DSMD form, finding the form "virtually unintelligible if read literally." The case, known as *Data Translation, Inc.*,[204] involved a GSA allegation that a Schedule vendor, Data Translations, Inc., had improperly priced the contract when it failed to disclose certain *ad hoc* discounts to "special customers" in its DSMD form.

Beyond the black-letter law, it is particularly instructive to review the human element of the *Data Translation* case because it provides a telling illustration of the dangers of diving into the MAS Program unprepared. Data Translation decided to pursue a MAS contract upon the urging of its Government customers.[205] The company's DSMD form, which consisted of a 78-page questionnaire, was completed by a well-meaning, but inexperienced, nineteen-year-old contracts employee who was assisted by GSA.[206] The employee was given no real training. To help her through the process, she contacted GSA, where she was informed (as still happens to this day in similar situations) that she did not have to comply with all of the elements of the questionnaire.[207]

The employee did the best she could, only to find her company on the receiving end of a federal investigation. In its defense, Data Translation argued that it had completed its DSMD form properly and that the challenged disclosures were not required. Ultimately, the court agreed with Data Translation (indeed, one asks how it could have been otherwise when GSA's own expert, who helped draft the DSMD form language, testified that, in his experience, no vendor fully complies with the requirements of the DSMD form[208]), marking the end of the DSMD form. One can be virtually certain, however, that Data Translation would have preferred not to have been put to the fight in the first place.

Subsequent to the *Data Translation* case, in December 1993, GSA launched Pilot II, yet another attempt to solve the problems with the DSMD form. Pilot II, known formally as the "National Performance Review Reinvention Pilot II," was issued in the form of a solicitation for information technology hardware and software products. Effective for the period April 1994—March 1995, Pilot II redefined the manner in which GSA conducted the MAS Program, as follows:

- Prior to Pilot II, the Schedule's commerciality requirement was met if a product was sold in "substantial quantities" to the general public, with the term substantial quantities having to be justified by the vendor and accepted by the Government. Pilot II made it clear that a product could be commercial if it regularly were used for other than Government purposes and were sold or traded in the course of normal business operations.

- Pilot II saw the beginning of GSA's use of an electronic format for listing Schedules—the precursor to GSA *Advantage!*

- Pilot II also revised the price negotiation objective from one of receiving the same or better than most favored customer prices to that of receiving "fair and reasonable" pricing. This change in objectives was met with approval from vendors. The Government's insistence upon receiving most favored customer benefits had long been an area of dissatisfaction.

Most importantly, however, Pilot II eliminated the DSMD form and its accompanying certification requirements. In its place, GSA required that offerors provide price lists, a summary of business practices, and information relating to non-standard discounts.

In November 1994, however, Pilot II was bypassed with the issuance of Pilot III. Like Pilot II, Pilot III was issued in the form of a solicitation for information technology hardware and software products. Again, notwithstanding the incorporation of a revised Price Reductions Clause, industry was disappointed with the change. Industry also was disappointed by the fact that Pilot III reverted back to the use of the old DSMD form and the data requirements related thereto.

The DSMD form finally was retired on August 21, 1997, when GSA issued the current CSP Format as part of a final rule.[209]

E. *Understanding The Price Adjustment— Failure to Provide Accurate Information Clause*

The Price Adjustment Clause, found at GSAR 552.215-72, is GSA's answer to the FAR's Defective Pricing Clause.[210] The Price Adjustment Clause affords GSA the right to demand a refund, make a forward price adjustment, or terminate a contract for default in the event a vendor provides inaccurate or incomplete data to GSA during the contract negotiation process.[211] After briefly reviewing the history of the clause and discussing the continuing attempts by industry to excise the clause from the regulations, this subsection analyzes the current clause and its application to Schedule vendors.

1. History Of The Price Adjustment Clause

In 1984, CICA applied the requirements of the Truth in Negotiations Act ("TINA")[212] to the MAS Program.[213] While a mainstay of traditional Government contracting, TINA, which requires an offeror submitting a bid of $500,000 or more to submit certified "cost or pricing data,"[214] is anathema to the more commercial-like world of MAS contracting. Ten years later, Congress exempted commercial item procurements from TINA's reach with the passage of the Federal Acquisition Streamlining Act of 1994 ("FASA"). The FAR Council incorporated this exemption into the FAR soon thereafter.[215]

Prior to the current version, the MAS contract contained the "Price Reduction for Defective Pricing" Clause.[216] The Price Adjustment Clause was promulgated in 1997.[217] However, FASA included, among other things, a mandate that contracts for the acquisition of commercial items contain only those clauses "that are required to implement provisions of law or executive orders applicable to acquisitions of commercial items or commercial components" or "that are determined to be consistent with customary commercial practice."[218] Since there was not a law or statute that required the Price Adjustment Clause and since such a clause was not part of customary commercial practice, industry had reason to expect that use of the clause would be discontinued. However, GSA continued—and, to a very minor extent, still continues—to include the Price Adjustment Clause in some MAS contracts, citing a need to assure that GSA receives accurate pricing information for its commercial items.

2. Industry's Efforts To Do Away With The Price Adjustment Clause

Over the years, the procurement industry has expressed substantial discontent with the Price Adjustment Clause. While most of this discontent manifested itself in the form of casual remarks to contracting officers or informal letters to GSA, on June 1, 1999, industry submitted a formal petition, filed by the Government Electronics and Information Technology Association ("GEIA") on behalf of its membership, to the Office of Federal Procurement Policy ("OFPP") challenging the legality of the clause.[219]

GEIA's petition, which was addressed to then-OFPP Administrator Deidre Lee, argued that the Price Adjustment Clause (and the Examination of Records Clause[220]) was inconsistent with the FAR and contrary to the direction of Congress to minimize the use of Government-unique contract requirements in the acquisition of commercial items. In support of its petition, GEIA argued that the FAR requires that commercial item contracts, "to the maximum extent practicable," include only those clauses that (i) are required to implement provisions of law or executive orders applicable to commercial items or (ii) are determined to be consistent with "customary commercial practice."[221] GEIA argued that the Price Adjustment Clause was not "required" to implement provisions of law or executive order because FAR 52.212-5 provides an exhaustive list of such required contract clauses and the Price Adjustment Clause is not identified thereon. Thus, reasoned GEIA, if the challenged clause is permissible, it must be because it constitutes "customary commercial practice." GEIA presented substantial evidence, however, much of which was gathered by GSA, to demonstrate that this was not so.[222]

On October 12, 1999, OFPP denied industry's request for relief from the Price Adjustment Clause.[223] In her decision, Ms. Lee suggested that the Price Adjustment Clause was a necessary tool to protect the interests of the Government in an environment where vendors do not compete in a head-to-head competition.[224] She explicitly dismissed GEIA's assertion that the clause was not in keeping with customary commercial practice. According to Ms. Lee, the Price Adjustment Clause was consistent with commercial practice to the "maximum extent practicable given the current objectives of the MAS Program."[225] Ms. Lee concluded that GSA's use of this clause represented a reasoned and careful decision that was in keeping with the requirements of the FAR.

We believe that the OFPP decision rests upon a tenuous foundation. A potential vendor seeking to challenge the incorporation of the Price Adjustment Clause into its MAS contract could bring the matter before the GAO, the United States Court of Federal Claims, or the district court. All three of these forums have entertained such pre-award protests in the past. The basis of such a protest would be that the incorporation of the Price Adjustment Clause violates FAR Part 12 because GSA has not shown that the clause is "required." While the OFPP's October 12, 1999 decision might one day be used by GSA as evidence against the protest, the decision is susceptible to challenge on several grounds.[226]

Notwithstanding these flaws in the OFPP decision,[227] however, the decision represented a major setback to industry's attempts to remove the Price Adjustment Clause from the MAS Program, and a major setback for reform generally. Time will tell just how major. From this point forward, however, the clause is alive; and, although GSA uses it sparingly, vendors would be wise to understand its workings.[228]

3. The Current Price Adjustment Clause

The current Price Adjustment Clause, found at GSAR 552.215-72, provides, in relevant part, as follows:

> The Government, at its election, may reduce the price of this contract or contract modification if the Contracting Officer determines after award of this contract or contract modification that the price negotiated was increased by a significant amount because the Contractor failed to:
>
> (1) Provide information required by this solicitation/contract or otherwise requested by the Government;
> (2) Submit information that was current, accurate, and complete; or
> (3) Disclose changes in the Contractor's commercial pricelist(s), discounts or discounting policies which occurred after the original submission and prior to the completion of negotiations.[229]

The clause goes on to make clear that the Government's rights specified in the Price Adjustment Clause are not exclusive "and are in addition to any other rights and remedies provided by law or under this contract."[230] In other words, the damages that could flow from a Price Adjustment Clause violation may very well exceed the price adjustment.[231]

The Price Adjustment Clause requires vendors to report even *contemplated* discounts to GSA.[232] Indeed, vendors are required to disclose all pricing information relating to discounts, including potential changes to pricing structures that are under consideration by the company at the time of negotiation. The case of *Millipore Corp.*[233] highlights this requirement. The vendor in *Millipore* failed to disclose to GSA the fact that it was "considering" modifications to its pricing structure involving dealers. This failure came to light during a post-award audit conducted by the GSA OIG. Consequently, the GSA OIG recommended a price adjustment.[234] The contracting officer agreed, Millipore challenged the final decision before the GSBCA, and the GSBCA found in favor of GSA.[235]

F. *Central Contractor Registration*

As of October 2003, all MAS vendors must register with the Central Contractor Registration (CCR) database.[236] This can be done on-line at *www.ccr.gov*. According to CCR, it takes the Government approximately 48 hours to process new registrations. CCR registration must be updated annually.

G. *eOffers, eMod, and Quick.Mod*

As of the submission of this Second Edition to the publisher, GSA had just rolled out its new "vendor electronic offer submission system" (*eOffer*) for new schedule contract proposals. The eOffer program is open only to Schedule IT 70 contract holders. According to GSA, initial reviews of the program were extremely favorable and GSA plans to make the program available to Financial and Business Services (520), Professional Engineering Services (871) and Advertising and Integrated Marketing (541) vendors by the end of fiscal year 2005, and to all other Schedule offers by fiscal year 2006.

GSA's *eMod program*, released in July, 2004, is an electronic method for vendors to make changes to schedule contracts, such as adding or deleting Special Item Numbers. Currently all GSA Schedule contracts are eligible for eMod. eMod requires an electronic signature and any changes must be approved before revisions may be posted on GSA Advantage.

Quick-Mod is a pilot program introducing a streamlined method of adding products to a schedule contract without specific Contracting Officer approval. Quick-Mod is not open to all vendors, only ITFO vendors. A contracting officer must ask a vendor to participate in the program, whereupon the vendor must modify its contract to include contract clause I-FSS-598.

From the vendor's point of view, GSA is touting these new systems as easier and faster than the current paper based systems. From the Government's point of view, the system was designed to improve efficiency, enhance GSA-to-applicant communications, enable better proposal tracking, eliminate a significant amount of data entry and reduce paper files.

Notes:

[180] *See, e.g., Qualimetrics, Inc.,* B-262057, Nov. 16, 1995, 95-2 CPD ¶ 228, in which the Comptroller General held that GSA had failed to use "full and open competition" in the context of the MAS Program when it failed to effectively solicit an incumbent contractor through the inadvertent misaddressing of a solicitation. GSA has prevented this problem from recurring by listing all solicitations on its web site.

[181] There are no closing dates for MAS solicitations. Prior to March 21, 2000, acquisition centers could continue to issue annual "open seasons." *See* FSS Acquisition Letter FC-97-5 (Oct. 13, 1997), Supplements 2 (May 22, 1998) and 4 (Mar. 21, 2000).

[182] Prior to October 11, 2000, the NAICS classification was known as the "Standard Industrial Classification" or "SIC" code.

[183] *See DSD Labs., Inc. v. United States,* 46 Fed. Cl. 467 (2000) (rejecting vendor's claim that contracting officer used the wrong Schedule or, alternatively, that vendor's bid should be considered because it is a Schedule contractor -- just not on the Schedule selected by contracting officer).

[184] Every product or service procured by GSA through the MAS Program is assigned a Group number. Most information technology, for example,

is assigned to Schedule Group 70, while telecommunications products are assigned to Schedule Group 58. A product's or service's specific Group number can be obtained through GSA's web site.

[185] The manual is found at *http://eps.gov/EPSVendorsManual/epsvendorsmanual.htm*. GSA also maintains a "help line" to assist vendors through the solicitation and proposal process. This number and other important GSA telephone numbers are listed in Appendix I of this book. Additionally, the SBA provides assistance to small businesses. The applicable telephone numbers for the SBA are listed in Appendix I as well.

[186] FAR 2.101.

[187] An IDIQ contract is binding as long as it reflects some minimum level of consideration. *See, e.g., Carr's Wild Horse Ctr.*, B-285833, Oct. 3, 2000, 2000 CPD ¶ 210 (holding that a guaranteed minimum quantity of 100 horses and/or burros constituted sufficient consideration to bind the parties in the context of the Bureau of Land Management's temporary horse/burro adoption program). *See also supra* note 13.

[188] Additionally, GSA's Federal Supply Service ("FSS") offers several useful training classes for which vendors may register through GSA's web site or the web site for the specific FSS center in which the vendor is interested.

[189] FAR 52.212-4 (Contract Terms and Conditions—Commercial Items) and FAR 52.212-5 (Contract Terms and Conditions Required to Implement Statutes or Executive Orders—Commercial Items).

[190] Until recently, vendors were required to obtain their Past Performance Evaluation Reports from Dun & Bradstreet. Dun & Bradstreet recently transferred the preparation of such reports to "Open Ratings." Questions regarding Past Performance Evaluation Reports may be directed to Open Ratings at 617.232.9660, ext. 162.

[191] *See infra* discussion regarding the Price Reductions Clause at Chapter XIV and the Commercial Sales Practices Format at Chapter VII.

[192] GSAR 552.216-73 (Sept. 1999) and Alternate II (Sept. 1999).

[193] GSA looks for a 30 percent post-consumer material standard for non-electronic submissions. FAR 52.204-4.

[194] Interestingly, in *US ex rel Vosika and Thompson v. Starkey Labs,* Civil No. 01-709, September 8, 2004, 2004 US Dist Lexis 18349, the United States District Court for the District of Minnesota agreed with the defendant that it was not required to disclose to GSA "every discount ever offered," but refused to dismiss the case because the agency alleged that the vendor failed to disclose "significant" discounts. While this case may be useful (after the fact) to a vendor facing Price Adjustment Clause or Price Reductions Clause allegations, vendors who rely on this apparent flexibility do so at their own risk since it is quite likely that vendors and contracting officers will have quite a different opinion as to the meaning of "significant" in this context.

[195] GSAR 538.270 (July 2000). On the topic of "fair and reasonable" pricing in the context of hourly rates, Professors Ralph Nash and John Cibinic make the following point: GSA's "determination that . . . hourly rates are 'fair and reasonable' is *not* made by comparing them to the rates charged by other contractors selling the same services. The GSA determination is merely that the rates are in line with or lower than the rates the company charges to commercial customers. This curious definition of 'fair and reasonable' does not seem to be understood by many COs and probably would not be accepted by them if they understood it." THE NASH & CIBINIC REPORT, Vol. 19, No. 4, April 2005 at ¶ 17.

[196] FSS Clause M-FSS-330 (1984), *supra* note 56.

[197] *See Millipore Corp.*, GSBCA No. 9453, 91-1 BCA ¶ 23,345 (1990) (upholding GSA's allegation of defective pricing); *see also P.A.L. Sys. Co.*, GSBCA No. 10858, 91-3 BCA ¶ 24,259 (Contractor had disclosed a higher discount than that negotiated with the Government, but an audit revealed discounts that were ever higher. GSBCA endorsed a refund that measured the difference between the disclosed and undisclosed discounts, even though the discounts were not the basis for the price negotiated.); *Gelco Space*, GSBCA No. 7916 *et al.*, 91-1 BCA ¶ 23,387 (1990) (distinguishing between defective pricing claim and Price Reductions Clause violation).

[198] 56 Fed. Reg. 56,956 (Nov. 7, 1991) (to be codified at 48 C.F.R. pts. 515 and 538).

[199] *See* Richard J. Wall, *Surviving Commercial Pricing Rules*, 23 Pub. Cont. L. J. 553 (Summer 1994).

[200] 57 Fed. Reg. 5862 (proposed Feb. 18, 1992) (to be codified at 48 C.F.R. pts. 515 and 538).

[201] 58 Fed. Reg. 32,085 (proposed June 8, 1993) (to be codified at 48 C.F.R. pts. 515 and 538).

[202] 58 Fed. Reg. 32,890 (proposed June 14, 1993) (to be codified at 48 C.F.R. pts. 538 and 552).

[203] FAR 8.405-4 (2004) ("Schedule contractors are not required to pass on to all schedule users a price reduction extended only to an individual ordering activity for a specific order.")

[204] *United States v. Data Translation, Inc.*, 984 F.2d 1256 (1st Cir. 1992).

[205] *Id.* at 1258.

[206] *Id.*

[207] *Id.* at 1263.

[208] *Id.* at 1261-62.

[209] 62 Fed. Reg. 44,518 (Aug. 21, 1997) (to be codified at 48 C.F.R. pts. 504, 507, 510, 511, 512, 514, 515, 538, 539, 543, 546, 552, and 570).

[210] *See* FAR 15.407-1 and 52.215-10.

[211] GSAR 552.215-72, Price Adjustment -- Failure to Provide Accurate Information (Aug. 1997).

[212] Ch. 1041, 70A Stat. 130 (1962) (codified as amended at 10 U.S.C. §§ 2306, 2306a); 41 U.S.C. § 254(d).

[213] Pub. L. No. 98-369, § 2711, 98 Stat. 1175 (codified as amended at 41 U.S.C. § 253).

[214] FAR 15.403-4.

[215] FAR 15.403-1(c)(iii)(2).

[216] Prior to 1997, the Price Reduction for Defective Pricing Data Clause was included in a "Basis for Price Negotiation" provision.

[217] GSAR 552.215-72 (Aug. 1997).

[218] GEIA Petition to OFPP Administrator, Review of GSAR MAS Pricing Clauses 2 (June 1, 1999).

[219] GEIA filed the petition under the administrative procedures established by Section 25 of the Office of Procurement Policy Act,

which allows private parties to seek OFPP's review of an agency procurement regulation for consistency with the FAR. GEIA was supported in this petition by other industry groups including the Aerospace Industries Association, the Coalition for Government Procurement, the National Defense Industry Association, and the American Electronics Association. GEIA also was supported by a thorough analysis drafted by Richard J. Wall, CPA, of Ernst & Young.

[220] Interestingly, the petition initially requested review of three clauses, including the "Price Reductions Clause." GEIA decided to drop its challenge of this clause in the final petition. *See* James J. McCullough & Jonathan S. Aronie, *Check or Checkmate? OFPP's Recent Decision Affirming the Legality of GSA's Post-Award Audit Clause*, CONTRACT MANAGEMENT (Dec. 1999), at 10 [hereinafter "McCullough & Aronie"]; *see also* Richard J. Wall & Robert J. Sherry, *Industry's Appeal to OFPP to Revoke the GSAR Clauses: What's All The Fuss About?* FED. CONTRACTS REP., at 161 (Aug. 2, 1999).

[221] FAR 12.301(a).

[222] McCullough & Aronie, *supra* note 200, at 12.

[223] *See* letter from Deidre Lee, Administrator of OFPP, Office of Management and Budget, to Government Electronics and Information Technology Association (Oct. 12, 1999).

[224] While OFPP also seemed to agree that the challenged clauses were not "customary commercial" clauses, it focused more attention on the requirement that clauses be commercial only to the "maximum extent practicable." *Id.*

[225] *Id.* at 2.

[226] McCullough & Aronie, *supra* note 200, at 13-14.

[227] *Id.* at 10; *see also* Wall & Sherry, *supra* note 200, at 161.

[228] Industry currently is pursuing legislative relief through the Acquisition Reform Working Group ("ARWG"). The ARWG's "2000 Legislative Package" seeks the prohibition of "defective pricing remedies on contracts for commercial items." *See* ARWG 2000 Legislative Package (Background Papers) at 8-9.

[229] GSAR 552.215-72(a) (Aug. 1997).

[230] *Id.* at (e).

[231] With respect to calculating a price adjustment, the GSBCA generally presumes that "the natural and probable consequence of a failure to disclose is that the negotiated price is inflated by the full amount of the omission." *Millipore Corp.*, GSBCA No. 9453, 91-1 BCA ¶ 23,345 at ¶ 117,069 (1990); *see also Sylvania Elec. Prods., Inc. v. United States*, 479 F.2d 1342, 1349 (1973).

[232] *See Millipore Corp.*, GSBCA No. 9453, 91-1 BCA ¶ 23,345 (1990).

[233] *Id.*

[234] The OIG relied upon Clause 330, Basis for Price Negotiations, which included a subsection entitled "Price Reduction for Defective Pricing Data." *Millipore Corp.*, 91-1 BCA at ¶ 117,066. The clause is analogous in many respects to GSA's current Price Adjustment—Failure to Provide Accurate Information Clause (GSAR 552.215-72).

[235] *But see United States ex rel. Thompson v. Starkey Laboratories, Inc.*, 2004 U.S. Dist. Lexis 18349 (September 8, 2004) ("The Court also agrees that Starkey would be entitled to dismissal of Plaintiffs' claims had Plaintiffs alleged that the terms offered to other purchasers were only slightly better than those offered to the VA. However, Plaintiffs have alleged that discounts whose terms were significantly better than those disclosed to the government were granted to certain purchasers and were in existence at the time the contract was being negotiated.")

[236] 68 Fed. Reg. 56669 (Oct. 1, 2003).

VII.

PRICING MULTIPLE AWARD SCHEDULE CONTRACTS
(by Richard J. Wall, Ernst & Young)

"I'll make him an offer he can't refuse."
-Vito Andolini (aka Don Vito Corleone)
in Mario Puzo's *The Godfather*

This chapter covers how MAS contracts awarded by the GSA are priced. It covers the Government's pricing rules in general and focuses more specifically on the rules adopted by GSA for its unique MAS Program. The chapter covers the pricing process—from proposal submission to price negotiation and contract award. Because MAS pricing is a continuous process throughout the period of performance, this chapter also covers pricing changes that occur after contract award. Finally, this chapter covers the special requirements of the MAS Program managed by the Department of Veterans Affairs.

A. *Government Pricing Policies And Procedures*

The FAR, which is applicable to all federal agencies, provides the basic foundation for the Government's policies and procedures on contract pricing. Federal agencies, such as GSA, may issue supplemental policies and procedures that are necessary to implement the FAR and satisfy a specific need of the agency.[237] With respect to the MAS Program, GSA has incorporated special policies, procedures, and contract clauses into the GSAM.[238] It is, nevertheless, important to understand the overall framework of the Government's pricing rules and the proper context for applying GSA's unique pricing rules and practices.

1. Fair And Reasonable Prices

Contracting officers at all federal agencies are responsible for purchasing supplies and services from prospective contractors at fair and reasonable prices.[239] "Fair and reasonable" is a term of art, and a substantive body of related law and regulation has been developed over the years. Surprisingly, as important as the term "fair and reasonable" is to Government policies and procedures on contract pricing, the term is not expressly defined in the FAR.

One guidepost for deciding what is fair and reasonable might be derived from the FAR Part 31 Cost Principles,[240] which state that a fair and reasonable price would be a price a reasonably prudent business person would pay in the conduct of competitive business for a particular supply or service. Another guidepost is contained in the Contract Pricing Reference Guides,[241] which state that a fair price would be a price in line with previous prices for same or similar supplies and services that have been negotiated between informed buyers and sellers under similar competitive market conditions, terms and conditions, and quality and quantity requirements. A fair price must also be realistic in terms of the contractor's ability to satisfy the terms and conditions of the contract. Economic factors, such as supply, demand, and competition, must be considered.

The contracting officer must be satisfied that a fair and reasonable price was obtained from the prospective contractor. The price negotiation memorandum prepared by the contracting officer must state this and document the basis for making such a determination.[242] Under the FAR's pricing rules, if the contracting officer cannot make a determination of a fair and reasonable price, then supplies or services may not be purchased from the prospective contractor. There may be exceptions for extraordinary circumstances, such as meeting critical needs or reacting to emergency situations, but this is not likely to be the case with MAS contracts.

Of course, how the contracting officer establishes what is a fair and reasonable price depends upon a wide range of factors, including the nature of the supplies or services being purchased, how the purchase is being conducted, the type of contract being used, the period of performance, the terms and conditions, and the relative risks being assumed by the parties. These factors determine the pricing approach to be used by the contracting officer, as well as the type of pricing proposal data that must be obtained from the prospective contractor. In recent years, the pricing process has significantly changed, particularly under the reforms enacted under the Federal Acquisition Streamlining Act ("FASA") and Clinger-Cohen Act for acquiring commercial items. Today, the contracting officer's determination of fair and reasonable is to be based on appropriate information about prices at which same or similar items previously have been sold.[243]

2. Government Pricing Approaches

There are two basic approaches to pricing Government contracts: cost-based approach and price-based approach. The cost-based approach (also called "cost analysis") is a cost build-up approach that requires estimates of material, labor, and other direct costs, plus overhead and general and administrative expenses, that would be incurred to accomplish the work required by the contract. In addition to these costs, the prospective contractor would add profit or fee. Because the cost build-up approach is reliant on estimated costs, the Government contractually imposes a number of protective provisions, such as the Truth in Negotiations Act (TINA) and the Cost Accounting Standards (CAS). As a basis for determining a fair and reasonable price, the contracting officer must obtain advisory services from functional experts (*e.g.*, engineering, manufacturing, information technology), price analysts, and auditors. As might be expected, this is a cumbersome process for all parties.

The price-based approach (also called "price analysis") is a market driven approach. This approach relies on prices at which same or similar items have previously been sold in the commercial marketplace. In evaluating what is fair and reasonable, the contracting officer considers catalog prices, market prices, or customary prices of commercial items that either are available or will be available in the commercial marketplace. The contracting officer is expressly prohibited from obtaining cost or profit information for commercial items.[244] Because the price-based approach is not reliant on estimated costs, it is not encumbered with the protective provisions associated with the cost-based approach. For example, the price-based approach is exempt from TINA and CAS.

3. Pricing Proposal Data

The pricing approach being used dictates the type of pricing proposal data that is to be submitted by the prospective contractor. The pricing proposal data required for the cost-based approach is called "cost or pricing data." The pricing proposal data required for the price-based approach is called "information other than cost or pricing data." Loosely defined, "information other than cost or pricing data" is anything that is not "cost or pricing data," as shown below.[245] Both are terms of art, and the distinction is significant to the risks assumed by the prospective contractor.

"Cost or pricing data" means all facts that . . . prudent buyers and sellers would reasonably expect to affect price negotiations significantly . . . . Cost or pricing data are more than historical

accounting data; they are all the facts that can
be reasonably expected to contribute to the
soundness of estimates of future costs and to the
validity of determinations of costs already
incurred. They also include such factors as—

(1) Vendor quotations;
(2) Nonrecurring costs;
(3) Information on changes in production methods
    and in production or purchasing volume;
(4) Data supporting projections of business
    prospects and objectives and related
    operations costs;
(5) Unit-cost trends such as those associated with
    labor efficiency, make-or-buy decisions;
(6) Estimated resources to attain business goals;
    and
(7) Information on management decisions that
    could have a significant bearing on costs.

* * *

"Information other than cost or pricing data" means
any type of information that is not required to be
certified [i.e., cost or pricing data] . . . and is
necessary to determine price reasonableness or
cost realism. For example, such information may
include pricing, sales, or cost information, and
includes cost or pricing data for which certification
is determined inapplicable after submission.[246]

The distinction is important. The type of pricing proposal
data establishes the Government's audit rights over the data
submitted by the prospective contractor. For "cost or pricing data,"
the Government's audit rights extend until three years after final
payment under the contract.[247] For "information other than cost

or pricing data," the Government's audit rights are limited to any time before award.[248] Prospective contractors should take care to mark pricing proposal data that is "information other than cost or pricing data" (*e.g.*, catalogs, price lists, commercial contracts, master agreements, invoices) with a rubber stamp and to place an appropriate footer on prepared text documents and worksheets.

Whether applying the cost-based approach or the price-based approach, the contracting officer is instructed to obtain no more information than is necessary.[249] The contracting officer is to place the provision, "Requirements for Cost or Pricing Data or Information Other Than Cost or Pricing Data," in solicitations that contemplate the need for proposal pricing data from prospective contractors.[250] Where it is known that "cost or pricing data" would not be required, such as in the acquisition of a commercial item, the contracting officer is to use Alternate IV of this notice, which in essence specifies that "information other than cost or pricing data" is required.[251] GSA uses Alternate IV for MAS contracts.

B. *GSA Pricing Policies And Procedures*

Conceptually, GSA's pricing polices and procedures for MAS contracts are no different from those contained in the FAR for all federal agencies. GSA contracting officers are similarly charged with the responsibility of securing prices from prospective contractors that are fair and reasonable. What is different, however, is how the GSA contracting officer determines fair and reasonable prices for supplies and services to be purchased under MAS contracts. As previously mentioned, because MAS contracts are unique, GSA has issued supplemental policies and procedures through the GSAM.

GSA's pricing policies and procedures for MAS contracts were first enunciated in the 1982 MAS Policy Statement,[252] which remained in effect until 1996, at which time the reforms legislated under FASA and Clinger-Cohen were implemented by GSA through the GSAR.[253] Although the GSA's pricing policies and procedures have undergone some refinement, their core objective has remained the same. Essentially, GSA requires that a most

favored customer price be obtained from the prospective
contractor and that a specific pricing relationship be maintained
over the life of the contract. That is, the GSA pricing process is
continuous, and it is important that prospective contractors
understand the need for installing the necessary infrastructure
to comply with these policies and procedures.

1. GSA Most Favored Customer Pricing

In its 1982 MAS Policy Statement, GSA's stated goal was to
obtain a discount equal to or greater than the discount given to
the prospective contractor's most favored customer. This discount
was defined as the best discount given to any customer, except
original equipment manufacturers ("OEMs"), dealers, and
distributors, because these customers were not ultimate end users
of the supplies or services. GSA recognized that there could be
situations where the terms and conditions of a purchase agreement
with the most favored customer would be substantively different
from what could be accepted by GSA or where there were
substantive differences in the relative bargaining positions.

Nonetheless, the 1982 MAS Policy Statement warned that
GSA would not award a MAS contract to a prospective contractor
that did not give GSA a price equal to its large volume end user
customers under comparable terms and conditions. The current
GSA pricing policy, as expressed in the GSAM, is not markedly
different from the 1982 MAS Policy Statement:

> The Government [GSA] will seek to obtain the
> offeror's best price (the best price given to the most
> favored customer). However, the Government
> [GSA] recognizes that the terms and conditions of
> commercial sales vary and there may be legitimate
> reasons why the best price is not achieved.[254]

GSA believes that its most favored customer pricing goal and
the FAR's stated obligation to seek fair and reasonable prices are

compatible. GSA accepts that legitimate differences in commercial terms and conditions should be considered by the GSA contracting officer when negotiating price.[255] Notwithstanding, the GSA contracting officer's negotiation objective should still be based on the best discount given to any commercial customer. It is important for the prospective contractor to understand that GSA's most favored customer pricing goal entails a disclosure obligation, even if most favored customer pricing will not be offered or accepted by the prospective contractor.

2. GSA Pricing Relationships

The structure of GSA's pricing policies and procedures requires the GSA contracting officer to establish at the time of contract award discrete relationships among the following three prices:

- The commercial list price,
- The most favored customer price for a given customer or category of customers (also called "Basis of Award" or "Relevant Category" customer), and
- The MAS contract price.

Once established, the relationship among these three prices is to be maintained throughout the MAS contract period of performance through the Price Reductions Clause of the MAS contract.[256] Simply put, if either the commercial list price or the most favored customer price subsequently decreases during the term of the contract, then the MAS contract price must also be decreased. There are a number of complexities to these pricing relationships that are discussed later in this chapter. However, it should be pointed out that maintaining a pricing relationship is a distinguishing feature of MAS contracts and the reason why MAS contract pricing must be viewed as a continuous process.

C. *GSA Pricing Proposal Requirements*

Because the MAS Program essentially entails the acquisition of commercial items, GSA uses the price-based approach to evaluate fair and reasonable pricing. Consistent with the FAR, GSA requires the prospective contractor to submit "information other than cost or pricing data," as modified for GSA's purposes. This is the process by which the GSA contracting officer establishes relationships among the three prices needed to operate the Price Reductions Clause.

1. Commercial Sales Practices Format

As previously mentioned, GSA uses Alternate IV to the "Requirements for Cost or Pricing Data or Information Other Than Cost or Pricing Data" solicitation provision.[257] The Commercial Sales Practices Format ("CSP Format") is the manner specified by the GSA contracting officer for the purpose of submitting "information other than cost or pricing data." It replaced the Discount Schedule and Marketing Data ("DSMD") format previously used by GSA. The key requirements of the CSP Format are shown below.

Commercial Sales Practices Format

(Figure 515.4-2)

Name of Offeror _____ SINs_____

(1)   Provide the dollar value of sales to the general public at or based on an established catalog or market price during the previous 12-month period or the offeror's last fiscal year. $_____. State the beginning and ending of the 12-month period. Beginning _____ ending _____. In the event that a dollar value is not an appropriate measure of the sales, provide and describe your own measure of the sales of the items.

(2) Show your total projected annual sales to the Government under this contract for the contract term, excluding options, for each SIN offered. If you currently hold a Federal Supply Schedule contract for the SIN, the total projected annual sales should be based on your most recent 12 months of sales under that contract.

SIN_____ $_____

SIN_____ $_____

SIN_____ $_____

(3) Based on your written discounting policies (standard commercial sales practices in the event you do not have written discounting policies), are the discounts and any concessions which you offer the Government equal to or better than your best price (discount and concessions in any combination) offered to any customer acquiring the same items regardless of quantity or terms and conditions? YES: _____ NO: _____.

(4) (a) Based on your written discounting policies (standard commercial sales practices in the event you do not have written discounting policies), provide information as requested for each SIN (or group of SINs for which the information is the same) in accordance with the instructions at Figure 515.4-2 which is provided in the solicitation for your convenience. The information should be provided in the chart below or in an equivalent format developed by the offeror. Rows should be added to accommodate as many customers as required.

Column 1 Customer	Column 2 Discount	Column 3 Quantity/ Volume	Column 4 FOB Term	Column 5 Concessions

(b) Do any deviations from your written policies or standard commercial sales practices disclosed in the above chart ever result in better discounts (lower prices) or concessions than indicated? YES: _____ NO: _____. If YES, explain deviations in accordance with the instructions at Figure 515.4-2, which is provided in this solicitation for your convenience.

The prospective contractor is required to prepare the CSP Format for each Special Item Number ("SIN") being offered. The CSP Format may be combined for SINs having the same information. Alternate formats are permitted, provided that the same information is furnished to the GSA contracting officer.

If the prospective contractor is offering GSA the best price or lower, then the prospective contractor only needs to prepare the CSP Format for the customers receiving the most favored price. If not, then the prospective contractor needs to prepare the CSP Format for all customers or categories of customers that receive better pricing based on agreements in effect on the date the offer is submitted or will be in effect during the proposed contract period. The disclosures are to be based on the prospective contractor's written discounting policies or standard commercial sales practices in the event the prospective contractor does not have written discounting policies. A description of each column follows.

a. CSP Format Column 1: Customer

"Customer" means any customer other than the Federal Government.[258] In a manner similar to the DSMD form previously required by GSA, CSP Column 1 must include all commercial customers—OEMs, resellers, dealers, distributors, state and local governments, educational institutions, national accounts, and any other customer grouping—with whom the prospective contractor does business. The prospective contractor is instructed to disclose information about specific customers, although the information may be disclosed by category of customers if the prospective contractor's written discounting policies or standard commercial sales practices are the same for all customers in that category.

Here the prospective contractor needs to be careful, especially if there are no written discounting policies. The prospective contractor should survey its marketing practices and customer base to identify homogeneous groupings that could form the basis of standard commercial sales practices. As a start, customers will typically fall into two groups: (1) customers that are not end users themselves and provide a value-added service for the prospective contractor, such as OEMs, dealers, distributors, etc., and (2) customers that are end users, such as state and local governments, educational institutions, and national accounts. Then, within these two groups, consistent patterns might emerge that form the basis of subgroups. If practical, disclosures should be made at the subgroup level or lower to the extent that characteristics in terms and conditions affecting price can be discerned.

The reason why this is an important step is that it will form the basis of selecting a given customer or category of customers for purposes of operating the Price Reductions Clause. One of the most common mistakes made by prospective contractors is not properly disclosing a customer or category of customers, assuming that the terms and conditions are irrelevant to GSA's bargaining position. The prospective contractor must recognize that there is a significant distinction between making disclosures and negotiating price. If there is doubt about any customer or category of customers, the prospective contractor should err on the side of disclosure.

b. CSP Format Column 2: Discount

"Discount" means a reduction to the catalog price or list price, whether it is published or unpublished.[259] Discounts include, but are not limited to, rebates, quantity discounts, purchase option credits, and any other term or condition that reduces the amount of money a customer ultimately pays for supplies or services ordered or received. Any net price lower than the list price is considered a discount by the percentage difference between the list price and net price.

For each customer and category of customers identified in CSP Format Column 1, the prospective contractor is required to disclose the best discount granted within a designated period (*e.g.*, previous twelve months), without regard to quantity or the terms and conditions of the agreements under which the discount was granted. The disclosures should be based on written discounting policies or standard commercial sales practices. Discounts are to be normalized. That is, discounts from other catalogs or price lists should be expressed as discounts from the catalog or price list that will serve as the basis of the offer (*e.g.*, distributor price list vs. end user price list). The other catalog or price list, however, must be identified by the prospective contractor, and submitting a copy to the GSA contracting officer is encouraged. If the disclosed discount is a combination of various discounts (regular, quantity, prompt payment, etc.), the discount percentage should be disclosed for each type of discount.

As with customer disclosures, this is an important step because it establishes the most favored customer price for a given customer or category of customers. It is a component needed to operate the Price Reductions Clause. Again, the most common error made by prospective contractors in this area is the failure to accurately disclose discounts actually granted, typically because the discounts were believed to be irrelevant to GSA's bargaining position or the discounts were not known. Failure to make accurate disclosures in this area should be viewed by the prospective contractor as a high risk condition.

c. CSP Format Column 3: Quantity/Volume

In CSP Format Column 3, the prospective contractor is to identify the minimum sales volume which the customer or category of customers identified in CSP Format Column 1 must purchase, either per order or within a specified period, to earn the discounts in CSP Format Column 2. When purchases must be placed within a specified period to earn a discount, the prospective contractor must indicate the required time period. The GSA contracting officer will use this information to evaluate differences in terms and conditions and make comparisons to GSA's bargaining position.

d. CSP Format Column 4: FOB Terms

The prospective contractor is to indicate the delivery term (*e.g.*, FOB origin, FOB destination, etc.) for each identified product.[260] This information will be used by the GSA contracting officer to evaluate the need for adjustments in discounts due to differences in shipping terms. The prospective contractor should also make the same evaluation. If, for example, the GSA solicitation requires FOB destination pricing and the prospective contractor's discounting is based on FOB origin, then it would be reasonable for the prospective contractor to reduce offered discounts to cover shipping costs.

e. CSP Format Column 5: Concessions

"Concession" means a benefit, enhancement, or privilege that either reduces the overall cost of a customer's acquisition or encourages a customer to consummate a purchase.[261] Concessions include, but are not limited to, freight allowance, extended warranty, extended price guarantees, free installation, and bonus supplies.

For each customer or category of customers identified in CSP Format Column 1, the prospective contractor is required to disclose concessions granted within the designated period, regardless of quantity. The disclosure should be made on a separate sheet with appropriate references if the space provided by the CSP Format is inadequate.

The GSA contracting officer will use this information as part of the overall evaluation of offered discounts. Sometimes this will result in the GSA contracting officer seeking greater discounts to compensate for the inability to take advantage of a commercial concession under normal MAS ordering procedures. For example, if a regularly available "buy three—get one free" concession could not be applied by GSA due to Government ordering patterns (*i.e.*, normally do not order in such quantities), the GSA contracting officer might instead seek a 25 percent discount overall for the applicable product.

Here, again, the prospective contractor should exercise great care, mostly because conventional sales order entry systems and accounting systems do not routinely track concessions. They tend to be *ad hoc* or irregular events that are not part of written discounting policies. The prospective contractor should survey its marketing practices to identify the nature and extent of concessions granted. This could provide a reasonable basis for disclosing the prospective contractor's standard commercial sales practices. As with discounts, failure to make accurate disclosures in this area should be viewed by the prospective contractor as a high risk condition.

f. Deviations

The CSP Format is intended to be based on the prospective contractor's written discounting policies or standard commercial sales practices. CSP Format Question 4 asks whether there are deviations that result in better pricing or concessions. If such deviations occur, the prospective contractor is required to explain the circumstances. The explanation should discuss situations that lead to deviations, how often they occur, and the controls employed by the prospective contractor that assure the integrity of pricing and compliance with written discounting policies or standard commercial sales practices. Examples of typical deviations might include, but are not limited to, one-time goodwill discounts to charity organizations or to compensate an unsatisfied customer, limited sale of obsolete or damaged supplies, sale of sample supplies to a new customer, or the sales of prototype supplies for testing purposes.

GSA warns prospective contractors that deviations from written discounting policies or standard commercial sales practices could affect the GSA contracting officer's ability to establish whether an offered price is fair and reasonable. The prospective contractor should be prepared to provide information to demonstrate that substantial sales of offered items have been made in the commercial market on terms consistent with the written discounting policies or standard commercial sales practices, as reflected in the CSP Format.

2. Manufacturer Sales Data

For resellers and dealers that do not have significant sales to the general public, the prospective contractor is instructed to complete the CSP Format with information supplied by the manufacturer for each SIN offered if the manufacturer's sales under any resulting MAS contract are expected to exceed $500,000. The manufacturer must provide written authorization that grants GSA access, at any time before award (or modification), to the manufacturer's sales records in order to verify the accuracy of the "information other than cost or pricing data" submitted by the manufacturer. The information may be provided by the manufacturer directly to the GSA contracting officer.

In addition, the prospective contractor must submit the information shown below for each of the manufacturers whose supplies and services are being offered:

- Manufacturer name
- Manufacturer part number
- Dealer or reseller part number
- Product description
- Manufacturer list price
- Dealer or reseller discount percentage from list price or net price

3. Certification

Because a MAS contract is a contract for a commercial item, a price-based approach is used by GSA. Thus, no "cost or pricing data" are required, nor is a "Certificate of Current Cost or Pricing Data" required. Also not required is GSA's previous "Certificate of Established Catalog or Market Price," associated with the 1982 MAS Policy Statement. Instead, the GSA solicitation notice informs the prospective contractor that the GSA contracting officer will consider information submitted by the prospective contractor to be current, accurate, and complete as of fourteen calendar days prior to the date the information was submitted.[262] As a practical matter, this is a *de facto* certification, and it should be regarded carefully by the prospective contractor.

The MAS contract contains the Price Adjustment—Failure to Provide Accurate Information Clause[263] under which the GSA contracting officer may reduce MAS contract prices if such prices were increased by a significant amount because the prospective contractor failed:

- To provide information required by the solicitation (*i.e.*, CSP Format) or otherwise requested by the GSA contracting officer or authorized representative;
- To provide information that was current, accurate, and complete as of fourteen calendar days prior to the date the information was submitted; or
- To disclose changes in the prospective contractor's commercial price list, discounts, or discounting policies that occurred after the original pricing proposal submission but prior to the completion of price negotiations.

The CSP Format is the means by which the GSA contracting officer obtains necessary "information other than cost or pricing data" for applying the price-based approach and performing a price analysis. It enables the GSA contracting officer to evaluate the offered price against the disclosed most favored customer price for a given customer or category of customers, as well as any disclosed deviations to either written discounting policies or standard commercial sales practices. Failure to provide the GSA contracting officer with current, accurate, and complete data may affect this evaluation and disturb the discrete pricing relationships established at the time of contract award. The MAS contract provides that, if this happens, the prospective contractor could be exposed to price reductions, demands for refunds and interest, and termination for default.

The prospective contractor must exercise prudent caution when preparing pricing proposals for MAS contracts. Not only should the prospective contractor have an adequate infrastructure, especially with regard to reliable information management systems, but all personnel involved should be adequately trained. The most common mistakes made by prospective contractors are not appreciating the rights granted to the GSA in MAS contracts, notwithstanding that the prospective contractor is providing a commercial supply or service, or assuming the irrelevance of certain types of data.

D. *GSA Fact-Finding And Preparation For Negotiations*

Once the pricing proposal and supporting CSP Format information is submitted by the prospective contractor, the GSA contracting officer undertakes a number of steps to conduct a price analysis and evaluate what would be a fair and reasonable price under the circumstances. Upon completion of these steps, the negotiation process begins.

1. Price Analysis

Price analysis is the process of evaluating the prospective contractor's proposed pricing without considering the details of cost and profit.[264] In performing a price analysis, the GSA contracting officer may be assisted by a contract specialist and functional specialists. Examples of price analysis techniques used for MAS contracts include, but are not limited to, the following:

- Comparison of prospective contractor's proposed prices to prices previously paid by the Government for same or similar supplies and services with consideration given to differences in terms and conditions (*e.g.*, predecessor MAS contract, other Government contracts);

- Comparison of prospective contractor's proposed prices to prices proposed by other prospective contractors for same or similar supplies and services (*e.g.*, other responses to the GSA solicitation);
- Comparison of prospective contractor's proposed prices to prices paid by prospective contractor's commercial customers for same or similar supplies and services with consideration given to differences in terms and conditions (*e.g.*, CSP Format information);
- Comparison of prospective contractor's proposed prices to competitor price lists, discount terms, or rebate arrangements (*e.g.*, competitor CSP Format information);
- Comparison of prospective contractor's proposed prices to published market prices and similar indexes (*e.g.*, market research); and
- Comparison of prospective contractor's proposed prices to independent estimates developed by the Government.

The CSP Format information submitted by the prospective contractor is usually sufficient for the GSA contracting officer to perform an effective price analysis. The CSP Format information informs the GSA contracting officer about the prospective contractor's written discounting policies or standard commercial sales practices for its major customers and categories of customers. The CSP Format information also informs the GSA contracting officer about the best discounts and concessions, as well as the related terms and conditions. Finally, the CSP Format information informs the GSA contracting officer about deviations to the prospective contractor's written discounting policies or standard commercial sales practices.

Notwithstanding the apparent comprehensiveness of the CSP Format and supplementary disclosures, the prospective contractor should expect a number of clarification questions and requests for additional pricing information. This would be the case particularly for resellers and dealers that do not have significant sales to the general public. The prospective contractor should take care to treat such questions and requests as extensions to the CSP Format and subject to the same standards for being current, accurate, and complete. If it is the prospective contractor's intent to submit corrected disclosures or pricing information that supersedes previously submitted disclosures or pricing information, the correspondence and documentation should be clearly marked accordingly.

2. Pre-Award Pricing Audit

In submitting an offer for a MAS contract, the prospective contractor grants the GSA contracting officer or authorized representative the right to examine, at any time before award of the MAS contract, the prospective contractor's books, records, documents, papers, and other directly pertinent records for the purpose of verifying the information submitted by the prospective contractor.[265] The solicitation notice makes it clear that such access does not extend to the prospective contractor's cost or profit information or other data relevant solely to the prospective contractor's determination of the prices to be offered in the catalog or marketplace. The pre-award audit is normally conducted by the GSA Office of Inspector General, although assist audits have been known to be performed by the Defense Contract Audit Agency.

Inasmuch as the expressed purpose of the pre-award audit is verification, the prospective contractor should expect to be required to provide additional details about the CSP Format information submitted to the GSA contracting officer. Although the CSP Format information is derived from written discounting policies or standard commercial sales practices, the auditor may take steps to test the accuracy of the representations being made by the prospective contractor. This could include providing transaction reports from the prospective contractor's sales order entry system, copies of commercial contracts and price lists, customer invoices, details of rebates and promotion programs, etc. Again, the prospective contractor should treat such requests as being made by the GSA contracting officer and subject to the same standards for being current, accurate, and complete. Requests that appear to be unreasonable or impractical should be referred to the GSA contracting officer as quickly as possible.

3. Negotiation Objective

After the GSA contracting officer has completed the price analysis and considered the results of the pre-award pricing audit, the GSA contracting officer will develop a negotiation objective. This will be used as a guide in conducting negotiations with the prospective contractor. Typically, the negotiation objective is subject to higher level review and approval.

The GSA contracting officer's negotiation objective is an extension of GSA's pricing policy. The GSA contracting officer can be expected to seek a price that is equal to or better than the best price paid by the prospective contractor's most favored customer with consideration given to differences in terms and conditions and bargaining positions. This generally translates into the best price paid by the largest volume end user customer or category of customers. GSA considers itself to be among the largest volume end users based on total sales made to the Government. GSA contracting officers normally recognize that non-end user customers, such as OEMs, dealers, and distributors, provide other value-added services that justify lower pricing.

When establishing negotiation objectives and determining price reasonableness, the GSA contracting officer must analyze differences in terms and conditions between the MAS contract and the prospective contractor's commercial contracts for given customers or categories of customers.[266] The following factors should be considered:

- Aggregate volume of purchases anticipated under the MAS contract

- Minimum quantity purchases and pattern of historic purchasing practices
- Discounted prices taking into account any combination of discounts and concessions offered to commercial customers
- MAS contract period of performance
- Purchase price of warranties, training, or maintenance
- Ordering and delivery practices

E. *Offer, Price Negotiations, And Contract Award*

From the prospective contractor's viewpoint, the negotiation process begins with the presentation of the pricing proposal. In fact, however, the prospective contractor is advised that, before an offer's expiration date, the GSA contracting officer may accept all or part of an offer without conducting negotiations.[267]

1. Offer

The prospective contractor is required to present a pricing proposal to the GSA contracting officer that is responsive to the solicitation's requirements. The prospective contractor is instructed to provide copies of the prospective contractor's current commercial catalog or price list that contain the offered supplies or services and to annotate the corresponding SIN next to each offered item. Any items in the prospective contractor's current commercial catalog or price list that are not being offered are to be marked "excluded," lined-out, and initialed by the prospective contractor.

If circumstances make it more practical to prepare a special catalog or price list, the special catalog or price list is to include a statement indicating that the special catalog or price list represents a verbatim extract from the prospective contractor's current commercial catalog or price list. The prospective contractor is to identify the current commercial catalog or price list from which the special catalog or price list has been prepared.

The prospective contractor is to describe the discounts being offered to GSA. The description is to include all discounts, such as regular discounts, volume discounts (quantity or dollar), prompt payment discounts, blanket purchase agreement[268] discounts, purchase option credits, etc. The description should indicate whether products may be combined to earn discounts. The prospective contractor should also describe any concessions being offered, such as an extended warranty, a return/exchange of supplies policy, or enhanced or additional services.

If the prospective contractor is a dealer or reseller or if the prospective contractor will use dealers to perform any aspect of the MAS contract, the prospective contractor is required to describe the functions, if any, that the dealer or reseller will perform. Examples might include assuming or sharing responsibilities for marketing, order processing, distribution, and invoicing.

There is no prescribed format for presenting an offer, and the method used should weigh practical considerations, such as the numbers of products being offered and the complexity of proposed pricing. However, this is another area where the prospective contractor needs to exercise abundant care so that the offer and ultimately the pricing relationships that will be used to operate the Price Reductions Clause are absolutely clear. The prospective contractor should not rely solely on the GSA contracting officer to provide this clarity or understanding. One suggested approach is shown in the table below (other columns should be added, as necessary).

Suggested Offered Pricing Format

Product Number and Description	SIN	List Price (1)	Offered Price (2)	Offered Discount (2)	Most Favored Customer Discount (3)

(1) Identify commercial catalog or list price
(2) Indicate whether or not the offered price and discount includes the industrial funding fee
(3) Based on CSP Format for proposed designated customer or category of customers

Additional discounts:
Explain other discounts being offered, if any.

Concessions:
Explain concessions being offered, if any.

The objective of this suggested approach is to make clear the offeror's proposed pricing, commercial catalog or price list upon which the offer is based, and proposed relationship to the most favored customer price for a given customer or category of customers. The approach lends itself to an electronic spreadsheet application and would be particularly useful if the offer contains numerous products. It should greatly reduce the number of errors in preparing the offer (*e.g.*, discount application and calculation, industrial funding fee application, proposed pricing relationships), facilitate preparation of the MAS price list, and provide a foundation for subsequent price changes. If an offer is structured by SIN or other product grouping, a summary of the information contained in the above table should also be provided in order to provide the appropriate perspective.

As previously discussed, the GSA contracting officer's price analysis will produce a negotiation objective that seeks a price that is equal to or better than the best price paid by the prospective contractor's most favored customer with consideration given to differences in terms and conditions and bargaining positions. In addition, the GSA contracting officer will develop a discrete pricing relationship among the commercial list price, most favored customer price, and MAS contract price. The prospective contractor should consider such pricing relationships to be negotiable, particularly in the selection of a customer or category of customers for operating the Price Reductions Clause. Several considerations are important.

a. Offered Price

The Government's pricing policy is to obtain a fair and reasonable price based on prices paid for same or similar supplies and services. GSA pricing policy equates fair and reasonable price to the most favored customer price. However, there is no law or regulation that compels a prospective contractor to offer the most favored customer price. Notwithstanding, the prospective contractor must realize that the GSA contracting officer will be intensely focused on the differences between the offered price and the most favored customer price. Ultimately, the GSA contracting officer will have to justify the differences and make a determination that the MAS contract price is a fair and reasonable price and that contract award is in the best interest of the Government.[269]

There are a number of legitimate reasons why GSA is justifiably not entitled to the prospective contractor's best price. Some examples follow:

- The commercial customer may perform a service involving substantive resources that is not performed by GSA (*e.g.*, marketing, warehousing, distribution).
- The commercial customer may make commitments that cannot be made by GSA (*e.g.*, purchase commitment, source commitment, design commitment).
- The commercial customer may historically make purchases in significantly greater volume than anticipated to be made by the Government.
- The commercial customer may take advantage of incentives or promotions not available to GSA (*e.g.*, advance payment, bundled purchase incentive, incremental volume incentive, lease to purchase credits).
- The commercial customer's higher discount may relate to definite-quantity contracts or orders above the maximum order threshold contained in the MAS contract.
- The commercial customer's higher discount may relate to special incentives to promote educational or research programs.
- The commercial customer's higher discount may relate to specific competitive opportunities where there was a teaming agreement to share economic contributions.

If the prospective contractor intends to offer additional discounts, incentives, or concessions, it must be made clear how they would be earned by GSA. Such offerings must recognize how the MAS ordering process works and whether actions needed to earn the offerings would be authorized. If conditions needed to earn the offerings are not likely to be present, the additional discounts, incentives, or concessions should not be offered.

b. Most Favored Customer (Basis Of Award)

The disclosure and designation of the most favored customer price for a given customer or category of customers is almost as important as the offered price itself. The most favored customer price forms the baseline for operating the Price Reductions Clause and, if not carefully considered, can result in a reduction of MAS contract prices almost immediately after contract award for the balance of the contract period. As a reasonable protective measure, the prospective contractor should propose a designated customer or category of customers in the pricing proposal submitted to the GSA contracting officer.

There are two important considerations. First, the prospective contractor must ensure that the designated customer or category of customers provides a realistic and manageable baseline for operating the Price Reductions Clause. Designations that are too broad (*e.g.*, all commercial customers, all national accounts) or incompatible (*e.g.*, non-end users, large differences in pricing, dissimilar business relationships) should be avoided. Second, it is imperative that the most favored customer price for the designated customer or category of customers be accurate. It is worthwhile to double-check even after contract award, and any discrepancies should be immediately brought to the GSA contracting officer's attention.

The prospective contractor should ensure that the underlying terms and conditions of the most favored customer pricing are clearly disclosed and understood. If the prospective contractor anticipates changes might occur that would increase the most favored customer discount, the prospective contractor should seek an understanding with the GSA contracting officer about their impact under the Price Reductions Clause. To illustrate, suppose the MAS contract price was based on a national account customer that received a 30 percent discount without any purchase commitment. Subsequent to contract award, the same national account customer negotiated a new contract and received a 50 percent discount but made a significant purchase commitment. Given the substantive difference in the terms and conditions of the commercial contract, the price differential should not trigger a price adjustment under the Price Reductions Clause. Again, however, to avoid disputes and provide predictability, this is an issue that should be addressed before contract award.

c. Pricing Relationships

At the conclusion of price negotiations, it will be imperative that there is absolute clarity as to the relationship between the MAS contract price and the most favored customer price for the designated customer or category of customers. This, too, could have a significant impact on the operation of the Price Reductions Clause. It is an issue that the prospective contractor needs to consider at the time of the offer.

Pricing relationships have generally been assumed to be proportional. For example, where a most favored customer discount was 50% and the MAS contract discount was 40%, the relationship was assumed to be 50%:40% or 80% of the most favored customer discount. Under this assumption, if the most favored customer discount increased to 60%, then the MAS contract discount would be proportionally increased to 48% (*i.e.*, 80% of 60%) under the Price Reductions Clause. [*Editor's Note*: See Chapter XIV for a detailed discussion of the Price Reductions Clause.]

There can be problems with this assumption. First, the MAS contract may not have been based on proportional relationships.

It may have been based on an absolute relationship. For example, where a most favored customer discount was 20% and the MAS contract discount was 5% more, the absolute relationship would be 20%:20% + 5% (*i.e.*, 25%). Under the Price Reductions Clause, if the most favored customer discount increased to 30%, then the MAS contract discount should be increased to 35% (*i.e.*, 30% + 5%). However, if a proportional relationship was assumed, the MAS discount could be erroneously increased to 37.5% (*i.e.*, 125% of 30%).

Second, the proportional relationship does not work equitably when the MAS contract discount is greater than the most favored customer discount, even if the proportional relationship was understood and agreed upon at the time of price negotiations. The proportional relationship has the effect of exaggerating the benefit granted to GSA if future price changes are made. It is also an indicator that there may be a mismatch in the designated customer or category of customers.

Other key pricing relationships that must be considered are additional discounts, incentives, or concessions that will be offered. The prospective contractor must be clear about the relationship baseline and how the offered benefits will be priced, particularly under the Price Reductions Clause.

d. Industrial Funding Fee

The prospective contractor will be required to pay GSA an industrial funding fee which is equal to a specified percentage of sales reported in the "Contractor's Report of Sales."[270] This is a cash payment made quarterly within thirty days of the end of the quarter. The Federal Supply Service Commissioner or designee determines the percentage (presently .75 percent) to be used by the GSA contracting officer and the percentage is stated in the Industrial Funding Fee Clause contained in the solicitation. The purpose of the industrial funding fee is to fund GSA's costs of operating the MAS Program from the orders placed by the Government or other authorized users. It is intended to be a user fee. [*Editor's Note*: See Chapter XIV for additional discussion of the industrial funding fee.]

2. Economic Price Adjustment

MAS contracts generally provide for economic price increases during the contract's period of performance under the "Economic Price Adjustment—FSS Multiple Award Schedule Contracts" Clause.[271] The price increases are associated with increases in the commercial catalog price upon which the MAS contract prices are based. It will not apply to static list prices or to changes in the prospective contractor's written discounting policies or standard commercial sales practices (*e.g.*, reduced discounting). The price increases are generally limited as follows:

- Only three increases will be considered during the contract period,
- Increases must be requested after the first thirty days of the contract period and prior to the last sixty days of the contract period,
- At least thirty days must elapse between requested increases, and
- The aggregate of the increases in any contract unit price shall not exceed a pre-established percentage of the initial MAS contract price. This percentage will normally be 10 percent,[272] unless trends, as measured by an appropriate index like the Producer Price Index, suggest otherwise. A percentage greater than 10 percent must be approved by the contracting officer. GSA reserves the right to raise this ceiling when changes in market conditions during the contract period support an increase.

Alternate I of the "Economic Price Adjustment—FSS Multiple Award Schedule Contracts" Clause provides for slightly different limitations to price increases. Its use is required on multiyear MAS contracts. Important differences are as follows:

- No more than three increases will be considered during each succeeding twelve-month period,
- Increases must be requested prior to the last sixty days of the contract period, and
- The aggregate of the increases during any twelve-month period shall not exceed a pre-established percentage of the initial MAS contract price.

Again, MAS contract pricing must be viewed as a continuous process that starts with the initial offer and ends with the final payment. In formulating an offer and negotiating MAS contract pricing, the prospective contractor should consider the availability of economic price adjustments. More importantly, to the extent that certain economic price adjustment factors are negotiable, such as the pre-established ceiling, this should be addressed by the prospective contractor at the outset.

If the prospective contractor's supplies and services are historically characterized by rising list prices, then it would be worthwhile for the prospective contractor to evaluate potential list price increases for the offered supplies and services for the term of the MAS contract. The result might lead the prospective contractor to either seek different terms for economic price adjustments or reconsider offering selected products. The time to do this is before the MAS contract is awarded.

3. Price Negotiations

As a practical matter, price negotiations commence almost immediately upon the GSA contracting officer's receipt of the pricing proposal. The CSP Format is designed to inform the GSA contracting officer whether the offered price is equal to or better than the best price paid by any commercial customer. If the answer is "yes," then the GSA contracting officer's fact-finding efforts are basically verification measures. If the answer is "no," then the GSA contracting officer will be persistent with the prospective contractor either to enhance the offer or to provide documentation justifying why the GSA should not receive the best price. This will be evident in the fact-finding questions asked by the GSA contracting officer and requests for copies of commercial contracts; sales histories of selected products; and explanations of rebates, promotions, and concessions.

Even though the GSA contracting officer's negotiation objective will be to obtain the prospective contractor's best price, GSA recognizes that the terms and conditions of commercial sales vary and that there may be legitimate reasons why the best price is not achieved. The GSA contracting officer will generally focus on the best prices received by large volume end users and make comparisons to total Government sales. However, GSA warns that discounts given to OEMs, dealers, and distributors are not considered "off limits" simply because the Government does not perform certain functions that these types of customers perform.[273]

The key is in distinguishing between the most favored customer price for a given customer or category of customers and GSA's ability to earn the same pricing under the terms of the MAS contract. The prospective contractor should not be induced into granting GSA a discount that is not consistent with the prospective contractor's written discounting policies or standard commercial sales practices. It must also be recognized, however, that GSA's negotiating leverage is its position to decide whether or not a MAS contract will be awarded (i.e., "offer best price or get no contract").

For prospective contractors offering multiple SINs or product groupings, GSA's most favored customer pricing goal will create an additional concern. The GSA contracting officer will be motivated to seek the best price for each SIN or product grouping (or even for each product). This produces a "cherry-picking" process by which the best pricing might involve several customers or categories of customers (e.g., national accounts for one SIN and state and local governments for another SIN). The obvious result is that the GSA contracting officer could possibly be seeking a better consolidated pricing arrangement than that enjoyed by any single customer or category of customers. Another problem for the prospective contractor in following this approach is the administrative difficulties that would be experienced for operating the Price Reductions Clause.

4. Final Offer

At the conclusion of negotiations, the GSA contracting officer will request a revised pricing proposal from the prospective contractor.[274] In a sense, the revised pricing proposal confirms the agreement already reached between the GSA contracting officer and the prospective contractor. The revised pricing proposal is to contain a number of items. Some of the key items related to MAS contract prices are as follows:

- Date on which price negotiations were concluded—this is the date of price agreement and is very important from a price adjustment perspective
- Commercial catalog or price list upon which the revised pricing proposal is based
- Discounts being offered in the revised pricing proposal, including quantity discounts or net prices
- Concessions being offered in the revised pricing proposal
- "Basis of Award" customer or category of customers and the relationship to the most favored customer price
- Prompt payment discount
- Economic price adjustment terms

The prospective contractor should use the revised pricing proposal as an opportunity to make the price agreement reached with the GSA contracting officer clear and executable. In many ways, the proposal will become one of the most important documents for administering the contract and resolving disputes. It is important to note that all of the information submitted up to this point might be covered by GSA's defective pricing provisions. It is a good opportunity to ensure that the information upon which the price agreement was reached would meet the standards of the "Price Adjustment—Failure to Provide Accurate Information" Clause.[275]

5. Contract Award

Upon award of a contract, the GSA contracting officer will send the contractor a copy of the contract and the approved MAS price list.[276] While this step in the process formalizes the price agreement already reached with the GSA contracting officer, the contractor should pay special attention to the award documentation. It should reflect the same terms as contained in the final offer. A suggested checklist is presented in the Table below.

Question	Yes	No
Does the contract award document accurately incorporate the CSP Format data and additional pricing information submitted by the prospective contractor?		
Have incorporated documents that the prospective contractor intended to be corrected or superseded been appropriately treated?		
Does the contract award document accurately incorporate the prospective contractor's commercial price list upon which the MAS contract prices are based?		
Does the contract award document accurately incorporate any other commercial price list upon which the MAS contract prices are based (*e.g.*, manufacturer)?		
Does the contract award document accurately reflect the base discounts negotiated on the date of price agreement?		
Does the contract award document accurately reflect other discounts negotiated on the date of price agreement?		
Does the contract award document accurately reflect concessions negotiated on the date of price agreement?		

Does the contract award document accurately reflect the treatment of the industrial funding fee (*i.e.*, embedded in MAS contract prices or waived)?		
Does the contract award document accurately reflect the agreed—upon terms of the economic price adjustment provisions?		
Does the contract award document accurately reflect customer or category of customer that will be used to operate the Price Reductions Clause?		
Does the designated customer or category of customer provide a realistic and manageable baseline for operating the Price Reductions Clause?		
Are the pricing relationships clear between the base discounts and designated customer or category of customer?		
Does the contract award document accurately reflect all limitations or restrictions on MAS contract pricing intended by the prospective contractor?		

If the answer to any of the above questions is "no" or there is uncertainty, the questions should be immediately brought to the attention of the GSA contracting officer. It must be kept in mind that, although discrepancies and uncertainties might appear to be minor at the outset, they can pose substantial financial risks to the prospective contractor during the MAS contract period of performance.

F. *Department of Veterans Affairs Federal Supply Service Contracts*

The VA has been delegated the authority to award MAS contracts for selected medical supplies and services. Examples of MAS contracts include professional medical healthcare services, pharmaceuticals and drugs, medical and dental equipment and supplies, *in vitro* diagnostics, reagents, and test kits and test sets. While the VA follows the basic pricing policies and procedures adopted by the GSA, there are a number of noteworthy exceptions. These are adopted through many means, such as the VA Acquisition Regulation ("VAAR"), "Dear Contractor" and "Dear Manufacturer" letters, master agreements, and special contract clauses, and are attributable to related legislation, commercial business practices of the health care industry, and the VA's administrative needs.

1. Pricing Policies And Procedures

VA's pricing polices and procedures for MAS contracts are basically the same as those contained in the GSAM, although it should be noted that the VA's pricing rules are not as well documented through a formal system of regulations. For the most part, the VA contracting officer can be expected to seek a price that is equal to or better than the best price paid by the prospective contractor's most favored customer with consideration given to differences in terms and conditions and bargaining positions. However, there are some differences in selected policies and procedures.

a. Price Negotiations

As with GSA's MAS proposal requirements, the prospective contractor is required to submit the CSP Format shown in the table earlier in this chapter. The flexibility of the CSP Format seems to have resolved an inherent problem with the structure of the previously used DSMD form that did not readily capture business practices common in the health care industry (*e.g.*, hospital purchasing groups, formulary business arrangements, etc.). The prospective contractor should follow the procedures previously described in this chapter to provide CSP Format information based on written discounting policies or standard commercial sales practices. However, special care should be taken to ensure that the CSP Format information provided adequately describes the groups and subgroups of customers, as well as the reasoning for various levels of discounting.

The prospective contractor should take notice of the "Examination of Records by VA (Multiple Award Schedule)" Clause contained in VA solicitations.[277] The VA Senior Procurement Executive has apparently determined that MAS contracts involve pricing risks that represent a likelihood of significant harm to the Government. The clause contains a provision for post-award audit rights of the prospective contractor's pricing proposal data, which are normally conducted by the VA Office of Inspector General. The clause grants the VA the right to initiate an audit until two years after (1) the date of contract award, (2) the date of modification adding the VA audit clause to an MAS contract, or (3) the date of modification adding the new CSP Format to an MAS contract. In the latter instance, post-award audit rights are limited to information contained in the modification.

The VA's audit clause should be viewed by the prospective contractor as a high risk condition. One noteworthy difference exists between the VA and GSA audit clauses: The VA's clause establishes the right to "initiate" an audit; the GSA clause does not refer to "initiate." In practice, this means that the prospective contractor's exposure on a VA MAS contract could last well beyond the periods contained in GSA's audit clause, if the audit is simply initiated within the prescribed period.

b. Industrial Funding Fee

Similar to GSA's requirement, the prospective contractor will be required to pay VA an industrial funding fee which is equal to a specified percentage of sales reported in the "Contractor's Report of Sales" (presently 0.5 percent). A notable difference, however, is that the VA requires that the fee be paid not only on sales to VA medical centers but also on sales of MAS contract supplies and services made to other Government agencies.[278] These include the following:

- Sales made under a VA MAS contract at or lower than a MAS contract price;
- Sales not made under a VA MAS contract but made at a MAS contract price;
- Sales made under a blanket purchase agreement derived from a MAS contract price;
- Sales made to pharmaceutical prime vendors under a distribution and pricing agreement using a VA MAS contract number or price; and
- Sales made to state veterans' homes using a VA MAS contract number or price.

The requirement that an industrial funding fee be paid on purchases made outside the MAS contract will probably place an additional data collection requirement on the prospective contractor. Where sales order entry systems are usually capable of identifying a customer's authorizing document (*e.g.*, contract), not all systems will readily establish a point of reference to a price contained in another authorizing document.

c. Price Reductions

Given the VA's trend in interpreting the application of the Price Reductions Clause, the selection of the most favored customer price for a given customer or category of customers will probably be more important than initially establishing MAS contract prices. This must be viewed as a high risk condition for the prospective offeror. It would be prudent to consider narrowing the designated customer or category of customers as much a possible. It will also be important to make the established pricing relationships as clear as possible.

2. Pharmaceuticals

One unique feature of VA MAS contracting is the pricing of pharmaceuticals. Not only are the normal MAS pricing policies and procedures applied to pharmaceuticals, but they are also subject to the pricing provisions of the Veterans Health Care Act ("VHCA").[279]

The VHCA was a consolidation of several legislative initiatives directed toward health care and, with respect to pharmaceuticals, attempted to remedy a problem created by previous legislation.[280] The VHCA prescribed a ceiling price that may be charged by manufacturers for covered drugs. Although the formula is somewhat complex, it basically establishes the ceiling price at 76 percent of the previous year's non-federal average manufacturer price (called "non-FAMP"). This is the weighted average price of a single dosage unit paid by wholesalers to the manufacturer, after taking into consideration discounts, rebates, and similar price reductions.

In the context of pricing MAS contracts for pharmaceuticals, the prospective contractor must be concerned with two sets of disclosures: (1) CSP Format information based on written discounting policies or standard commercial sales practices and (2) the previous year's non-FAMP for each covered drug. The prospective contractor must also be concerned with negotiating from two pricing perspectives. On one hand, the VA contracting officer will seek the best price paid by the prospective contractor's most favored customer (percentage discount from list price); on the other hand, the negotiated MAS contract price must not be more than 76 percent of the previous year's non-FAMP.

The complexity increases significantly after contract award. The VHCA requires that the 76 percent ceiling be recalculated each year and that MAS contract prices be adjusted accordingly, subject to other restrictions on allowable price escalation. At the same time, the contractor must monitor the prices paid by the designated customers or category of customers. Thus, at any time during the post-award period, the MAS contract price is controlled by either the VHCA or the Price Reductions Clause.

Implementing the provisions of the VHCA must be a priority consideration at the time of initially negotiating MAS contract prices. If the best price for a large volume end user customer

under comparable terms and conditions is near the non-FAMP
ceiling price, then the prospective contractor should consider
establishing a pricing relationship to the non-FAMP ceiling rather
than to the end user customer or category of customers. In this
instance, no customer or category of customers would be
designated for purposes of the Price Reductions Clause. If this
approach is not workable, then the prospective contractor should
consider offering a price substantially less than the non-FAMP
ceiling price to reduce compliance risks.

There is a note of caution that should be made with respect
to the non-FAMP ceiling price. If the prospective contractor
intends to sell a drug whose price will increase substantially in
excess of the Consumer Price Index for urban products, the
prospective contractor should be aware that a flaw in the
prescribed formula for computing non-FAMP ceiling prices in
subsequent years could cause unacceptable decreases in the
MAS contract price.[281] The prospective contractor should
carefully weigh the benefits of including the drug in the MAS
contract, notwithstanding the possible restriction of sales to other
Government customers.

G. *Contract Modifications*

MAS contract pricing is a continuous process that lasts for
the full period of performance. Changes in MAS contract pricing
can occur almost immediately after contract award and can result
from provisions of contract clauses, changes in market conditions,
changes in technology, etc. Prospective contractors should
understand that the ability effectively to administer such price
changes is largely dependent upon the baseline established at
the time of initial contract award.

1. Adding And Deleting Products

Inevitably, the contractor will desire to add or delete products
from the MAS contract. The operative provision in the MAS

contract is the "Modifications (Multiple Award Schedule)" Clause.[282] The contractor may request a contract modification by submitting a request to the GSA contracting officer with a description of the proposed change and supporting rationale. The contractor is also required to submit a pricing proposal with the same information as required by the CSP Format, previously discussed. If the CSP Format information has not changed since the initial award, the contractor may make that representation to the GSA contracting officer. However, the contractor should be careful here since there could be substantial difference in the time periods used to support the CSP Format information.

Any pricing proposal for added items will be subject to the same processes as used by the GSA contracting officer for the initial award (*e.g.*, fact-finding, pre-award audit, price negotiation, and formalization). The contractor should treat the processes as being the same and appropriately weigh the advantages and disadvantages of adding products. The contractor should also be aware that the pre-award audit for added products could result in a *de facto* post-award audit of other products. For example, if a product were to be added to the MAS contract six months after initial award and a pre-award audit covered twelve months of commercial contracts and sales transaction data, the pre-award audit would also cover the six-month period prior to the date of the initial contract award.

With respect to product deletions, the contractor must explain the deletion to the GSA contracting officer. While the contractor certainly has the right to delete products from the MAS contract, GSA reserves the right to reject any subsequently proposed addition of same or similar items to the MAS contract at higher prices. By the same token, the contractor is not compelled to offer same or similar items at previous prices. Obviously, the contractor would have to justify the higher prices.

The addition or deletion of products from the MAS contract is formally executed through a contract modification. It is suggested that the contractor apply the suggested checklist set forth earlier in this chapter to the extent appropriate. An updated

MAS price list should be distributed as quickly as possible after requisite approval is obtained from the GSA contracting officer.

2. Price Reductions

As previously mentioned, the structure of GSA's pricing policies and procedures requires the GSA contracting officer to establish at the time of contract award discrete relationships between three prices:

- Commercial list price,
- Most favored customer (Basis of Award) price to a given customer or category of customers, and
- MAS contract price.

The Price Reductions Clause is the means by which GSA maintains these relationships during the MAS contract's period of performance. The clause requires the contractor to inform the GSA contracting officer when these relationships have been disturbed, which means when commercial list prices have been reduced or a better most favored customer price occurs for the designated customer or category of customers. In the latter instance, the presence of better most favored customer prices should not, in and of itself, be considered determinative. The better pricing might be related to circumstances or substantive revisions to terms and conditions. At the present time, practical guidance is lacking in this area.

Although Chapter XIV will focus on the operation of the Price Reductions Clause more specifically, it is worthwhile to address a few points from the perspective of MAS contract pricing. It is absolutely imperative that the pricing relationships are clearly established at the time of initial award (or at the time a product is added). The time to do this is at the time of the final offer, if not the initial offer, and the contract award documents must be unambiguous. Waiting to sort out relationships well after contract award should be viewed as a high risk condition for the contractor. It would be prudent for the prospective contractor to consider possible future changes in pricing relationships before agreeing to a designated customer or category of customers.

3. Economic Price Adjustment

Also as previously discussed, the MAS contract may provide for economic price increases under the "Economic Price Adjustment—MAS Multiple Award Schedule Contracts" Clause. Such increases must be related to changes in the commercial catalog or price list upon which the MAS contract prices were initially established. The price increase will be limited in the manner previously described and should be managed by the contractor accordingly, even perhaps to the point of considering the timing of list price changes and requests for economic price adjustments.

To effect an economic price adjustment, the contractor must submit the following to the GSA contracting officer.

- Commercial list price showing the price increase and the effective date,
- A completed CSP Format regarding the contractor's commercial pricing practices related to the revised commercial list price or a certification that no change has occurred in the data since completion of the initial price negotiations or a subsequent submission, and
- Documentation supporting the reasonableness of the price increase.

GSA reserves the right either to accept the requested price increases, renegotiate more favorable discounts from revised commercial list prices, or remove the affected products from the MAS contract under the "Cancellation Clause." The contractor should be careful here to the extent that negotiated prices might disturb the pricing relationships previously established. GSA guidance on the relationship between economic price adjustments and the Price Reductions Clause is lacking. As always, it is prudent to maintain a high level of clarity and understanding, and the contractor should not rely solely on the GSA contracting officer to provide this.

H. *Summary*

In order to manage risk effectively and provide reasonable financial returns, prospective contractors must view MAS contract pricing as a continuous process. MAS contracts are characterized by constantly changing prices, whether the changes are made on a temporary or permanent basis. Changes are inevitable, and the time to plan for changes is at the time of the initial offer.

Prospective contractors must take care to understand the critical pricing relationships that are established at the outset, particularly between the MAS contract price and the most favored customer price for the designated customer or category of customers that will be used to operate the Price Reductions Clause. There must be total clarity in the offer correspondence and contract award documents. The prospective contractor must not rely solely on the contracting officer to provide that clarity.

The contracting officer can be expected to seek a price that is equal to or better than the best price paid by the prospective contractor's most favored customer with consideration given to differences in terms and conditions and bargaining positions. However, there is no requirement that the prospective contractor offer the most favored customer price. The only requirement is that the MAS contract price be fair and reasonable. Of course, the prospective contractor must also understand that the contracting officer will have to justify why a most favored customer price was not achieved.

The prospective contractor must appreciate the relationships between the various clauses that affect pricing. The most significant clause is the Price Reductions Clause, and the prospective contractor must be careful to accept a designated customer or category of customers that provides a realistic and manageable baseline. Designations that are not relevant or too broad will inevitably become a problem during the period of performance. Prospective contractors must also understand the relationships of clauses related to the industrial funding fee, economic price adjustments, etc.

Prospective contractors wanting to do business through the MAS Program must ensure that they have an adequate information management system that is capable of providing reliable information to prepare the CSP Format, as well as administering the clauses affecting MAS contract prices. It would be prudent for the prospective contractor to consider MAS contract pricing as a high risk condition deserving of the same level of senior management attention and internal control as any other high risk area. Particular attention should be directed to the audit clauses contained in MAS contracts, especially if post-award audit rights are extended to pricing proposal data.

Notes:

[237] FAR 1.302.

[238] The GSAM encompasses numerous GSA-unique regulations collectively known as the GSAR. *See supra* Chapter III for a discussion of the GSAM and GSAR.

[239] FAR 15.402(a).

[240] There is corollary guidance at FAR 31.201-3 (2001) for determining whether an incurred cost is reasonable.

[241] The Contract Pricing Reference Guides were published by the Air Force Institute of Technology and the Federal Acquisition Institute in May 1996 with participation by GSA. FAR 15.404-1(a)(7) (2001) states that the guides, although not directive in nature, may be used for instruction and professional guidance and should be considered as informational only.

[242] FAR 15.406-3(a)(11).

[243] FAR 15.403-3(a)(1). *See* 10 U.S.C. § 2306a and 41 U.S.C. § 254b.

[244] FAR 52.215-20(a)(2); GSAR 515.408(a) (Sept. 1999).

[245] FAR 2.101.

[246] *Id.*

[247] FAR 52.215-2(d)(2).

[248] FAR 52.215-20(a)(2).

[249] FAR 15.402(a).

[250] FAR 15.408(l); FAR 52.215-20.

[251] FAR 15.408(l)(4); FAR 52.215-20, Alternate IV.

[252] 47 Fed. Reg. 50,242 (Nov. 5, 1982) (to be codified at 41 C.F.R. Ch. 5).

[253] Interim Rule, 61 Fed. Reg. 6164 (Feb. 16, 1996) (to be codified at 48 C.F.R. pts. 501, 504, 507, 510, 511, 512, 514, 515, 538, 539, 543, 546, 552, and 570); 62 Fed. Reg. 44,518-44,525 (Aug. 21, 1997) (to be codified at 48 C.F.R. pts. 504, 507, 510, 511, 512, 514, 515, 538, 539, 543, 546, 552, and 570).

[254] GSAR 538.270(a) (Sept. 1999).

[255] 62 Fed. Reg. 44,518, 44,519 (Aug. 21, 1997) (to be codified at 48 C.F.R. pts. 504, 507, 510, 511, 512, 514, 515, 538, 539, 543, 546, 552, and 570).

[256] GSAR 552.238-75 (Sept. 1999).

[257] GSAR 515.408(a) (July 2000).

[258] GSAR 515.408(c) (July 2000).

[259] GSAR 552.212-70(a) (Aug. 1997).

[260] *See* FAR Subpart 47.3.

[261] GSAR 552.212-70(a) (Aug. 1997).

[262] GSAR Figure 515.4 and GSAR 552.215-72(b) (Aug. 1997).

[263] GSAR 552.215-72 (Aug. 1997); *see supra* Chapter VI, Section E.

[264] FAR 15.404-1(b).

[265] GSAR 515.408(a) (July 2000).

[266] GSAR 538.270(c) (July 2000).

[267] GSAR 552.212-73(b) (Aug. 1997).

[268] Blanket purchase agreements are discussed more fully *infra* in Chapter XV.

[269] GSAR 538.270(d) (July 2000).

[270] GSAR 552.238-76 (Sept. 1999); GSAR 552.238-74 (Sept. 1999).

[271] GSAR 552.216-70 (Sept. 1999).

[272] This percentage can differ from Schedule to Schedule.

[273] The Contractor Guide, Section C: Preparation of a Federal Supply

Service Multiple Award Schedule contract, *available at http://www.fss.gsa.gov/vendorguide/*.

[274] *Id.*

[275] GSAR 552.215-72 (Aug. 1997).

[276] The Contractor Guide, Section C, *supra*.

[277] Clause AS13. *See* VA Solicitation Nos. RFP-797-FSS-99-0025 (Medical Equipment and Supplies) and M5-Q52C-00 (In Vitro Diagnostics, Reagents, Test Kits, and Test Sets).

[278] *See, e.g.*, Dear Contractor letter, "Contract Sales Reporting for GSA Form 72," June 28, 1995.

[279] Veterans Health Care Act of 1992, Pub. L. No. 102-585, § 603(a)(1), 106 Stat. 4971 (codified as amended at 38 U.S.C. § 8126).

[280] For more background, *see* Richard J. Wall & Christopher B. Pockney, *Pricing Pharmaceuticals for the Government*, A.B.A. PUB. CONTRACT L. J. (Fall 1999).

[281] *Id.*

[282] GSAR 552.243-72 (July 2000).

VIII.

CONTRACT NEGOTIATIONS

(by William Gormley and Larry Allen)

"A smile is the chosen vehicle for all ambiguities."
-Herman Melville

Many would-be MAS vendors, and some federal purchasers, assume that the Government awards Schedule contracts to every company that makes an offer. This attitude fosters the dangerous belief that getting "on Schedule" requires little preparation by the company and minimal scrutiny by the Government. This belief is not reality.

As discussed in the prior chapter, companies considering whether to obtain a MAS contract need to consider carefully how they will prepare and position their company (and structure their offer) prior to entering into negotiations with the Government in order to ensure maximum opportunity to obtain a satisfactory business result at the conclusion of the process. This need for careful consideration, however, applies with equal force during contract negotiations, as such negotiations can be protracted and difficult, especially if the initial offer is not prepared carefully.

Generally, offerors can expect the negotiation process to take several months, depending on the complexity of the offer, the GSA contracting officer's workload at the time the offer is submitted, and, most importantly, how well the company has defined its end goal (*i.e.*, pre-determined for itself a range of what it will consider to be a successful outcome) in advance. This chapter examines several important elements of the MAS negotiation process.

A. *The Importance Of Creating An Internal Team*

Just as it is important to bring together a group of corporate officials to ensure proper collection of company commercial sales information, it also is important to have a team examine the company's existing commercial and Government business practices to determine the acceptable discount that will allow the company to make a fair and reasonable profit from Schedule sales. This team can be comprised of the same individuals as the team that collected the company's sales information, but it should have some familiarity with company policies on establishing price points for different markets and distribution methods as well.

In addition to an internal examination, a review of the prices offered by competitors already on the GSA Schedule may provide a guide as to how GSA has dealt with similar companies. The results of this investigation, however, should be viewed as no more than general guidance. Although an analysis of competitor pricing may yield some clues as to what a company may be getting itself into, GSA will negotiate a vendor's Schedule contract based on *that vendor's* commercial sales practices. Too many companies assume that, because their competitor has the service or product on Schedule for "X," this means they will be able to have the same service or product on Schedule for "X" plus or minus a few dollars. This is not the case. The actual discounts a vendor negotiates with GSA, based on the vendor's own established business practices, will determine whether the vendor will be successful in obtaining a Schedule contract and at what prices and terms.

Outside assistance, even for experienced Schedule vendors, can also be an important part of this initial analysis. Independent third parties can provide information on current GSA negotiation strategies, a guide to current sticking points, and a dispassionate analysis about how the company's initial negotiation position may or may not match up with current GSA negotiation positions. (The Vendor Resource Guide at the conclusion of this book lists a number of experienced consultants.)

B. *Preparing A Negotiation Strategy*

After the internal team has reached an agreement on what the vendor will consider to be a successful range of outcomes, the vendor must prepare a strategy that will help ensure that those outcomes are actually realized. As Stephen Covey puts it in the context of personal leadership, "begin with the end in mind."[283] The same rule applies here. Company objectives need to be clearly defined and matched against those likely to be put forward by the Government negotiator. The stronger the case is made up front, the easier it may be for the vendor to obtain a satisfactory outcome.

If the vendor plans to offer GSA its very best prices and discounts, this step will take little time and thought. GSA generally expedites offers that can be shown to be the best deal the vendor offers to any customer under any terms and conditions. Such offers are typically rare and come from vendors offering a limited number of items for sale through the MAS Program.

Additionally, most experienced Schedule vendors know that Government buyers routinely will ask for "spot discounts" below the awarded Schedule price. Indeed, pursuant to the terms of the applicable regulations, larger dollar purchases or any especially competitive situation typically will spark such a request. GSA contracting officers also are required by regulation to seek (but not to achieve) the vendor's most favored customer price. Thus, Schedule contract negotiations can begin with the parties being very far apart because of these countervailing forces. As a result, most vendors do not offer the Government their best and final discount at the start of negotiations.

Understanding (i) the GSA contracting officers' mandate, (ii) the reality that many federal buyers will ask for spot discounts after award, and (iii) the vendor's own financial and strategic position, therefore, are all important factors in setting and executing an effective negotiation strategy. To render such a strategy even more effective, however, it is important to know some of the factors influencing how *the Government* will look at the vendor's offer. Knowing these factors and being able to address them up front can be key elements of a successful and timely negotiation process.

Who at the GSA or the Department of Veterans Affairs Manages Contracts for the Vendor's Service or Product? Though this question is easily answered for VA vendors since that agency has one centralized location for all Schedule offers, it is more complex at GSA. The proliferation of service contracts and the overlap in offerings that result can make it very confusing as to the most appropriate place for the vendor to submit its offer. In addition, different GSA acquisition centers negotiate in slightly different ways. Examining alternatives and discussing the vendor's approach with GSA—or an experienced outside party—can help determine the most appropriate or advantageous location at which to submit the offer.

Industrial Funding Fee: The industrial funding fee ("IFF") (.75 percent at GSA and 0.5 percent at VA) is added to every vendor's Schedule contract price in order to fund the management of the MAS Program. (*See* Chapter XIV for a detailed discussion of the IFF.) Vendors need to be aware that, though the original intent of the Program was for companies that so chose to be allowed to raise their prices by the IFF amount at the conclusion of negotiations, Government contracting officers routinely now *expect that the price they negotiate includes the IFF*, unless it is otherwise made clear by the vendor throughout the course of negotiations.

Most Favored Customer Price: As described in greater detail in Chapter VII, the Government's objective in most MAS negotiations is to obtain the vendor's most favored customer price. If the vendor's best corporate customer is extended a 50 percent discount from the vendor's standard commercial rates, for example, the contract specialist will seek that same discount for GSA. While Government negotiators have the flexibility to consider differing terms and award less than the most favored customer price, they will not award a contract unless they determine that the discount(s) offered are fair and reasonable and in the best interest of the Government.

Pre-Award Audits: The contract specialist sometimes will order a pre-award audit of the vendor's offer to determine whether the information included in the offer is accurate, current, and complete. Though it is unusual for new offerors to be selected for a pre-award audit, it is not out of the question. More likely, an incumbent Schedule vendor that realizes significant Schedule sales will be selected. If ordered, a pre-award audit usually will take place after the offer is submitted and before negotiations have begun. In addition to examining the sales records and other documents used to prepare the offer, the pre-award audit also will provide the negotiator with an outline of the sales practices from which the Government's negotiation position will be established. This outline may or may not be available to the vendor prior to negotiations. Occasionally, an impasse in negotiations may result if the Government misreads or misinterprets the vendor's information. (Chapter XXII provides a detailed discussion of GSA Office of Inspector General audits.)

C. *What Happens When the Offer Is Submitted?*

Once the vendor has completed its offer, checked it to ensure that it is accurate, current, and complete, and developed a negotiation strategy, the offer then must be submitted to the appropriate GSA acquisition center that manages the Schedule contracts for the type of service or product the vendor provides.

(The Vendor Resource Guide at the conclusion of this book lists contact information for each GSA acquisition center.)

The vendor's offer will be assigned to a "contract specialist" soon after it is submitted. Each acquisition center has a relatively short time frame within which it must assign newly received offers. The vendor's offer may be one of a dozen, or one of hundreds, for which the contract specialist is responsible, depending on what type of service or product the vendor is offering and GSA's workload. An initial contact should be made by the contract specialist, however, within thirty days of the submission of the vendor's offer.

This contact may be no more than a perfunctory introduction or it may be to alert the vendor to missing documents or to request additional clarification of the vendor's offer. Any reasonable request by the contract specialist, whether oral or in writing, should be handled promptly to avoid delays in the negotiation and award process. Not all requests, though, may seem reasonable, as discussed below.

D. *Negotiating The Offer*

Once the contract specialist has reviewed the vendor's offer and determined that all necessary information has been submitted, the vendor will be notified and the negotiation process will begin.

The GSA contract specialist will have already prepared an official Government negotiation position prior to this time based on the information the vendor supplied regarding the vendor's sales and discounting practices and, perhaps, some broad-based market research (yet another reason why vendors should define their own "negotiation position" prior to meeting with GSA). This information likely will not be provided to the vendor prior to or during negotiations. Remember, however, that the contract specialist's goal is to obtain the vendor's most favored customer price—*i.e.*, to cut the best deal possible *for the Government*.

Negotiations need not be in person. As a general rule, however, face-to-face discussions can help expedite the negotiation process and create a stronger business relationship. It is not at all uncommon, however, for Schedule contracts to be awarded without the offeror and negotiator meeting. Several companies report that they negotiate good contracts via telephone and e-mail. Such a process can help reduce travel costs and minimize lost service or productivity in a company where the Schedule negotiator wears several hats.

Negotiations on discounts may be swift or protracted depending on the complexity of the offer and how far apart the offeror and contract specialist are. In addition, it is not uncommon for the human relations element to enter into the negotiation process. Again, this can be a positive or negative influence. If, however, each side can work within reasonable boundaries, an agreement on a fair and reasonable Schedule price usually can be achieved.

This does not mean, though, that this is the conclusion of negotiations. The final discount structure agreed to by the contract specialist must be approved by a supervisory contracting officer actually warranted to bind the Government to the terms negotiated. While this supervisory contracting officer usually will be part of the negotiation process before an agreement is reached, it is possible that he or she merely will review the contract specialist's work. If he or she is not convinced that the terms negotiated by the contract specialist are in the best interest of the Government, additional negotiations and discussions must take place.

E. *Negotiations On Factors Other Than Price*

While discount and pricing terms are certainly important parts of Schedule contract negotiations—and are discussed in detail in Chapter VII—they are by no means the only aspect of the vendor's offer that will be negotiated. The following are some examples of contract elements a contract specialist will examine in determining whether the vendor's entire offer is in the Government's best interest.

Delivery Terms: GSA contract specialists will examine the vendor's commercial delivery terms and may ask the vendor to improve upon them, at least for certain items.

Warranty: The vendor's commercial warranty terms also will be reviewed. It is likely that the vendor will be asked to improve upon its commercial warranty, though the extent to which this becomes a key sticking point varies widely by vendor.

Industrial Funding Fee: Vendors planning to add the additional IFF (.75 percent for GSA) to their prices at the conclusion of negotiations must make sure that Government officials are aware of this intent throughout the negotiation process. Failure to do this may result in a net price the contract specialist believes already to include the fee.

Small Business Subcontracting Plan: Large businesses whose Schedule contract is estimated to be worth more than $500,000 will be required to submit a small business subcontracting plan showing how small businesses will benefit from the award of this contract. Government negotiators have recently paid increased attention to these plans, requiring vendors to increase small business usage. The vendor's plan needs to show how this will be accomplished. A representative of the Small Business Administration will be assigned to monitor the implementation of the vendor's plan. (Small business subcontracting plans are discussed in greater depth in Chapter XIII.)

Government Commercial Purchase Card Acceptance/ Prompt Payment Discounts: GSA contracting officers encourage vendors to accept the Government's commercial purchase card for Government purchases.[284] Some contracting officers ask whether the vendor will provide for a prompt payment discount either tied to purchase card usage or for all invoices paid within thirty days.

End-Of-Contract Discount: Though this type of discount is more rare than it used to be, some contracting officers still ask whether a vendor will provide the Government with a percentage-based rebate at the conclusion of the contract term if certain business volumes are met.

F. _What Happens When Things Go Wrong?_

Occasionally, the offeror and Government negotiator will reach an impasse in the negotiation process. This can happen for a variety of reasons. Disagreements over appropriate discount levels and misunderstandings as to what is being offered or how the service or product is sold are the most frequent causes. In these cases, offerors need to have the ability to seek assistance from the supervisory contracting officer or other GSA officials.

Each contract specialist works for a supervisory contracting officer or branch manager. Each supervisor typically manages a team of four or five contract specialists. While it may not be advisable routinely to bypass the vendor's contract specialist, it is not uncommon to have the supervisory contracting officer or branch manager be a part of the negotiations, especially those that are complex and time-consuming. The supervisor may have a different perspective from the contract specialist and is often integral to the resolution of problems that may arise.

Above the supervisory level, each acquisition center has a center director and deputy center director. At the VA, these are the Executive Director of the National Acquisition Center and the head of Federal Supply Service operations, respectively. These directors are typically senior managers and are available to assist in particularly difficult situations. In some exceptional cases, the center director may re-assign the vendor's offer to a different contract specialist, though this may result in re-starting the negotiation process.

Above the center directors, there are more senior GSA and VA executives. It is not normally advisable, though, to contact these officials for all but the most intractable problems.

G. _What Happens When Things Go Right?_

The vendor has consulted with its attorney and/or consultant, obtained a corporate commitment, developed its policies, organized its sales force, negotiated its contract, and received an award—what happens next?

Once the vendor receives notification of award, the vendor must forward authorized price lists to user agencies on the mailing list for the contract code.[285] Vendors have the option of providing a paper copy of the price list to each addressee on the mailing list or may send a self-addressed, postage-paid envelope or postcard to be returned by the agency if they want a paper price list (distribution must be made within twenty days after receipt of returned requests).[286] Immediately upon the contracting officer's approval of the vendor's price list, the vendor must return two paper copies of the price list along with a copy of the list in electronic medium as required by the contracting officer.[287]

During the life of the contract, the vendor must provide, upon the request of any authorized user, an authorized price list. Vendors are prohibited from using the mailing list for any other purpose.

Advice From The Trenches

(Deborah Lague, GSA FSS ITAS Division Director)[288]

The FAR provides that a contracting officer is responsible for "ensuring performance of all necessary actions for effecting contracting, ensuring compliance with the terms of the contract, and safeguarding the interests of the United States in its contractual relationships." I would add something to this list. MAS contracting officers also are responsible for promoting mutually beneficial partnerships between GSA and the thousands of vendors that offer their goods and/or services through the Schedule Program.

Clearly, contracting officers, known more colloquially as COs, play a critical role in protecting the interests of the Government (and, thus, the taxpayers). But we also play an important role in helping contractors understand the MAS program, submit compliant offers, and, once an award is in hand, market their products to federal users across the country and the world. Thus, establishing a good working relationship with your CO is a good idea on many levels.

Over the years, I have seen contractors succeed and fail in this regard. Consequently, I have learned a lot about what helps make a positive working relationship between a contractor and his or her CO. The following short list of "Do's" and "Don'ts" is drawn from my 12 years of experience working within GSA.

DO carefully review all the requirements of the solicitation prior to submitting your offer. This not only will save you time, money, and aggravation, it also will help achieve the professional respect of your CO. Your understanding of the requirements of the MAS Program also will facilitate the proposal review and contract negotiation process. Much of the information you will need in this regard is found in the section of the solicitation entitled "Instructions to Offerors—Commercial Items." Be sure also to pay close attention to GSAR 552.212-70, which describes how to summit a MAS offer.

DO take time to understand the proposal process. Your understanding of what goes on behind the scenes within GSA will help you understand why the process may not always work quite as fast as you would like. Remember that the day you submit your proposal is not the day it finds its way into the hands of your CO. First, the proposal package hits our common delivery dock. Then it goes through x-ray. Then to the mailroom to be sorted. Then to the appropriate acquisition center. If that center is the IT Acquisition Center, it then is forwarded to a non-contracting review team for an initial review. This team reviews all offers to verify that the required documentation has been submitted. The review team also looks for obvious deficiencies in order to alert the offeror in advance of CO review. Once the proposal passes the review team, it then is logged into an electronic database and passed on to a supervisor, who then assigns it to the cognizant CO. From an IT contractors point of view, the initial review step is especially important because, if a proposal is significantly incomplete, it can be rejected and returned.

DO call the CO assigned to your proposal a few weeks after submission to introduce yourself as the primary point-of-contact for your company. This will help kick off your relationship on a good foot and personalize the process so that your proposal is seen as something more than a number.

DON'T pressure the CO for a specific contract award date. Keep in mind that, at any given time, your CO has multiple proposals sitting on his or her desk awaiting action. Typically, a CO reviews from three to eight offers at one time. New proposals are put at the bottom of the pile and must work their way to the top. So be patient!

DON'T call the CO on a daily basis. There is nothing wrong with "checking in" from time to time, but when such checking becomes nagging, you risk damaging your relationship.

DO respond to CO requests completely and in a timely manner. If you cannot meet a due date, you should contact your CO *prior to the due date* and discuss the possibility of securing an extension. You should be prepared to justify your request and to propose a new due date. Once this new due date has been established, you should make all reasonable efforts to ensure that you meet it since it is less likely that a further extension will be granted absent truly extenuating circumstances.

DON'T let the CO make unreasonable demands. If you feel that a certain request for information or documents is unnecessary or unreasonable, it is within your right to contact the CO's supervisor. You should exercise great discretion in this area, however, and try hard to resolve the matter directly with the CO first. Remember that the CO is the only government official authorized to award your contract.

DO take advantage of the MAS Contracts Helpdesk. The Helpdesk (available at 800.488.3111) was established as an entry point to GSA for questions regarding the requirements of the MAS Program. While the Helpdesk is not manned by contracting personnel, the Helpdesk staff is knowledgeable regarding the requirements of the MAS solicitation, as well as what product and services should be offered through which Schedule(s).

In the end, remember that the MAS Program was designed to benefit the Government and its contractors. The time you take to understand and comply with the rules governing that Program will be time well spent. Likewise, the time you spend developing a relationship with your CO that is based upon trust, respect, and a common interest in serving the needs of the various departments and agencies that look to the MAS Program to meet their procurement needs also will be time well spent.

Notes:

[283] Stephen R. Covey, THE 7 HABITS OF HIGHLY EFFECTIVE PEOPLE 97 (Simon & Schuster 1989).

[284] GSAR 552.232-77 (Mar. 2000) requires vendors to accept the Government's commercial purchase card for purchases at or below the micro-purchase threshold (currently $2,500) and encourages vendor acceptance of the card for purchases above the micro-purchase theshold.

[285] FSS Clause I-FSS-600(9) (Sept. 2000) provides general information regarding the customer mailing list format. In compliance with this clause, contractors are required to distribute the authorized price list at least fifteen calendar days prior to the beginning of the contract or within thirty days after the contracting officer has approved the list for printing, whichever is later. GSAR 552.238-71(d) (Submission and Distribution of Authorized FSS Schedule Pricelists) (Sept. 1999).

[286] GSAR 552.238-71(c)(2)(ii) (Sept. 1999).

[287] See FSS Clause I-FSS-600 for details as to the price list requirements.

[288] Deborah Lague is a warranted contracting officer currently serving as a Contracting Officer within the Information Technology Acquisition Center of GSA's Federal Supply Service. She has been active in the MAS Program for more than 12 years. The opinions set forth herein are her own and may not reflect the opinions of GSA, the FSS, or the IT Acquisition Center.

IX.

CERTIFICATIONS AND REPRESENTATIONS

"The vow that binds too strictly snaps itself."
-Alfred Lord Tennyson

The Government Contracts Reference Book defines a certification as a "signed representation that certain facts are accurate."[289] MAS vendors, like all Government contractors, should become very familiar with this definition for several reasons. First, every MAS contract requires the execution of several certifications. Second, a knowingly inaccurate certification can lead to severe penalties. Third, these penalties can be imposed upon not only the vendor, but also upon the individuals who signed the certifications or representations. Thus, it is with good reason that this area of Government contracting is the subject of significant discussion within the contracting community.

Certifications and representations generally come in two forms. Some require an explicit, affirmative statement regarding compliance. An offeror's certification that it never has been debarred or suspended provides an apt example of an explicit certification. On the other hand, some representations are implicit—that is, they are deemed executed by the performance of an act. The submission of a Schedule proposal, for example, carries with it an implicit representation that the vendor will comply with the terms and conditions thereof.

This chapter examines the primary certifications and representations that a Schedule vendor must execute in order to participate in the MAS Program.

A. *Size Representation*

Vendors must certify whether they are small or large businesses under the applicable standards that govern each Schedule procurement. Because different procurements define "small" and "large" differently, vendors must assess their size against the applicable threshold *prior* to submitting any certification in this regard.[290] Generally, a solicitation will have only one business size associated with it; but, in some instances, there may be more than one applicable business size and each may have a different dollar or size standard associated with it. If the vendor is a small business under one North American Industry Classification System code and a large business under another, the vendor should certify as to the larger size or submit two separate proposals.

Vendors wishing to be considered a small disadvantaged business ("SDB") must file a separate application with the Small Business Administration and be accepted into the SDB program. More information regarding the SBA's SDB program can be found at *http://www.sba.gov/sdb/*.

Previously, a vendor's business size was determined at the time of the vendor's initial MAS offer and lasted the life of the contract.[291] Given that MAS contracts now may extend twenty years (a 5-year base contract plus three 5-year options), this allowed a vendor that had outgrown its original business size (because of a merger, for example) still to certify itself as small—and claim the benefits of being small—under its MAS Contract. Recognizing that this was not how the small business programs was intended to function,[292] GSA and SBA moved to address this unintended result.

GSA moved first by implementing a deviation to the FAR that required small businesses to recertify their small business size each time their MAS contract came up for renewal.[293] According to GSA, the new policy was designed "to address a loophole in Federal contracting that has allowed businesses to retain their status as 'small' (and all the sub-categories) even after they no longer meet the requirements for being classified as small."[294] Consequently, MAS vendors (as well as those vendors operating under other multiple award contracts, such as the FTS FAST program) now must recertify that they qualify as a small business each time their contract or contracts come up for renewal.

The SBA was not far behind. On April 25, 2003, SBA issued a proposed rule requiring small businesses to re-certify their size *every year*.[295] Additionally, the SBA's proposed rule also establishes guidelines for protesting size certifications. Under the rule, agencies must publish a list of vendor size recertifications within ten days of receipt.[296]

The issuance of the proposed SBA rule in 2003 was foreshadowed by two specific events taking place in 2002. First, in March 2002, the SBA Office of Hearing and Appeals (OHA) held that a Schedule RFQ for award of a Blanket Purchase Agreement properly was considered a _new_ small business set-aside procurement that required a _new_ size certification from competing contractors. The SBA was not swayed by GSA's strenuous objection that a BPA is an account established with a contractor, not a "new procurement."[297] Second, in August 2002, the Government Accountability Office held that an agency properly may require contractors to recertify their small business size status as of the time they submit their quotations in response to an RFQ issued under a Schedule contract.[298]

As of the submission of the text of this Second Edition to the publisher, the SBA rule had not yet been finalized.

B. _Equal Opportunity Clause Certification_

Vendors are required to certify as to whether they have participated in a previous contract that was subject to the Equal Opportunity Clause. If the answer to this question is in the affirmative, then the vendor must certify that it submitted all required compliance reports.[299]

C. *Non-Segregated Facilities Certification*

Most Schedule solicitations include FAR 52.222-21, which relates to non-segregated facilities. This clause prohibits the vendor from segregating any of its facilities on the basis of race, color, religion, sex, or national origin. This is an implicit certification that is incorporated into the contract by reference. By submitting its proposal, the vendor implicitly certifies that it does not—and will not—(i) maintain segregated facilities or (ii) permit its employees to work in a segregated facility. This clause is required to be included in all subcontracts or purchase orders under the contract.

D. *Payments To Influence Federal Transactions Certification*

Vendors are required to certify that, to the best of their knowledge and belief, no appropriated funds have been used to influence or attempt to influence an officer or employee of any federal agency, a member of Congress, or an officer or employee of a member of Congress in connection with the award of any Government contract.[300]

E. *Taxpayer Identification Number Representation*

Schedule vendors are required to provide, among other things and subject to certain exceptions, a Taxpayer Identification Number ("TIN").[301] The purpose of the TIN is to ensure that the vendor is a properly registered taxable entity. The TIN identifies the entity and provides a tracking mechanism for the Government and the IRS. The contracting officer generally must submit the TIN, along with information relating to the dollar value of the contract, to the IRS. Along with an offeror's TIN representation, vendors must certify their organizational structure. If an organization is a subsidiary of another organization, for example, this information must be disclosed to GSA along with the TIN of the parent organization.

F. *Service Contract Act Certification*

See Chapter XVI for a discussion of the Service Contract Act.

G. *Veterans Employment Certification*

FAR 52.222-37 requires vendors to execute annually a form entitled "Federal Contractor Veterans' Employment Report VETS-100" ("VETS-100"). This form accounts for (1) the number of disabled veterans and veterans of the Vietnam era employed by the vendor and (2) the total number of new employees hired during the period covered by the report and, of that total, the number of disabled veterans or veterans of the Vietnam era.[302] The certification requires that the vendor represent whether its most recent VETS-100 was submitted to the Government. (Effective January 12, 1999, no contract valued in excess of $25,000 may be awarded or option exercised until the contracting officer has determined that the vendor has submitted its most recent VETS-100.) The Department of Labor maintains a hotline (703.461.2460) and a web site (*http://vets100.cudenver.edu*) for questions in this area.

H. *Trade Agreements Act Certification*

Prospective MAS vendors must certify that their products are compliant with the Trade Agreements Act ("TAA"). If the MAS solicitation includes a TAA certification (or if the solicitation includes the clause at FAR 52.225-6, "Trade Agreements Certification"), then the vendor must assess whether its products conform to the definitions under the TAA. As discussed in detail in Chapter XIV, the TAA precludes the Government from purchasing noncompliant supplies when the value of the solicitation is above a certain threshold.[303] Currently, the threshold for application of the TAA in supply contracts is $175,000.[304]

I. *Buy American Act Certification*

The Buy American Act ("BAA"), discussed more fully in Chapter XIV, applies to Schedule contracts that incorporate FAR 52.225-1. As most Schedule contracts exceed the threshold for application of the TAA—because the threshold is calculated based upon the estimated value of the acquisition (including option periods)—the BAA will be inapplicable to most Schedule contracts. Where the BAA is applicable, however, the vendor must certify that each end product is a domestic end product as defined in the FAR.[305]

J. *Economic Price Adjustment Certification*

MAS vendors seeking a Schedule price increase pursuant to the Economic Price Adjustment Clause must certify that the proposed increase does not result from a change to the vendor's disclosed pricing/discount policies or procedures.[306] The Economic Price Adjustment Clause is discussed in more detail in Chapters VII and XIV.

K. *Online Representations And Certifications*

A recent addition to the list of representations and certifications is one that aims to eliminate the redundancy of the process and to reduce paperwork. The Online Representations and Certifications Application (ORCA), implemented as part of the E-Government initiative, is a streamlined electronic method for reusing certifications and representations in multiple procurements. This is accomplished through a web-based environment, found at *http://orca.bpn.gov*, that the Government uses to collect, store, and view many of the representations and certifications required by the FAR in both commercial and non-commercial items acquisitions.

For vendors of commercial items under the GSA MAS program, the revised FAR 52.212-3, now includes paragraph (j), requiring registration and completion of the online representations and certifications in ORCA. Once the contractor has entered its information into the online system, FAR 52.212-3(j)(2) provides that the submission of an offer operates as a verification that the information in ORCA was entered or updated within the last twelve months and that all the information in ORCA is current, accurate and complete. If, for whatever reason, the contractor needs to deviate from the information on file in ORCA for the purposes of a particular solicitation, the impacted representations and certifications must be so identified in the offer. Any such change, however, is specific to a single solicitation only and does not change the information on file with ORCA.[307] Permanent changes need to be made online and will be effective for all prospective solicitations. ORCA information is active for 365 days from the date of submission or update, and email reminders are sent sixty, thirty, and fifteen days prior to expiration.

Notes:

[289] GOVERNMENT CONTRACTS REFERENCE BOOK 87.

[290] Vendors are cautioned to check the North American Industry Classification System code (formerly Standard Industrial Classification code) under which the solicitation falls.

[291] *See* GSA Procurement Information Bulletin 00-16 (June 14, 2000).

[292] GSA Press Release (Nov 15, 2002).

[293] *Id.* According to the press release, GSA's Senior Procurement Executive issued the deviation on October 10, 2002.

[294] GSA Press Release (Nov. 15, 2002).

[295] *See* 68 Fed. Reg. 20350 (Apr. 25, 2003).

[296] *Id.* (the list must be published "on their agency's website, and may

also publish it in the Federal Register, or otherwise").

[297] *See Size Appeal of SETA Corp.*, Mar. 1, 2002.

[298] *See CMS Info. Servs., Inc.*, B-290541, Aug. 7, 2002.

[299] FAR 22.807(b)(6) requires that, for indefinite-quantity contracts, the Equal Opportunity Clause shall be required for contracts with orders exceeding $10,000 in any twelve-month period.

[300] FAR 52.212-3(e).

[301] FAR 52.212-3(b)(3).

[302] On October 11, 2001, the Department of Labor ("DOL") issued a final rule implementing provisions of the Veterans Employment Opportunity Act of 1998 ("VEOA") (Pub. L. No. 105-339), including new requirements for submission of the VETS-100. 66 Fed. Reg. 51,998 (Oct. 11, 2001) (to be codified at 41 C.F.R. pt. 61-250). On October 22, 2001, the Civilian Agency Acquisition Council and the Defense Acquisition Council (the "FAR Council") issued a final rule that revises related FAR provisions. 66 Fed. Reg. 53,487 (Oct. 22, 2001) (to be codified at 48 C.F.R. pts. 2, 12, 13, 22, and 52). The VEOA and the implementing DOL and FAR rules create new reporting requirements and a potential risk for contractors. For additional information regarding these changes, *see* James J. McCullough & Catherine E. Pollack, *Veterans Legislation Creates New Obligations for Government Contractors and New Opportunities for Veterans*, Dec. 12, 2001, *available at* http://www.ffhsj.com/cmemos.htm.

[303] *See infra* note 599.

[304] FAR 25.403(b).

[305] 41 U.S.C. §§ 10a-10d (1933, as amended in 1988).

[306] GSAR 552.216-70(d)(2) (Sept. 1999). Vendors must certify that there has been no change in data submitted on the CSP Format since initial negotiation or subsequent submission.

[307] FAR 52.212-3(j)(1).

X.

MULTIPLE AWARD SCHEDULE PROTESTS

(by James J. McCullough and Deneen J. Melander,
Fried, Frank, Harris, Shriver & Jacobson LLP)

> *"Show me a good and gracious loser and I'll show
> you a failure."*
>
> -Knute Rockne

Traditional competition for federal contracts is a zero-sum game: When one competitor wins, all other competitors lose. This is not the case with MAS contracting, where all vendors have the opportunity to sell their commercial products on the Schedule. The resulting absence of disappointed bidders creates an environment where bid protests are unusual. However, they are not unknown. Since the inception of the MAS Program, at least a few Schedule vendors have found reason to pursue their complaints before the GSA, the Government Accountability Office ("GAO"), or the federal courts; and these protests have helped shape the boundaries of the current MAS Program.

The Competition in Contracting Act of 1984 ("CICA") defines "protest" as

> a written objection by an interested party to a
> solicitation by a Federal agency for bids or
> proposals for a proposed contract for the
> procurement of property or services or . . . to a
> proposed award or the award of such a contract.[308]

The Federal Acquisition Streamlining Act of 1994[309] expanded this definition to make clear that the term "protest" encompassed a challenge to any of the following agency actions:

(a) A solicitation or other request by a federal agency for offers for a contract for the procurement of property or services.

(b) The cancellation of such solicitation or other request.

(c) An award or proposed award of such a contract.

(d) A termination or cancellation of an award of such a contract, if the written objection contains an allegation that the termination or cancellation is based in whole or in part on improprieties concerning the award of the contract.

Currently, the FAR and the GAO's own regulations incorporate the foregoing definition.[310]

Notwithstanding the statutory and regulatory definition of "protest," the GAO historically has taken a very narrow view of the aspects of a MAS procurement that can be protested. This view derives, in part, from the fact that purchases of supplies and services from the Schedule are considered to be made pursuant to full and open competition and, thus, are excepted from the competition requirements of CICA and FAR Part 15.[311] In this regard, the Schedule process involves the negotiation of reasonable prices from each vendor[312] and requires vendors to treat purchasers under the Schedule as favored customers.[313] Since the equivalent of full and open competition has already been achieved through the negotiation of reasonable prices, some have argued that there is no basis for protesting a Schedule

procurement.[314] In recent years, however, the GAO has evidenced a much greater willingness to hear certain types of protests brought by Schedule vendors. This upswing in Schedule protest activity has escaped some vendors, who are so accustomed to GAO's traditional aversion toward Schedule bid protests that they fail to consider this avenue for relief even when a protest may be warranted. In light of GAO's recent shift, new attention to this area of dispute resolution is important. Indeed, a thorough understanding of the rules and regulations that govern bid protests is essential for Schedule vendors both from an offensive and a defensive point of view.

A. *Where Can I Protest?*

A MAS vendor, like most government contractors, can initiate a bid protest in three different forums: the GAO (sometimes referred to as the Comptroller General), the United States Court of Federal Claims ("COFC"), or the agency itself. Historically, bid protests also could be lodged with the General Services Administration Board of Contract Appeals ("GSBCA") or with a federal district court, but the GSBCA's authority to hear bid protests was eliminated in 1996[315] and the district courts' statutory protest authority was eliminated in 2001.[316]

Of the two protest forums outside of the agency, GAO offers the least expensive and most efficient alternative. Additionally, GAO possesses the greatest experience—and, thus, many would say, the greatest expertise—in resolving protest matters. But this is not to say that the GAO necessarily should be the protest forum of choice for every aggrieved Schedule vendor. Each forum offers advantages and disadvantages, as discussed below.

1. Agency Level Protests

Both the FAR and the agency supplements to the FAR, e.g., the GSAR, set forth procedures for protests that are filed directly with the agency. Agency protest procedures are relatively fast, flexible, and informal. Some typical highlights of those procedures are discussed below. However, we urge readers to review carefully the requirements of the applicable agency, e.g., GSAR 552.233-70, before filing any protest. In general, agency level protests should be filed with the agency that issued the relevant RFQ, or if no RFQ was issued, with the agency issuing the relevant order.

- *Timeliness and content.* The mechanics of filing a protest with an agency are governed in the first instance by the FAR, which is applicable to all executive branch agencies. The FAR requires that protests of solicitation improprieties (any problem related to the solicitation itself, for example, an agency's decision to limit a competition to Schedule vendors, or the agency's statement of its requirements) be filed before the solicitation's scheduled closing date. Protests of anything other than solicitation improprieties (generally, issues that arise after the closing date) must be filed no later than ten calendar days after the basis of protest is known or should have been known, whichever is earlier.[317] FAR 33.103(d)(2) and agency supplements such as GSAR 552.233-70(c) set forth specific information that the protester must provide, including solicitation information, point-of-contact information, and a detailed factual and legal statement of the protest grounds.

- *Where to file.* GSA's rules note that a protest is "filed" when it is received in the office designated in the solicitation for receipt of protests. (This designation is usually made in a solicitation provision entitled "Service of Protest." In many, but not all, cases, the designated office is the same one listed on the front page of the RFQ or relevant order.) Any protest received after 4:30 p.m. will be considered filed on the next business day.[318]

- *Automatic stay of award or performance.* FAR 33.103(f) requires the contracting agency, upon receipt of a protest, to refrain from awarding a contract (in the case of a pre-award protest) or suspend performance of the contract (in the case of a post-award protest). However, the agency may proceed with award or performance of the contract by executing a written determination that award or performance is justified by urgent and compelling reasons or is in the best interest of the Government.[319] This written determination must be executed at a level above the contracting officer.[320] It should be noted that some agencies may take the position that the automatic stay of award does not apply to orders issued under a GSA MAS contract.

- *Procedural requirements and time frames*. The agency-level process is designed to move quickly, for example, the GSAR provides that the deciding official must conduct a scheduling conference with the protester within three calendar days after the protest is filed in order to establish deadlines for oral or written arguments by the protester and by agency officials.[321] GSA's procedures encourage, but do not require, the parties to exchange information they submit to the deciding official, except that, if the agency makes a written response to the protest, it must file this response with the deciding official within five calendar days after the protest is filed and it must provide a copy of the response to the protester.[322] If the agency wants to redact or withhold any information in the response from the protester, it must first obtain permission from the deciding official.[323]

- *The protest decision*. The deciding official is required to make "best efforts" to render a decision within 35 calendar days after the protest is filed.[324] Specific agency rules may shorten this time period. However, there is no requirement that the decision be in writing.[325] The GSAR, however, provides that if the decision is communicated orally to the protester, the deciding official is required to confirm the decision in writing within three (3) calendar days after the oral decision is issued.[326] This requirement for a written confirmation, however, does not expressly provide for any articulation of the legal basis for the agency's decision.

The advantages of filing a protest with the agency are that such protests are decided much more quickly than in other forums, they are relatively inexpensive, and the agency action may be automatically stayed until a decision is rendered. In addition, at GSA, as at some other agencies, there is no provision for intervention by a third party (*e.g.*, an awardee whose contract is being protested). The disadvantages are that there is no discovery of evidence that could support the protester's case, there is no reimbursement for legal fees, and the relative informality of the proceedings may not allow for complex legal issues to be to be explored and resolved effectively. In addition, there is a procedural wrinkle that may be a strong deterrent to an agency-level protest: Once the agency acts on the protest, the automatic stay of award or performance ends. If the protest is denied, and the protester chooses to pursue relief at the GAO, the protester will not be able to obtain the benefit of GAO's automatic stay.

2. Government Accountability Office

Of the three bid protest venues—the contracting agency, the COFC, and the GAO—the GAO is by far the most popular. This is primarily due to GAO's accessibility, relative speed, and long-standing reputation for expertise in procurement matters. Although the GAO process usually is not as speedy, informal, or inexpensive as the agency-level process, it provides protesters with an independent, impartial review of the agency's procurement action.

The GAO's protest procedures are set forth in the Code of Federal Regulations at 4 C.F.R. § 21.0 *et seq.* Some of these requirements are also included at FAR 33.104. Again, we urge readers to review these requirements carefully prior to filing any protest rather than relying on this discussion, particularly with respect to the requirements setting forth the information that the protest must contain. Readers may also wish to review the GAO's publication, *Bid Protests at GAO: A Descriptive Guide*, GAO-03-539SP (7th ed. 2003), which can be obtained through the GAO's web site at *http://www.gao.gov*. This guide includes the text of the Bid Protest Regulations, along with a discussion of the regulatory requirements and helpful "practice tips."

Following is a brief outline of the GAO's procedures and some of their idiosyncrasies:

While the GAO has been reviewing and deciding bid protests for approximately seventy-five years, its current statutory authority to render bid protest decisions is based on CICA.[327] The GAO's mandate under CICA is to ensure that statutory requirements for "full and open competition" are met. Understanding this fundamental concept can help a protester or prospective protester understand the GAO's approach to carrying out its bid protest function.

- *Standing to protest*. In order to have a protest considered by the GAO, the protester must qualify as an "interested party." The GAO defines "interested party" as an "actual or prospective bidder or offeror whose direct economic interest would be affected by the award of a contract or by the failure to award a contract."[328] In other words, the interested party must potentially suffer an injury as a result of losing the contract or receive a benefit if the protest is sustained. For example, depending on the nature of the issues raised in the protest, the GAO may find that a non-Schedule holder is not an interested party to challenge the award of an order to a Schedule holder.[329]

- *Protective orders*. If the protest contains proprietary or confidential information that should be withheld from persons outside the Government, the protester may request a protective order or the GAO may issue such an order on its own initiative.[330] Protesters need to know, however, that the issuance of a protective order usually has the effect of limiting the information to which the protester itself (as opposed to its counsel) will have access. This is because only a protester's outside counsel, and in some cases in-house counsel and consultants, may apply for access to protected material. When an agency deems material produced in response to the protest to be protected, as is generally the case with competitive proposals, evaluation documents, and source selection information, only the individuals admitted under the protective order will have access to those protected materials. That is, the protester itself (as opposed to its counsel) will not be able to see much of the agency's response to the protest. This can be problematic in cases where the protester elects to file and pursue its protest without counsel. In such cases, the GAO makes efforts to ensure that the agency provides the protester with enough information to argue its case, but such *"pro se"* protesters still cannot gain access to information such as other offerors' proposals or the agency's evaluations of those proposals.

- *Timeliness requirements.* It is critical to understand the GAO's timeliness requirements for two reasons: (1) Some of the deadlines are very short and therefore are easy to miss, and (2) the GAO almost never waives its timeliness rules.

The basic timeliness rules are the same as at the agency level: Protests of solicitation improprieties must be filed before the solicitation's scheduled closing date,[331] and protests of anything other than solicitation improprieties must be filed within ten calendar days after the protester knew or should have known of the basis for protest.[332] There is one exception to the latter requirement. Where the protest concerns a competitive procurement under which a debriefing is requested and required, the protest must be filed no later than ten calendar days after the debriefing (even if the protester knew of at least some of its protest grounds before the debriefing).[333] The purpose of this rule is twofold: to preclude protesters from unnecessarily filing "protective" protests before they are fully informed about the basis for the agency's procurement decision and to encourage agencies to provide thorough, informative debriefings that may resolve a potential protester's concerns so that there is no need for a protest.

The GAO has a further requirement where the protest challenges the agency's denial of an agency-level protest: Such a protest must be filed within ten calendar days after the protester knew or should have known of the agency's initial adverse action on the agency-level protest.[334] In addition to dismissing protests that do not comply with these requirements, the GAO applies these requirements to protest grounds that are newly raised during the course of an ongoing protest. Thus, if information provided by the agency during the course of a protest raises a new protestable issue, the protester must protest to the GAO within ten calendar days of learning of the new information or forfeit that protest basis.

- *Automatic stay of award or performance.* The filing of a timely protest at the GAO may require the agency to suspend or "stay" contract award or performance while the protest is pending.[335] In general, the filing of a protest before award requires the agency to refrain from making award until after the protest is resolved, and the filing of a post-award protest either within ten calendar days after award or within five calendar days after a "requested and required" debriefing requires the suspension of contract performance.[336] This sounds straightforward enough. However, the process is complicated by the fact that the suspension is triggered not by the filing of the protest, but by *the GAO's telephonic notice to the agency* that the protest has been filed. Although the GAO undertakes commendable efforts to make agency notifications promptly, some notifications cannot be made on the same day the protest is filed. If the protest was filed on the last possible day for obtaining the automatic suspension (for example, the fifth day following a post-award debriefing), and the GAO does not notify the agency of the protest until the following day, the agency is not required to suspend the award or the performance of the contract. There are no exceptions to this statutory requirement. Prospective protesters should always try to file their protests the day before the last possible day, even if this means drafting and filing a protest in just four calendar days following a post-award debriefing. At least the protester does not have to allow much additional time for delivery since GAO accepts filings by fax (202.512.9749), but the risk of incomplete transmission or technical difficulties with the fax transmission, or a busy signal on GAO's end, is on the protester.

As is the case in agency-level protests, agencies may authorize award or continued performance in the face of the protest by executing a written determination that award or performance is justified by urgent and compelling reasons or is in the best interest of the Government.[337] This written determination must be made by the head of the contracting activity.[338] In general, agencies have conformed with CICA's automatic stay requirements with respect to protests challenging the award of orders under GSA MAS contracts. However, there is no definitive caselaw, to date, holding that CICA's stay provisions apply to the award of orders under GSA MAS contracts.

- *Agency report, protester's comments, and further proceedings*. The GAO's telephonic notice also triggers the "agency report" requirement—that is, the agency must produce a report responding to the protest allegations within thirty calendar days following the GAO's telephonic notice.[339] The report must include any documents that are relevant to the protest and that support the agency's position, as well as any relevant documents that are specifically requested by the protester.[340] The agency must provide copies of the report to the protester and any intervenors.[341] The protester's and intervenor's responses, which are called "comments" in GAO parlance, must be filed within ten calendar days after receipt of the report.[342] In many cases, the GAO closes the record after receiving the protester's comments. However, if the protester's comments set forth new protest issues, the agency must respond with a supplemental agency report. In other cases, agencies simply request leave to respond to arguments raised in the protester's comments, or the GAO itself asks the agency to do so. The GAO establishes expedited schedules for such supplemental filings on a case-by-case basis. Finally, the GAO may decide that it cannot render a protest decision based on the written record and may convene a hearing to obtain testimony from witnesses, such as the source selection official.[343] The GAO generally requires all parties to file post-hearing comments, generally within five calendar days after the hearing.[344]

- *GAO's Decision*. The GAO is required by statute to issue a decision on the protest within 100 calendar days after the protest was filed. There are several possible outcomes: The protest can be dismissed, denied, or sustained. As an initial matter, the GAO will only sustain a protest if it finds that the protester was *prejudiced* by any improper agency action—that is, but for the agency's improper action, the protester would have a substantial chance of receiving the award. In many cases, the GAO finds that the agency acted improperly but denies the protest because the protester would not have been awarded a contract in any case.

If the GAO sustains the protest, it will recommend that the agency take some type of corrective action. It is important to note that the GAO can only recommend a remedy; it does not have the authority to direct a contracting agency to take any particular action. However, it is extremely rare for agencies to ignore the GAO's recommendation. The statute requires that the agency report to the GAO on the implementation of its corrective action within sixty calendar days of the decision. If the agency declines to implement the GAO's recommendation, it must so inform the GAO. The GAO then reports the matter to Congress. Since agencies do not want to put themselves in the position of having to answer Congressional inquiries concerning their failure to implement the GAO's recommendations, they nearly always follow the recommendations.

However, the GAO's recommendation often leaves the agency with some latitude in implementing corrective action. For example, if the protest involved the agency's failure to apply the evaluation criteria set forth in the Request for Proposals, the GAO may give the agency the option of either re-evaluating proposals in accordance with the stated criteria or amending the solicitation to reflect the actual evaluation criteria and allowing offerors to submit revised proposals. As long as the agency's corrective action does not itself violate procurement laws or regulations, it generally is not subject to further challenge.

- *Protest costs, attorneys' fees, and bid and proposal costs.* In connection with sustaining a protest, the GAO generally awards the protester the costs of filing and pursuing its protest, including reasonable attorneys' fees.[345] These costs and fees must be documented in a detailed claim to the contracting officer within sixty calendar days after receipt of the protest decision. If it is not possible for the agency to take corrective action that puts the protester in a position to be considered for award, the GAO will also recommend that the agency reimburse the protester's costs of bid and proposal preparation. Note that for protesters that are not small business concerns, the recovery of attorneys' fees generally is capped at $150 per hour.[346]

- _Alternative Dispute Resolution_. The GAO's regulations also provide for the use of "flexible alternative procedures," including establishing accelerated schedules or issuing summary decisions.[347] One other technique that the GAO frequently has employed is a dispute resolution process known as "outcome prediction." In an outcome prediction case, the parties agree that the GAO will render an oral opinion as to the likely outcome of the protest, usually in a telephone conference conducted after the agency report is filed. If the GAO informs the parties that it is likely to sustain the protest, the agency has the opportunity to take corrective action before the GAO issues a formal written opinion. If the GAO informs the parties that it is likely to deny the protest, the protester has the opportunity to withdraw the protest before it expends additional resources in pursuit of a losing protest.

As the foregoing points illustrate, the GAO offers protesters a number of advantages over the agency-level process, including the automatic stay, standardized procedures, the opportunity for protester's counsel to review and respond to the agency's position on the protest, and a vast body of published case law that helps protesters know what to expect. In addition, GAO offers certain advantages over the COFC process, including generally lower costs, a statutorily mandated time frame for resolution, and decision makers with extensive experience in procurement law. On the other hand, the GAO process is usually more costly and time-consuming than the agency-level process; it is difficult to pursue a protest involving protected material without counsel admitted under a protective order; and there is no discovery beyond the documents in the agency's written record, with the possible exception of oral testimony at a hearing.

3. United States Court Of Federal Claims

The COFC is the only judicial forum in the United States currently authorized by statute to resolve bid protests.[348] The COFC's jurisdiction is limited by statute to (a) objections to a solicitation, a proposed award of a contract, or an award of a contract and (b) alleged violations of a statute or regulation in connection with a procurement or a proposed procurement.[349]

As at the GAO, only "interested parties" may file protests at the COFC. The term "interested party" has the same meaning at the COFC as it does at the GAO—that is, an actual or prospective offeror with a direct economic interest in the award or failure to award a contract.[350] The term "federal agency," however, does not have the same meaning at the COFC as it does at the GAO. The COFC defines "federal agency" more broadly than the GAO, so that COFC has jurisdiction over Government entities that the GAO does not. For example, the COFC will hear a protest concerning a U.S. Postal Service procurement,[351] while the GAO will not.[352] As discussed below, there are other significant differences between protests at the Court of Federal Claims and protests at the GAO.

- *Representation by counsel*. Unlike the GAO, which allows parties to represent themselves without counsel, the COFC requires that companies be represented by counsel. Individual plaintiffs, however, may represent themselves.[353]
- *Timeliness requirements*. The COFC does not have stringent timeliness requirements like the GAO. However, in its decisions, the COFC has often held, that improprieties apparent on the face of a solicitation must be protested before the solicitation's closing date, just as at the GAO. In at least one case, however, the COFC rejected efforts to import the GAO's strict timeliness rules and was willing

to consider the issue of a solicitation's improprieties after the solicitation's closing date.[354] Protestors should be warned that as a practical matter, a protester that waits an unreasonably long time to file a protest (e.i., waiting until after award to complain about an obvious solicitation defect) may be unable to obtain relief at the COFC. In such a case, the government may be able to assert an equitable defense referred to as laches.

- *COFC procedures generally.* The COFC follows the Federal Rules of Civil Procedure. However, the COFC also has it's own set of rules and there are some differences between the Rules of the Court of Federal Claims ("RCFC") and the Federal Rules of which protesters should be aware.[355]

- *Filing a protest.* The filing of a protest at the COFC is more complicated than at the GAO or the agency. First, the protester must file a "prefiling notice" at least twenty-four hours before filing a protest action in the court.[356] Then the protest is filed, in the form of a complaint[357] accompanied by a "civil cover sheet."[358] If the protester is seeking the withholding of contract award or suspension of contract performance, the protester should file a motion for a temporary restraining order ("TRO") and/or a motion for preliminary injunction ("PI"), as appropriate, with the complaint. As with most motions, the motion for TRO and/or the motion for PI should be accompanied by a memorandum in support, proposed orders, and any affidavits or other documents upon which the protester intends to rely.[359] All documents must be served on the appropriate parties in accordance with the RCFC, Appendix C.

- *Protective orders.* Like the GAO, the COFC has a protective order procedure. The COFC model protective order is similar to the GAO's standard protective order. Again, however, the COFC procedure is more complicated. If the protester wishes to protect any information in the

234 Chierichella & Aronie

complaint or other pleadings, the protester must file with those documents a motion for leave to file under seal and redacted versions of the pleadings for public release.[360] The protester also should file a *motion for a protective order*.[361]

- *Intervention.* Intervention in a COFC protest—*e.g.*, by an awardee or another offeror—is not automatic as it is at the GAO. For example, while an awardee of a contract may simply inform the GAO that it is intervening in a protest because of its status as awardee, at the COFC the awardee must file a motion for leave to intervene.[362] At least one COFC judge has denied motions by awardees to intervene, although such a party may be allowed to participate in the proceedings as an *amicus curiae* ("friend of the court").[363]

- *Discovery and supplementation of the record.* COFC bid protests are subject to the requirements of the Administrative Procedures Act of 1996 ("APA").[364] The APA generally requires that actions filed in a federal court pursuant to the APA be decided based on the "administrative record"—the record that was before the agency at the time the agency made the decision being challenged.[365] However, a court may make exceptions to this requirement where the record is somehow inadequate to allow the court to decide the case.[366] The COFC in some cases has allowed parties to put additional evidence into the record through the discovery process—for example, by taking depositions[367]—or through the submission of sworn affidavits.[368]

- *Standard of review.* By statute, the COFC applies the APA standard of review to bid protests. The APA standard provides, in part, that a court shall set aside agency action found to be "arbitrary, capricious, an abuse of discretion, or otherwise not in accordance with law"[369] The COFC, therefore, has indicated that there are two general categories of protest grounds. First, a protester may allege that an agency *violated an applicable procurement statute or regulation*. Second, a protester may allege that an agency's actions were *arbitrary, capricious, or an abuse of discretion*. Most protests in the COFC will involve an application of the "arbitrary, capricious . . . abuse of discretion" standard of review. This standard is highly deferential to the agency and requires the court to uphold any agency action that is reasonably based on a consideration of the relevant information.[370] In either case, as in a GAO protest, it is not enough to demonstrate that the agency acted improperly; the protester also must establish that it was prejudiced by the agency's improper action. [371]

- *Remedies*. One difference between a COFC protest and GAO or agency-level protests is that the COFC's decision is binding on the agency. If the COFC determines that the protester is entitled to relief, the agency must comply with the remedy that the COFC provides or risk sanctions for contempt of court. The COFC may award any nonmonetary relief that it considers proper, including declaratory judgments and injunctive relief.[372] In addition, the COFC, by statute, may award bid and proposal preparation costs.[373]

    However, unlike the GAO, the COFC generally is not inclined to award attorneys' fees to prevailing protesters.[374] The COFC is only required to award attorneys' fees to a prevailing party when the party meets certain specific requirements of the Equal Access to Justice Act ("EAJA").[375] Generally, EAJA awards of attorneys' fees (and other costs, such as expert witness costs) are only available to parties that do not exceed maximum net worth limitations,[376] that meet the strict EAJA definition of "prevailing party,[377] and that submit, under oath, the required application and supporting statements.[378] In addition, the agency must fail to show that its litigation position was "substantially justified."[379]

- *Appeals to the Federal Circuit*. Another difference between COFC protests and those filed in the GAO or at the contracting agency is the availability of an appeal from a COFC protest. A party wishing to appeal a COFC decision must file a notice of appeal at the United States Court of Appeals for the Federal Circuit within sixty calendar days after the COFC's decision is entered.[380] The Federal Circuit's decision is binding on the COFC and the contracting agency.

To summarize, the COFC offers some potential advantages over the GAO and agency-level processes, including the possibility of obtaining discovery and the binding nature of the COFC's remedies.[381] Some cases also may benefit from the more exhaustive and formal procedures in the federal court setting. However, corporate plaintiffs must be represented by counsel; and, if the corporation uses outside rather than in-house counsel, the process can be expensive.

B. *Where Should I Protest?*

The decision *where* to file a protest is far more objective, and therefore easier to make, than the decision *whether* to file a protest. A pros-and-cons analysis can be helpful in determining where to file a protest. While this chapter is not intended to provide legal advice, a summary of the pros and cons of each of the three bid protest forums is set forth below.

The agency-level protest is the simplest, fastest, and least antagonistic to the agency, but protesters generally are not provided access to information in the record that will help them to better understand the agency's procurement decision. The GAO process is substantially more time-consuming and costly, and the timeliness requirements are strict. On the other hand, the GAO's process provides for an automatic stay of award or performance, it provides the protester and/or the protester's lawyer with a record of the procurement and the agency's decision-making process, and it results in a detailed written decision explaining the basis for the GAO's conclusions. If a protester wants all these procedural safeguards (without the automatic stay, but with the opportunity to request a stay) plus the opportunity to request discovery from the agency and the prospect of a binding judicial remedy, the COFC is the best choice. Also, as noted above, a protester may file at the COFC after being denied relief at the GAO.

The next section addresses issues that may arise in a MAS protest situation. Those discussions may be helpful in an assessment of the likelihood of success of a protest (but they should not be substituted for legal advice).

C. *What MAS-Related Issues May Be Addressed In Protests?*

The universe of possible protest issues is vast, and all protestable issues cannot be addressed here. However, certain issues either are unique to MAS procurements or have arisen in MAS protests in the past and, therefore, warrant some brief exploration.

- *Non-Schedule vendor protests against Schedule procurements*. Although an agency's decision to purchase a product or service from the Schedule instead of conducting an off-Schedule competition for that product or service generally is not protestable by a non-Schedule vendor,[382] and an agency's decision to conduct a competition only among Schedule vendors instead of opening the competition to all potential offerors is similarly non-protestable,[383] there are exceptions to these general principles. For example, a protester may allege that a Schedule purchase does not meet the agency's actual requirements[384] or that an agency intends to order products or services that are beyond the scope of a vendor's MAS contract.[385]

· *Timeliness.* As discussed above, protests of alleged solicitation defects should be filed before the solicitation closes (or, where an alleged defect is incorporated into a solicitation after the initial closing date, the next closing date after the defect is incorporated). Sometimes, however, it is difficult to determine whether the defect was apparent on the face of the solicitation and therefore subject to the "closing date rule." If the defect is not apparent on the face of the solicitation, the agency and GAO "ten-day rule" applies—that is, the protester must raise the protest allegation within ten calendar days after the protester "knew or should have known" of the basis for protest. Thus, where a solicitation issued to MAS vendors did not properly state the agency's basis for award, but the protester could not have known that until after award, the GAO has held that the protest was timely.[386]

• *Standing to protest.* In some cases, a non-Schedule vendor has tried to protest some aspect of an agency's attempt to purchase supplies or services from a Schedule. In such cases, the Government may take the position that a non-Schedule vendor is not an "interested party" as defined by CICA and therefore does not have standing to protest. If the non-Schedule vendor would not be eligible for an order even if it had a Schedule contract (because, for example, it did not offer a product meeting the agency's needs), it is not an interested party to challenge the procurement.[387]

• *Agency's failure to solicit a vendor.* When an agency decides to conduct a competition among Schedule vendors, it may be required to furnish a copy of the Request for Quotation ("RFQ") to certain vendors or to a certain number of vendors. For example, GAO sustained a protest where GSA sent copies of the RFQ to only two of thirteen vendors of furniture systems, even though the applicable Schedule required GSA to furnish copies of the RFQ to all vendors for whom it had brochures on hand.[388] GAO also has sustained a protest where an agency issued a Schedule order to a company that was the only vendor on one particular Schedule, but where identical services were available at a lower price from the protester on a different Schedule.[389]

On the other hand, if an agency properly determines that only one Schedule vendor offers a product that meets its needs, the agency is not required to solicit any other vendors or to seek further competition.[390] A disappointed vendor may protest the agency's determination of what its needs are, but the protester has the burden of demonstrating that its product can meet the agency's needs at the lowest overall price.[391]

- *GSA failure to award Schedule contract*. Just as the GAO generally will review an agency's rejection of a vendor's proposal pursuant to a competitive solicitation, GAO also will review GSA's rejection of a vendor's proposal pursuant to a MAS solicitation. In one such case, where GSA rejected the protester's offer after lengthy negotiations because the protester failed to provide information establishing the reasonableness of its offered prices, the GAO stated that it will question an agency's determination of price reasonableness "only where it is clearly unreasonable or there is a showing of bad faith or fraud."[392]

- *Non-Schedule purchases disguised as Schedule purchases*. Agency purchases from Schedules are not subject to statutory "full and open competition" requirements. In at least one case, a protester turned this proposition around to argue that a procurement was not really a Schedule procurement as claimed by the contracting agency and that the procurement therefore was subject to competition requirements that were not met.[393] The protester did not succeed, as the procurement was properly conducted as a MAS procurement and was not subject to competition requirements.

- *Reasonableness of vendor selection*. The GAO will review an agency determination for reasonableness.[394] As discussed above, the COFC reviews agency determinations to determine whether they were "arbitrary and capricious" or in violation of law and regulation. In practice, the COFC's "arbitrary and capricious" standard is essentially the same as GAO's "reasonableness" standard: Both are extremely deferential to the agency.[395] However, the GAO occasionally has found an agency's decision to be unreasonable.[396]

- *Reasonableness of time given to respond to solicitation*. GAO has held that there may be circumstances where an agency's failure to afford offerors a reasonable amount of time to respond to a solicitation may support a bid protect.[397]

- *Agency's use of a particular schedule*. In some cases involving requirements for services, the services an agency needs are not described precisely by any one Schedule, and the agency selects the Schedule that most closely describes its needs. A vendor that is not on the selected Schedule, but is on a different Schedule, may wish to protest the agency's choice of Schedule. In one such case at the COFC, the court found the agency's determination of the appropriate schedule to be reasonable.[398] On the other hand, the GAO has sustained a protest where an agency failed to review similar offerings available under a different Schedule.[399]

- *Blanket purchase agreement ("BPA") awards*. A BPA is a simplified agreement that allows an agency to satisfy recurring needs by placing successive orders with a Schedule vendor. (BPAs are discussed in detail in Chapter XV of this book.) While BPAs can make repetitive ordering easier for the agency, they can mean fewer orders for the Schedule vendors that are not holders of such BPAs. Therefore, vendors sometimes bring protests against BPA awards. However, a protest against the award of a BPA itself is not likely to be successful at either the GAO or the COFC since there are virtually no restrictions on an agency's award of a BPA,[400] and a BPA award involves a discretionary agency decision.[401]

- *Defining the agency's requirements*. Whether or not an agency is making a purchase against a Schedule, it must properly define its needs in order to ensure that it identifies vendors that can meet those needs and that the vendors can compete intelligently and fairly.[402] Vendors that can prove their product could satisfy the agency's requirements have been successful in protesting the agency's decision not to consider their product. Thus, the GAO has held that, where an agency decides not to consider a particular vendor's product because the agency concludes that the product does not meet its needs, the vendor whose product was excluded from consideration may protest the exclusion, and GAO will determine whether the agency had a reasonable basis for determining that the excluded product did not meet its needs.[403] Similarly, GAO has sustained a protest against an agency's failure adequately to define what it meant by "technically acceptable."[404]

- *Purchase of incidental items in connection with a Schedule purchase*. When an agency conducts a competition among Schedule vendors, the vendors may not offer items that are not included in their Schedule contracts. An agency's purchase of such non-Schedule items, sometimes called "incidental items," as part of a purchase from a Schedule vendor, violates the competition requirements of CICA.[405] Thus, items that are not on a Schedule must be procured separately using the competitive procedures appropriate to that purchase. While this issue historically most often arose in the context of product procurements, recent case law makes clear that GAO will strictly examine the nature of services offered as well.[406] Both the GAO and the COFC (products and services) have sustained protests challenging agency attempts to purchase "non-schedule" items in connection with Schedule purchases.[407] However, if the value of the incidental items is less than the $2,500 micro-purchase threshold, the agency may procure those items from the Schedule vendor or any other supplier without regard to any other competition requirements.[408]

- *Applicability of FAR Part 15 requirements*. FAR Part 15 sets forth detailed procedural requirements for procurements based on the submission and evaluation of competitive proposals. While an agency generally is not required to comply with the procedural requirements of FAR Part 15 when it makes a Schedule purchase,[409] if it holds itself out as following such rules, it must abide by them.[410] Thus, some protesters have attempted to argue that an ordering agency failed to comply with certain FAR Part 15 requirements, such as rules for selecting the "best value" proposal,[411] conducting discussions with offerors,[412] or adhering to stated evaluation criteria.[413]

- *Agency evaluation of past performance*. Agencies conducting competitive acquisitions under the FAR must consider vendors' past performance in evaluating proposals for award. This is true even if the vendors are Schedule vendors. Thus, agency past performance evaluations are a frequent subject of protests. At the GAO, past performance evaluations are reviewed only to determine whether the agency's evaluation was reasonable. In one recent case involving the past performance of Schedule vendors, the GAO found an agency's past performance evaluation unreasonable where it was based on a mechanical comparison of past performance scores for incumbent vendors that was unfair to non-incumbents.[414] The agency re-evaluated the proposals in accordance with the GAO's recommendation, and the GAO found the re-evaluation reasonable.[415]

D. *Conclusion*

Although the GSA's MAS procedures are modeled on commercial practices in many ways, the MAS process does offer vendors the opportunity—unavailable in the commercial world—to challenge a buyer's ordering decision, especially where the buying agency chooses to conduct a competition among Schedule vendors. Indeed, such vendors should be cognizant of the available protest alternatives—not only so that they can exercise their protest rights if necessary, but also so that they can operate within the protest framework if they find themselves on the receiving end of a protest.

Notes:

308 Pub. L. No. 98-369, § 2741(a), 98 Stat. 1175, 1199 (codified as amended at 31 U.S.C. § 3551(1)).

309 Pub. L. No. 103-355, 108 Stat. 3287 (codified as amended at 31 U.S.C. § 3551(1)).

310 4 C.F.R. § 21.1(a); 48 C.F.R. § 33.101.

311 41 U.S.C. § 259(b)(3); FAR 6.102(d)(3); *see also, e.g., Computer Universal, Inc.*, B-291890 *et al.*, Apr. 8, 2003 ("The procedures established for the FSS program satisfy the general requirement for full and open competition.").

312 FAR 15.402(a).

313 GSAR 538.270(a) (June 2000).

314 It should be noted that Section 803 of the National Defense Authorization Act for Fiscal Year 2002 imposes additional competition requirements for DoD orders for services exceeding $100,000. *See* DFARS 208.404-70.

315 From 1985 to 1996, the Brooks Act, 40 U.S.C. § 759, as amended by CICA, gave the GSBCA the authority to resolve bid protests involving procurements for automated data processing equipment and related services. In 1996, the Information Technology Management Reform Act of 1996, Pub. L. No. 104-106, § 5101, 101 Stat. 679, 680 (1996), abolished the GSBCA's bid protest

jurisdiction, leaving the GAO, the district courts, the United States Court of Federal Claims, and the contracting agency as possible protest forums.

[316] From 1970 to 1997, district courts exercised jurisdiction over post-award bid protests under the doctrine set forth in *Scanwell Labs. v. Shaffer*, 424 F.2d 859 (D.C. Cir. 1970). District courts in some federal judicial circuits also took jurisdiction over pre-award protests, while the COFC entertained pre-award, but not post-award, protests. From 1997 to 2001, the Administrative Dispute Resolution Act of 1996 ("ADRA") gave the district courts and the COFC concurrent jurisdiction over both pre-award and post-award bid protests. 28 U.S.C. § 1491(b). The ADRA called for the expiration, or sunset, of the district courts' statutory bid protest jurisdiction on January 1, 2001, arguably leaving the COFC as the only judicial forum for bid protests.

[317] FAR 33.103(e).

[318] GSAR 552.233-70(b) (July 2000).

[319] FAR 33.103(f)(1), (f)(3).

[320] *Id.*

[321] GSAR 552.233-70(f) (July 2000).

[322] GSAR 552.233-70(h)(4), (5) (July 2000).

[323] GSAR 552.233-70(h)(5)(ii) (July 2000).

[324] FAR 33.103(g).

[325] FAR 33.103(h).

[326] GSAR 552.233-70(l) (July 2000).

[327] The portion of CICA relating to the GAO's bid protest jurisdiction is codified at 31 U.S.C. §§ 3551-3556.

[328] 4 C.F.R. § 21.0(a).

[329] *See, e.g., Draeger Safety, Inc.*, B-285366 *et al.*, Aug. 23, 2000, 2000 CPD ¶ 139 (A Schedule holder that does not have a Schedule product that meets the agency's needs is not an "interested party" to raise issues with regard to the agency's cost evaluation and request for a price decrease from the awardee.).

[330] 4 C.F.R. §§ 21.1(d)(1), 21.4.

[331] *Id.* § 21.2(a)(1).

[332] *Id.* § 21.2(a)(2).

333 *Id.*

334 *Id.* § 21.2(a)(3).

335 31 U.S.C. § 3553(c), (d); 4 C.F.R. § 21.6.

336 31 U.S.C. § 3553(c), (d); 4 C.F.R. § 21.6.

337 31 U.S.C. § 3553(d)(3).

338 FAR 33.104(b), (c)(2).

339 4 C.F.R. § 21.3(c). The timeframes discussed here apply to the GAO's standard procedures. The GAO has an alternative "express option" procedure that has shorter timeframes, leading to a decision on the protest within sixty-five calendar days. 4 C.F.R. § 21.10.

340 *Id.* § 21.3(d).

341 *Id.* § 21.3(c). The regulations define an intervenor as "an awardee if the award has been made or, if no award has been made, all bidders or offerors who appear to have a substantial prospect of receiving an award if the protest is denied." *Id.* § 21.0(b).

342 4 C.F.R. § 21.3(i).

343 *Id.* § 21.7. While the protester may request a hearing, the GAO alone decides whether or not one is needed.

344 *Id.* § 21.7(g).

345 *Id.* § 21.8(d).

346 31 U.S.C. § 3554(c)(2)(B); FAR 33.104(h)(5)(ii). The GAO may authorize payment of fees above $150 per hour based on cost of living or special factors such as the limited availability of qualified attorneys. *Id. See Sodexo Management, Inc.—costs*, B-289605.3, Aug. 6, 2003 (granting request for cost of living adjustment based on U.S. Department of Labor's Consumer Price Index).

347 4 C.F.R. § 21.10(e).

348 The COFC's current statutory authorization to hear and decide bid protests comes from the Administrative Dispute Resolution Act of 1996. 28 U.S.C. § 1491(b). One apparent exception to this exclusive judicial jurisdiction involves bid protests regarding maritime contracts. Exclusive jurisdiction over maritime contract disputes, including bid protests, historically has been vested in the U.S. District Courts under the Suits in Admiralty Act. *See Asta Eng'g, Inc. v. United States*, 46 Fed. Cl. 674, 676 (2000) (concluding that this is "no evidence that Congress determined, in enacting the

ADRA, to vary this long-standing exclusive relegation of maritime contract matter involving the United States to the district courts"). [349] *Id.*

[350] *American Fed'n of Gov't Employees v. United States*, 258 F.3d 1294 (Fed. Cir. 2001), *petition for cert. filed* (Oct. 22, 2001); *Alaska Cent. Exp., Inc. v. United States*, 50 Fed. Cl. 510 (2001).

[351] *Hewlett-Packard Co. v. United States*, 41 Fed. Cl. 99, 103 (1998).

[352] 4 C.F.R. § 21.5(g).

[353] Rule 83.1(c)((8) of the COFC.

[354] *Consolidated Engineering Services, Inc., v. United States*, 64 Fed. Cl. 617 (2005).

[355] The RCFC are available at *http://www.law.gwu.edu/fedcl/rules.htm.* In addition, the COFC has promulgated specific bid protest procedures in its Appendix C "Procedure on Procurement Protest Cases Pursuant to 28 USC § 1491(b)" ("Appendix C") (May 1, 2002).

[356] G.O. No. 38, app. I, ¶ 2 (May 7, 1998).

[357] *See* RCFC 3, 10.

[358] *See* RCFC Form 2.

[359] *See* RCFC 65; *see also* RCFC 7(b), Appendix C.

[360] Appendix C, ¶¶ 16-17, Form 8.

[361] *See id.*¶¶ 17, RFFC 10.

[362] *See* Appendix C ¶ 12; RCFC 24(a)(2).

[363] *See, e.g., Envirocare of Utah, Inc. v. United States*, 44 Fed. Cl. 474, 476 (1999); *Advanced Data Concepts, Inc. v. United States*, 43 Fed. Cl. 410, 413 n.3 (1999), *aff'd*, 216 F.3d 1054 (Fed. Cir. 2000).

[364] 28 U.S.C § 1491(b).

[365] 5 U.S.C. § 706; *see Cubic Applications, Inc. v. United States*, 37 Fed. Cl. 345, 349-50 (1997).

[366] *Esch v. Yeutter*, 876 F.2d 976 (D.C. Cir. 1989).

[367] *See, e.g., Antarctic Support Assocs. v. United States*, 46 Fed. Cl. 145, 148, *aff'd*, 251 F.3d 171 (Fed. Cir. 2000); *Ellsworth Assocs., Inc. v. United States*, 45 Fed. Cl. 388, 392 (1999); *CCL Serv. Corp. v. United States*, 43 Fed. Cl. 680, 682-83 (1999).

[368] *See, e.g., Myers Investigative & Sec. Servs. v. United States*, 47 Fed. Cl. 288, 294-95 (2000); *Ryan Co. v. United States*, 43 Fed. Cl. 646, 651 n.3 (1999).

369 5 U.S.C. § 706.

370 See *Advanced Data Concepts*, 216 F.3d at 1057; *Mangi Env't Group, Inc. v. United States*, 47 Fed. Cl. 10, 14-15 (2000).

371 See *MVM, Inc. v. United States*, 46 Fed. Cl. 137, 141 (1999) (citing *Statistica, Inc. v. Christopher*, 102 F.3d 1577, 1582 (Fed. Cir. 1996)).

372 28 U.S.C. § 1491(b)(2).

373 *Id.*

374 See *MVM, Inc. v. United States*, 47 Fed. Cl. 361, 363-65 (2000).

375 28 U.S.C. § 2412(d).

376 *Id.* § 2412(d)(2)(B).

377 See *id.* § 2412(d); RCFC 54(d), *see also* RCFC Form 5.

378 See 28 U.S.C. § 2412(d); RCFC 54(d); *see also* RCFC Form 5.

379 See 28 U.S.C. § 2412(d); RCFC 54(d); *see also* RCFC Form 5.

380 See Fed. R. App. P. 4(a).

381 It should be noted that a protester may pursue a protest first at the GAO and then, if unsuccessful, file a second challenge to the agency action in the COFC. *See, e.g., Cubic Applications, Inc.*, 37 Fed. Cl. 345.

382 See *Advance Bus. Sys.*, B-237728, Mar. 16, 1990, 90-1 CPD ¶ 300, *aff'd*, B-237728.2, 90-2 CPD ¶ 78 (agency was not required to accept protester's unsolicited offer rather than purchase item from Schedule, even where protester offered a lower price than Schedule vendor).

383 See *Sales Resources Consultants, Inc.*, B-284943, June 9, 2000, 2000 CPD ¶ 102 (protester that did not have Schedule contract for required item was not an interested party to challenge agency's conduct of a limited competition among Schedule vendors for the required item). The reason MAS procurements generally are not protestable is because GSA is considered to have already conducted a competitive process by awarding Schedule contracts in the first instance. Therefore, ordering agencies are not required to conduct further competition for products or services that may be ordered from a Schedule in accordance with the terms (*e.g.*, the maximum order limitation) of a vendor's Schedule contract.

[384] *See, e.g., Intelligent Decisions, Inc.*, B-274626 *et al.*, Dec. 23, 1996, 97-1 CPD ¶ 19, at 8, *reconsideration denied*, B-274626.3, May 15, 1997, 97-1 CPD ¶ 185.

[385] *See, e.g., Marvin J. Perry & Assocs.*, B-277684, Nov. 4, 1997, 97-2 CPD ¶ 128.

[386] *COMARK Fed. Sys.*, B-278343 *et al.*, Jan. 20, 1998, 98-1 CPD ¶ 34.

[387] *See CHE Consulting v. United States*, 47 Fed. Cl. 331 (2000).

[388] *Knoll North Am., Inc.*, B-259112 *et al.*, Mar. 8, 1995, 95-1 CPD ¶ 141; *see also Savantage Financial Services, Inc.*, B-292046, June 11, 2003 (Digest: "A protester may challenge an agency's decision not to provide the protester with a solicitation for a purchase under the Federal Supply Schedule, where this decision was based upon the agency's determination, pursuant to Federal Acquisition Regulation § 8.404(b)(3) (which applies to orders expected to exceed the maximum order threshold), that the protester did not appear to offer best value, as determined by the agency from market information obtained from schedule vendors and product demonstrations; GAO will review the reasonableness of the agency's determination."); *GMA Cover Corporation*, B-288018, Aug. 17, 2001 (Digest: "Agency's failure to solicit a quote from the protester for an urgently needed item under an oral solicitation conducted under simplified acquisition procedures is unobjectionable where the contracting officer solicited the sources that she was aware had supplied the item and she was unaware of the protester's interest in submitting a quote, notwithstanding that the protester had supplied the item for another agency and had submitted quotes on prior agency simplified procedure acquisitions of the item.")

[389] *REEP, Inc.*, B-290665, Sept. 17, 2002 (GAO found that the agency had knowledge that the services were available under the second schedule and; since it was supposed to review "information reasonably available" before awarding a Schedule delivery order, it should have reviewed the prices available on the second schedule.) *But see Computer Universal, Inc.*, B-291890, Apr. 8, 2003 (Digest: "Protester was not unfairly denied opportunity to compete under Federal Supply Schedule acquisition, where it does not hold

schedule contract to provide requested services, and agency reasonably determined that protester was not capable of providing such services.").

[390] *See Card Tech. Corp.*, B-275385 *et al.*, Feb. 18, 1997, 97-1 CPD ¶ 76.

[391] *Id.; see also Delta Int'l, Inc.*, B-284364.2, May 11, 2000, 2000 CPD ¶ 78; *Computer Universal, Inc.*, B-291890 *et al.*, April 8, 2003 ("Here, we find that the agency reasonably determined that [protester] could not meet its needs . . . . [Protestor] does not currently have a contract under the schedule for program management services, and therefore could not have submitted a quote under the RFQ.").

[392] *Concepts Bldg. Sys., Inc.*, B-281995, May 13, 1999, 99-1 CPD ¶ 95. It is extremely difficult to maintain a claim of "bad faith" against a Government official. *See, e.g., Allworld Language Consultants, Inc.*, B-291409.3, Jan. 28, 2003 ("In order for a protester to succeed in a claim of bias on the part of a contracting official, the record must establish that the official intended to harm the protester, since government officials are presumed to act in good faith; our Office will not attribute unfair or prejudicial motives to procurement officials on the basis of inference or supposition. Moreover, in addition to producing credible evidence of bias, the protester must show that the agency bias translated into action that unfairly affected the protester's competitive position." *Citing Docusort, Inc.*, B-254852.2, Feb. 22, 1995, 95-1 CPD ¶ 107 at 3.); *Computer Universal, Inc.*, B-291890 *et al.*, Apr. 8, 2003 ("Because contracting officials are presumed to act in good faith, [protestor's] speculation provides us with no basis to conclude that the failure to solicit [protestor] was due to bad faith.").

[393] *See, e.g., Intelligent Decisions, Inc.*, B-274626 *et al.*, Dec. 23, 1996, 97-1 CPD ¶ 19.

[394] *See, e.g., Spacesaver Sys., Inc.*, B-284924 *et al.*, June 20, 2000, 2000 CPD ¶ 107; *Amdahl Corp.*, B-281255, Dec. 28, 1998, 98-2 CPD ¶ 161 (agency's technical evaluation of vendor quotations on computer systems was reasonable where performed in accordance with stated evaluation criteria and based on valid assessments of

proposed systems); *Design Contempo, Inc.*, B-270483, Mar. 12, 1996, 96-1 CPD ¶ 146 (agency reasonably determined that only the awardee's Schedule items met its minimum needs).

[395] *See supra* note 358.

[396] *See Delta Int'l, Inc.*, B-284364.2, May 11, 2000, 2000 CPD ¶ 78. In one of the most extreme cases of GAO involving itself in a Schedule procurement, GAO sustained Delta's protest challenging the FBI's determination that it needed a digital rather than a digital/analog portable x-ray system. The GAO found unreasonable the FBI's assumptions concerning its needs and Delta's alleged inability to meet those needs.

[397] *Warden Associates Inc.*, B-291440, Dec. 27, 2002 ("FAR Subpart 8.4 does not require that vendors be permitted a specific minimum amount of time to respond to an RFQ; what is reasonable and sufficient depends on the facts and circumstances of the case. We recognize that issuing a solicitation late on Friday, September 27, 2002, and requiring submission by midday on the next business day (Monday, September 30) allows very little time, particularly where, as here, a "technical proposal" is sought. There could be circumstances where such action by an agency would lead us to sustain a protest." * * * Here, the RFQ's call for "technical proposals" due on the next business day may well have been objectionable in other circumstances. In the context of the unique facts of this case, however, we do not find the agency's actions to be objectionable.").

[398] *DSD Labs. v. United States*, 46 Fed. Cl. 467 (2000).

[399] *REEP, Inc.*, B-290665, Sept. 17, 2002 (GAO found that the agency had knowledge that the services were available under the second schedule and; since it was supposed to review "information reasonably available" before awarding a Schedule delivery order, it should have reviewed the prices available on the second schedule.)

[400] *See Contracting Methods: Square Pegs and Round Holes*, The Nash & Cibinic Rep., ¶ 48, Vol. 15, No. 9 (Sept. 2001).

[401] *See, e.g., Labat-Anderson Inc.*, B-287081, Apr. 16, 2001, 2001 CPD ¶ 79; *Labat-Anderson Inc. v. United States*, 50 Fed. Cl. 99 (2001); *BTG, Inc. v. Riley*, No. 00-1069-AA (E.D.Va. Sept. 22,

Multiple Award Schedule Contracting | 251

2000) (unpublished); *Pfizer, Inc.*, B-276362, June 6, 1997, 97-1 CPD ¶ 205.

[402] *See Draeger Safety, Inc.*, B-285366 *et al.*, Aug. 23, 2000, 2000 CPD ¶ 139.

[403] *Delta Int'l, Inc.*, B-284364.2, May 11, 2000, 2000 CPD ¶ 78; *see supra* note 360.

[404] *Garner Multimedia, Inc.*, B-291651, Feb. 11, 2003.

[405] *ATA Defense Indus. v. United States*, 38 Fed. Cl. 489 (1997); *Pyxis Corp.*, B-282469 *et al.*, July 15, 1999, 99-2 CPD ¶ 18; *T-L-C Sys.*, B-285687.2, Sept. 29, 2000, 2000 CPD ¶ 166; *The CDM Group, Inc.*, B-291304.2, Dec. 23, 2002 ("An agency cannot properly select an FSS vendor for an order of items on the vendor's schedule and then include in the order items not included in that vendor's FSS contract where, as here, the non-FSS items are priced above the micro-purchase threshold." *Citing T-L-C Sys.*, B-285687.2, Sept. 29, 2000, 2000 CPD ¶ 166 at 4.); American Systems Consulting, Inc., B-294644, Dec. 13, 2004, 2004 CPD ¶ 247 (protest sustained where award of BPA in competition between FSS Vendors included service not covered awardee's by FSS contract; KEI Pearson, Inc., Comp Gen., B-294226.3 *et al.*, 2005 WL 1457668 (Comp. Gen. Jan. 10, 2005) (protest sustained where task order issued to vendor whose quotation improperly included products outside of FSS contract).

[406] *See, e.g.*, *American Systems Consulting, Inc.*, B-294644, Dec. 13, 2004, 2004 CPD ¶ 247. (Labor categories offered to schedule customer must match precisely the labor categories listed on Schedule.

[407] *Id*. In *Pyxis* and *TLC*, GAO reversed its earlier position, illustrated in *ViON Corp.*, B-275063.2 *et al.*, Feb. 4, 1997, 97-1 CPD ¶ 53, that agencies may procure non-Schedule items that are incidental to the Schedule items so long as the items as a total package meet the needs of the ordering agency at the lowest overall cost.

[408] *See SMS Sys. Maint. Servs., Inc.*, B-284550.2, Aug. 4, 2000, 2000 CPD ¶ 127.

[409] *See Ellsworth Assocs., Inc. v. United States*, 45 Fed. Cl. 388 (1999); *see also KPMG Consulting*, B-290716, Sept. 23, 2002 ("Under

the FSS program, an agency is not required to issue a solicitation to request quotations, but rather may simply review vendors' schedules and, using business judgment to determine which vendor's goods or services represent the best value and meet the agency's needs at the lowest overall cost, may directly place an order under the corresponding vendor's FSS contract." *citing OSI Collection Servs., Inc.; C.B. Accounts, Inc.*, B-286597.3 *et al.*, June 12, 2001, 2001 CPD ¶ 103 at 4).

[410] *Digital Systems Group, Inc.*, B-286931 *et al.*, Mar. 7, 2001, 2001 CPD ¶ 50; *Uniband Inc.*, B-289305, Feb. 8, 2002 ("Where an agency intends to use the FSS vendors' responses to a solicitation as the basis of a detailed technical evaluation and price/technical tradeoff, it may elect, as INS did here, to use an approach that is like a competition in a negotiated procurement. When an agency takes such an approach, and a protest is filed, we will review the protested agency actions to ensure that they were reasonable and consistent with the terms of the solicitation." *citing Labat-Anderson, Inc.*, B-287081 *et al.*, Apr. 16, 2001, 2001 CPD ¶ 79 at 5.); *KPMG Consulting*, B-290716, Sept. 23, 2002 ("While we recognize that the procedures of Federal Acquisition Regulation (FAR) Part 15, governing contracting by negotiation, do not govern competitive procurements under the FSS program, *Computer Prods., Inc.*, B-284702, May 24, 2000, 2000 CPD ¶ 95 at 4, where the agency has conducted such a competition and a protest is filed, we will review the record to ensure that the evaluation is reasonable and consistent with the terms of the solicitation and with standards generally applicable to negotiated procurements. *OSI Collection Servs., Inc.; C.B. Accounts, Inc., supra* at 4-5; *Amdahl Corp.*, B-281255, Dec. 28, 1998, 98-2 CPD ¶ 161 at 3."); *see also COMARK Fed. Sys.*, B-278343 *et al.*, Jan. 20, 1998, 98-1 CPD ¶ 34 at 4-5; *Warden Associates*, B-291238, Dec. 9, 2002; *KPMG Consulting LLP*, B-290716, Sept. 23, 2002; *OSI Collection Services et al.*, B-286597 *et al.*, June 12, 2001; *Verizon Federal, Inc.*, B-293527, 2004 CPD ¶ 186, March 26, 2004.

[111] *Computer Prods., Inc.*, B-284702, May 24, 2000, 2000 CPD ¶ 95 (agency announced a "best value" evaluation, but then made award to the low-cost, technically acceptable offeror. GAO sustained protest, holding that the evaluation must be consistent with the terms of the solicitation)

[112] *BTG, Inc. v. Riley*, No. 00-1069-AA (E.D.Va. Sept. 22, 2000) (unpublished).

[113] *OSI Collection Servs., Inc.*, B-286597.3 *et al.*, June. 12, 2001, 2001 CPD ¶ 103.

[114] *OSI Collection Servs., Inc.*, B-286597 *et al.*, Jan. 17, 2001, 2001 CPD ¶ 18.

[115] *OSI Collection Servs., Inc.*, B-286597.3 *et al.*, June 12, 2001, 2001 CPD ¶ 103.

XI.

TEN STEPS TO
EFFECTIVE SCHEDULE SELLING

"The trouble with using experience as a guide is that the final exam often comes first and then the lesson."

-Anonymous

Because MAS contracts are indefinite-delivery/ indefinite-quantity ("IDIQ") contracts, award guarantees nothing more than a relatively minor guaranteed level of sales and an *opportunity to compete* for Government business. In other words, award does not guarantee much. In the context of the MAS Program, revenue comes to the vendor that markets, promotes, advertises, and, in a word, "sells."

Because the number of books currently written on how to market and sell to the Federal Government could fill a small library, this book will not attempt to pave new ground in this regard. Instead, we simply offer ten "tried and true" steps to effective selling.[416]

A. *STEP ONE—Ensure Information Finds Its Way Into The Right Hands*

Upon contract award, the MAS vendor must notify Schedule purchasers of its Schedule offerings. To this end, GSA provides the vendor a mailing list identifying thousands of Government agencies that have indicated a desire to receive such notification. Unfortunately, this mailing list is coded for the United States Postal Service and, thus, is valueless as a direct marketing tool. Fortunately, proactive Schedule vendors can turn the mailing list into a marketing tool.

Vendors should consider including in each notice a postage-paid "bounce back" card. Indeed, many vendors rely strictly upon such a card, choosing not to bear the expense of including a complete MAS catalog or price list. A "bounce back" card is simply a postcard-sized response form upon which a prospective customer may request additional information regarding the vendor's supplies or services. Such cards typically request the customer's name, address, and telephone number. Additionally, such cards often ask a few routine marketing questions such as: "How many people are in your office?"; "Are you planning to purchase the product or service in the future?"; or "Would you like a sales representative to call you?" Upon the return of the card, the vendor then can have a sales representative hand-deliver the GSA contract catalog and price list to the potential customer, thereby accomplishing two tasks at once: (1) putting the right information in the right hands and (2) arranging a face-to-face meeting with the right individual.

B. *STEP TWO—Identify Potential Customers*

While GSA will arrange for the distribution of a vendor's price list to potential Schedule purchasers, the responsibility for identifying interested customers falls primarily upon the vendor. A vendor has many sources of assistance in this regard.

First, and perhaps most simply, the telephone directory's Blue Pages provide a ready list of potential customers. A vendor simply can identify an agency that might be interested in its products. From there, a quick review of the agency's web site typically will give an indication of the types of supplies and services that the particular agency procures.

Second, the Government publishes a wealth of reports and directories that can serve as a useful road map toward increased MAS sales. These resources include, but are not limited to, the following:

- *Commerce Business Daily*. The "CBD," published by the Department of Commerce, serves as the Government's official announcement of proposed and actual federal procurements.
- *FedBizOpps.gov*. This on-line directory identifies a number of Government business opportunities.
- *Forecast of GSA Contracting Opportunities*. This annual guide identifies anticipated GSA contracting opportunities.
- *GSA Subcontracting Directory*. Of special interest to small vendors, this official directory lists large MAS vendors (and vendors holding other Government contracts) with plans requiring the vendor to contract with small, small-disadvantaged, and women-owned small businesses. (*See* Chapter XIII for a discussion of the MAS clauses that require subcontracting with small businesses.)

Each of these publications can be obtained via the Internet.

Finally, a vendor interested in digging a little deeper might want to follow publicly-announced shifts in Government policy and infer what that means for a given agency's procurement needs. Congress or the Administration frequently announces new policies or modifies old ones. A Senate bill increases funding for education. A House subcommittee debates the need to explore alternative energy sources. The President expresses a commitment to modernize veterans hospitals. Each of these events represents a potential expenditure of Government funds and, consequently, a potential source of revenue for MAS vendors. MAS vendors on Schedule 69 (Training Aids & Devices, Instructor-Led Training; Course Development; Test Administration—Programmed learning devices) might want to set their sights on the Department of Education following the passage of the Senate bill. Vendors offering services on Schedule 871 II (Energy Management Services) might want to check with the Department of Energy following the House debate. Pharmaceutical vendors will want to keep in close contact with their contacts at the Department of Veterans Affairs following the President's statement.

Fortunately, this information is readily available to any interested party. Indeed, much of the information can be found in the headlines of any national newspaper. For the more adventurous vendors, GSA publishes an annual report, known as the Federal Data Systems Division Report, that compiles data on all federal contracts. This free report, available on-line and in hard copy, provides a wealth of information from which a vendor can track federal demand for a specific category of product or service. Additionally, the Internet offers a host of additional resources, some of which are described in greater detail in Appendix I.

Whichever approach the vendors adopt—and there are many more not discussed here—they must resist the temptation to limit their sales aim to federal agencies. The list of authorized Schedule purchasers goes well beyond the executive branch of the United States Government. Congress, independent agencies, most federal vendors, most Indian tribes, and even a few universities represent legitimate customer targets. Vendors should develop a comprehensive list of potential Schedule purchasers and update this list regularly.

C. *STEP THREE—Hire Competent Staff And Train Them Well*

As with most businesses, a vendor's public face is its sales force, but the need to hire and retain competent staff goes far deeper than these front-line employees. The contracts manager, the bid and proposal staff, and the Small Business Plan Administrator all play a role in ensuring a successful Schedule experience. There are few more effective revenue generating techniques than hiring and retaining top-notch people.

This task is not as simple as it at first sounds. Many sales representatives are extremely uncomfortable selling to the Government. This discomfort stems in part from fear and in part from the uniqueness of the Government marketplace. In a sense, if the vendor is new to the MAS Program, it is a little like trying to sell a product in a foreign country without a working knowledge of the country's language or customs.

Several reputable organizations exist that can assist vendors (i) identify potential customers, (ii) cut through red tape, and (iii) make the sale. Additionally, many of these organizations can be retained to train a vendor's in-house sales force or work with a vendor's in-house sales force in a "team sales" approach. A vendor must resist the temptation to believe that its in-house commercial sales force is up to the job of selling to the Government without additional training. Remember, the Government is by far the largest purchaser of supplies and services in the world. A little extra training can go a long way.

Vendors looking for sales and marketing assistance need not look far. GSA, for example, offers informative publications, holds regular seminars, and provides telephone (and drop-by) assistance. For small businesses, GSA's Office of Enterprise Development maintains twelve "Regional Small Business Centers," which GSA touts as the "front door to contracting opportunities with GSA."[417] The assistance available through these centers extends beyond the relatively narrow scope of the MAS Program and includes helping vendors:

- Enroll on a GSA Bidders Mailing List.
- Introduce a new item for Government purchase.
- Learn more about current GSA bidding opportunities.
- Obtain publications and other documents about federal procurements, and even receive business counseling.

Vendors can find out more information about these—and other— federal programs by visiting the GSA's Office of Enterprise Development web site at *http://hydra.gsa.gov/oed*.

Within the private sector, vendors looking for a little assistance in marketing themselves to the Federal Government only need go as far as the Internet, where a multitude of consultants tout their ability to bring vendors and customers together.[418]

D. *STEP FOUR—Advertise, Market, And Promote*

As with any business, advertising is an essential component of any marketing plan. Schedule vendors may direct their advertising at agency buyers or agency users. The potential avenues of advertising are limited only by the creativity of the Schedule vendors. Direct mailings, dedicated Schedule web sites, specialized catalogs, visits to Government facilities, and billboards all represent legitimate forms of Schedule advertising. Advertising in Government-focused publications (including military publications) offers an exceptional opportunity to reach Government purchasing officials. Many of these are first-class publications that offer reasonable advertising rates. For vendors looking to save money, GSA's "MarkeTips" publication provides vendors free space on a limited and approved basis.[419]

Trade shows also provide an excellent opportunity to market a vendor's supplies and services. GSA itself hosts several product expositions that see extremely high attendance within the Government purchasing community. On the other side of the spectrum, several agencies host "table-top" shows that are open to buyers of the hosting agency only. Typically, such shows are expensive and provide only limited exposure to potential customers.

One of the most effective marketing methods is to present a vendor-specific "show" at a military base or agency. Such shows typically are held on-site and cost little more than the rental fee for the conference room and the fee for the advertisement in the base or agency newspaper. Vendors that go this route might even want to obtain a copy of the organization's telephone directory and send personal invitations directly to potential customers. Two caveats, though: First, in order to avoid accusations of impropriety, vendors should not provide anything of value to attendees; second, vendors may not suggest that the Government "endorses or has given a stamp of approval" to a vendor's products.[420]

Regardless of the marketing approach undertaken by the vendor, experience has demonstrated the wisdom of adopting a "little steps for little feet" approach in this context. Vendors— especially those new to the world of Government contracting—are wise to initiate their identification efforts by targeting one or two particular agencies before setting their sights on the federal marketplace as a whole. As time passes and experience builds increased confidence—and competence— vendors might want to expand their advertising horizons. But, even in this circumstance, vendors typically are rewarded by focusing their efforts narrowly, rather than applying a scattershot approach.

Finally, it is worth saying a word here that should be of interest to small vendors. Both GSA and the SBA offer several official avenues for small businesses to promote themselves. The Small Business Administration, for example, maintains an electronic database known as the Procurement Automated Source System, or PASS. The purpose of PASS is to assist large vendors identify small vendors for subcontracting purposes. Thus, small vendors should ensure that they are included in this important database.

E. *STEP FIVE—Consider Entering Into A Contractor Team Arrangement*

Companies just starting out may find it advantageous to enter into a teaming agreement with a more experienced vendor. Many of today's most successful companies began federal business in this way. Teaming can be very effective. An information technology vendor, for example, might team with a furniture vendor to offer computers and computer workstations. A building materials vendor might team with a vendor offering architectural or design services. The key is to achieve synergy in the hope of achieving a "win-win" relationship. Additionally, teaming agreements allow vendors unfamiliar with the Government market a great way to gain important knowledge while minimizing risk. Small and small disadvantaged businesses particularly should have little difficulty in finding larger teaming partners as those companies look for ways to meet their contractual socio-economic requirements. Teaming also allows new companies a way to build solid past performance records.

F. *STEP SIX—Be On The Lookout For Blanket Purchase Agreements*

As discussed in Chapter XV, a blanket purchase agreement ("BPA") is "a simplified method of filling anticipated repetitive needs for supplies or services by establishing 'charge accounts' with qualified sources of supply."[421] BPAs provide the opportunity for a vendor to lock in a Schedule purchaser for a length of time— up to a full fiscal year—without having to compete continuously against rival vendors. As discussed in Chapter XV, BPAs allow a vendor and the Government to negotiate for a specific amount of business using tiered pricing. The Government agency typically ends up receiving the vendor's best pricing for each order placed, and the vendor receives a continuing source of orders.[422]

Over the past few years, several agencies have established BPAs under the umbrella of the MAS Program. The Air Force's IT2 BPA and the Army's new BPA are two of the more popular. Schedule vendors compete to be included as a source under these BPAs. The business revenue that may to be derived from these BPAs is potentially significant.

G. *STEP SEVEN—Take Advantage Of GSA Advantage!*

Recently made mandatory for all MAS vendors, GSA *Advantage!* is an electronic tool with which the Government identifies and purchases Schedule supplies and services on-line.[423] Establishing a GSA *Advantage!* account and uploading products and prices is easy and advantageous (it also is mandatory). However, pursuant to Section 508 of the Rehabilitation Act, a vendor that provides a direct link from the GSA *Advantage!* web site to its own web site (something that is highly recommended) must ensure that its web site is compliant with all applicable Access Board regulations (*see* Chapter XIII).

H. *STEP EIGHT—Take Care Of Your Customers Or Your Competitors Will*

Government customers, like commercial customers, seek the best product or service they can purchase, at the best price available, with the best customer service. It is essential that vendors learn the importance of service when it comes to Government purchasers. Vendors that learn this lesson will find that Government purchasers can be very loyal and valuable allies, returning often to make repeat purchases, expanding the breadth of supplies and services purchased, and even recommending the vendor to other Government agencies.

To this end, vendors should keep in mind that few activities come close to matching a face-to-face encounter as a powerful sales tool. Vendors that put this principle into practice are well rewarded. One of the simplest methods for doing so is to make an appointment with a purchasing officer who handles the product or service offered on Schedule. Each federal agency employs purchasing officers of its own, most of whom would be more than happy to schedule some time to meet with a prospective vendor. Federal purchasers like to know that their suppliers are here today and still will be here tomorrow. And with strong weight now being given to past performance ratings and with performance-based contracting already being pilot-tested, it is all the more important to maintain strong business relationships with current, and even previous, federal buyers. Sound federal relationships create a comfort level with federal buyers that can be among the most important of intangibles when the Government makes its best value determination. While these relationships may differ in some ways from those a company has with commercial business partners, they can be just as important—if not more important—to nurture.

In addition to developing a relationship with Schedule purchasers, however, vendors should seek to establish a positive relationship with the GSA's Federal Supply Service ("FSS") and the many people who make this service one of the best within the Government. The FSS has become quite sophisticated in recent years as the MAS Program has expanded. And, with the advent of the industrial funding fee, FSS has retained a top-notch marketing and customer staff to help promote the MAS Program throughout the Government. As a result, the FSS often is able to assist vendors identify potential sales leads or, on occasion, may even go so far as to recommend a vendor to a particular agency.

I. *STEP NINE—Join An Industry Association*

Whether the American School Food Service Association, the Chlorine Institute, the Leather Industries of America, or the National Stone Association, every industry has a related association.[424] Many of these associations offer their members a variety of useful sales resources. In the area of Schedule contracting generally, for example, the Coalition for Government

Procurement (*http://www.coalgovpro.org*) offers its members a multitude of resources and services, including a newsletter, frequent training programs, and two annual conferences that typically feature, among other experts in the field, speakers from within GSA, the VA, the Office of Federal Procurement Policy, and other Government agencies.

While industry associations can provide an excellent opportunity to rub elbows with influential Government officials (as well as to learn about the MAS Program and to take a unified stance regarding issues of interest to Schedule vendors generally), vendors also should keep in mind that they will be rubbing elbows with their competitors. Thus, vendors should consult with their legal departments to ensure that the activities of a given association are appropriate. Additionally, whenever interacting with Government officials, vendors should avoid even the slightest hint of impropriety. Thus, vendors should avoid entertaining Government officials, providing gifts to Government officials, or otherwise seeking improperly to influence Government officials.

Finally, vendors should be mindful that, over the years, some Government agencies and industry associations have developed an adversarial relationship. Vendors would be wise to query GSA contracting personnel regarding a particular association, or even particular association members, before signing up.[425]

J. *STEP TEN—Understand And Comply With The Terms And Conditions Of The MAS Program*

Vendors should take great effort to ensure that they understand the MAS solicitation and contract "inside and out." Additionally, vendors must have an understanding of how they will deal with the applicable rules and regulations *before* a proposal is submitted to GSA. To this end (and as discussed in greater detail in Chapters VI and XX), vendors should appoint a team within the company to ensure contract compliance. While few MAS vendors set out to ignore the terms and conditions of their contracts, many forget or overlook their responsibilities in the heat of doing battle with their competitors. Unfortunately, "I forgot" is no defense in the face of a Government audit, investigation, or prosecution. Experience suggests that complying with the terms and conditions of the MAS Program is far cheaper than the consequences of not complying. Vendors that know the rules and regulations and keep up to date with changes give themselves a terrific advantage over their competitors. If a vendor believes that it is unable to ensure compliance on its own, it should contact an organization (whether a consulting firm or a law firm) to obtain assistance.

Granted, this is more of a step to avoid problems than a step to generate sales, but the point is important enough to warrant restating it here. In addition to whatever other problems it may cause (as discussed in Chapter XXIV), a failure to comply with the terms and conditions of the MAS Program can drastically reduce sales.

* * *

In the end, each Schedule vendor must adopt the sales/ marketing approach that works for it. Clearly, no "Ten Steps" will work for every vendor. An emphasis on targeted direct mail might work for one vendor, but produce disappointing results for another. A full-page advertisement in a Government-focused publication might produce impressive sales for some, but not for others. The key to generating sales is to identify the *combination of approaches* that fits a vendor's product, culture, market—and budget—and to pursue that approach with creativity, consistency, and discipline.

Advice From The Trenches:
Biting the Hand that Feeds You

(by Anne B. Perry of Sheppard, Mullin, Richter & Hampton)

You have successfully negotiated your GSA MAS Contract, you have spent a significant portion of your marketing budget trying to sell to the Government, you have competed under a solicitation, offering deep discounts and a superior product and service, and you are informed that your competitor won. What should you do? The following seven steps should help you decide.

Step One: Determining Why You Lost

Immediately upon receipt of the notice of award, you must send a written request to the contracting officer asking for a debriefing. Your mission at the debriefing is to learn as much as possible from the agency concerning the evaluation of your proposal and the basis for award. Come to the debriefing prepared with relevant questions and a very good understanding of the Solicitation, the evaluation criteria listed therein, and your proposal. A tip: don't "lawyer up." In other words, if you want to have a free and open dialogue with the agency concerning the details of the evaluation and the award, don't show up with your lawyer who, even if he/she never opens his/her mouth, will lead the contracting officer to bring his/her lawyers, and then nothing of substance will thereafter pass between you. Tip 2: accept the first date offered to you by the agency because the requirements for obtaining an automatic stay of contract performance (which precludes the awardee from performing during the pendency of your protest) should you choose to file a protest are in large part tied to this date.

Step Two: Assessing Whether The Award Was Flawed

Once you have been debriefed, you must compare what the agency told you they *did* <u>*with*</u> what the Solicitation told you the agency was *going to do*. In other words, you must examine the agency's evaluation of your proposal and the award determination to determine whether they are consistent with the express and explicit terms of the Solicitation. Examples of obvious flaws include situations in which the Solicitation stated that technical merit was more important than price, but the agency informs you that it made award to the lowest-priced, technically acceptable offeror. Similarly, if the agency tells you that your proposal was downgraded for failing to provide X functionality, make sure that such functionality was either expressly called out in the Solicitation or at least reasonably related to the factors that were expressly stated. One other key error—if the agency limited the competition to products and services currently on schedule, but awarded to a contractor who does not hold a schedule contract for the purchased product or service.

Step Three: Determining Whether You Were Harmed By The Flawed Award

Even assuming that you determine the agency's evaluation of your proposal was flawed, or that the award was inconsistent with the Solicitation's disclosed criteria, you still have one more significant legal hurdle to overcome. Did the flaw(s) deprive you of the contract? This question is not as easily answered as one might expect. Not all errors in a procurement cause the award to go to the wrong entity. Or even if the error in the process lead to the wrong awardee, the correct awardee may be yet another competitor. Hence, it is important to take an honest look not only at the flaws in the procurement process, but also, at your own proposal and answer the question "but for the error, would I have been the awardee or would I have had a substantial chance for award?" If the answer to the question is no—for example, if there is a higher rated, lower-priced offeror who sits between you and the awardee—then challenging the award would not be in your best interests unless the evaluation of that intervening offeror is also flawed.

Step Four: Evaluating How Important The Contract Is To Your Company

Not all contracts are equal, and size is not the only relevant factor. Some contracts are more important than others for a variety of reasons, and it may depend on the nature of your business or the timing of the award. While it is obvious that very large dollar contracts are important to all businesses, there are small contracts that are critical to a company's continued success. For example, even a small procurement can be important if it has the potential to lead to a much larger follow-on contract, or if it serves as a basis for breaking into a new market and proving to other potential customers that you have a viable and competitive product line. So it is important to assess whether this is a contract you can lose without harming your business base or whether it is sufficiently critical that you are willing to undergo the expense, both in time and money, of formally challenging the award.

Step Five: Determining Whether This Is The Battle To Pick

While a particular contract might not be critical to your company's success, it has been suggested by commentators that if you simply allow agencies repeatedly to award contracts to your competitors without any fear that you might challenge the propriety of the award, you might not be treated fairly in the end. Here, you need to ask yourself, "Have I been shut out of other similar contracts unfairly?" If the answer is yes, then perhaps you need to make it known to the agency that you will not "roll over." In addition, sometimes you believe that the agency committed errors that deprived you of the award, but the errors involve areas of technical judgment. Here, you should consider your likelihood of success on the merits of your challenge. Were the procurement errors so profound or fundamental and so objectively determinable that it is clear you were unfairly denied a fair opportunity to compete? If the answer is yes, then the likelihood that you may be successful is enhanced. Overall, you want to ensure that you seriously consider how often you challenge awards because (1) not every contract is worth the turmoil caused by a protest and (2) for purposes of client relations and credibility, it is better not to be known as a company that protests every award, regardless of merit.

Step Six: Deciding Whether You Are Willing To Incur The Expense

Okay, you have now determined that (a) the agency did not reasonably evaluate your proposal or make an award based on the disclosed evaluation criteria, (b) but for the errors you would have received the contract, (c) this is a very important contract to your company, and (d) you think you have a decent likelihood of success on the merits of your challenge. Now all you have to do is decide whether you are willing to pay the price, both in terms of time and money, for the privilege of suing your potential client. In almost every case, the first question asked from a client is "How much is this going to cost me?" The answer, as flip as it could be interpreted, is "How much is it worth?" Not surprisingly, in typical situations, the larger the procurement, the more costly a protest. On the other hand, there are some expenses that all protests share, regardless of size. For example, all must incur the expense of preparing and filing the protest. This itself is not an expensive endeavor. The expensive portion of the protest comes when the agency responds to the protest and serves your lawyer with the agency report. Depending on the size and nature of the procurement, that report could consist of a single three-ring binder *or* hundreds of boxes of documents. Obviously, review of the former will take much less time, multiplied by your lawyer's hourly rate, than review of the latter.

You might ask, why do I have to hire a lawyer? The answer is simply that it is impossible to file and pursue effectively a protest in a negotiated procurement without the assistance of counsel because, typically, only counsel, and in limited circumstances outside consultants working under the direction of counsel, are able to gain access to the relevant documentation necessary to prove your case. Counsel is permitted to review the materials and make arguments based thereon under what is commonly known as a Protective Order. This Protective Order precludes the attorney from disclosing outside of the protest process, to any party, the substance of the documentation provided. This Protective Order is put in place to protect your data from being released to your competitors and theirs to you. Without access to protected information and documentation, it is virtually impossible to argue, with any substantive or persuasive basis, the flaws in the procurement and their impact on your proposal and standing. In other words, while you can file and pursue a protest without being given access to the relevant documents, you are then at the mercy of a busy judge or hearing officer to review the record in detail to determine whether you have a good case. If that is your strategy, one suggestion: don't waste the ink in preparing and filing the protest. However, even with counsel, *you* can reasonably manage your protest expenses by treating your protest as an incremental endeavor.

Step Seven: Knowing When To Quit

Simply because you decide to file a protest does not mean that you have to continue to pursue it to its bitter end. You are free to withdraw the protest at a later point if you determine either that (1) the award was not as materially flawed as you had believed, or (2) your chances of success in the protest are sufficiently small so as to not warrant the incurrence of additional protest expenses. Any lawyer who you retain to handle your protest should be willing to advise you during the protest process, and at various stages, whether the agency's evaluation and/or award is so seriously flawed that you have a reasonable chance for overturning the award, and whether, even if you do win the protest, you have a reasonable prospect of becoming the awardee. In managing your case, therefore, you will have the opportunity to monitor and control your expenses and only expend additional resources when it continues to make sense. One caveat, remember that your lawyer will be precluded from giving you any specifics regarding the bases for his/her recommendation if the details arise from the information to which the lawyer has access under the protective order. Rather, your counsel will be permitted to inform you only in general terms of the nature of the issues and his/her assessment of your likelihood of success.

In sum, when "just being considered" is not enough, and it was the contract you were after and were wrongly denied, then there is a remedy. Whether that remedy works for you, and in what circumstances, is a fact and contractor specific determination that requires consideration of a variety of factors. You should seriously and thoroughly consider each element described above before making this decision. One final note, however—if you plan to file a protest either at the agency or the GAO, make sure you think fast because the filing deadlines to enter into the game are short and inflexible.

Notes:

[416]   Douglas B. Parker, of the GSA consulting firm of Parker, Chaney & Anderson, contributed significantly to this chapter. *See* the Vendor's Resource Guide at Appendix I for more information on Mr. Parker's firm.

[417]   Additionally, small businesses should keep in mind that, since 1998, federal agencies have been permitted to count purchases from MAS small businesses toward their internal small business goals. GSA

Procurement Information Bulletin 98-1 (Jan. 15, 1998). This change in Government policy created tremendous opportunities for small businesses looking to break into the MAS marketplace.

[418] *See* the Vendor Resource Guide at Appendix I.

[419] For more information on GSA's "MarkeTips, log on to *http:// www.fss.gsa.gov/pub/marketips.cfm.*

[420] GSAR 552.203-71 (Restriction on Advertising) (Sept. 1999).

[421] FAR 13.303-1.

[422] Other BPAs contemplate further competition in connection with each order.

[423] *See http://www.gsaadvantage.gov.*

[424] A simple search for the words "trade association" on an Internet search engine will provide an excellent starting point in this regard.

[425] On a related note, one of the many benefits of joining an industry association is the fact that the Government need *not* know of the membership. Consequently, association members may take politically unpopular positions simply by relying on association management to make the arguments and push the agenda for them.

XII.

FEDERAL ACQUISITION REGULATION PART 12

"[T]he less government we have, the better—the fewer laws, and the less confided power."
                                                -Ralph Waldo Emerson

T he terms and conditions of a MAS contract are the product of many sources. The primary source, however, is FAR Part 12, which governs the acquisition of commercial items.[426] After briefly reviewing the history of FAR Part 12, this chapter discusses the more significant FAR clauses incorporated into all Schedule contracts.

A. *A Brief History Of FAR Part 12*

In an effort to streamline the way the Government buys supplies and services, Congress, in 1990, directed the Department of Defense ("DOD") to establish an advisory panel (which became known as the "Section 800 Panel") to recommend measures to revise the nation's procurement laws and regulations.[427] On January 12, 1993, the Section 800 Panel presented its recommendations to Congress (by way of a nine-volume report). Among other things, the Section 800 Panel recommended numerous reforms in the area of commercial item acquisitions.[428]

Not surprisingly, "Congress took many of the findings and recommendations of the Section 800 Panel to heart in developing reform legislation, culminating in the Federal Acquisition Streamlining Act of 1994 (FASA)."[429] As a result, FASA mandated that commercial item contracts include, to the maximum extent practicable, only (i) clauses required to implement the provisions of law or executive orders applicable to the acquisition of commercial items or (ii) clauses determined to be consistent with customary commercial practice.

Following the passage of FASA, the Government was faced with the rather daunting task of implementing its provisions in the FAR. The Government undertook this task through the creation of unique *ad hoc* Government-wide implementation teams. The FAR Part 12 team (*i.e.*, the team assigned to implement FASA's commercial item requirements) involved representatives from the Office of the Secretary of Defense, each branch of the military, GSA, the Department of State, and the National Aeronautics and Space Administration. The team was tasked with reviewing comments from interested Government agencies, discussing implementation strategy, and proposing language for inclusion in the Federal Register. The various federal agencies were given little say in the way the team handled (or even *if* it handled) their comments.

As a model, the FAR Part 12 team looked to the recommendations of the Section 800 Panel, FASA, and Part 211 of the Defense FAR Supplement, a DOD regulation that preceded FASA and sought to streamline commercial contracting within DOD, but which met with only minimal success. Pressed for time, much of the team's work involved internal discussions and compromise. The primary result of the team's activities is reflected in four FAR clauses that *must* be inserted into solicitations and contracts for the acquisition of commercial items, 52.212-1, 52.212-3, 52.212-4, and 52.212-5.[430]

B. *Solicitation Provisions And Contract Clauses Applicable To Commercial Item Contracts*

FAR Part 12 has streamlined the process of negotiating and awarding Schedule contracts. This streamlining primarily is the result of four clauses that limit the number of clauses that must be incorporated into a commercial item contract.

1. FAR 52.212-1

FAR 52.212-1 provides a "single, streamlined set of instructions to be used when soliciting offers for commercial items . . . ."[431] While this FAR clause may be tailored by the contracting officer under appropriate circumstances, the MAS solicitation adheres to the requirements identified in FAR 52.212-1.

2. FAR 52.212-3

FAR 52.212-3 provides a "single, consolidated list of certifications and representations for the acquisition of commercial items . . . ."[432] Unlike FAR 52.212-1, this clause may be tailored only in very limited circumstances. Chapter IX provides a detailed discussion of the several certifications and representations applicable to MAS vendors.

3. FAR 52.212-4

FAR 52.212-4 sets forth "terms and conditions which are, to the maximum extent practicable, consistent with customary commercial practices . . . ."[433] Among other things, this clause covers inspection/acceptance, assignments, changes, disputes, terminations, and warranties. (Several of these provisions are discussed in Chapter XIV.) Additionally, this clause identifies several laws that are "unique to Government contracts" and with which the vendor must comply. (These laws are also discussed in Chapter XIV.)

While some form of FAR 52.212-4 will be included in every MAS solicitation and resulting contract, contracting officers have the authority to tailor FAR 52.212-4. The FAR provides contracting officers with this discretion in recognition of the fact that, like commercial items themselves, the nature of commercial contracts differs from situation to situation. Thus, subject to certain exceptions, and only after all necessary market research has been performed, contracting officers may tailor many of the clauses identified in FAR 52.212-4 better to suit the nature of the particular acquisition. However, the following provisions may *not* be tailored by the contracting officer:

(1) Assignments;
(2) Disputes;
(3) Payment (except as provided in Subpart 32.11);
(4) Invoice;
(5) Other compliances; and
(6) Compliance with laws unique to Government contracts.[434]

Additionally, contracting officers are precluded from tailoring any clause to include any additional terms or conditions that are inconsistent with customary commercial practices unless a formal waiver is obtained in advance.[435]

4. FAR 52.212-5

FAR 52.212-5 serves several purposes. First, paragraphs (a), (b), and (c) identify clauses that must be incorporated into commercial item contracts in order to "implement statutes or executive orders." Specifically, paragraph (a) sets forth two specific clauses that must be included in commercial item contracts, *i.e.*, FAR 52.233-4, clarifying that U.S. law will apply to any breach of contract claim, and FAR 52.233-3, establishing the procedures for pursing a protest following the award of a contract.[436] Paragraph (b) sets forth several clauses, some of which must be incorporated into commercial item contracts, *e.g.*, FAR 52.219-9 (Small Business Subcontracting Plan), FAR 52.222-26 (Equal Opportunity), and FAR 52.225-5 (Trade Agreements).[437] (The more important of these provisions are described elsewhere in this book.) It is the contracting officer's responsibility to indicate, by checking the applicable clauses, which clauses are applicable to the particular procurement. Paragraph (c) sets forth several clauses applicable to commercial services, such as FAR 52.222-41, implementing the Service Contract Act, and FAR 52.222-43, implementing the Fair Labor Standards Act. As with paragraph (b), it is the contracting officer's responsibility to indicate, by checking the applicable clauses, which clauses are applicable to the particular procurement.

Second, FAR 52.212-5 grants the Comptroller General access to a vendor's records for audit purposes.[438] This element of FAR 52.212-5 is discussed in Chapter XXI.

Third, FAR 52.212-5 limits the number of clauses that a vendor must flow down to its subcontractors.[439] This final purpose is discussed below.

C. *Laws Inapplicable To Commercial Item Contracts*

In an effort to make the Government's contracts for commercial acquisitions more like industry's commercial contracts, FAR Part 12 exempts commercial vendors from compliance with certain statutes. These statutes, which are set forth at FAR 12.503(a), include the Walsh-Healy Act,[440] certain laws relating to the payment of contingent fees,[441] and the Drug-Free Workplace Act of 1988,[442] among others. Additionally, FAR Part 12 exempts commercial item contracts from certain requirements of other laws, including the Contract Work Hours and Safety Standards Act,[443] the Anti-Kickback Act of 1986,[444] and the Fly American Act.[445] For example, commercial item contracts will not include the clause at FAR 52.222-4 relating to overtime for laborers and mechanics, even though other elements of the Contract Work Hours and Safety Standards Act may apply. Likewise, commercial item contracts will not include the clause at FAR 52.247-63 relating to vouchers, even though other elements of the Fly American Act may apply. Vendors are encouraged to read these (and all other) clauses carefully to determine which clauses and aspects of clauses apply to a given Schedule contract.

D. *Flow Downs*

A "flow-down clause" is a clause that a prime contractor must incorporate into its subcontracts. For example, MAS vendors are required to comply with the FAR's Equal Opportunity Clause.[446] Among other things, this clause requires that the vendor "not discriminate against any employee or applicant for employment because of race, color, religion, sex, or national origin."[447] The Equal Opportunity Clause also requires that the vendor "include the terms and conditions [of the clause] in every subcontract or purchase order that is not exempted by the rules . . . ."[448] In other words, the vendor must "flow down" the substantive requirements of FAR 52.222-26 into all applicable subcontracts.

Historically, MAS vendors—like Government contractors generally—were required to flow down a significant number of prime contract clauses. In an effort to streamline the process for the procurement of commercial supplies and services, however, Congress incorporated within FASA a limitation on the number of clauses that a commercial contractor must flow down to its commercial subcontractors. This limitation is found at FAR 52.212-5(e), a clause that is incorporated into every new Schedule contract.

FAR 52.212-5(e) identifies six clauses that a vendor must flow down to its commercial subcontractors.[449] Notwithstanding any other provision in the FAR, vendors are required to flow down only these six clauses. As a matter of sound practice, however, vendors would be well advised to confirm that their contracting officers have the same reading of FAR 52.212-5(e). Experience has shown that, notwithstanding the clear language of this clause, some contracting officers have misinterpreted what the clause requires.

As of the publication of this book, a MAS vendor (and, for that matter, any other commercial item prime contractor) must flow down to its commercial subcontractors only the following clauses:

- FAR 52.222-26, Equal Opportunity, which requires that contractors not discriminate against any person because of "race, color, religion, sex, or national origin" in either their hiring or employment practices.
- FAR 52.222-35, Affirmative Action for Disabled Veterans and Veterans of the Vietnam Era, which requires that the vendor comply with the requirements of the Vietnam Era Veterans' Readjustment Assistance Act of 1972. The vendor is required to "[t]ake affirmative action to employ, advance in employment, and otherwise treat qualified disabled veterans, veterans of the Vietnam era, and other eligible veterans without discrimination based upon their disability or veterans' status in all employment practices . . . ."[450]
- FAR 52.222-36, Affirmative Action for Workers with Disabilities, which requires that the vendor "[t]ake affirmative action to employ, advance in employment, and otherwise treat qualified individuals with disabilities without discrimination based upon their physical or mental disabilities in all employment practices . . . ."[451]
- FAR 52.222-41, Service Contract Act of 1965, as Amended, which governs the wages a vendor must pay its service employees.
- FAR 52.219-8, Utilization of Small Business Concerns, which requires the contractor to maximize subcontract awards to various types of small businesses "to the fullest extent consistent with efficient contract performance" and

to cooperate in any studies or surveys conducted by the SBA or the awarding agency to determine the extent of the contractor's compliance with this clause.

- FAR 52.222-39, Notification of Employee Rights Concerning Payment of Union Dues or Fees, which requires the contractor to post standardized notices informing employees of their right to refrain from joining a labor union and to decline to pay any portion of union dues not related to collective bargaining efforts.

The requirements of each of these clauses are described in detail in Chapters XIII and XVI.

Notably absent from the foregoing list is FAR 52.219-9, Small Business Subcontracting Plan. As described elsewhere in this book, FAR 52.219-9 includes a flow-down provision that requires commercial item contractors to incorporate into their subcontracting plans assurances that they will include the FAR's "Utilization of Small Business Concerns" Clause in certain commercial item subcontracts and will require certain commercial subcontractors to adopt and comply with subcontracting plans of their own.[452] As currently drafted, FAR 52.212-5 preempts this provision and relieves contractors of this particular flow-down requirement. As noted above, however, MAS vendors should be aware that some contracting officers take a different view of the interaction between these two clauses. For example, some will argue that each vendor's Subcontracting plan incorporates a flow-down requirement regarding such plans that is distinct from FAR 52.219-9. Additionally, because some long-standing MAS contracts still do not include FAR 52.212-5, some contracting officers will argue that the flow-down limitation in paragraph (e) is completely inapplicable. Although vendors have a legitimate argument that the provisions of FAR 52.212-5 are incorporated into every contract as a matter of law,[453] vendors would be well advised to (i) read their MAS contracts carefully to ensure the incorporation of FAR 52.212-5 and (ii) consult their contracting officers to assess their understanding of its impact.

Recently, certain Government officials have described the absence of FAR 52.219-9 from the list of required flow-down provisions in FAR 52.212-5 as an "implementation oversight." GSA has indicated that, at some point in the not too distant future, the FAR Council will propose a modification to FAR 52.212-5 to add FAR 52.212-9. Until that time, however, vendors have a strong basis for not flowing down requirements to subcontractors. But, again, talking to the cognizant contracting officer first is not a bad idea.

One final word on the subject of flow downs and the possibility that the FAR Council will move to increase the number of clauses set forth in FAR 52.212-5(e). While flow-down clauses serve a purpose, they also require additional infrastructure, increase the cost of doing business (and, thus, the cost of the products offered for sale), and increase the risks of noncompliance. These clauses also affect the willingness of subcontractors to enter into contracts with Schedule vendors. In an environment that, pursuant to the direction of Congress, is supposed to be moving toward the adoption of greater commercial practices, one must question the wisdom of increasing the number of clauses that must be flowed down to subcontractors.

Notes:

426 FAR 12.102(a) (2001) provides that "[t]his part shall be used for the acquisition of supplies or services that meet the definition of commercial items . . . ."

427 National Defense Authoriziation Act for Fiscal Year 1991, Pub. L. No. 101-510, § 800, 1990 U.S.C.C.A.N. (104 Stat.) 1485, 1587.

428 For an excellent overview of FASA's and FARA's commercial item modifications, *see* Lynda Troutman O'Sullivan & Douglas E. Perry, *Commercial Item Acquisitions, in* Briefing Papers 3, No. 97-5 (Fed. Pub'ns Inc. Apr. 1997).

429 *Id.*

430 FAR 12.301.

431 FAR 12.301(b)(1).

[432] FAR 12.301(b)(2).

[433] FAR 12.301(b)(3).

[434] FAR 12.302(b).

[435] FAR 12.302(c).

[436] FAR 52.212-5(a)(1) and (2).

[437] FAR 52.212-5(b).

[438] FAR 52.212-5(d).

[439] FAR 52.212-5(e).

[440] 41 U.S.C. § 43.

[441] *Id.* § 254(a);10 U.S.C. § 2306(b).

[442] 41 U.S.C. § 701(a).

[443] 40 U.S.C. § 329(b).

[444] 41 U.S.C. §§ 57(d) and 58.

[445] 49 U.S.C. § 40118.

[446] FAR 52.222-26.

[447] FAR 52.222-26(b)(1).

[448] FAR 52.222-26(b)(10).

[449] FAR 52.212-5(e) includes one additional clause -- FAR 52.247-64, Preference for Privately-Owned U.S. Flag Commercial Vessels -- that is applicable only to subcontracts awarded prior to May 1, 1996. *See* FAR 47.504(d).

[450] FAR 52.222-35(b)(1).

[451] FAR 52.222-36(a)(1).

[452] FAR 52.219-9(d)(9).

[453] FAR 12.301 (2001) provides that the contracting officer "shall" insert FAR 52.212-5 into "solicitations for the acquisition of commercial items, and clauses in solicitations and contracts for the acquisition of commercial items . . . ." *See G.L. Christian & Assocs. v. United States*, 320 F.2d 345 (Ct. Cl. 1963), regarding the incorporation of mandatory procurement clauses into contracts as a matter law.

XIII.

SOCIO-ECONOMIC PROVISIONS

"I believe in equality for everyone, except reporters and photographers."

-Mahatma Gandhi

T he MAS Program incorporates many clauses designed to ensure that no segment of society is precluded from participating in the benefits of Government contracting and that many are affirmatively included. These clauses encourage the hiring and retention of disabled Vietnam era veterans and handicapped individuals, mandate products accessible to persons with physical disabilities, and promote the participation of small and small disadvantaged businesses and women-owned and HUBZone small businesses. This chapter reviews these various clauses and examines the obligations they impose on MAS vendors.

A. *FAR 52.222-26 (Equal Opportunity)*

In an effort to instill equality in the workplace, the Government requires that all vendors holding contracts over $10,000 comply with FAR 52.222-26, under which vendors are required to take affirmative action to ensure that candidates for employment and employees are not subject to discrimination because of race, color, religion, sex, or national origin. Once a vendor exceeds $50,000 in Government sales, it will be required to develop an affirmative action program for each of its facilities.[454] If the vendor expects that it will receive Government contracts in excess of $10 million, it is required to undergo a pre-award audit to determine compliance with the Equal Opportunity Clause.[455]

Vendors are also required to flow down this requirement to all applicable subcontractors (*i.e.*, for subcontracts over $10,000 that are not otherwise exempted). Vendors must post notices regarding equal employment opportunity requirements conspicuously in the workplace and also must indicate in any employment advertisements that they are an equal opportunity employer.[456] Sanctions for noncompliance include administrative sanctions, penalties, and publication of the names of noncompliant vendors.[457] More severe sanctions include suspension, cancellation, or termination of the vendor's contracts and debarment from future contracts or modifications or extensions of existing contracts until the contractor is in compliance.[458] In addition, the DOJ may institute civil or criminal proceedings.[459]

B. *FAR 52.222-36 (Affirmative Action For Workers With Disabilities)*

Another socio-economic goal of the Government is to eliminate discrimination by employers against workers with disabilities, either physical or mental. To further this goal, the Government requires that its contractors and subcontractors holding contracts worth $10,000 or more comply with FAR 52.222-36. Under the terms of this FAR clause, vendors are required in their hiring and retention practices to take affirmative action in ensuring that discrimination because of a person's physical or mental disability does not occur.

The vendor must post its obligations and the rights of employees under this clause in a conspicuous place where they will be available to both applicants and employees. As with the Equal Opportunity Clause, the Government has several remedies for noncompliance. Sanctions for noncompliance include withholding of payments, termination or suspension of the contract, or debarment.[460]

C. *FAR 52.222-35 (Affirmative Action for Disabled Veterans And Veterans Of The Vietnam Era)*

In FAR 52.222-35, the Government seeks to address any discrimination by employers regarding eligible veterans and disabled veterans. To comply with this clause, the employer is required to make an affirmative effort to prevent any discrimination in either its hiring or retention policies and practices. Vendors must ensure that employment openings are provided to the appropriate office of the State employment service system.[461] A Veterans of the Vietnam Era is a person who:

(1) Served on active duty for a period of more than 180 days, any part of which occurred between August 5, 1964, and May 7, 1975, and was discharged or released therefrom with other than a dishonorable discharge; or

(2) Was discharged or released from active duty for a service-connected disability if any part of such active duty was performed between August 5, 1964, and May 7, 1975.[462]

Vendors must file on an annual basis a report regarding the number of veterans and disabled veterans hired and the total number of employees hired for the reporting period.[463] Both of these clauses must be flowed down to subcontractors receiving contracts for $10,000 or more. Failure to comply with the requirements of FAR 52.222-35 will subject the vendor to sanctions including withholding of payments, suspension, and termination and also may result in debarment.[464]

D. *The Energy Star Program*

The Federal Government is the largest consumer of energy in the United States, spending over $7 billion a year.[465] As a leading consumer, the Government is in the position to effect energy saving programs and policies, and the Energy Star Program is one such program. On June 3, 1999, President Clinton signed Executive Order No. 13123, which requires that federal agencies select Energy Star products when choosing energy-using products.[466] If Energy Star products are not available, then agencies "shall select products that are in the upper 25 percent of energy efficiency as designated by FEMP."[467] Vendors whose products qualify may advertise using the Energy Star label. Vendors interested in the Energy Star Program should visit the Environmental Protection Agency's web site at *http://www.energystar.gov*.

E. *Section 508*

More formally known as Section 508 of the Rehabilitation Act of 1973,[468] Section 508 refers to two sets of recently implemented regulations intended to ensure that people with disabilities have access to "electronic and information technology" ("EIT," defined *infra*) that is *comparable* to the access afforded to people without disabilities. First, Section 508 refers to a series of EIT regulations published by the Architectural and Transportation Barriers Compliance Board (more commonly known as the "Access Board"), "an independent Federal agency whose primary mission is to promote accessibility for individuals with disabilities."[469] These regulations outline the technical standards that EIT must meet in order to be considered "accessible." Second, Section 508 refers to recent amendments to the FAR establishing regulations for the procurement of EIT.[470]

In sum, Section 508 imposes two primary obligations upon agencies. Agencies must ensure that "[f]ederal employees with disabilities have access to and use of information and data that is comparable to the access and use by Federal employees who are not individuals with disabilities."[471] Agencies must also ensure that "[m]embers of the public with disabilities seeking information or services from an agency have access to and use of information and data that is comparable to the access to and use of information and data by members of the public who are not individuals with disabilities."[472] In short, agencies must ensure that all acquisitions of EIT (except where an exception applies) meet the applicable Section 508 technical accessibility standards.[473]

It is important to understand, however, that agencies need not provide the same access to individuals with disabilities as is available to others but, rather, "comparable access." According to GSA,

> an agency's obligation to provide comparable access
> under section 508 is satisfied by acquiring EIT
> that meets the applicable technical provisions . . .
> of the Access Board's standards, either directly
> or through equivalent facilitation . . . . [474]

"Equivalent facilitation" refers to the permissibility of accepting EIT offered by a vendor that employs designs or technologies that do not meet the specific technical provisions of the Section 508 standards, but that provide "substantially equivalent or greater access to and use of product for people with disabilities."[475]

Likewise, it is important to understand that Section 508 requires procured EIT to be *compatible with* assistive technology, rather than being fully accessible as purchased. For the most part, this is because Section 508 requires agencies to provide assistive technology only to those individuals requiring such assistance. Thus, an information technology vendor, for example, need not sell only computers with a refreshable Braille display terminal. Rather, it simply must ensure that its computers are compatible with such terminals. While this principle likely causes little concern among computer hardware manufacturers, it may present obstacles for manufacturers of products that are less easily rendered compatible, such as handheld calculators, facsimile machines, personal organizers, and the like.

1. What Is Electronic And Information Technology?

Any attempt to understand Section 508 must begin with an understanding of EIT. In short, EIT has the same meaning as "information technology," except that is also includes "any equipment or interconnected system or subsystem of equipment that is used in the creation, conversion, or duplication of data or information."[476] Additionally, the term includes "telecommunication products (such as telephones), information kiosks and transaction machines, worldwide web sites, multimedia, and office equipment such as copiers and fax machines."[477]

But EIT is not just limited to products. Services can qualify as EIT as well. Consider the following example offered by GSA:

> [A]gencies acquiring help desks must ensure that providers are capable of accommodating the communications needs of persons with disabilities, consistent [with the Access Board's standards]. An agency help desk may need to communicate through a teletypewriter (TTY)—*i.e.*, equipment that transmits coded signals across a telephone network. The help desk provider must also be familiar with such features as keyboard access and other options important to people with disabilities.[478]

Thus, the application of Section 508 is broader than many vendors initially believed.

2. Does Section 508 Apply To You?

Section 508 governs the development, procurement, maintenance, and use of all EIT by the United States Government. The effective date of the new regulations was June 21, 2001. With respect to contracts other than indefinite-delivery/indefinite/quantity ("IDIQ") contracts, the Section 508 procurement regulations apply "to contracts awarded on or after the effective date . . . ." With respect to IDIQ contracts, the regulations apply to "delivery orders or task orders issued on or after the effective date." Of particular interest to MAS vendors, the Federal Register preamble to the new regulations notes that the Access Board's EIT standards do not apply to (1) the taking of delivery of items ordered prior to the effective date of this rule, (2) within-scope modifications of contracts awarded before the effective date of this rule, (3) unilateral options for contracts awarded before the effective date of this rule, or (4) multiyear contacts awarded before the effective date of this rule.

When a contract is awarded after the Section 508 effective date, the next task is to determine whether the regulations apply to a given federal procurement.[479] As implemented at FAR Part 39, Section 508 includes five specific exceptions. These five situations in which agencies need not acquire EIT are as follows:

- Purchases made prior to January 1, 2003 with a total value below the micro-purchase threshold.[480] This exception applies to a "one-time purchase that totals $2,500 or less, made on the open market as opposed to under an existing contract."[481]
- Purchases of national security systems, as defined at FAR 39.002.[482]
- Purchases of EIT that are incidental to a Government contract.[483] The following example of this exception, provided by GSA, is illustrative: "[I]f a Federal agency enters into a contract to have a web site developed, the

web site is required to meet the applicable technical provisions of the Access Board's standards because the web site is a deliverable that is being acquired by the agency . . . . However, the vendor's office system used to develop the web site does not have to meet the technical provisions, since its equipment is incidental to the contract."[484]

- Purchases of EIT to be used in spaces frequented only by service personnel for maintenance, repair, or occasional monitoring of equipment. This is more commonly known as the "back office exception."[485]
- Purchases that would impose an "undue burden" on the agency if EIT were required.[486] Due to the complexity of this exception, it is discussed in greater detail below.

Additionally, while not technically an exception, the procurement regulations implementing Section 508 provide that, "[w]hen acquiring commercial items, an agency must comply with those accessibility standards that can be met with supplies or services that are available in the commercial marketplace in time to meet the agency's delivery requirements."[487] Thus, if a commercial product that meets a certain standard is unavailable in time to meet the agency's delivery requirements, an agency need not procure that item. As GSA cautions in its "Frequently Asked Questions," however, "[i]f products are available that meet some, but not all applicable provisions, agencies cannot claim a product as a whole is nonavailable just because it does not meet all of the applicable provisions. Agency acquisitions must comply with those applicable technical provisions that can be met with supplies or services that are available in the commercial marketplace in time to meet the agency's delivery requirements."[488]

Importantly, even where an exception applies, agencies still have an obligation to "provide reasonable accommodation for employees with disabilities and provide program access to members of the public with disabilities."[489]

3. What Does "Undue Burden" Mean?

Of all the exceptions to Section 508, the "undue burden" exception has received the most attention—and for good reason. Following the publication of the proposed Section 508 procurement rules, several commenters suggested that the FAR Council elaborate on the meaning of the term. Finding that "[s]ubstantial case law exists on this term, which comes from disability law,"[490] however, the FAR Council turned down the suggestion.[491] As a result, vendors and Government officials have had to muddle their way together through the learning process.

While the FAR does not define "undue burden," it does offer a starting point by providing that the term contemplates "a significant difficulty or expense" in complying with the accessibility standards.[492] Likewise, the FAR instructs agencies faced with making undue burden determinations to consider (1) the difficulty or expense of compliance and (2) the agency resources available to its program or component for which the supply or service is being acquired. Beyond these general guiding principles, disability law offers the following useful lessons regarding the meaning of undue burden:

- First, case law in the disability context (Section 504 of the Rehabilitation Act and Title III of the Americans with Disabilities Act ("ADA")) makes it clear that an undue burden determination must be made on a case-by-case basis. This is consistent with the Access Board's comments accompanying the final Section 508 standards.[493]
- Second, ADA case law suggests that several factors may be considered in determining whether an undue burden exists in a given situation. These factors include (i) the nature and cost of compliance, (ii) the overall financial resources of the agency conducting the procurement, and (iii) the nature of the agency's mission.[494]
- Third, an undue burden can arise even where compliance would not require a "fundamental alteration" of program resources.[495]

- Fourth, when considering the cost of complying with the Section 508 technical requirements, an agency properly may limit its analysis to the budget available to that agency for the program to be supported by the acquisition.[496]

But, even with the foregoing guidance, the *application* of the term likely will prove to be contentious and very well could serve as a source of future disappointed bidder protests.

4. What Does Section 508 Mean To You?

Section 508 means different things to different audiences. From the Government's perspective, Section 508 requires compliance with the entirety of the applicable regulations (governing activities from procurement planning to market research to source selection to actual use of the supplies and services procured) unless an exception applies. From a vendor's perspective, Section 508 is more straightforward. It requires simply that the vendor (1) design or manufacture products that meet the Access Board's technical standards and (2) be able to identify such products to the Government.

a. Design And Manufacture

The Access Board's technical standards are set forth at 36 C.F.R. part 1194. The standards establish general requirements and component specific requirements. For example, with respect to general requirements, the standards provide, among other things, that (1) color coding not be used as the only means of conveying information; (2) freestanding, non-portable products be accessible to persons in wheelchairs; (3) the flash rate of blinking text not exceed two Hertz to prevent seizures in people with epilepsy; (4) interactive features requiring timed responses allow additional time as needed; (5) biometrics not be the only means of user identification; and (6) touch-operated controls not be the only means of controlling operations and functions.

With respect to component specific requirements, the standards include technical criteria unique to certain types of features and products, including (1) input devices (such as keyboards and keypads), (2) non-embedded software, (3) web-based information or applications, (4) telecommunications functions, (5) video or multimedia products, and (6) information kiosks and transaction machines. The criteria for input devices, for example, address access for people with vision impairment or with limited motor control. As another example, the criteria for telecommunications functions address access for people who are deaf or hard of hearing.

Additionally, the Access Board's technical standards require procuring agencies to ensure that any "product support documentation provided to end-users be made available in alternate formats upon request, at no additional charge."[497] The term "product support documentation" includes user guides, installation guides, and customer support documentation. Thus, vendors will have to ensure that such documentation is available in formats such as Braille, audio recordings, large print, and other accessible media.

b. Identification

With respect to identification, it is interesting to note that the new FAR regulations do not include any certification requirement, such as those imposed upon vendors in the Y2K and Energy Star contexts. Notwithstanding this intentional omission, FAR 39.203(b)(2) provides that "[c]ontracting offices that award indefinite-quantity contracts must indicate to requiring and ordering activities which supplies and services the vendor indicates as compliant, and show where full details of compliance can be found (e.g., vendor's or other exact website location)." Likewise, the Federal Register preamble to the new regulations notes that "[i]t is expected that almost all products will comply with the standards within the next two years, and be labeled by the manufacturer accordingly." Thus, one can assume that, even without a FAR certification requirement, agency-specific representation requirements—at least with respect to agencies that routinely deal with indefinite-quantity contracts, such as GSA—are not far off.

5. Will Section 508 Become A Source For Disappointed Bidder Protests?

The provisions of Section 508 are enforceable primarily through private suits in federal court.[498] But from a procurement perspective, Section 508 also is enforceable through bid protests. Specifically, the new Section 508 regulations open at least three doors to such protests.

First, a protester could argue that a competing offeror cannot provide products that comply with the accessibility requirements or that the features of the EIT sought in the solicitation do not comport with the new requirements. Notable in this regard is the fact that the final rule does not provide for a best-value assessment, where a product's ability to meet the accessibility requirements is one factor among many. Rather, to the dismay of industry, which lobbied to the contrary, a product's ability to meet the accessibility requirements seems to be a mandatory requirement that is subject to a "go/no go" evaluation, assuming no "equivalent facilitation."

Second, a protester could challenge the invocation of any of the five exceptions set forth above.[499] The FAR explicitly provides that "[e]xception determinations [for other than IDIQ contracts] are required prior to contract award . . . ."[500] This requirement is a clear source of potential protests.

Third, as noted above, the subjectivity of the "undue burden" standards appears to be yet another potential avenue for protests. A vendor offering assistive technology, for example, might contest an agency's invocation of the undue burden exception. Likewise, a vendor offering a product or service that lacks assistive technology might protest an agency's failure to conduct an undue burden analysis.

As of the submission of this text to the publisher, the only reported case that has been decided raising Section 508 as a protest ground proved to be unsuccessful for the protestor. In *CourtSmart Digital Systems, Inc.*,[501] the GAO dismissed a protest alleging, among other things, that a particular software product offered by the awardee did not comply with Section 508. The GAO declined to sustain the protest, noting that the awardee's software was the "most Section 508 compliant" (the criteria included in the RFQ) and that the Section 508 evaluation of each offeror's product was consistent with the methodology outlined in the RFQ. CourtSmart had asked the GAO to hold that both quotations were "equally and substantially non-compliant" with the Section 508 standards. The GAO, however, noted that because the RFQ allowed for award to the "most Section 508 compliant" product, and because the agency followed the stated criteria in evaluating the software, the mere fact that the software was not fully Section 508 compliant did not prohibit the award.

* * *

Section 508 represents a positive step in an ongoing effort to ensure that disabled persons may participate fully and actively in public life. But it is a step that has brought with it a fair amount of confusion and unanswered questions. Vendors would be well advised to contact their in-house counsel to assess how Section 508 affects their ongoing contract compliance efforts.

F. *GSA Small Business Subcontracting Program*

It is the GSA's policy (indeed, the United States' policy) to afford classes of businesses historically underrepresented in the Government contracting community the maximum practicable opportunity to participate in the MAS Program.[502] These underrepresented classes include the following:

- Small businesses,
- Small disadvantaged businesses,
- Women-owned small businesses,
- HUBZone small businesses,
- Vietnam veteran-owned small businesses, and
- Service disabled veteran-owned small businesses.

GSA's primary means of ensuring such maximum practicable opportunity is through the FAR's Small Business Subcontracting Program.[503]

Mandated by the Small Business Act and implemented at FAR Subpart 19.7, the Small Business Subcontracting Program provides that:

> Any contractor receiving a contract for more than the simplified acquisition threshold must agree in the contract that small business, veteran-owned small business, service-disabled veteran-owned small business, HUBZone small business, small disadvantaged business, and women-owned small business concerns will have the maximum practicable opportunity to participate in contract performance consistent with its efficient performance.[504]

FAR 19.702 adds additional detail to this general statement by requiring that every solicitation in a negotiated acquisition (of which the MAS Program is one),[505] where the award is expected to exceed $500,000 and provide for subcontracting opportunities, shall require the awardee to "submit an acceptable subcontracting plan. If the apparently successful offeror fails to negotiate a subcontracting plan acceptable to the contracting officer within the time limit prescribed by the contracting officer, the offeror will be ineligible for award."[506]

GSA incorporates two FAR clauses into Schedule contracts to implement these requirements—FAR 52.219-8 (Utilization of

Small Business Concerns) and FAR 52.219-9 (Small Business Subcontracting Plan). MAS vendors must be familiar with their obligations under both clauses, which require them, among other things, to:

- Draft and submit an annual subcontracting plan setting forth, among other things, subcontracting goals and a description of the means the vendor plans to employ those goals.
- Submit annual reports to GSA (and the Small Business Administration ("SBA")) identifying the vendor's progress toward meeting its subcontracting goals.
- Undertake proactive efforts to maximize the use of small business subcontractors.

GSA will not award a Schedule contract that does not satisfy these requirements.

This chapter examines these, and other, subcontracting requirements of the MAS Program, as well as the penalties for noncompliance with such requirements.

1. What Is A Small Business?

The definitions of the various categories of small business concerns encompassed by the Small Business Subcontracting Program are set forth at FAR 2.101, 19.001, 19.101, 19.102, 19.701, and 52.219-8(c) and the Small Business Act. Fortunately, from the MAS vendor's point of view, ascertaining whether a subcontractor is small requires simply asking the subcontractor because the FAR permits vendors, in most cases, to rely upon the size representations of their subcontractors. The following bullet points, however, provide the general requirements for each size category.

- *Small Business.* A small business is an independently owned and operated concern that, including its affiliates, satisfies certain criteria set forth at FAR 19.102. Generally speaking, small businesses are not dominant (*i.e.*, they do not exert a controlling or major influence in an area in which there are a number of other companies competing) in the field of operation in which they operate.[507] To determine whether a business is dominant, GSA considers the following factors: volume of business, number of employees, financial resources, competitive status or position, and ownership or control of materials.[508] Because the threshold for a small business varies from procurement to procurement, vendors always should refer to the applicable North American Industry Classification System ("NAICS") for the specific product or service being procured.[509]

- *Small Disadvantaged Business ("SDB")*. An SDB is a small business that satisfies certain additional requirements, one of which is that the business has been certified by the SBA as an SDB.[510] Generally speaking, an SDB (1) is a small business, (2) is unconditionally owned and controlled (at least 51 percent) by one or more socially and economically disadvantaged individuals who are citizens and of good character, and (3) has demonstrated a potential for success. The net worth of any of the disadvantaged owners upon which the certification is based must not exceed $750,000 after taking into account all applicable exclusions.[511]

- *Women-Owned Small Business ("WOSB")*. A WOSB is a small business that has at least 51 percent ownership (or stock if a publicly owned business) held by women *and* one or more women must control the management and daily business operations.[512]

- *HUBZone Small Business*. A HUBZone small business is a small business located in a HUBZone area. (HUBZones are historically underutilized business zones designated as such by the Department of Housing and Urban Development or lands within the external boundaries of an Indian reservation.) The SBA maintains a list of qualified HUBZone businesses.[513]

- *Vietnam Veteran-Owned Small Business.* A Vietnam veteran-owned small business is a small business concern where one or more such veterans own at least 51 percent of the business or control at least 51 percent of the stock if a publicly owned business and the management and daily business operations are controlled by one or more such veterans.[514]
- *Service-Disabled Veteran-Owned Small Business.* A service-disabled veteran-owned small business is a small business where one or more service-disabled veterans own at least 51 percent of the business or control at least 51 percent of the stock of a publicly owned business and the management and daily business operations are controlled by one or more service-disabled veterans or the spouse or permanent caregiver of a seriously disabled veteran.[515]

As noted above, a vendor is permitted to rely *in good faith* upon the written size representation of its subcontractors (except for SDBs, which must be certified by the SBA).[516]

2. The Subcontracting Plan

Schedule vendors that are not small businesses must prepare an annual subcontracting plan.[517] In general terms, the subcontracting plan sets forth the vendor's subcontracting goals for the forthcoming contract year, expressed in dollars and as a percentage of total planned subcontracting dollars. Along with the statement of subcontracting goals, the vendor also must describe its plan to meet its goals. Additionally, the vendor must identify a subcontracting plan administrator. The duties of the administrator are regulatorily prescribed to ensure that vendors provide maximum practicable subcontracting opportunities to small businesses.

Subcontracting plans can be either "contract specific" or "commercial." Most MAS vendors employ commercial plans, which shall relate to the offeror's planned subcontracting generally, for both commercial and Government business, rather than solely to the Government contract.[518]

A commercial plan covers the vendor's fiscal year and "applies to the entire production of commercial items sold by either the entire company or a portion thereof (*e.g.*, division, plant, or product line)."[519] FAR 52.219-9(g) provides that commercial plans are the "preferred type of subcontracting plan for contractors furnishing commercial items."

The elements of a subcontracting plan are set forth in detail at FAR 19.704 (and the implementing clause at FAR 52.219-9). A few of these elements, however, are worthy of additional discussion here.

3. Subcontracting Goals

The heart of a subcontracting plan is a vendor's subcontracting goals. Goals are expressed as a percentage of total planned subcontracting dollars for each class of small business concerns. For example, a vendor may set its subcontracting goals for women-owned small business concerns at 5 percent. This means that the vendor expects—and will make good faith efforts to ensure—that 5 percent of its total subcontracting dollars are attributable to women-owned small businesses.

Selecting reasonable goals is essential for a number of reasons. Goals that are too low likely will be rejected by GSA, thereby delaying the execution of a Schedule contract. Goals that are too high, on the other hand, can cause the vendor problems down the road if it turns out that the vendor cannot meet the goals. (Additionally, goals that are too high can be counterproductive from a Government policy perspective as well, in that they could foster a "we'll never make it so why try" attitude.)[520] Thus, vendors must undertake good faith efforts to identify subcontracting goals that are aggressive, yet attainable. In short, a vendor's goals should be reasonable and realistic.

Perhaps the most difficult task in identifying subcontracting goals is determining what constitutes a subcontract for purposes of the subcontracting plan. Unfortunately, the FAR and GSAM do not provide adequate guidance on this topic. The FAR defines a subcontract as follows:

> "Subcontract" means any agreement (other than one involving an employer-employee relationship) entered into by a Government prime contractor or subcontractor calling for supplies and/or services required for performance of the contract, contract modification, or subcontract.[521]

This definition clearly provides *some* useful information.

- It makes clear that the salaries a vendor pays to its employees do not constitute subcontract dollars for subcontracting reporting purposes.
- It makes clear that, to constitute a subcontract, the agreement must call for "supplies and/or services required for performance of the contract."
- It makes clear—at least when read in conjunction with the "general instructions" of the standard form on which a vendor reports its use of subcontractors—that only subcontracts involving domestic performance are encompassed by the definition.[522]

In practice, however, this element of the definition raises as many questions as it answers. What is a "supply and/or service?" What does it mean to be "required for performance of the contract?"[523] Are payments to a vendor's outside janitorial company subcontracts? Are payments to a vendor's insurance company or HMO subcontracts? What about payments to the catering company that runs the in-house cafeteria?

Unfortunately, neither the definition of "subcontract" nor the text of the FAR or GSAR answers these questions.[524]

In the absence of clear regulatory guidance, vendors typically look to the experiences of other vendors (and frequent telephone conversations with GSA and/or the SBA). In this context, the following items reflect the experience of some vendors in some situations. Each item is based upon the actual experience of a MAS vendor or the advice of GSA and/or SBA personnel. It is essential to keep in mind, however, the following: The information below is *not* confirmed by regulation or case law. Rather, it is based upon experience. Different contracting officers may very well give different guidance on these issues.

- *OEM Purchases*. The Small Business Administration and GSA will likely view products purchased for resale as falling within the meaning of "subcontract."
- *Industry Association Dues*. Dues paid to chambers of commerce may *not* fall within the meaning of "subcontract."
- *Donations to Charitable Organizations*. Donations typically do *not* fall within the meaning of "subcontract."
- *Employee Incentive Awards*. Such awards probably do *not* fall within the meaning of "subcontract" because such awards stem from agreements involving an employer-employee relationship.[525]
- *Company Airplane Flight Crew Costs*. Such payments may constitute payments for "services" within the meaning of the term "subcontract."
- *HMO Costs*. HMO costs typically do not fall within the meaning of "subcontract" because such awards stem from agreements involving an employer-employee relationship.[526]
- *Facilities Rent Payments*. Such payments probably constitute payments for "services" within the meaning of the term "subcontract."
- *Telephone Bills*. Payments made to telephone companies may *not* fall within the meaning of "subcontract."

- *Intra-Company Purchases*. Such purchases do not constitute subcontracts for purposes of the vendor's subcontracting plan.[527]

Because even the foregoing items are subject to differing interpretations, the keys to ensuring compliance with MAS subcontracting requirements are (1) full disclosure, (2) reasonableness, and (3) consistency. With respect to full disclosure, out of an abundance of caution, a vendor would be well advised to specify in its subcontracting plan the categories of payments that are not included in the reported figures.[528] For example, if a certain vendor were not going to include utilities contracts in its subcontracting calculations, then that vendor should disclose that fact in its subcontracting plan. Such a disclosure could be included in Section III of the subcontracting plan (entitled "Goals"). With respect to consistency, vendors should ensure that their annual subcontracting reports reflect the same categories of payments used to calculate the goals identified in the annual subcontracting plan.

While a failure to achieve subcontracting goals, in itself, will not bring about contractual or regulatory penalties, the failure to undertake good faith efforts to meet those goals can. As described below, a failure to exercise good faith efforts to meet subcontracting goals (or, sometimes, even the perception of such a failure) can lead to liquidated damages, contract termination, and even suspension from Government contracting. The most effective way to avoid such consequences is to adhere assiduously to the terms of the subcontracting plan. While such adherence will not guarantee a finding of good faith by GSA should the vendor's subcontracting efforts ever come into question, it will provide strong evidence of good faith.

4. Flow Downs

FAR 52.219-9 encompasses several requirements relating to the relationship between a MAS vendor and its subcontractors. These requirements include the following:

- Vendors must "assure" GSA that they will include FAR 52.219-8 (Utilization of Small Business Concerns) "in all subcontracts that offer further subcontracting opportunities . . . ."[529]
- Vendors must "assure" GSA that they will "require all subcontractors (except small business concerns) that receive subcontracts in excess of $500,000 ($1,000,000 for construction of any public facility) to adopt a subcontracting plan that complies with the requirements of this clause."[530]
- Vendors must "assure" GSA that their subcontractors have agreed to submit Standard Form ("SF") 294s and/ or SF 295s.[531]

Obviously, these "flow-down" requirements can be quite burdensome. Many subcontractors vehemently resist the inclusion of any such Government regulations in their subcontracts. From their perspective, they have entered into a standard commercial contract and should not be weighed down with Government-unique terms and conditions—no matter how noble the goal.

Schedule vendors have a strong argument, as explained in Chapter XII, that the foregoing subcontracting flow-down requirements are *inapplicable* to commercial item contracts. The argument stems from FAR 52.212-5, which explicitly limits the clauses that a commercial item contractor must flow down to its subcontractors.[532] Many GSA contracting officers, however, take the position that Schedule vendors must comply with the flow downs notwithstanding the terms of FAR 52.212-5.[533]

In October 2000, the clause at FAR 52.219-8 (Utilization of Small Business Concerns) was added to the list of clauses that a vendor may be required to flow-down to its subcontractors. FAR 52.219-9, however—the clause that actually requires subcontractors to develop Subcontracting Plans of their own— still is not among the prescribed flow-down clauses. Thus, the argument mentioned above has not been diminished. Against the background of GSA's contrary view, however, Schedule vendors should make sure that they (1) determine whether FAR 52.212-5 is incorporated into their Schedule contracts and (2) ascertain the contracting officer's position regarding the applicability of the clause's flow-down requirements.

5. Compliance Generally

While developing an acceptable (and attainable) subcontracting plan can be a difficult task, the vendor's real work begins subsequent to GSA's acceptance of the plan. It is at that point that the vendor must undertake *good faith efforts* to satisfy the requirements incorporated into the plan. The following activities, derived from GSA's regulations and the experience of a number of Schedule vendors, have proved over time to be essential elements in any subcontracting plan compliance policy.[534]

- *Develop Policies and Procedures*. Vendors should draft and implement policies and procedures specifically designed to assure the success of their subcontracting plans. Such policies and procedures should be made accessible to all individuals within the company who have responsibilities relating to subcontracting.
- *Ensure that the Creation of the Subcontracting Plan is a Group Effort*. Because compliance is a product of a number of different business units (*e.g.*, manufacturing, contract administration, procurement, etc.), it is essential that those same groups participate in the creation of the plan.
- *Keep Files Organized*. A vendor frequently finds itself in noncompliance simply because certain elements of the company never knew what compliance entailed. Maintaining the subcontracting plan in an organized and readily accessible manner is one means toward solving this sort of noncompliance.
- *Survey Subcontractors as to their Size Status*. Vendors must adopt a reasonable means of ascertaining the size of their subcontractors. While GSA's regulations do not require

that such information be updated annually, an annual update procedure likely will enhance a vendor's efforts to comply with the subcontracting provisions of the MAS contract.

- *Maintain a Database and Records.* The subcontracting regulations obligate vendors to maintain records reflecting the procedures it has adopted to comply with the subcontracting plan and the other subcontracting requirements of the MAS contract. These records must include *at least* the following:

    - Source lists, guides, and other data that identify small businesses;
    - Organizations contacted in an attempt to identify small businesses;
    - Specific records on each subcontract solicitation resulting in an award of more than $100,000 (for example, for each subcontract awarded in excess of $100,000, the subcontracting file must include a record indicating whether each of the small business categories were solicited and, if not, why);[535]
    - Records of outreach efforts to trade associations, business development organizations, and trade fairs; and
    - Records of internal guidance and encouragement to a vendor's buyers through workshops, seminars, training, evaluations, and performance monitoring.[536]

- *Search Diligently for Qualified Small Businesses.* This requirement lies at the heart of GSA's subcontracting requirements. To satisfy their obligations in this regard, MAS vendors should, among other things, undertake the following activities:

    - Review publications relating to small businesses such as those published by the SBA;

- Contact the SBA's local and national associations and councils for assistance in identifying potential small business subcontractors;
- Participate in trade fairs and industry meetings;
- Advertise in industry and local publications;
- Perform a periodic historical analysis of their subcontracting patterns to assess the use of small businesses; and
- Join local and national associations that promote the use of small business subcontractors.

- *Submit All Necessary Forms to GSA.* Most vendors' primary obligation in this regard is to submit SF 294s and SF 295s to GSA on an annual basis. These forms inform GSA whether the vendor has reached the subcontracting goals identified in its subcontracting plan.
- *Conduct Training.* Buyers and other individuals having a role in making or administering purchasing decisions should receive periodic training relating to MAS subcontracting obligations. This training not only should cover the requirements of the MAS contract and the vendor's subcontracting plan but also should focus on ways in which the vendor can increase to the maximum practicable extent the subcontracting opportunities available to small businesses.
- *Support Activities that Help Buyers to Find Small Businesses.* Closely related to a vendor's obligation to train its buyers, vendors also must support activities that assist buyers in identifying and retaining small businesses. In this context, a vendor might consider sending buyers to minority trade fairs, subscribing to minority contractor publications, and increasing the vendor's ties with minority trade associations.
- *Conduct Outreach Efforts.* Outreach efforts comprise those activities undertaken by the vendor to promote the use of small businesses to the maximum practicable extent.

Such efforts may include offering to relax deadlines at non-critical times for small businesses or providing managerial, technical, quality control, and production assistance to small businesses where appropriate.

While these activities will not guarantee compliance with the subcontracting terms and conditions of a MAS contract, they will place a vendor intent on satisfying those terms and conditions on the path toward compliance.

6. Submission Of Standard Form 294 Or Standard Form 295

MAS vendors typically report their subcontracting activity on a federal form known as an SF (for Standard Form) 295.[537] The SF 295 typically is submitted annually to GSA and the SBA and must include all subcontracts—as defined above—awarded under the subcontracting plan. Among other things, the SF 295 requires vendors to report (in whole dollars and percentages), for each fiscal year ending September 30, their "cumulative fiscal year subcontract awards" to each category of small business concerns. The SF 295 must be filed by October 30. While the Office of Management and Budget estimates the "public reporting burden" for these forms to be "12.9 hours per response," most vendors devote a significantly greater number of hours to ensuring comprehensive and accurate reporting.

A vendor must calculate the figures reported on its SF 295s on the same basis as that used to calculate the figures included in its subcontracting plan. In other words, a vendor must ensure that, when GSA compares the SF 295 to the subcontracting plan, it is not comparing "apples to oranges." For example, if the vendor includes the cost of temporary secretarial support in its subcontracting goals then that cost also should be included in its subcontracting reports. Likewise, if a vendor does not include advertising costs in its goals, then those costs should not be included in its reports. Indeed, this is a critical element of contract compliance.

In addition to the standard SF 295s, vendors now also must submit specially detailed information regarding their use of small disadvantaged subcontractors. Specifically, in conjunction with all end-of-fiscal-year subcontracting reports, vendors must

> include a breakout, in the Contractor's format, of subcontract awards, in whole dollars, to small disadvantaged business concerns by North American Industry Classification System (NAICS) Industry Subsector. For a commercial plan, the Contractor may obtain from each of its subcontractors a predominant NAICS Industry Subsector and report all awards to that subcontractor under its predominant NAICS Industry Subsector.[538]

Consequently, vendors are well advised to add a question regarding NAICS Industry Subsector to their Vendor Survey Forms.

7. Noncompliance

As with most aspects of the MAS Program, a failure to comply with the subcontracting obligations can subject a vendor to significant legal exposure. Not only may such a failure be a violation itself, but it also may evidence a lack of good faith in meeting subcontracting goals. And in the context of the Schedule's subcontracting requirements, lack of good faith can bring with it significant penalties. The FAR defines a "failure to make a good faith effort" as a

> willful or intentional failure to perform in accordance with the requirements of the subcontracting plan, or willful or intentional action to frustrate the plan.[539]

The FAR directs that the contracting officer consider the following facts as "indicators" of a failure to make a good faith effort:

- Failure to attempt to identify, contact, solicit, or consider for award any of the small business categories;
- Failure to designate and maintain a company official to administer the subcontracting program and monitor and enforce compliance with the plan;
- Failure to submit the SF 294 or SF 295 in accordance with the instructions on the forms or as provided in agency regulations;
- Failure to maintain records or otherwise demonstrate procedures adopted to comply with the plan; or
- Adoption of company policies or procedures that have as their objectives the frustration of the objectives of the plan.[540]

The following are the potential consequences of a Government finding that a vendor failed to undertake a good faith effort to provide small businesses with maximum practicable subcontracting opportunities. Some of these consequences may arise even as a result of *perceived* noncompliance.

- *Liquidated Damages.* MAS contracts contain a Subcontracting Plan Liquidated Damages Clause,[541] described in greater detail below. The clause subjects vendors to prescribed financial liabilities if the contracting officer determines that the vendor failed to make *good faith efforts* to meets its subcontracting goals. These liquidated damages will be assessed in an amount equal to the actual dollar amount by which the vendor failed to achieve each subcontracting goal.
- *Breach of Contract.* Since a vendor's subcontracting obligations stem from the terms and conditions of the MAS contract itself, GSA could consider a failure to comply with those obligations to be a breach of contract.[542] Among other consequences, such a breach could prompt

GSA to terminate the vendor's MAS contract. Likewise, it could prompt GSA to refuse to renew or renegotiate a vendor contract in future years.

- *Qui Tam Action*. MAS vendors have found themselves the subjects of lawsuits filed by *qui tam* plaintiffs alleging violations of the False Claims Act as a result of an alleged failure to comply with the subcontracting provisions of the MAS contract.

- *Loss of Good Will*. A vendor's failure to undertake good faith effort to comply with the MAS subcontracting provisions can lead to the loss of good will with GSA and its Schedule customers.

- *Suspension or Debarment*. While unlikely in the absence of egregious circumstances, a failure to comply with the subcontracting terms and conditions of the MAS contract could result in a vendor's suspension or debarment (*i.e.*, the vendor's elimination) from all Government contracting. Additionally, because many states base their debarment decisions on the decisions of the Federal Government, a federal suspension or debarment also could prompt any number of states to take similar action.

The foregoing potential adverse actions make clear that the MAS subcontracting requirements are important elements of contract compliance.

8. Liquidated Damages

As discussed briefly above, FAR 19.705-7 authorizes the contracting officer to impose liquidated damages where a vendor has failed to undertake good faith efforts to comply with its subcontracting plan. Liquidated damages, however, do *not* come into play merely upon a vendor's failure to meet its subcontracting goals. Indeed, pursuant to the explicit terms of the applicable regulations, liquidated damages cannot be imposed unless and until a variety of judgments, affirmative decisions, and actions occur. Until the contracting officer has progressed through each of the steps specified in the regulations and made a final determination, the "obligation" to pay liquidated damages is purely "inchoate," or potential.[543]

Specifically, FAR 19.705-7 establishes a multi-step process that must be undertaken prior to the possible imposition of liquidated damages by a contracting officer. This multi-step process illustrates well the inchoate nature of liquidated damages. The process is as follows:

- **Step One:** "If . . . at the close of the fiscal year for which the [subcontracting] plan is applicable, a contractor has failed to meet its subcontracting goals, the contracting officer shall review all available information for an indication that the contractor has not made a good faith effort to comply with the plan."[544]

- **Step Two:** "If the contracting officer decides . . . that the contractor failed to make a good faith effort to comply with its subcontracting plan, the contracting officer shall give the contractor written notice specifying the failure, advising the contractor of the possibility that the contractor may have to pay to the Government liquidated damages, and providing a period of 15 working days . . . within which to respond."[545]

- **Step Three:** "If, after consideration of all the pertinent data, the contracting officer finds that the contractor failed to make a good faith effort to comply with its subcontracting plan, the contracting officer shall issue a final decision to the contractor to that effect and require the payment of liquidated damages in an amount stated."[546]

- **Step Four:** "The contracting officer's final decision shall state that the contractor has the right to appeal under the clause in the contract entitled Disputes."[547]

Liquidated damages cannot be imposed before the foregoing actions take place.

Liquidated damages are calculated by deriving the actual dollar amount by which the vendor failed to achieve its subcontracting goals.[548] The contracting officer will undertake this calculation for each subcontracting category for which the goals were not achieved. Liquidated damages for vendors subject to a commercial subcontracting plan are calculated on a pro rata basis. In other words, the contracting officer will assess liquidated damages only against that portion of subcontracting dollars that flow from Government contracts. Whether a contract-specific plan or a commercial plan, the regulations make clear that "[l]iquidated damages shall be in addition to any other remedies that the Government may have."[549]

* * *

Many within GSA and SBA readily acknowledge the lack of subcontracting guidance available to vendors. Many further acknowledge that the regulations that do exist are complicated and confusing. Against this background, there has been discussion within the Government of opening a FAR case file in an effort to clarify and explicate the small business subcontractor reporting regulations. Should such a case be initiated, however, there is no assurance that the FAR Council will act with dispatch. In the face of such uncertainty, vendors likely will continue to find themselves in awkward situations, not knowing what full compliance requires, yet being subject to Government audits, whistleblower suits, and the host of liabilities they can occasion. To mitigate at least some of this risk, vendors should not hesitate to contact GSA or SBA (or their company's attorneys) whenever questions arise.

G. *Small Business Set-Asides*

GSA has set aside certain elements of certain GSA Schedules exclusively for small businesses.[550] Special Item Number 66-614 on Schedule 66 II Q (Geophysical, Environmental Analysis

Equipment and Services) is such an example. This means that only vendors that qualify as "small businesses" pursuant to the applicable regulations (*see* Section F of this chapter) may offer such products to the Government through the MAS Program.

Additionally, the FAR advises ordering activities that they "may consider socio-economic status when identifying contractor(s) for consideration or competition for award of an order or BPA," and instructs that they "should consider, if available, at least one small business, veteran-owned small business, service disabled veteran-owned small business, HUBZone small business, women-owned small business, or small disadvantaged business."[551] To this end, many procuring agencies will establish a certain portion of its orders to be available to small businesses only.[552] In situations where two or more items are available at the same delivered price and the order exceeds the micro-purchase threshold, such agencies should give preference to the small business.[553]

Chapter IX discusses recent changes to GSA's and SBA's certification requirements regarding a vendor's business size.

While GSA and SBA both have worked to increase small business participation in the MAS Program over the years, the two agencies have not always seen eye to eye regarding the means toward that end. For example, GSA has resisted SBA's efforts to have more MAS contracts set aside for small businesses. In 1997, when GSA announced its intention to consolidate five information technology Schedules into a single Schedule, SBA vehemently opposed the idea as harmful to small businesses.[554] SBA's objection delayed the information technology solicitation for many months.[555] Interestingly, many small businesses favored GSA's proposed consolidation and viewed the SBA's efforts as a hindrance.[556] In the end, however, GSA and SBA reached an accommodation. GSA agreed to increase its efforts supporting small businesses by "(1) encouraging agencies to use the broad array of small businesses that hold MAS contracts and (2) enhancing GSA efforts to provide significant subcontracting opportunities to small businesses that do not wish to offer directly to the MAS Program."[557] SBA dropped its objections to the consolidation.

Advice From The Trenches

(Murray Schooner, Unisys Corporation)

Webster's Dictionary defines a mentor as a trusted counselor or guide, a tutor or a coach. As Director of Unisys Corporation's Corporate Supplier Diversity Program, I receive many calls from small, minority, and women-owned suppliers asking if Unisys has a mentoring program and whether I would be their mentor. In my particular case, I typically answer "yes." I am a mentor to all qualified disadvantaged subcontractors that follow my advice—advice that is based on twenty-two years of experience. Moreover, Unisys maintains a supplier diversity web site that provides extensive assistance to disadvantaged suppliers.

Many subcontractors, however, are looking for more than an informal mentor. Rather, they are looking to participate in a formal "mentor-protégé" program with an established prime contractor that will give them a contract and provide them with financial, managerial, and technical assistance. Unisys, like many other large Government contractors, participates in a number of such programs. After a short discussion of the background of mentor-protégé programs generally, I provide a brief explanation of the most popular of these programs.

Public Law No. 95-507, enacted in 1978, basically required large firms doing business with the Federal Government to provide subcontracting opportunities to socially and economically disadvantaged businesses. The ten years that followed the passage of Public Law No. 95-507, however, saw very little progress on the part of the DOD and large prime contractors.

About twelve years later, realizing that there existed too few prime contractors possessing the technical expertise necessary to meet DOD and industry demands, Senator Sam Nunn set about to create a formal program that would foster the inclusion of disadvantaged business subcontractors in Government contracts. He sought out and received the advice of industry and Government groups and soon came to realize that, while industry possessed the necessary expertise to assist disadvantaged companies, it would take some "incentivizing" on the Government's part to see that such expertise was put to good use. The result of this realization was the DOD Pilot Mentor-Protégé Program, developed with the personal cooperation of then-Secretary of Defense William Perry.

The DOD Pilot Mentor-Protégé Program was established to encourage major DOD contractors to act as mentors to disadvantaged businesses. The "encouragement" comes in the form of, among other things, reimbursement of the costs of the assistance furnished by the mentor to the protégé. The bottom-line goal of the program is to increase the participation of disadvantaged businesses in Government contracts. There are currently over 120 firms participating in DOD's program, with nearly 70 mentors. DOD protégé firms represent a wide range of industries, including information technology, manufacturing, telecommunications, engineering services, environmental remediation, and health care services.

Following the creation of DOD's mentor-protégé program, other federal agencies have followed suit and created similar programs of their own. Each program is unique, however. The National Aeronautics and Space Administration ("NASA"), for example, administers the NASA Mentor-Protégé Program. While NASA's mentors provide technical, managerial, and financial assistance similar to DOD's mentors, NASA's focus is on the provision of "high-tech" expertise. Unlike DOD's program, which encourages mentor participation through cost reimbursability, NASA encourages mentors through the use of "award fee" incentives. Still other agencies have adopted programs that encourage mentors with credit toward subcontracting goals or additional evaluation points toward the award of new contracts.

The Federal Aviation Administration ("FAA") administers yet another popular mentor-protégé program. Currently comprised of 26 mentor firms, the FAA's program is designed to motivate and encourage firms to (i) assist small, socially and economically disadvantaged businesses, historically Black colleges and universities, minority institutions, and women-owned small businesses enhance their capabilities to perform FAA prime contracts and subcontracts; (ii) foster the establishment of long-term business relationships between these entities and mentor firms; and (iii) increase the overall number of these entities that receive FAA prime contract and subcontract awards. The FAA program—like some other mentor-protégé programs—encourages mentors to provide disadvantaged subcontractors facility and equipment use on a rent-free basis and personnel temporarily assigned to the protégé firm.

Yet another successful mentor-protégé program is the Treasury Department's Success Partnership Program, which is designed to motivate and encourage firms to assist small businesses, including HUBZone small businesses. Additionally, the program was created to improve the quality of Treasury's contracts and subcontracts, foster the establishment of long-term business relationships between contractors and the agency, and increase the overall number of disadvantaged businesses that receive Treasury contracts and subcontracts. Treasury implemented its program in three "phases," the final phase of which became effective in October 2000 and opened the program to HUBZone subcontractors. Currently, Treasury has approximately 35 agreements with 5 of its bureaus. Half of the Treasury partnerships are with the Internal Revenue Service.

While by no means the end of the list, the last program that I will mention is the SBA's Mentor-Protégé Program, which was created to encourage approved mentors to provide various forms of assistance to eligible protégé participants, to enhance the capabilities of protégé firms, and to improve the ability of protégé firms to compete successfully for federal contracts. The SBA has about 116 mentor-protégé agreements covering a wide variety of industries, including maintenance, construction, consulting services, and many more.

* * *

While all mentor-protégé programs have many similarities, they all have differences as well. On the similarity side, all encompass some sort of application process and performance reporting process. On the difference side, each program relies upon a slightly different form of "encouragement" to secure the participation of mentor firms. The Internet provides a treasure trove of information regarding the specifics of each program. Some useful sites in this regard include *http://www.nasa.gov*, *http://www.faa.gov*, *http://www.acq.osd.mil*, *http://www.treas.gov*, *http://www.sba.gov*, *http://www.disa.mil*, and *http://www.sadbu.com*.

Notes:

[454] FAR 22.804-1.

[455] FAR 22.805; FAR 52.222-24.

[456] FAR 52.222-26(b)(3) and (4).

[457] FAR 22.809; FAR 52.222-26(b)(9).

[458] FAR 22.809(b) and (c).

[459] FAR 22.809(d).

[460] FAR 22.1407.

[461] FAR 52.222-35(c). Listing employment openings with the Department of Labor's America's Job Bank satisfies this requirement.

[462] FAR 52.222-35(a).

[463] FAR 52.222-37.

[464] FAR 22.1307.

[465] *See* Federal Energy Management Program Overview, *available at* http://www.eren.doe.gov/femp/aboutfemp/fempoverview.html.

[466] Exec. Order No. 13123, 64 Fed. Reg. 30,851 (June 8, 1999). "Energy Star" refers to products that must meet Governmentally-prescribed energy efficient standards. Energy Star products should be selected when such selection is life-cycle cost effective. The

Federal Energy Management Program ("FEMP") is part of the U.S. Department of Energy and helps agencies reduce their costs, increase energy efficiency, use renewable energy, and conserve water.

467 *Id.* at 30,854.

468 Pub. L. No. 99-506, § 603(a), 100 Stat. 1830 (codified as amended at 29 U.S.C. § 794d).

469 29 U.S.C. § 794d(a)(2); 65 Fed. Reg. 80,500 (Dec. 21, 2000) (codified at 36 C.F.R. pt. 1194); *see also Acquisition of Electronic and Information Technology Under Section 508 of the Rehabilitation Act—Frequently Asked Questions* at A.5, published by GSA, *available at http://www.section508.gov/docs/508QandA.html* [hereinafter "Section 508 FAQ"].

470 29 U.S.C. § 794d(a)(3). On April 25, 2001, the Civilian Agency Acquisition Council and the Defense Acquisition Regulations Council issued final amendments to the Federal Acquisition Regulation ("FAR") relating to Section 508. *See* 66 Fed. Reg. 20,894 (Apr. 25, 2001) (codified at 48 C.F.R. pts. 2, 7, 10, 11, 12, and 39).

471 FAR 39.201.

472 *Id.*

473 *See* 36 C.F.R. pt. 1194, *available at http://www.access-board.gov/sec508/508standards.htm.*

474 Section 508 FAQ at B.2.i; 36 C.F.R. § 1194.5.

475 Section 508 FAQ at B.3.i; *see also* 36 C.F.R. § 1194.5.

476 FAR 2.101; *see also* 36 C.F.R. § 1194.4.

477 36 C.F.R. § 1194.4.

478 Section 508 FAQ at B.1.ii.

479 Section 508 does not govern non-Government sales.

480 FAR 39.204(a).

481 Section 508 FAQ at G.2.i.

482 FAR 39.204(b); 36 C.F.R. § 1194.3(a).

483 FAR 39.204(c); 36 C.F.R. § 1194.3(b).

484 Section 508 FAQ at G.4.i.

485 FAR 39.204(d); 36 C.F.R. § 1194.3(f).

486 FAR 39.204(e); 36 C.F.R. § 1194(a).

487 FAR 39.203(c)(1).

[488] Section 508 FAQ at F.1.

[489] 36 C.F.R. § 1194.2(a)(1); Section 508 FAQ at G.10; *see also Dopico v. Goldschmidt*, 687 F.2d 644, 650 (2d Cir. 1982).

[490] *See, e.g.*, 42 U.S.C. § 12182(b)(2)(A)(iii) (Americans with Disabilities Act).

[491] For a detailed discussion of the undue burden exception, *see* James J. McCullough, Jonathan Aronie, & Abram Pafford, *Section 508 Accessibility: The "Undue Burden Exception,"* CONTRACT MANAGEMENT (August 2001). *See also* James J. McCullough, Jonathan Aronie, & Abram Pafford, *The New Section 508 Accessibility Rules: Threshold Compliance Issues for Both Federal Agencies and Contractors*, 75 FED. CONTRACTS REP. 21 (May 22, 2001).

[492] FAR 39.202.

[493] *See* 65 Fed. Reg. 80,500, 80,505-80,506 (Dec. 21, 2000).

[494] *See* 28 C.F.R. § 36.104; *Roberts v. KinderCare Learning Ctrs. Inc.*, 86 F.3d 844, 846 (8th Cir. 1996).

[495] *See Onishea v. Hopper*, 171 F.3d 1289, 1304 (11th Cir. 1999).

[496] 28 C.F.R. pt. 35, App. A at 492 (July 1, 1999 ed.); *Pascuiti v. New York Yankees*, 87 F. Supp. 2d 221, 224 (S.D.N.Y. 1999).

[497] 36 C.F.R. § 1194.41(a).

[498] 29 U.S.C. § 794d(f).

[499] *See* FAR 39.204.

[500] FAR 39.203(b)(1). Exception determinations for IDIQ contracts generally are required at the time of issuance of task or delivery orders.

[501] In *CourtSmart Digital Systems, Inc.*, B-292995.8, Dec. 9, 2004, even though CourtSmart's final quotation was nearly $5 million less than its closest competitor, the SSA awarded the contract to CourtSmart's competitor because the competitor's software was better "rated" under Section 508, although not fully compliant.

[502] FAR 19.702; FAR 52.219-8.

[503] In 2001, the Government implemented a new subcontracting goal requirement for service-disabled veteran-owned small businesses. *See* 66 Fed. Reg. 53,492 (Oct. 22, 2001). Specifically, FAC 2001-01 expanded the small business subcontracting plan requirements at FAR 19.704 and 52.219-9 to include separate subcontracting goal

and reporting requirements for this category of veteran-owned small businesses. This change stems from Section 803 of the Small Business Reauthorization Act of 2000 (Pub. L. No. 106-554).

[504] FAR 19.702.

[505] 15 U.S.C. § 637(d).

[506] FAR 19.702(a)(1).

[507] *See* FAR 19.001.

[508] *Id.*

[509] The industry size standards are published by the SBA on the Internet at *http://www.sba.gov/size/NAICS-cover-page.htm.* The manual is available on the Internet at *http://www.osha.gov/oshstats.* The North American Industry Classification System ("NAICS") classifies and defines activities by industry categories. *See* FAR 19.102(h). The SBA uses the manual as a guide for defining industry standards. There will be assigned to each NAICS a number of employees and/or annual receipts. These numbers represent the maximum numbers for a concern, including its affiliates. To qualify, a business must not exceed these numbers.

[510] *See* FAR 19.001.

[511] *See* FAR 19.001. *See* 13 C.F.R. § 124.104(c)(2) for applicable exclusions.

[512] *See* FAR 19.001.

[513] *See id.*

[514] FAR 2.101.

[515] FAR 2.101. Service-disabled veterans must meet the definition of veteran set forth in 38 U.S.C. § 101(2) and the service-related disability must meet the requirements of 38 U.S.C. § 101(16).

[516] *See* FAR 19.703(b). The FAR requires that Schedule vendors confirm the SDB status of subcontractors by accessing SBA's PRO-NET database or by contacting the SBA directly. *Id.* In contrast, the FAR clause actually incorporated into Schedule contracts provides that "Contractors acting in good faith may rely on written representations by their subcontractors regarding their status as a small business concern, a veteran-owned small business concern, a service-disabled veteran-owned small business concern, a HUBZone small business concern, a small disadvantaged business concern,

or a women-owned small business concern." FAR 52.219-8(d) (emphasis added). GSA's position is that a Schedule vendor must confirm the SDB status of its subcontractors and cannot simply rely on their written representation.

517 FAR 19.702(b) provides that the following entities are not required to submit subcontracting plans: small business concerns, vendors entering into personal service contracts, and vendors entering into contracts that will be performed entirely outside the United States.

518 FAR 52.219-9(g).

519 FAR 52.219-9(b).

520 See Jonathan S. Aronie, "Foolish Inconsisstency," FEDERAL COMPUTER WEEK (April 18, 2005).

521 FAR 19.701.

522 FAR 53.301-295 (Standard Form 295).

523 This question is particularly perplexing when one considers that a commercial subcontracting plan is meant to encompass the entire production of commercial items sold by a vendor.

524 Other questions are left unanswered as well. For example, FAR 52.219-9(d)(6) asks vendors to declare whether indirect costs have been included in establishing subcontracting goals. The directions to the SF 295, however, state that reported amounts "must include both direct awards and an appropriate prorated portion of indirect awards." In light of this particular contradiction, vendors with commercial plans probably are best served by stating that they have included indirect awards in their goals and including such awards in their reports as well.

525 Id.

526 See FAR 52.219-9(b).

527 See General Instruction 8, FAR 53.301-295.

528 Additionally, vendors should include indirect costs in their goals and reports. See FAR 53.301-295, Specific Instructions for Blocks 10a through 15b.

529 FAR 52.219-9(d)(9).

530 Id.

531 FAR 52.219-9(d)(10)(iv).

532 *See* Jonathan S. Aronie, "Small Business Confusion," FEDERAL COMPUTER WEEK (April 14, 2003).

533 Others within GSA and the SBA "unofficially" disagree with this position and read FAR 52.212-5 in precisely the same way expressed in the text above.

534 Obviously, consideration of these activities also is important in setting the vendor's subcontracting goals in the first place.

535 FAR 52.219-9(d)(11)(iii)(A)-(E).

536 Additionally, vendors without a "commercial plan" must maintain "records to support award data submitted by the offeror to the Government, including the name, address, and business size of each subcontractor." FAR 52.219-9(d)(11)(vi).

537 Located at FAR 53.301-295. MAS vendors that do not have an approved "commercial plan" submit the SF 294 on an individual contract-by-contract basis. *See* FAR 53.301-294.

538 FAR 52.219-9(j)(2).

539 FAR 19.701; *see also* FAR 52.219-16(a).

540 FAR 19.705-7(d).

541 FAR 52.219-16. FAR 19.702(c) provides that "a contractor's failure to make a good faith effort to comply with the requirements of the subcontracting plan shall result in the imposition of liquidated damages."

542 FAR 19.702(c) provides that "any contractor or subcontractor failing to comply in good faith with the requirements of the subcontracting plan is in material breach of its contract."

543 "Inchoate" obligations are outside of the scope of the False Claims Act. *See, e.g., United States ex rel. American Textile Mfrs. Inst., Inc. v. Limited, Inc.*, 190 F.3d 729, 738 (6th Cir. 1999) (the False Claims Act does not impose liability for "contingent" obligations to the Government); *United States v. Q Int'l Courier, Inc.*, 131 F.3d 770, 773 (8th Cir. 1997) (stating that, to recover under a reverse false claim, a plaintiff must allege that defendant "had a present duty to pay money or property" to the United States). *Cf. United States v. Pemco Aeroplex, Inc.*, 195 F.3d 1234 (11th Cir. 1999) (allowing a case to proceed under a "reverse" false claims theory of

liability because the defendants allegedly made false statements to avoid an obligation that was not inchoate, but rather was based upon a specific contractual obligation to the Government). *See also* John T. Boese, CIVIL FALSE CLAIMS AND QUI TAM ACTIONS, § 2.01[G] (Aspen Law & Business 2d ed., 2001-2 Supp.).

[544] FAR 19.705-7(c).

[545] *Id.*

[546] FAR 19.705-7(e).

[547] *Id.*

[548] FAR 19.705-7(b).

[549] FAR 19.705-7(g).

[550] *See* FAR 19.501.

[551] FAR 8.405-5 (2004).

[552] *See* GSA Procurement Information Bulletin 98-1 (Jan. 15, 1998). As of Fiscal Year 1998, agencies may include GSA Schedule buys in their goals.

[553] FAR 8.405-5(c) (2004).

[554] *GSA Issues IT Schedule Overruling SBA Objections*, THE GOVERNMENT CONTRACTOR, Vol. 40. No. 12, ¶ 140, at 5 (Mar. 25, 1998).

[555] *Id.*

[556] *See* Paul Caggiano, *Small Business Administration gets it wrong on GSA schedules*, FEDERAL COMPUTER WEEK, at 25 (Mar. 23, 1998).

[557] *See* THE GOVERNMENT CONTRACTOR, *supra* note 506.

XIV.

TERMS AND CONDITIONS

"A verbal agreement isn't worth the paper it's written on."

-Samuel Goldwyn

A contract has been defined by one source as "an agreement, enforceable by law, between two or more competent parties, to do or not to do something not prohibited by law, for a legal consideration."[558] The things that the parties must "do or not do" and the manner in which they must be done (or not done) are encompassed by the contract's "terms and conditions." Indeed, a contract is little more than its terms and conditions.

Historically, Government contracts were filled to the brim with unique and complex terms and conditions that one never would find in a commercial item contract. With the passage of the Federal Acquisition Streamlining Act of 1994,[559] however, the number of such clauses has been reduced. And, while GSA claims that MAS contracts incorporate only those clauses required by law or clauses found to be "consistent with customary commercial practice,"[560] most vendors will agree that Government contracts, including MAS contracts, are more burdensome and more risky than commercial contracts.

The terms and conditions applicable to MAS contracts come from a variety of sources. Some flow directly from statutes, such as the Trade Agreements Act; some are made applicable by the incorporation of a FAR provision, such as the rules relating to subcontracting plans; and some come from GSA's own agency supplement to the FAR, such as the Price Reductions Clause. Still other terms and conditions have been incorporated into MAS contracts by the Federal Supply Service ("FSS") and do not appear in the FAR or the GSAM. Regardless of the source, however, vendors must comply with all terms and conditions. Noncompliance can lead to stiff penalties.

This chapter reviews several common terms and conditions that frequently cause problems for Schedule vendors. This chapter does *not* discuss the entire panoply of terms and conditions relating to the MAS Program. Some clauses—the Price Adjustment Clause, for example—are discussed elsewhere in this book. Other clauses are self-explanatory and are not addressed in this book at all. Whether a given clause is or is not in this book, however, vendors must keep in mind that, to some extent, terms and conditions vary from contract to contract. Frequently, they also vary from the language used in the FAR due to a tailored clause or to a deviation. Thus, no book should be used as a substitute for reading firsthand the explicit language of the contract itself.

A. *The Industrial Funding Fee*

In 1995, looking for an avenue through which to turn the MAS Program into a self-supporting venture, GSA implemented an "industrial funding fee" ("IFF") designed to recoup the costs associated with administering the MAS Program from the agencies that purchase supplies and services through the Program.[561] To facilitate this result, all Schedule vendors must embed within their published Schedule prices a ¾ percent (until 2003, 1%)

fee that the vendor then collects from the ordering offices and refunds to GSA on a quarterly basis.[562] Think of it as a legal kickback to GSA. GSA monitors compliance through special reviews and audits designed to ensure that the vendor is, in fact, rebating ¾ percent of its total quarterly Schedule sales.

While the IFF is supposed to be paid by the ordering agency and simply collected and remitted by the Schedule vendor, some contracting officers attempt to force the vendor to "absorb" the IFF (*i.e.*, pay the IFF itself) in order to obtain a contract award. This is inappropriate. The Coalition for Government Procurement, the primary industry association for Schedule vendors, raised this precise issue with GSA in June 2003.[563] In response, GSA made clear that it is GSA's intention that "the IFF cost be borne by the customer and merely collected and remitted by the schedule contractors."[564] Vendors should not hesitate to remind their contracting officers of this issue if necessary.

From a customer's viewpoint, the IFF is invisible. Schedule purchasers simply order from a vendor's Schedule price list and pay the advertised price that already incorporates the IFF. At the end of each quarter, the vendor tallies its total Schedule sales, submits an electronic report to GSA, writes a check for ¾ percent of the total, and transmits it to GSA.[565] A vendor is required to submit an IFF payment only for supplies and services that are purchased through the MAS Program.[566] Many vendors end up overpaying the IFF through a failure to properly segregate Schedule sales from other Government sales, such as open market purchases.[567]

Many vendors also end up overpaying the IFF because GSA Industrial Operations Analysts ("IOAs"), the GSA personnel charged with reviewing contractor compliance with the IFF reporting and payment provisions of the MAS Contract, often take an over-zealous view of what constitutes a Schedule sale.

Pursuant to the terms of the applicable regulation, a contractor's IFF payment is calculated on the value of sales "under [the Schedule] contract."[568] Obviously, a sale made under a different contract is not made under the Schedule contract.

Federal purchasers, however, do not always clearly identify the contract under which they are purchasing. Indeed, sometimes a purchaser does not know under what contract he or she is purchasing. Where an order does not clearly identify the relevant contract number, the IOAs will look to the "totality of the circumstances" surrounding the purchase.[569] In practice, this often means that, when an IOA identifies a Schedule product or service being sold to the federal Government, he or she will presume that the sale is a Schedule sale unless there exists affirmative contrary evidence. GSA does not view the absence of a Schedule contract number on an order as evidence that a purchase is not a Schedule purchase.[570] Regardless of the fairness of this view, it is a view supported by some case law.[571]

The same issue also may arise in the context of open market purchases. Since an open market sale, by definition, is not a Schedule sale,[572] GSA should not require the inclusion of or payment of the IFF in such a situation. Some within GSA, however, still espouse a contrary view from time to time.[573]

In its generally excellent publication entitled "The Steps to Success—How to Be a Successful Contractor," GSA sets forth seven "common indicators" that demonstrate when "a sale is a MAS sale." Unfortunately, the publication states that a sale is a Schedule sale when "[a]ny one or more" of these "indicators" are present. This is incorrect. While the indicators may form a part of the picture regarding the nature of a given sale, most of them do not alone qualify a sale as a Schedule sale. For example, the publication states that a sale is a MAS sale when "the customer made contact with you through GSA Advantage! or e-Buy," when the "product or service is on your GSA contract," when "pricing is at or below the schedule price," and when "the customer pays with the government purchase card."[574] In fact, none of these "indicators" necessarily qualifies a sale as a MAS sale.

They may be sufficient, however, to raise a question regarding the nature of the sale. And since, as noted above, GSA will presume a sale to be a MAS sale in the absence of contrary evidence, any of the factors may be sufficient to prompt an IOA to take a position regarding the nature of a sale regardless of its correctness.

Against this background, vendors are well advised to take steps to ensure that they clearly distinguish between Schedule and non-Schedule sales. Such steps might involve the following:

- Instructing federal sales representatives to ask purchasers directly whether they are buying under the vendor's Schedule contract, and recording the response on the proposal and invoice.
- Referencing the appropriate contract number, if available, on the purchase order and invoice. If unavailable, vendors should clearly identify whether the purchase is a Schedule purchase or not.
- Explicitly identifying open market items on official GSA price lists and making clear that the price of such items does not include the IFF, if that is the case.
- Maintaining clear and complete records regarding all federal sales and distinguishing between Schedule and non-Schedule sales. Embedding a Schedule/Non-Schedule field in the internal order processing database will go a long way in this regard.
- Discussing the issue with the contracting officer and the IOA to ensure that all parties are operating with the same understanding of the applicable rules.

While these steps will not necessarily move GSA from its sometimes overly broad interpretation of the IFF clause, it will put contractors on more solid ground to defend themselves, should the need arise, as GSA works to promote greater consistency within the ranks of its IOAs.[575]

Vendors are obligated to make their IFF payments within thirty days of the end of each contract reporting period.[576] Payment must be made in U.S. dollars. Vendors may make a single payment even if they offer multiple Special Item Numbers ("SINs") on Schedule. Vendors can make payment by check or electronically, through GSA's 72A Quarterly Reporting System web site.[577] All payments must be directed to the GSA. To ensure proper credit, vendors must identify the payment as an IFF payment and must include their contract number(s), report amount(s), and reporting period(s) on the check or electronic payment.

If a vendor does not pay the full IFF amount due within thirty calendar days after the end of the reporting period, the unpaid portion constitutes a "contract debt" to the United States Government under the terms of FAR 32.6, which provides the policies and procedures for ascertaining and collecting contract debts and charging interest on the debts owed to the Government. FAR 32.6, in relation to the Industrial Funding Fee Clause, provides notification procedures for debts and allows interest to accrue against any unpaid debt. Any debts remaining unpaid thirty days after demand will be subject to interest charges at a rate established by the Secretary of the Treasury under Public Law No. 92-41. As such, the Government may exercise all rights afforded it under the Debt Collection Act of 1982, including withholding or setting off payments and interest on the debt.[578] Moreover, if a vendor fails to pay the IFF in a timely manner, the Government may terminate or cancel the contract.[579] An intentional or reckless underpayment of an IFF can constitute a violation of the False Claims Act[580] and could lead to significant financial penalties, suspension, debarment, or some combination thereof.

B. *The Contractor's Report Of Sales Clause*

To facilitate a vendor's IFF payment and to monitor a vendor's compliance with the IFF requirements, MAS contracts incorporate the Industrial Funding Fee and Sales Reporting Clause that requires vendors to report the "quarterly dollar value" of all sales "under this contract" by calendar quarter.[581] The use of the language "under this contract" is important because it states that only Schedule sales come within the scope of the provision. In other words, non-Schedule sales, or open market sales, need not be reported to GSA.

In accordance with this clause, vendors must record the total value of all Schedule sales, rounded to the nearest whole dollar, of the preceding calendar quarter. Vendors then submit this information to GSA electronically on a form known as a 72A.[582] The reporting periods are January-March, April-June, July-September, and October-December. Figures must be separated by SIN and must be shown in U.S. dollars.[583] (Thus, when the vendor is paid in foreign currency, it must convert the payment into U.S. dollars, using the "Treasury Reporting Rates of Exchange" in effect on the last day of the calendar quarter, before reporting the revenue on its sales report.[584]) Reports are due thirty days after the close of each reporting period. The reported sales value must include the 1 percent IFF paid by the Schedule user agencies that, ultimately, will be forwarded to GSA. As described above, vendors calculate the applicable IFF payment based upon the figure reported on this Contractor's Report of Sales.

As of 1999, the completed sales report must be submitted electronically to the FSS Vendor Support Center ("VSC").[585] Contracts issued prior to 1999 allowed submission both in hard copy and electronically. Vendors seeking to submit their 72As electronically must register in advance with the VSC. To register, an authorized vendor representative simply contacts the VSC and provides the vendor's name, a designated contact's name, and relevant telephone numbers. Subsequently, the VSC will issue the vendor a 72A-specific password and provide all information necessary to access and use the system.

As with most provisions of the MAS contract, compliance with the Contractor's Report of Sales Clause requires the existence of an effective infrastructure. A vendor must ensure that it has a system in place that captures all Schedule sales in an accurate and timely fashion. Additionally, from the vendor's point of view, it is extremely useful if this system (i) segregates Schedule sales from non-Schedule sales and (ii) processes refunds and returns accurately and in a timely manner.

The Industrial Funding Fee and Sales Reporting Clause—provides fertile ground for a GSA audit. More than any other aspect of the MAS Program, this clause again and again proves to be the source of vendor noncompliance, the consequences of which can be significant. Penalties range from an administrative penalty, to termination, to suspension or debarment, to actions under the False Claims Act.

C. *The Economic Price Adjustment Clause*

While the Price Reductions Clause governs the *reduction* of a vendor's prices, the Economic Price Adjustment Clause governs increases of a vendor's prices. Found at GSAR 552.216-70,[586] the Economic Price Adjustment Clause permits a vendor to increase its Schedule prices only in limited circumstances.[587] First, the clause prohibits a vendor from increasing its prices within the first twelve months of contract performance. For price increases subsequent to the first twelve months of performance, the clause sets forth the following rules:

- The increase must result from a reissue or other modification of the catalog/list price that was used as a basis for the contract award.
- A vendor is permitted only three price increases for every twelve-month period.
- All price increases must be requested before the last sixty days of the contract performance period.
- There must be at least thirty days between requested increases.
- The total value of all increases during any twelve-month period cannot exceed a percentage that is determined by the contracting officer at the time the solicitation is issued. The cap is usually 10 percent unless the contracting officer, using an appropriate index, such as the Producer Price Index, finds that there is a trend in the most recent six months indicating that another percentage is appropriate. The Government must approve ceilings for other than 10 percent.[588]

To lodge a request for a price increase pursuant to the Economic Price Adjustment Clause, a vendor submits a price list or catalog showing the proposed increase and the effective date.[589] If the proposed increase involves a change to the pricing practices or procedures that were disclosed to GSA during contract negotiations, the vendor must submit a revised CSP Format.[590] If the proposed increase involves no change to a disclosed practice or procedure, then the vendor must certify that no change has occurred.[591] In connection with any submission, GSA will expect the vendor to provide documentation supporting the reasonableness of the price increase.[592]

Upon receipt of a request for an economic price adjustment, the contracting officer has three choices. He or she may accept the increase, accept the increase but attempt to negotiate a greater Schedule discount, or reject the increase and, if the vendor does not maintain the current price, remove the item from the MAS Program.[593] Any change in pricing, however, must be reflected in a contract modification signed by the contracting officer.[594] Subsequently, the vendor must notify the contracting officer that any revised price lists have been furnished to authorized Schedule purchasers.[595] GSA will require that the revised prices apply to orders placed on or after the effective date of the contract modification.[596]

D. *The Inspection/Acceptance Clause*

FAR 52.212-4(a) sets forth the Government's authority to inspect and accept (or not accept) supplies or services procured through the MAS Program. This clause applies to MAS contracts pursuant to FAR 8.402. In relevant part, the Inspection/ Acceptance Clause provides as follows:

> The Contractor shall only tender for acceptance those items that conform to the requirements of this contract. The Government reserves the right to inspect or test any supplies or services that

have been tendered for acceptance. The Government may require repair or replacement of nonconforming supplies or reperformance of nonconforming services at no increase in contract price. The Government must exercise its post-acceptance rights—

(1) Within a reasonable time after the defect was discovered or should have been discovered; and

(2) Before any substantial change occurs in the condition of the item, unless the change is due to the defect in the item.[597]

Notably, this clause encompasses two related elements. First, the clause requires a vendor to provide the specific supplies and services it agreed to provide. Second, the clause affords the Government the right to inspect the supplies or services provided by the vendor and to compel the vendor to remedy (through repair or replacement) any problems discovered during such inspection as long as the Government acts swiftly.

FAR 8.405-3 sets forth additional provisions relating to inspection and acceptance. Primarily, these provisions relate to when the Government can inspect products at the vendor's facility versus when it must conduct an inspection at its own facility.

E. *The Excusable Delay Clause*

In the context of a Government contract, the term "excusable delay" refers to a delay that is caused by an event "that is beyond the control of and without the fault or negligence of the contractor or its subcontractors at any tier."[598] Typically, excusable delays encompass events such as acts of God or the public enemy, acts of the Government in either its sovereign or contractual capacity, fires, floods, epidemics, quarantine restrictions, strikes, unusually severe weather, and delays of common carriers. In the event of an excusable delay, a MAS vendor must notify the Contracting Officer in writing as soon as it is reasonably possible after the commencement of any excusable delay, setting forth the full particulars in connection therewith, [and] shall remedy such occurrence with all reasonable dispatch, and shall promptly give written notice to the Contracting Officer of the cessation of such occurrence.[599]

Out of an abundance of caution, and as a matter of sound business practice, a vendor should notify its GSA contracting officer as well as the contracting officers of the affected purchasing entities.

F. *The Warranty And Indemnity Clauses*

The standard MAS contract incorporates several warranty and indemnity clauses. These clauses provide as follows:

- The Patent Indemnity Clause provides that the vendor will indemnify the Government "against liability, including costs, for actual or alleged direct or contributory infringement of, or inducement to infringe, any United States or foreign patent, trademark or copyright, arising out of the performance of this contract, provided the Contractor is reasonably notified of such claims and proceedings."[600]
- The Warranty Clause provides that the vendor "warrants and implies that the items delivered hereunder are merchantable and fit for use for the particular purpose described in this contract."[601]
- The Limitation of Liability Clause provides that, "[e]xcept as otherwise provided by an express or implied warranty, the Contractor will not be liable to the Government for consequential damages resulting from any defect or deficiencies in accepted items."[602]

These three clauses are in addition to any additional warranty or indemnity provisions negotiated between the vendor and the particular purchaser.[603] Unless specified otherwise in the contract, the vendor's commercial warranty as stated in the vendor's commercial price list applies. As a practical matter, however, Government purchasers infrequently will agree to a warranty provision beyond that required by FAR 52.212-4.

G. *The Ethics Clauses*

All Government contracts are subject to multiple clauses designed to ensure that vendors act in an ethical manner. MAS contracts are no different. Violation of any of the following clauses can have significant consequences.

1. Kickbacks

The Anti-Kickback Act of 1986,[604] incorporated into Government contracts through FAR 3.502 and 52.203-7, prohibits the practice of giving "kickbacks" to the United States Government. The Act defines the term "kickback" quite broadly:

> The term "kickback" means any money, fee, commission, credit, gift, gratuity, thing of value, or compensation of any kind which is provided directly or indirectly, to any prime contractor, prime contractor employee, subcontractor, or subcontractor employee for the purpose of improperly obtaining or rewarding favorable treatment in connection with a prime contract or in connection with a subcontract relating to a prime contract.[605]

The purpose of the Act is to inhibit practices that impede competition.

The penalties associated with prohibited behavior are particularly harsh and include civil, criminal, and administrative sanctions. Violators who *knowingly and willfully* engage[606] in a kickback scheme are subject to imprisonment for a period of up to ten years and/or may be subject to a fine. In addition, participants who *knowingly* engage in prohibited conduct[607] are subject to civil penalties of "twice the amount of each kickback involved in the violation and not more than $10,000 for each occurrence."[608]

2. Conflicts Of Interest

FAR Subpart 9.5 provides the rules regarding "organizational conflicts of interest" ("OCIs") and the methods of handling any such conflicts that arise in the course of a federal contract. In the context of FAR Subpart 9.5, an organizational conflict of interest means

> that because of other activities or relationships with other persons, a person is unable or potentially unable to render impartial assistance or advice to the Government, or the person's objectivity in performing the contract work is or might be otherwise impaired, or a person has an unfair competitive advantage.[609]

In short, the rules are designed to prevent a situation where a vendor's conflicting roles could bias its judgment and give it an unfair competitive advantage.[610] An unfair competitive advantage results when a contractor submitting a bid for a federal contract possesses:

> (1) Proprietary information that was obtained from a Government official without proper authorization; or
>
> (2) Source selection information . . . that is relevant to the contract but is not available to all competitors, and such information would assist that contractor in obtaining the contract.[611]

The conflict of interest rules apply to all Government contractors.

As an example of how the organizational conflict of interest rules apply in practice, consider the following illustration taken from the FAR:

> Before an acquisition for information technology is conducted, Company A is awarded a contract to prepare data system specifications and equipment performance criteria to be used as the basis for the equipment competition. Since the specifications are the basis for selection of commercial hardware, a potential conflict of interest exists. Company A should be excluded from the initial follow-on information technology hardware acquisition.[612]

In the context of the MAS Program, a similar situation could arise where a vendor participates in the preparation of an agency's statement of work (*e.g.*, for professional services) or the terms of an agency's Request for Proposals to be issued under the MAS Program. In such a situation, the vendor would be wise to consult its legal department to consider requesting a waiver pursuant to FAR 9.503, or implementing an internal mitigation plan in an attempt to alleviate the organizational conflict of interest.

Although the FAR places the primary burden for determining whether a conflict of interest exists on the Government,[613] it is in the vendor's best interest to establish internal procedures to monitor and mitigate against the possibility of such conflicts. One incentive for companies to develop these internal controls is the threat of a protest because of a conflict of interest. Although rare, the courts have sustained such protests, resulting in the termination of award.[614]

3. Bribes And Illegal Gratuities

In 1988, as a result of Operation Ill Wind, the Pentagon's infamous procurement fraud investigation that uncovered serious violations of the procurement process and resulted in numerous prosecutions and convictions against Government officials and Government contractors, Congress amended 18 U.S.C. § 201 to establish strict new requirements governing "gratuities."[615] The amendments affect MAS vendors (and all Government contractors) in ways that may seem strange to companies new to Government contracting.

Section 201(1)(a) of 18 U.S.C. prohibits anyone from directly or indirectly giving, offering, or promising anything of value to any official "for or because of any official act performed or to be performed."[616] The gratuities statute sets forth criminal penalties for a violation.

The FAR also speaks directly to the issue of gratuities. Specifically, FAR 3.101-2 and its companion clause FAR 52.203-3 prohibit a vendor from offering or giving a gratuity to any officer, official, or employee of the Government when that gratuity is intended to influence an award decision or obtain favorable treatment under a contract. A Government contractor engaging in such behavior is subject to having its contract terminated. Additionally, such behavior may constitute a breach of contract, bringing with it exemplary damages of "not less than 3 nor more than 10 times the cost incurred by the Contractor in giving gratuities . . . ."[617]

In order to establish a violation of the gratuities statute, the Government must prove a link between the item given to the federal official and a specific official act "for or because of which" the item was given. Historically, this link could be somewhat weak and still support a gratuities violation allegation. Recently, however, in the widely reported *Sun-Diamond* case,[618] the United States Supreme Court issued a decision that reestablished the importance of this link as a substantive element of the gratuities statute.

In *Sun-Diamond*, the United States, represented by a Special Prosecutor, alleged that Sun-Diamond Growers of California gave illegal gifts to then-U.S. Secretary of Agriculture Mike Espy, while Espy had two matters pending before him in which Sun-Diamond had a substantial interest.[619] Count One of the indictment alleged that Sun-Diamond violated 18 U.S.C. § 201 by providing gratuities such as tickets to the 1993 U.S. Open, luggage, and free meals. The Special Prosecutor did not, however, allege any specific connection between these gifts and the matters that were pending before Espy.

In an opinion by Justice Scalia, the Court held that the inclusion of the term "official act" in the statutory text mandated some specific, identifiable, official act linked to the gratuity in order to establish liability under the statute. The Court based its holding on two grounds. First, adoption of the Government's reading would produce absurd results by criminalizing the giving of any kind of gift—even tokens— to a Government official. Second, the Court reasoned that, if Congress had intended to adopt such a broad criminal prohibition on gift-giving, it would have done so explicitly.

The Court's decision is of significance to Government contractors that have had to grapple with a seemingly impossible harmonization of the gratuities statute, if broadly read, with customary business courtesies. In this regard, the Court rejected an argument by the Special Prosecutor that a free lunch provided to the Secretary by a trade association in connection with a speech he delivered to the association on matters within his purview violated the statute, irrespective of the absence of a link between the lunch and any specific official act. The *Sun-Diamond* decision demonstrates the Court's view that the establishment of "good will" with an official that might prove useful for some undefined future benefit is not within the purview of the gratuities statute. This fact notwithstanding, MAS vendors must remain circumspect in their dealings with Government officials as a courteous gesture very well could be interpreted as a gratuity in connection with a contract benefit.

4. Lobbying

The Government has an interest in preventing federal contractors from using Government funds, including profit or fee, to influence any member of Congress or agency official in connection with a specific contract. In order to ensure that such misuse of federal funds does not occur, the Government requires that Government contractors execute a declaration that is both a disclosure and a certification.[620] In executing the declaration, a potential MAS vendor is certifying that no appropriated funds have been paid or will be paid in violation of the prohibitions in 31 U.S.C. § 1352.[621]

A vendor must also identify in its disclosure statement whether

> any funds other than Federal appropriated funds (including profit or fee received under a covered Federal action) have been paid, or will be paid, to any person for influencing or attempting to influence an officer or employee of any agency, a Member of Congress, an officer or employee of a Member of Congress, or an employee of Member of Congress in connection with a Federal contract, grant, loan, or cooperative agreement.[622]

Lobbying is not totally forbidden as long as the lobbying activity does not fall within any of the proscribed activities.[623] For instance, vendors may have in-house employees who act as agency and legislative liaisons as long as the employees' activities are not directly related to a covered federal transaction. If the declaration's accuracy is affected by an event, the vendor is required to update the declaration in the calendar quarter in which it occurred.[624]

Vendors that make payments to influence federal transactions in violation of 31 U.S.C. § 1352 are subject to civil penalties "of not less than $10,000 and not more than $100,000 for each such expenditure."[625] It is very important that declarations be updated as needed as a failure to file or amend a declaration carries a civil penalty of "of not less than $10,000 and not more than $100,000 for each such failure."[626]

5. Procurement Integrity

The Government has a vested interest in ensuring the integrity of its procurement activities and employs a host of laws and regulations to meet this interest. FAR 3.104 deals directly with the interactions between the vendor and Government employees involved in the acquisition process by requiring any Government employee who is "participating personally and substantially"[627] in a procurement that is in excess of the simplified acquisition threshold[628] and is contacted by a bidder or offeror for that contract regarding possible employment to report such offer immediately in writing to his or her supervisor and ethics official.[629] Withdrawal from the procurement is required unless the vendor is no longer bidding on that contract or the discussions regarding employment have ended "without an agreement or arrangement for employment."[630]

The procurement integrity rules also prohibit the employment in any capacity of any agency official who has participated in the award of or modification of a contract for $10,000,000 or more for one year from the date of participation.[631] The rules also prohibit the employment of a former Government employee who served as the program manager on one of the vendor's contracts.[632] These prohibitions are contract or service specific; thus, former officials may be hired to work in a division of the contractor that does not "produce the same or similar products or services" as the division having the pre-existing relationship with the official.[633]

A vendor that violates these rules may be disqualified as a bidder if the violation is discovered prior to award.[634] If the contract has been awarded, the Government may cancel the contract and seek other available remedies including recovery of profits.[635] In addition, both the vendor and the agency employee may be subject to criminal and civil penalties. Criminal penalties include imprisonment for up to five years and/or a fine.[636] Civil penalties for individuals include fines of up to $50,000 per violation plus twice the amount of compensation that the individual received.[637] Organizations may be fined up to $500,000 per violation plus twice the compensation paid.[638]

FAR 3.104 and 41 U.S.C. § 423 (the statute FAR 3.104 implements) are hardly the sole word on the retention of former Government employees. Specifically, 18 U.S.C. § 207, and the implementing regulations set forth at 5 C.F.R. § 2637.201, encompass a host of additional restrictions, including:

- A lifetime restriction against employing or retaining a former Government employee to represent the vendor before the United States in connection with any particular matter involving the vendor in which the official "participated personally and substantially" while a Government employee.[639]

- A two-year restriction against employing or retaining a former Government employee to represent the vendor before the United States in connection with any particular matter that was "pending under [his or her] responsibility" within a period of one year prior to the official's departure from the Government.[640]

- A two-year restriction against employing or retaining a former "senior" Government employee to assist in representing the vendor before the United States in connection with any particular matter involving the vendor in which the employee participated "personally and substantially" while employed by the Government.[641]

- A one-year restriction against employing or retaining a former "senior" Government employee to represent the vendor before the employee's "former department or agency" in connection with any particular matter regardless of the employee's prior involvement.[642]

While the Code of Federal Regulations provides a few exemptions for certain employees in certain circumstances, the restrictions, as illustrated above, are quite broad. Vendors seeking to retain or employ a former Government employee would be well advised to (i) review the applicable regulations carefully, (ii) consult with the law department or outside counsel, and (iii) have the former Government employee request a written opinion from his or her agency's ethics counsel.

H. *Assignment Of Claims Clause*

The Assignment of Claims Clause gives MAS vendors the ability to transfer their right to receive payment of $1,000 or more under the MAS contract to a bank, a trust company, or other financial institution.[643] Such a transfer, however, becomes effective only once the assignee (the entity to which the right is transferred)

> files written notice of the assignment together with a true copy of the instrument of assignment with the contracting officer issuing the order and the finance office designated in the order to make payment.[644]

Because MAS vendors typically accept orders from a large number of Government agencies, a comprehensive assignment will involve notifying each cognizant contracting officer and each finance office within each ordering agency. Merely notifying the vendor's GSA contracting officer is not sufficient. The potential difficulties inherent in this process are obvious.

I. *Change-Of-Name And Novation Agreements*

The realities of the business world are such that, from time to time, companies change names and/or corporate structures. The reasons for such changes are varied. One company might change its name for marketing reasons, another might create an independently incorporated subsidiary for tax reasons. Schedule vendors are not immune from the need to make such changes, and the FAR provides the means to do so.

1. Change-Of-Name Agreements

FAR 2.101 defines a "change-of-name agreement" as a

> legal instrument executed by the contractor and
> the Government that recognizes the legal change
> of name of the contractor without disturbing the
> original contractual rights and obligations of the
> parties.

MAS vendors effect a change-of-name agreement by submitting a written request to the GSA contracting officer.

Upon confirming that the change-of-name request does not disturb the Government's and the vendor's rights and obligations, the contracting officer "shall" execute the change-of-name agreement.[645] Upon execution, the vendor must submit to GSA three signed copies of the change-of-name agreement and one copy of each of the following:

(1) The document effecting the name change, authenticated by a proper official of the State having jurisdiction.

(2) The opinion of the contractor's legal counsel stating that the change of name was properly effected under applicable law and showing the effective date.

(3) A [detailed] list of all affected contracts and purchase orders remaining unsettled between the contractor and the Government . . . . [646]

FAR 42.1205 includes a suggested format for change-of-name agreements that may be adapted for specific cases as necessary.

Change-of-name agreements are routine administrative matters for GSA. As long as the vendor has compiled all of the necessary information prior to making its written request, the process typically is quick and painless.

2. Novation Agreements

The law precludes an outright transfer of a Government contract from the vendor to a third party.[647] The law, however, permits the Government to recognize a third party as a "successor in interest" to a Government contract when the third party's interest arises out of the transfer of all of the original vendor's assets *or* the entire portion of the vendor's assets involved in the performance of the contract.

FAR 2.101 defines a novation agreement as a legal instrument executed by the contractor (the transferor), the successor in interest (the transferee), and the Government by which, among other things

> the transferor guarantees performance of the contract, the transferee assumes all obligations under the contract, and the Government recognizes the transfer of the contract and related assets.[648]

Note that, notwithstanding the transferee's assumption of all contractual obligations (and, while not mentioned in the definition, the transferee's waiver of all rights under the contract against the Government),[649] the transferor continues to guarantee contract performance. This should be distinguished from a typical commercial novation between two non-Government contractors, the essence of which is a complete discharge of the prior obligation.[650]

The process to effect a novation begins with a written request to the vendor's GSA contracting officer. The vendor's request must include the following information:

- Three signed copies of the proposed novation agreement. (The FAR includes a suggested novation agreement format that may be adapted to specific cases at FAR 42.1204(i).)
- A document describing the proposed transaction.

- A detailed list of all affected contracts between the vendor and the Government as of the date of sale or transfer.
- Evidence of the transferee's capability to perform the contract.
- "Any other relevant information requested by the responsible contracting officer."[651]

Additionally, as the following documents become available, the vendor must submit them to its cognizant GSA contracting officer to supplement its initial submission:

- An *authenticated* copy of the instrument effecting the transfer of assets.
- A *certified* copy of each resolution of the corporate parties' boards of directors authorizing the transfer of assets.
- A *certified* copy of the minutes of each corporate party's stockholder meeting necessary to approve the transfer of assets.
- An *authenticated* copy of the new entity's certificate and articles of incorporation if a corporation was formed for the purpose of receiving the assets involved in performing the Government contracts.
- Opinions of legal counsel for the transferor *and* the transferee stating that the transfer was properly effected under applicable law and the effective date of transfer.
- Balance sheets for the transferor and transferee as of the dates immediately before and after the transfer of assets, audited by independent accountants.
- Evidence that any security clearance requirements have been met.
- The consent of sureties on all contracts being transferred if bonds are required or a statement from the transferor that none is required.

As with change-of-name agreements, GSA contracting officers typically are quite helpful throughout the novation process. The key is advance notice and communication.

J. *The Trade Agreements Act Of 1979*

The Trade Agreements Act of 1979[652] ("TAA") functions to promote *non*-discrimination in Government procurements by preempting the application of certain discriminatory laws, such as the Buy American Act ("BAA"), for certain categories of supplies coming from certain "designated countries."[653] In contrast to the BAA, which imposes an evaluative penalty on foreign offerors but allows them to be considered as so evaluated, the TAA bars the Government from purchasing noncompliant supplies and services.[654] Under the TAA, the Government may purchase products only if those products are, as described below, wholly the growth, product, or manufacture of the United States or other "designated country" or have been "substantially transformed" in the United States or other "designated country."[655] Services may be procured only from companies "established" in the United States or other designated country.[656]

1. Applicability

The TAA gives the President the authority to waive the BAA and other discriminatory rules normally applicable in government procurement. The President has delegated this authority to the U.S. Trade Representative ("USTR"), who has waived these restrictions with respect to countries that have signed an international trade agreement with the United States or that meet certain other criteria, such as being a "Caribbean Basin" country or a "least developed" country. International trade agreements serving as the basis for the TAA waiver are the World Trade Organization Government Procurement Agreement ("WTO GPA"), Free Trade Agreements, and the Israeli Trade Act. [657]

Until recently, the FAR equated the TAA with the WTO GPA[658]— a multilateral international treaty, signatories to which promise not to discriminate against each other in acquisitions covered by the agreement.[659] The current version of the FAR draws a distinction between the two: acquisitions covered by the WTO GPA receive nondiscriminatory treatment under the authority provided by the TAA.[660] Conversely, in acquisitions covered by the WTO GPA, the contracting officer is prohibited from selecting products or services from countries to which the TAA waiver does not apply.[661] Moreover, the nondiscriminatory treatment for products and services from the Caribbean Basin countries and least developed countries is limited to the acquisitions covered by the WTO GPA.[662]

Except where inapplicable for other reasons, the TAA applies to any federal acquisition of supplies and services where the "estimated value of the acquisition" is over the threshold set periodically by the USTR.[663] While identifying the threshold is supposedly simple, currently, for acquisitions covered by the WTO GPA, the USTR has set this at $175,000 for the acquisition of supplies or services and $6,725,000 for construction contracts—determining the "estimated value of the acquisition" historically has proven to be a source of much confusion to vendors and Government agencies alike.

In its most recent pronouncement on the subject, the General Services Administration Board of Contract Appeals ("GSBCA") affirmed the propriety of valuing acquisitions on an *item-by-item* basis.[664] That case involved a protester's argument that DOJ should have rejected the awardee's proposal because "the total value of the procurement" exceeded the TAA threshold and, thus, according to the protester, "none of the items procured can be from a non-designated country."[665] The GSBCA denied the protest, holding that the DOJ's practice of applying the TAA threshold on a line item-by-line item basis was consistent with the requirements of the TAA and the FAR.[666] The GSBCA's interpretation of the TAA is supported by the current TAA certification that states that the Government will evaluate "line items covered by the WTO GPA."[667]

In calculating the value of a given line item, the FAR instructs agencies to include the estimated value "of all options."[668] Additionally, in the context of a procurement involving multiple awards, it is proper to use the total combined estimated value of all projected awards for each line item.[669]

Thus, because the FAR applies the TAA threshold on a line item-by-line item basis, a single Schedule procurement may be subject to both the TAA and the BAA in cases where GSA has not determined that the TAA applies to the entire procurement. Fortunately for MAS vendors, GSA typically makes a formal determination that the TAA applies to its Schedule contracts. Whenever a solicitation or contract is not clear in this regard, however, *e.g.*, when the contract references both the TAA and the BAA, it is imperative that the vendor seek clarification and guidance from the contracting officer.

2. Requirements

To determine whether a given item satisfies the requirements of the TAA, the vendor must determine (a) whether the item is wholly the growth, product, or manufacture of the United States or a "designated country" and (b) if not, whether that item has been "substantially transformed" in the United States or another "designated country."[670] Recent decisions have provided some clarification in the application of the "substantial transformation" test of the TAA. Customs Service decisions that apply the substantial transformation test provide guidance to tribunals applying the TAA.[671] In addition, vendors may seek from the Customs Service an advisory opinion or a final determination of an article's country of origin under the substantial transformation test.[672] Consequently, Customs Service rulings should represent an integral part of a vendor's analysis of the country of origin of its products.

To determine whether a product has been substantially transformed, the Customs Service typically asks whether there has been a change in the product's name, character, or use.[673] In a recent case, for example, a manufacturing process for surgical equipment involved two main stages. In the first stage, which occurred in the United States, stainless steel bars were cut and forged into shape. The forgings were inspected, annealed, trimmed, and cold stamped. The forgings then were shipped to Pakistan, where they were machined and ground, assembled into the intended surgical instrument, given an initial finish, and then re-ground. The jaw and teeth were beveled and blade edges sharpened. The completed instruments then were heat treated and aligned.

The Customs Service determined that the country of origin of the surgical instrument was the United States, concluding that the initial cutting and forging that took place in the United States constituted a substantial transformation, while the processes that took place in Pakistan did not. As described by the Customs Service, "prior to the operations performed in Pakistan, each forging has the final shape of the finished surgical instrument . . . [and] the surgical instrument forging [produced in the United States] is not changed in Pakistan to such a degree to result in a new and different article with a new name, character or use."[674]

This is consistent with a number of cases that conclude that substantial low-tech manufacturing and assembly processes, even though necessary to create a functioning product, are insufficient to constitute the substantial transformation of component parts that look and act no different after those processes.[675] This refusal to recognize low-level assembly of constituent parts under these circumstances is reflected also in the high-tech arena of computers. In one well-known case, a computer company sought a final determination of origin of two types of laptop computers.[676] The manufacturer emphasized that (a) each computer was "customized" and (b) the assemblers must attend training and be certified to perform the tasks necessary to assemble both types of laptops.

With respect to the first laptop, the vendor explained to the Customs Service that it received the chassis from overseas with the LCD and CPU already installed in the base plastics. The BIOS chip and memory modules, as well as other components, including the chassis, hard drive, floppy drive, AC adapter, CD-ROM, fax modem cards, docking station, and memory board, were not installed. The components were purchased from suppliers around the world.

The vendor went on to explain that the assembly process for the first laptop involved receiving the parts and identifying them with a customer's order, installing the BIOS chip and memory modules, preparing and installing the hard drive into the notebook chassis, installing the PCMCIA modem card, plugging in the AC adapter, removing the PCMCIA card, and inserting a network interface card. The computer then would be booted and the BIOS flash burned into a non-volatile RAM. After undergoing diagnostic tests, defects were repaired, peripherals were added, random checks on the line occurred, and the computer then would be shipped.

Manufacture of the second laptop entailed a similar process. In the second scenario, however, the vendor received the notebook chassis with the LCD, floppy disk drive, and the BIOS chip installed. The CPU and keyboard, along with other parts similar to those in the first laptop, were imported and installed subsequently.[677]

The Customs Service framed the relevant question as whether "the imported foreign components are substantially transformed as a result of the operations performed in the U.S. That is, does the name, character or use of the foreign components change as a result of the processing and assembly operations performed to manufacture the notebook computers,"[678] which are "complex and meaningful." The Customs Service concluded that the foreign components used in the assembly of both laptops were "substantially transformed as a result of the operations performed in the U.S." In other words, the name, character, and use of the foreign components in each scenario "change[d] as a result of the processing and other assembly operations," and the components lost "their separate identities and [became] an integral part of a notebook computer."[679]

To understand the Customs Service's decision in the foregoing case properly, however, it is important to understand that, in the world of computers, all components are not created equal. Notwithstanding the Customs Service's discussion of hard drives, floppy disks, and CD-ROM drives, its substantial transformation analysis apparently was based principally upon the status of three particular components—the processor (including the CPU and

BIOS chip), the input device (whether a keyboard, a touch pad, or some other device that allows the user to input commands to the processor), and the output device (*i.e.*, a display screen). Customs Service case law suggests that, when these three components are combined (*i.e.*, installed on a laptop chassis), a "system" is created.[680] As a result, a chassis imported from overseas with a pre-installed CPU, BIOS chip, keyboard (or other input device), and display screen constitutes a computer system upon its arrival in the United States and, therefore, in most cases, cannot be "substantially" transformed further into a computer system in the United States—regardless of the incorporation of additional components. Because each of the laptop computers in the example discussed above was imported without at least one of the three critical components, both systems were capable of being substantially transformed in the United States after import.

While the Trade Agreements Act applies to services as well as to products, the regulations and case law relating to services are far less established. The FAR provides that "[t]he contracting officer shall determine the origin of services by the country in which the firm providing the services is established."[681] The FAR, however, does not provide an explanation of what it means to be "established" in a given country. Thus, until this issue is clarified by the regulators or by the courts, vendors are advised to come to an agreement with their cognizant contracting officer on this issue prior to offering services performed by non-U.S. companies.

K. *The Buy American Act*

The BAA and its implementing regulations function to give an advantage to domestic products over foreign products in the acquisition of supplies and construction materials.[682] This advantage is effected through the application to foreign products of an "evaluative differential" that increases the cost of the foreign product solely for bidding purposes.[683]

Beginning in 1998, the FAR Secretariat began a substantial revision of FAR Part 25 and portions of FAR Part 52, rewriting the regulations that implement the BAA, the TAA, and other domestic preference statutes.[684] While the overall structure of the regulations remains the same, a number of changes appear to require significantly different analysis, especially with regard to the sale of supplies. Newly redrafted definitions of "component," "end product," and "domestic offer" (a) grant contracting officers wider discretion in controlling the application of BAA price differentials; (b) require the vendor to analyze and certify every single line item in a contract; and (c) compel the vendor to consider not only the components of an end product, but also its sub-components and, possibly, sub-elements of the sub-components in executing its certificate.[685]

Because the BAA can apply to Schedule purchases, vendors should understand the requirements imposed by the BAA. Such an understanding is particularly important when dealing with the DOD as many DOD contracting officers will ask for a BAA assurance when making Schedule purchases. A comprehensive discussion of the BAA, however, is beyond the scope of this book. Interested vendors should refer to the Briefing Papers article from which this section was derived.[686]

L. *The Price Reductions Clause*

Just as the CSP Format helps GSA secure uniquely favorable pricing from the vendor during the negotiation phase, the Price Reductions Clause helps GSA ensure that it continues to receive such pricing throughout the life of the contract. To understand the Price Reductions Clause, one must remember that its purpose is to maintain the pricing structure negotiated by the vendor and GSA prior to contract award. Recall that, as discussed in Chapter VII, before contract award, in most cases at least, GSA (through its contracting officer) and the vendor agree upon (1) the Basis of Award customer or category of customers and (2) the Government's price or discount relationship to the identified customer or category of customers. The Price Reductions Clause serves to maintain this *relationship* throughout the contract period and to secure for the Government the benefits of any changes to this relationship.

In short, and depending on the precise nature of the pre-award negotiations, the Price Reductions Clause requires vendors to maintain a firm relationship between the discounts it offers the Government and the discounts it offers its Basis of Award.[687] Except where an exception applies, a change in this relationship typically requires that a corresponding "price reduction" be given to all Schedule purchasers purchasing that same product.[688] After providing a brief history of the Price Reductions Clause, this section examines the mechanics of the clause as well as the several exemptions to the clause.

1. History

The Price Reductions Clause, like the MAS Program itself, has undergone significant changes since its inception. As originally implemented, the clause operated to reduce the price to the Government *any time* the vendor reduced the price it offered *any* customer—whether federal or commercial.[689] In such circumstances, GSA would demand a price equivalent to the price offered the other customer. In a landmark case, soon mooted by changes in GSA's agency level regulations, the GSBCA held that the term "equivalent price reduction" did not entitle the Government to a percentage discount equivalent to that which the vendor gave its commercial customers. Thus, unlike today, GSA received a reduction only large enough to bring the Government's price down to the commercial customer's price.[690] Limiting the price reduction to the actual monetary reduction granted by the vendor to that granted other customers, the GSBCA noted that, if the Government, which authored the Price Reductions Clause, had desired to have the Price Reductions Clause be punitive in nature, then evidence of that intent should have been apparent in hearings on the subject.

Taking its cue from the GSBCA, GSA significantly revamped the Price Reductions Clause in 1982. One major feature of the

1982 clause was the removal of the requirement that a drop in price to *any* customer (including federal agencies[691]) would trigger a price decrease to the Government. Instead, the 1982 MAS Policy Statement created the concept of the Basis of Award customer or category of customers. The Basis of Award, which could apply to an individual customer or a category of customers, would serve as the means of comparison for Government pricing. From this point forward, it would be the *relationship* between a vendor's Basis of Award customers or categories of customers and its Schedule purchasers that would determine whether the Price Reductions Clause had been triggered. The clause would be triggered only if the reduced price, which had been agreed to during contract negotiations, were granted to a Basis of Award customer or category of customers.

Notwithstanding this positive change, vendors still were required to *report* to GSA all price reductions to any customer or category of customer (including federal agencies). The 1982 clause also retained the provision requiring a vendor to report all reductions in its commercial catalog, price list, or other documents used to establish the prices under the contract. In such situations, the resulting price reduction would apply to the Government until the end of the contract or until the price was further reduced. Counteracting at least some of the burden created by this requirement, the 1982 Price Reductions Clause provided that, if the vendor treated the price reduction as temporary and reported it to GSA, then the reduction to the Government would be in effect for the same period only, as opposed to the life of the contract.[692] If the vendor did not report such reductions, however, the price would be reduced retroactively and the vendor would at least be required to refund the overcharge amount plus interest.

Subsequently, in 1994, GSA modified the GSAM (then known as the GSAR) to include yet a new Price Reductions Clause.[693] The purpose of the revision, which came about in part as a result of industry dissatisfaction with the 1982 MAS Policy Statement, was to clarify the clause's applicability, reduce contractor reporting requirements, and eliminate price reductions based on sales to a federal agency. The 1994 clause required *only* that reductions to Basis of Award customers or categories of customers be reported to GSA. Furthermore, the 1994 clause allowed reductions to federal agencies without requiring the reduction to be Government-wide. The period for reporting a price reduction was extended from ten to fifteen calendar days after its effective date.

2. What Constitutes A Price Reduction?

GSAR 552.238-75 currently sets forth the text of the current Price Reductions Clause. The clause defines a "price reduction" as "any change in the Contractor's commercial pricing or discount arrangement applicable" to the Basis of Award that "disturbs" the Government's price/discount relationship to the Basis of Award. The clause further identifies three distinct events that trigger a price reduction. The clause provides that a price reduction will be required if the vendor:

(i)   Revises the commercial catalog, pricelist, schedule or other document upon which contract award was predicated to reduce prices;

(ii)   Grants more favorable discounts or terms and conditions than those contained in the commercial catalog, pricelist, schedule or other documents upon which contract award was predicated; or

(iii) Grants special discounts to the customer (or category of customers) that formed the basis of award, and the change disturbs the price/discount relationship of the Government to the customer (or category of customers) that was the basis of award.[694]

The clause goes on to provide that vendors must "report to the Contracting Officer all price reductions to the customer (or category of customers) that was the basis of award" and that the "Contractor's report shall include an explanation of the conditions under which the reductions were made."[695]

Because failure to comply with the Price Reductions Clause can have significant consequences, vendors must understand fully each of the triggering events.

The first triggering event relates only to revisions to documents "upon which contract award was predicated" and only where those revisions "reduce prices." While the phrase "upon which contract award was predicated" is not defined in the GSAM, it typically is understood to encompass documents presented to (or reviewed by) GSA during contract negotiations. For example, information presented to GSA in connection with a vendor's CSP Format could be information "upon which contract award was predicated." A modification to such information during contract performance can trigger the Price Reductions Clause. However, it is important to keep in mind that the first triggering event relates only to revisions to documents, not specific sales activities.

The second triggering event, perhaps the most inartfully written of the three, also relates to documents "upon which contract award was predicated." Unlike the first triggering event, however, the second can be implicated without a change to a document. Although the language is far from a model of clarity, this triggering event usually is viewed as occurring when a contractor's actual pricing/discounting practices are so inconsistent with the pricing documents upon which award was predicated as to render them inherently suspect. Whether the Price Reductions Clause will or will not be triggered in any given circumstance, however, depends upon the nature of the vendor's pre-award negotiations with GSA—something that is unique to each vendor. It also depends upon the specific factual circumstances surrounding the potential triggering event. For example, if the terms and conditions that accompany the more favorable discount are not as favorable as those afforded the Government, then the vendor will have an argument that the Price Reductions Clause ought not be triggered.

Finally, the third triggering event is unrelated to documentation at all—whether provided to GSA or not—and simply provides that discounts to the vendor's Basis of Award that disturb the *relationship* between the Schedule price and the Basis of Award price negotiated at the outset of contract performance may trigger the Price Reductions Clause. As noted above, it is essential to understand that a discount can be less favorable than a vendor's Schedule discount and yet still disturb the *relationship* between the Schedule price and the Basis of Award price negotiated at the outset of contract performance. However, as with the second triggering event, it is essential to consider any potentially triggering event in the context of the surrounding facts. The nature of the agreement negotiated with GSA and the nature of the terms and conditions offered may suggest that what appears to be a Price Reductions Clause triggering event on its face, in reality, is not (for example, where the terms and conditions of the sale are significantly different).

3. How Does One Compute A Price Reduction?

The Price Reductions Clause is implicated not only when a Basis of Award customer is granted a greater discount than the Government receives, but, in many cases, when the *relationship* between the Government discount and the commercial discount changes. Except in the few circumstances described below, the Government will assert that it is entitled to a price reduction whenever this relationship changes—even when the resulting price falls below the vendor's own cost.[696] The resulting reduction to the Government typically is calculated as a *ratio* rather than by subtraction and must be offered to the Government "with the same effective date, and for the same time period, as extended to the commercial customer (or category of customers)."[697]

The hypothetical scenario set forth below will serve to illustrate the mechanics of the Price Reductions Clause: Assume that vendor Sorebottom Inc. (a manufacturer of office chairs) and the

Government negotiate a contractual discount structure whereby the Government receives a 6% discount on desk chairs, while Sorebottom's Basis of Award customers receive only a 3% discount. Assume also that, for whatever reason, Sorebottom grants one of its Basis of Award customers a discount of 4% on desk chairs— a 33% increase. Thus, the scenario looks like this:

	Disclosed Discount	New Discount
Basis of Award	3%	4%
Government	6%	?%

Notwithstanding the fact that the Basis of Award customer still pays more than the Government, the *relationship* between the two discounts has changed. The discount offered to the Basis of Award customer has increased by 33%. Thus, pursuant to the Price Reductions Clause, the Government will assert that it is entitled to a 33% increase to its discount as well—in this scenario, an additional 2% as shown below—even though something else, such as a change in terms and conditions, might suggest that the relationship did not change.

	Disclosed Discount	Ratio	New Discount	% Increase	Ratio
Basis of Award	3%	1	4%	**33%**	1
Government	6%	2	**8%**	**33%**	2

Importantly, as noted above, this new discount must be offered to the Government "with the same effective date, and for the same time period, as extended to the commercial customer (or category of customers)."[698] It suffices to say that many Schedule vendors that offer discounts to their Basis of Award customers are oblivious to the long-term increased discount that may henceforward apply to all Schedule sales. As noted earlier in this section, vendors are well advised to attempt to negotiate an absolute, rather than a proportional, Basis of Award relationship.

4. What Are The Exceptions To The Price Reductions Clause?

To many Schedule vendors, compliance with the Price Reductions Clause ultimately becomes a case of the tail wagging the dog. In other words, many vendors allow the Price Reductions Clause to guide their entire sales strategy. This sort of inflexible reaction, while shared by many Schedule vendors, is unnecessary. While the Price Reductions Clause can be confusing and burdensome, it is not as invasive as some vendors believe. Several exceptions exist that, if used properly, could relieve vendors of much of the burden of the clause. Understanding fully these several exceptions, however, is essential to ensure compliance.

a. Orders Outside The Basis Of Award Do Not Trigger The Clause

The Price Reductions Clause is triggered only by sales to customers in a vendor's Basis of Award category of customers. This could be a single customer (such as End User X), a small group of customers (such as the top three customers in terms of sales volume), or an entire category of customers (such as all corporate customers). Vendors can grant whatever discounts they want to customers outside its Basis of Award, so long as such discounts are consistent with the vendor's disclosed commercial practices. If the vendor entirely modifies the policies and practices disclosed to GSA during contract negotiations, however, it runs the risk of triggering the Price Reductions Clause.

b. Orders Above The Maximum Order Threshold Do Not Trigger The Clause

Customers entering into firm, fixed-price/definite-quantity contracts of more than $X (where X is the value of the maximum order threshold) with specified delivery are excepted from the Price Reductions Clause. In order for a sale to fall within this exception, *the sale must satisfy each of the exception's three elements.* Merely having the potential to exceed $X, for example, is not enough. Thus, for a sale to be excepted from the Price Reductions Clause, the agreement must set forth:

1. A firm, fixed-price in excess of $X,
2. A definite quantity of products to be purchased, and
3. A specified delivery date or period.

Frequently, vendors enter into blanket purchase agreements ("BPAs") with non-federal purchasers. A BPA is a simplified procurement method through which the buyer can fill its anticipated recurring needs for services and supplies. BPAs can be thought of as accounts established with Schedule vendors. Typically, BPAs incorporate a "not-to-exceed" purchase ceiling. They rarely contemplate a definite quantity or a specified delivery. Such agreements, thus, generally are *not* firm, fixed-price contracts and, regardless of the *potential* value of the BPA, are not exempt from the Price Reductions Clause.[699]

Vendors, however, are not helpless in the face of a BPA. By instituting—and abiding by the terms of—a "reverse rebate" system, a vendor with an adequate internal infrastructure and disciplined employees should be able to bring a BPA within the scope of the maximum order threshold exception to the Price Reductions Clause. A reverse rebate simply is a contractual provision that establishes a minimum contract value and requires the purchaser to rebate the value of any discount that would trigger the Price Reductions Clause were the purchase not exempt if that minimum is not met. Savvy vendors have been relying on this approach for years with great success.

While the text of the Price Reductions Clause itself does not explicitly authorize such an approach, its validity is supported by case law, agency pronouncements, and experience. For example:

- The GSBCA has held that a commercial contract for an estimated quantity of products in excess of the maximum order threshold is equivalent to a definite-quantity contract in excess of the maximum order threshold as long as the contract contains a "price redetermination" provision should orders fall below the estimated quantity.[700]

- GSA itself (through the director of the Systems Furniture Division of the National Furniture Center) previously declared that a commercial agreement permitting the aggregation of multiple orders over an extended period of time qualifies as an "acceptable variation" to the typical single-order requirement "as long as the agreement stipulates a minimum amount to be purchased and includes billback requirements on purchases that fall below the minimum or includes other remedies that have the same effect in making the seller whole."[701]

Additionally, as noted above, many vendors have been employing the reverse rebate approach for years.

Vendors should keep in mind, however, that, as with any contracting approach not explicitly permitted by regulation, the reverse rebate approach *is not without an element of risk*. Notwithstanding the clear supporting authority, a given contracting officer or federal auditor might see things differently. To minimize this risk, therefore, a vendor should apprise its contracting officer of its intent to use the reverse rebate approach in writing *prior* to actual use.

c. Quotation And Billing Errors, If Reported, Do Not Trigger The Clause

MAS contracts provide that "[t]here shall be no price reduction for sales . . . [c]aused by an error in quotation or billing, provided adequate documentation is furnished by the Contractor to the Contracting Officer."[702] Unfortunately, the Price Reductions Clause is silent as to what constitutes an "error in quotation or billing." Thus, vendors are left with some latitude to argue that such discounts resulted from an error in quotation or billing.

This approach, obviously, is subject to limitations. Few would argue that, pursuant to the contractual language set forth above, clerical errors—such as order-entry errors, typographical errors, and mathematical errors—are not exempt from the Price Reductions Clause (as long as they are properly documented and disclosed as discussed above). GSA's Office of Acquisition Policy ("OAP"), however, has indicated that the scope of this exemption may be broader. As one secondary source has pointed out, "GSA's OAP has indicated that errors committed by a salesperson in improperly passing on excessive discounts may . . . fall within the billing error exception."[703] According to this same secondary source,

> [s]ituations such as this will be examined more carefully, but generally contractors will be granted the benefit of the doubt. Such leniency is granted because GSA recognizes the enormity of the task of preventing the overzealous salesperson from disobeying the discounting policies of a large corporation.[704]

Obviously, the more frequently these situations occur, the less likely GSA will be to find that they constitute mere quotation or billing errors.[705]

Like its silence regarding the nature of the errors encompassed by this exception, the Price Reductions Clause also is silent as to the meaning of "adequate documentation." Most likely, this phrase would include an explanation of (i) the reasons for, (ii) the extent of, and (iii) the steps taken to correct the quotation or billing error.

d. Charitable Donations Should Not Trigger The Price Reductions Clause

Donations to charity should not trigger the Price Reductions Clause.[706] Vendors should be warned, however, that a "donation" to a Basis of Award customer might be viewed differently by GSA. For example, when a donation can be viewed as being tied to a purchase by a relevant customer or a category of customers, the Government could take the view that the donation constitutes a price reduction. Thus, vendors should adopt—and adhere to—a policy of avoiding this risk. At a minimum, an effective policy probably should provide that donations are to be handled by a separate department within the company. In addition, vendors should exercise care in adopting a practice of providing *permanent* evaluation units—a common practice among information technology manufacturers, for example.

e. No Charge Items ("Freebies")

Occasionally, vendor sales representatives offer a commercial customer a free product or service to "apologize" for a delay or some other problem for which the vendor has accepted responsibility. In the information technology context, for example, these no-charge items might take the form of a free sound card or extra memory. In the furniture marketplace, they might take the form of a better fabric on a chair or more expensive veneer on a desk. While a literal reading of the Price Reductions Clause might suggest that this practice could trigger the clause, a reasonable contrary argument can be made.

As discussed in Chapter VII, the GSAR distinguishes between "discounts" and "concessions" as those terms are used in connection with MAS contracting. The definitions distinguish between those pricing strategies that give additional value for the catalog or list price paid (concessions) and those that reduce the payment received to something less than the catalog or list price (discounts). Under these definitions, "bonus goods" are defined as "concessions," not discounts.[707] The Price Reductions Clause, however, applies only when the vendor (i) revises its commercial catalog or price list, (ii) grants more favorable *discounts or terms and conditions*, or (iii) grants *special discounts* to the customer or category of customers identified in negotiations.

Thus, one could argue, concessions—not being "discounts"—should not be covered.

The flip side of this coin, however, is that GSA could argue that "bonus goods" constitute more favorable "terms and conditions" pursuant to GSAR 552.238-75(c)(1)(ii). Common usage and a careful reading of the applicable regulations, however, cast doubt on the validity of such an argument. First, common usage of the phrase "terms and conditions" usually connotes reference to contract provisions. The phrase generally relates to clauses incorporated into the contract, not the products or services to be provided. Such usage is consistent with the usage of the phrase in the Price Reductions Clause, which clause is invoked if a vendor offers terms and conditions more favorable than those contained in its "commercial catalog, price list, schedule, or *other documents* upon which the contract award was predicated."[708]

Second, and more importantly, the GSAR definitions of "concessions" and "discount" make clear that advantageous terms and conditions are to be considered "discounts" rather than "concessions." The regulatory definition of "discount" includes "rebates, quantity discounts, purchase option credits, and any other terms or conditions [(]other than concessions) which reduce the amount of money a customer ultimately pays . . . ."[709] "Concessions," on the other hand, are defined to be distinct from "discounts." A concession is "a benefit, enhancement, or privilege (other than a discount), which either reduces the overall cost of a customer's acquisition or encourages" a sale.[710] Read together, "concessions" and "discounts" are separate and distinct; there is no overlap. Terms and conditions which reduce the amount of money a customer pays are discounts.

Based on this interpretation of the regulations, therefore, it appears that vendors could argue that a no-charge item is a "concession" that does not disturb the price relationship provision of the Price Reductions Clause. The pricing strategies enumerated in the definition of "concessions" would be the safest strategies to adopt. In a manufacturer's context, "freight allowances" and "bonus goods" appear most relevant. Under the "bonus goods" exception, as long as supplies are sold to relevant customers or categories of customers at the standard discount rate, the vendor can offer particular software or peripheral equipment at no additional cost. To maximize the success of this strategy, such offers should be *ad hoc* rather than a stated, continuing policy. The policy might state that certain concessions could be made in order to achieve a sale or overcome a problem if the concession is approved at some level within a company's management. The *ad hoc* nature of the concession would tend to confirm the standard discount policy.

Should a vendor adopt the approach set forth above, it is important that all records associated with the transaction memorialize the nature of the transaction accurately. It is important that the incentive offered be consistently labeled a "concession" or "bonus good." In addition, the transaction should be reflected in the company's accounting records as a "concession" and not as a "credit" against individual sales. These warnings highlight the importance of carefully drafted internal policies and an internal infrastructure that ensures that such policies are followed consistently. Companies lacking such an infrastructure often find themselves unnecessarily on the defensive in circumstances where the underlying transaction, in actuality, is not problematic.[711]

Finally, on a more basic level, when a no-charge item is given to a customer in response to a legitimate complaint, its purpose is to compensate the customer for a diminution in the value of his or her purchase. In this light, the freebie constitutes no increase in the value of the purchased product—it merely makes the customer whole. For this reading of the Price Reductions Clause to make logical sense, however, vendors must ensure that freebies are provided only in response to legitimate customer satisfaction issues. To police this process, the company should implement a policy that sets forth, at a minimum, (i) the circumstances under which a freebie may be given and (ii) the maximum value of the freebie that may be given.

As stated at the outset, while the analysis set forth above describes a reasonable interpretation of the applicable MAS regulations, vendors should be aware that the lack of confirming judicial interpretation makes it impossible to guarantee that GSA will not take a contrary view.

5. Price Reductions Clause Reporting Requirements

The Price Reductions Clause requires that vendors track and report any discounts, concessions, or changes in terms and conditions that disturb the Basis of Award relationship. Specifically, the MAS contract incorporates the following reporting requirements relevant to the Price Reductions Clause:

> During the contract period, *the Contractor shall report to the Contracting Officer all price reductions* to the customer (or category of customers) that was the basis of award. The Contractor's report shall include an explanation of the conditions under which the reductions were made.[712]

The MAS contract provides further that vendors shall

> notify the Contracting Officer of any price reduction subject to this clause as soon as possible, but *not later than 15 calendar days after its effective date.*[713]

Failure to comply with this requirement could expose the vendor to various administrative actions such as a price adjustment (as noted in each of the foregoing sections), a breach of contract claim, or, possibly, a termination for default. Furthermore, the vendor could be deemed liable under the civil or criminal False Claims Act, the criminal False Statements Act, or other criminal statues and could be barred from contracting with the Government (federal and state). Each of these possibilities is described in further detail in Chapters XXIII and XXIV.

M. *Unique Identification*

Following the example of the aerospace, automotive, and health care industries, the DOD has developed its own Unique Identification ("UID") program. DOD's aim is that its UID Program will lead to the unique identification of all personal property, real property, persons, organizations and programs, allowing for their more effective management and resulting in increased overall productivity. As of the submission of this text to the publisher, however, the DOD UID initiative primarily is focused on requiring contractors to affix a specially coded stamp on the items they deliver to DOD. This new program should allow DOD to monitor with increased intelligence the supply of each item from manufacturer to end-user.

The DOD UID requirement applies to items delivered under all contract types, including MAS Contracts, T&M contracts, and GWACs. Where DOD procures items from a small business or purchases commercial items, the contracting activity has the authority to waive the identification requirement only after it makes a determination that it is more cost effective for the Government itself to apply the identifier after delivery. While the interim version of the rule was issued on January 1, 2004, the requirements operate prospectively and apply only to contracts or delivery orders that specifically include the DFARS Clause 252.211-7003.

Under the DOD UID policy,[714] contractors are required to provide unique item identifiers ("UII") for all items delivered to DOD that have a unit acquisition cost of $5,000 or more. If the cost is below $5,000, the UII is required if the item is DOD serially managed, mission essential, controlled inventory, or if required by the Requiring Activity. Regardless of the value, all DOD serially managed parts, components and subassemblies embedded within an item, as well as the parent item itself, also must have the UII.

The UII must be unambiguous, permanent, and unique for each item, allowing differentiation from all other items that DOD buys, owns, or leases. The UII must be a machine readable, two-dimensional data matrix that is inscribed directly on the item or on a label affixed to the item. DOD recognizes the "EAN.UCC Asset Identifiers," the "Vehicle Identification Numbers," and the "Electronic Serial Numbers" as equivalents of UII as long as they are encoded in the "ECC 200 Data Matrix" using "ISO 15434 Syntax," terms that likely will have meaning to a range of individuals. The component data elements of the UII must include the enterprise identifier, *e.g.*, CAGE Code or Dun & Bradstreet number. For items that are serialized within the enterprise identifier, the UII also must include a unique serial number. For items that are serialized within the part, lot, or batch number within the enterprise identifier, the UII must include the original part, lot, or batch number.

N. *Radio Frequency Identification*

In parallel with its UID initiative, the DOD also has launched a gradual implementation plan for adopting passive Radio Frequency Identification ("RFID") technology. Passive RFID tags reflect radio frequency signals emitted by "tag reader." The reader then is able to capture the reflected data, thereby identifying the tag and the item to which it is attached. Like UID, RFID technology is expected to increase DOD's efficiencies in inventory management and asset tracking. But unlike UID, which provides information on each item throughout its life cycle, the purpose of the RFID technology is to better track and trace packages of the items through the supply chain.

Under the first stage of the implementation plan, published as a proposed rule on April 27, 2005,[715] DOD contractors are required to affix passive RFID tags to shipments of items at the case and palletized unit load packaging levels. This requirement affects only certain DOD delivery locations and classes of supplies, as listed in the proposed rule, and applies only if the contract contains the RFID Clause, as prescribed by DFARS 211.275-3. According to the implementation plan, more locations and more classes of supplies will fall under the RFID tagging requirement starting January 1, 2006. By January 1, 2007, the requirement will apply to all contracts that contain the RFID Clause, and will extend to the individual item packaging level. Notably, the item packaging RFID tag will be required in addition to any UID affixed to the item itself.

O. *Contract Bundling*

An issue that received significant attention in the late 1990s and throughout the early and mid 2000s, is the effect of contract bundling on small businesses. In 1997, the Small Business Reauthorization Act defined contract bundling as

> consolidating two or more procurement requirements for goods or services previously provided or performed under separate, smaller contracts into a solicitation of offers for a single contract that is unlikely to be suitable for award to a small business concern[.][716]

The purported harm in bundling, according to the statute at least, is that a small business may not be able to receive an award because of the consolidated contract requirements for size, specialized expertise, or geographical dispersion. Accordingly, the Act requires that each federal department and agency (1) structure contracting requirements to facilitate competition by and among small business concerns, taking all reasonable steps to eliminate obstacles to their participation; and (2) avoid unnecessary and unjustified bundling of contract requirements that may preclude small business participation in procurements as prime contractors.[717]

Prior to the rise in popularity of the GWACs, little thought was given to what exactly constitutes "a single contract" in the definition of "bundling." Following recent FAR revisions,[718] however, it is clear that the anti-bundling rules apply even to single orders placed against a MAS contract. Under the revised FAR definition of "bundling," the "single contract" includes

> (i) multiple awards of indefinite-quantity contracts under a single solicitation for the same or similar supplies or services to two or more sources; and (ii) an order placed against an indefinite quantity contract under a—(A) Federal Supply Schedule contract, or (B) Task-order contract or delivery-order contract awarded by another agency (*i.e.*, Governmentwide acquisition contract or multi-agency contract).[719]

The DOD has gone even a step further. Section 801 of the National Defense Authorization Act for Fiscal Year 2004 provides that a DOD department, agency, or activity may not execute an acquisition strategy that includes a consolidation of contract requirements with a total value exceeding $5,000,000, unless the Senior Procurement Executive concerned conducts market research, identifies any alternative contracting approaches that would involve a lesser degree of consolidation, and determines that the consolidation is necessary and justified. [720] Pursuant to the interim rule implementing the statute, "consolidation of contract requirements means the use of a solicitation to obtain offers for a single contract or a multiple award contract . . . ."[721] Under the definition of "multiple award contract," the interim rule specifically includes the GSA MAS contracts.[722]

Notes:

[558] GOVERNMENT CONTRACTS REFERENCE BOOK 121.

[559] 60 Fed. Reg. 48,231, 48,246, 48,247 (Sept. 18, 1995) (to be codified at 48 C.F.R. pts. 2, 3, 5, 6, 7, 8, 9, 10, 11, 12, 14, 15, 16, 22, 23, 31, 36, 42, 44, 46, 47, 49, 52, and 53).

560 FAR 12.301(a).

561 The creation of the IFF was not strictly the product of GSA's unprompted creative thinking. In 1994, the House Committee on Appropriations directed GSA to examine alternatives for reimbursable funding for several of its programs. 59 Fed. Reg. 66,545 (Dec. 27, 1994) (to be codified at 48 C.F.R. pt. 552); see GSAR 552.238-76 (Sept. 1999).

562 60 Fed Reg. 19,360, 19,361 (Apr. 18, 1995) (to be codified at 48 C.F.R. pts. 538 and 532). Interestingly, when GSA first implemented the IFF, the Office of Acquisition Policy suggested that "[t]he fee is currently 1%. As schedule volume increases, we expect the fee to decrease." FSS Acquisition Letter FC-95-3 (Apr. 11, 1995). Since 1995, Schedule volume has increased by more than 1,000 percent, yet the IFF remained at 1 percent until it recently was reduced to ¾ %. 68 Fed. Reg. 41286 (July 11, 2003).

563 Letter from Patricia M. Mead to Coalition for Government Procurement (June 26, 2003).

564 Id.

565 See GSAR 552.238-74 (Sept. 1999).

566 On July 27, 2001, the GSBCA upheld a contractor's challenge to the GSA's application of the IFF under a MAS contract. *Xerox Corp. v. GSA*, GSBCA No. 15190, 01-2 BCA ¶ 31,528. Xerox had calculated its IFF payments and paid the IFF based on the amount of the *net* payments it received each quarter from Schedule sales. An audit by the GSA Office of Inspector General concluded that Xerox had underpaid the IFF by failing to include the value of trade-ins associated with each sale. The contracting officer thereafter asserted a claim for the underpaid IFF and Xerox appealed to the GSBCA. Arguing before the GSBCA, GSA asserted that Xerox's IFF payment should have been derived from the total amount paid for a product, including the value of any trade-ins. (In other words, GSA argued for the following formula: Cash Paid + Value of Trade-in = Total Price of Product.) Based upon this formula, GSA claimed that Xerox owed the Government $163,362 in IFF underpayments. The GSBCA rejected GSA's argument based upon the language of the Industrial Funding Fee Clause and the course

of dealings between the parties (which, fortunately for Xerox, was memorialized in writing). Specifically, the GSBCA gave significant weight to correspondence between Xerox and the Government whereby Xerox informed the Government that, in accordance with its standard practice, it planned to treat trade-ins as "open market" discounts from the customer's purchase price that would not be subject to the terms and conditions of the Schedule contract. Although the contract was awarded prior to the inception of the IFF, the GSBCA found that the subsequent incorporation of the IFF requirement did not alter the mutual understanding of the parties regarding the nature of trade-ins.

[567] However, where an authorized purchaser references the MAS contract number on its purchase order notwithstanding the existence of a pre-existing, non-MAS contractual relationship with the vendor, the vendor must treat the sale as a Schedule sale. *See Contemporaries, Inc. v. GSA*, GSBCA No. 15660, Nov. 29, 2001 (holding that MAS vendor underpaid IFF by failing to treat sales under NIH blanket purchase agreement as Schedule purchases).

[568] 48 C.F.R. 552.238-74 (July 2003).

[569] Letter from Assistant FSS Commissioner Patricia M. Mead to Coalition for Government Procurement (June 26, 2003).

[570] *Id.*

[571] *See, e.g., Photon Technology International, Inc. vs. General Services Administration*, GSBCA 14918, June 23, 1999 (holding that contractor has burden of identifying Schedule purchasers).

[572] *See, e.g.*, FAR 8.402(f).

[573] Vendors should be aware that at least one GSA Schedule Acquisition Center (PES) takes the position that the IFF applies to "other direct costs." Unless ODCs are negotiated, priced, and explicitly included on Schedule, however, such costs should not include an IFF. Nonetheless, the PES Solicitation says what it says, and vendors should take care to comply with the terms of the contract or to seek to have the questionable provision removed.

[574] "The Steps to Success" (Spring 2003) at 24.

[575] Letter from Assistant FSS Commissioner Patricia M. Mead to Coalition for Government Procurement (June 26, 2003) ("I do agree

with you that we need to keep promoting greater consistency and communication in ensuring a common understanding of what constitutes a schedule sale both within my office and in our relationship with our contractors.").

576 GSAR 55d.238-74(b)(1) (July 2003)

577 *See* http://72a.gsa.gov.

578 *See* GSAR 552.238-74(d) (July 2003) and FAR 52.232-17.

579 *Id.*

580 *See infra* Chapter XXIII for a detailed discussion of the False Claims Act.

581 GSAR 552.238-74(a)(1) (July 2003).

582 Form 72A can be found at *http://VSC.gsa.gov*. It is mandatory that vendors submit the 72A form to GSA electronically.

583 GSAR 552.238-74(a)(1).

584 Exchange rate information is available from the Treasury by calling 202.874.7994 or visiting *http://www.fms.treas.gov./intn.html*.

585 The VSC website is *http://VSC.gsa.gov*.

586 GSAR 516.203-4(a)(2) requires uses of GSAR 552.216-70, ALT 1 for multiyear contracts.

587 *See supra* Chapter VII for additional discussion regarding the Economic Price Adjustment Clause.

588 GSAR 552.216-70(c) ALT I (Sept. 1999). The Government reserves the right to raise the ceiling when market conditions during the contract period support such a change.

589 *Id.* at (d)(1).

590 *Id.* at (d)(2).

591 *Id.*

592 *Id.* at (d)(3).

593 *Id.* at (e).

594 *Id.* at (f).

595 *Id.*

596 *Id.*

597 FAR 52.212-4(a).

598 GOVERNMENT CONTRACTS REFERENCE BOOK 221.

599 FAR 52.212-4(f).

600 FAR 52.212-4(h).

[601] FAR 52.212-4(o).

[602] FAR 52.212-4(p).

[603] *See* GSAR 552.246-73, Warranty (MAS) (Mar. 2000).

[604] 41 U.S.C. §§ 51-58.

[605] FAR 3.502-1.

[606] In *Howard v. United States*, 345 F.2d 126 (1st Cir. 1965), the court, applying the predecessor statute, construed the scienter element of the Act to require specific intent. *See also* John Cibinic, Jr. & Ralph C. Nash, Jr., ADMINISTRATION OF GOVERNMENT CONTRACTS 108 (3d ed.1995).

[607] Cibinic & Nash, *supra* note 549.

[608] 41 U.S.C. § 55(a)(1)(A), (B).

[609] FAR 2.101.

[610] FAR 9.505(a) and (b).

[611] FAR 9.505(b).

[612] FAR 9.508(e).

[613] FAR 9.504.

[614] *See, e.g., Johnson Controls World Servs., Inc.*, B-286714.2, Feb. 13, 2001, 2001 CPD ¶ 29 (OCI protest sustained where agency had not determined that OCI could be resolved and where contractor had no procedure in place to mitigate against the OCI).

[615] *See* Andrew D. Irwin, *Ethics in Government Procurement/Edition III*, in BRIEFING PAPERS, No. 99-8 (July 1999).

[616] 18 U.S.C. § 201(c)(1)(a).

[617] FAR 52.203-3(c)(2).

[618] *United States v. Sun-Diamond Growers of Calif.*, 526 U.S. 398 (1999).

[619] Portions of this section were taken from Fried Frank Government Contracts Alertä News Brief No. 99-4-1, *at http://www.ffhsj.com/ govtcon/ffgalert/Index.htm.*

[620] *See* FAR 52.212-4(r), referencing 31 U.S.C. § 1352, relating to limitation on the use of appropriated funds to influence certain federal transactions. This limitation is applicable to contracts expected to exceed $100,000.

[621] 31 U.S.C. § 1352.

[622] FAR 3.802(b)(2), as implemented by FAR 52.203-11(b)(2). A "covered Federal action" is defined as any of the following: (a) the

awarding of any Federal contract, (b) the making of any Federal grant, (c) the making of any Federal loan, (d) the entering into of any cooperative agreement, or (e) the extension, continuation, renewal, amendment, or modification of any Federal contract, grant, loan, or cooperative agreement. FAR 3.801.

[623] *See* 31 U.S.C. § 1352 for prohibited and allowed lobbying activities.

[624] *Id.* § 1352(b)(4)(C).

[625] *Id.* § 1352(c)(1).

[626] *Id.* § 1352(c)(2)(A). Filing an amendment after action is initiated to impose a civil penalty will not prevent the imposition of a civil fine for a failure occurring before that date.

[627] FAR 3.104-4(c).

[628] Currently $100,000 or less.

[629] FAR 3.104-4(c).

[630] FAR 3.104-4(c)(2)(ii).

[631] FAR 3.104-4(d).

[632] FAR 3.104-4(d)(1)(ii).

[633] FAR 3.104-4(d)(2).

[634] FAR 3.104-10(d).

[635] FAR 3.104-10(d)(2)(i).

[636] 41 U.S.C. § 423(e)(1).

[637] *Id.* § 423(e)(2).

[638] *Id.*

[639] 5 C.F.R. § 2637.201.

[640] *Id.* § 2637.202.

[641] *Id.* § 2637.203.

[642] *Id.* § 2637.204.

[643] GSAR 552.232-23 (Sept. 1999).

[644] *Id.*

[645] FAR 42.1205.

[646] FAR 42.1205(a).

[647] 41 U.S.C. § 15; FAR 42.1204(a).

[648] FAR 2.101.

[649] FAR 42.1204(h).

[650] 58 Am. Jur. 2d *Novations* § 14 (1997).

[651] FAR 42.1204(e)(4).

652 19 U.S.C. § 2501 *et seq.*; H.R. Rep. No. 103-826(I), at 146 (1994), *reprinted in* 1994 U.S.C.C.A.N. 3773, 3918.

653 19 U.S.C. § 2511.

654 *Id.* §§ 2511, 2512.

655 This section was previously published by West Group and is reprinted here with the permission of West Group. John Chierichella, Jonathan Aronie, & Andrew Skowronek, *Domestic and Foreign Product Preferences*, *in* Briefing Papers No. 00-13 (West Grp. Dec. 2000).

656 FAR 25.402(a)(2).

657 FAR 25.402(a) and 25.405.

658 69 Fed. Reg. at 77871.

659 The WTO GPA is available at http://www.wto.org/english/tratop_e/gproc_e/gp_gpa_e.htm.

660 FAR 25.402(a).

661 FAR 25.403(c).

662 FAR 25.404 and 25.405.

663 FAR 25.402(b).

664 *Laptops Falls Church, Inc. v. Dep't of Justice*, GSBCA No. 12953-P, 95-1 BCA ¶ 27,311 (1994).

665 *Id.* at 136,126.

666 *See also Data Transformation Corp.*, GSBCA No. 8982-P, 87-3 BCA ¶ 20,017 (holding that agency's decision to apply the TAA threshold on an end item-by-end item basis did not violate the statute or the FAR).

667 FAR 52.225-6. *But see RMTC/Microware*, GSBCA No. 10060-P *et al.*, 89-3 BCA ¶ 21,985 (referring to USTR's position that, in applying the TAA threshold, agencies should "[u]se total contract amount unless multiple awards will be made . . .").

668 FAR 25.403(b)(2).

669 *Id.* at (b)(3). *See also Int'l Bus. Machs. Corp.*, GSBCA No. 10532-P, 90-2 BCA ¶ 22,824, at 114,604 (valuing a GSA non-mandatory Schedule contract, for TAA threshold purposes, according to the total estimated sales of the entire contract); *Tic-La-Dex Bus. Sys., Inc.*, B-235016.2, October 6, 1989, 89-2 CPD ¶ 323 (stating that the value, for dollar threshold purposes, of a non-mandatory GSA

Schedule contract is equal to the estimated dollar value of the entire contract for the whole of the contracting period).

[670] 19 U.S.C. § 2518; FAR 25.001. *See also CompuAdd Corp. v. Dep't of Air Force*, GSBCA No. 12021-P, 93-2 BCA ¶ 25,811, for an excellent discussion of the TAA substantial transformation test. *See* FAR 25.003 for a list of "designated countries."

[671] *See, e.g., Becton Dickinson Acutecare*, B-238942, July 20, 1990, 90-2 CPD ¶ 55.

[672] 19 U.S.C. § 2515(b)(1) (The "Secretary of the Treasury shall provide for the prompt issuance of advisory rulings and final determinations on whether, under [the substantial transformation test] an article is or would be a product of a foreign country or instrumentality" for whom application of discriminatory procurement laws has been waived.); 19 C.F.R. §§ 177.21-177.31 (Manufacturers, among others, may seek either an advisory ruling or a final determination from the U.S. Customs Service as to an article's country of origin as defined by the substantial transformation test.); 19 C.F.R. § 177.22(a); FAR 25.001(d).

[673] U.S. Customs HQ 563131 (Feb. 11, 2005); U.S. Customs HQ 561661 (July 20, 2000); U.S. Customs HQ 560677 (Feb. 3, 1998); U.S. Customs HQ 735608 (Apr. 27, 1995).

[674] U.S. Customs HQ 561661 (July 20, 2000).

[675] *Id.* and cases cited therein.

[676] U.S. Customs HQ 560677 (Feb. 3, 1998).

[677] *Id.*

[678] *Id.*

[679] *Id.; see also* U.S. Customs HQ 735608 (Apr. 27, 1995) (concluding that "the foreign components that are used in the manufacture of desktop computers [in the proposed scenarios] are substantially transformed as a result of the operations performed").

[680] *See, e.g.,* U.S. Customs NY C85792 (a chassis imported with a pre-installed processing unit, an input device (in this case, a pointing device), and an output device qualified as a "system" under the Harmonized Tariff Schedule ("HTS"); a chassis imported with a pre-installed processing unit, output device, hard disk drive/CD-ROM drive, and battery, but without an input device, did *not*

qualify as a "system" under the HTS); U.S. Customs NY C88416 (May 29, 1998) (a chassis imported with a pre-installed motherboard/CPU chip, display screen, keyboard/keyboard BIOS, hard drive, floppy drive, modem, and CD-ROM drive, but without a BIOS chip, did *not* qualify as a "system" under the HTS).

[681] FAR 25.402(a)(2).

[682] Ch. 212, §§ 1 to 3, 47 Stat. 1520 (codified as amended in 41 U.S.C. §§ 10a-10c and 19 U.S.C. §§ 2511, 2515); FAR 25.101.

[683] FAR 25.101.

[684] 63 Fed. Reg. 51,642, 51,643 (Sept. 28, 1998) (to be codified at 48 C.F.R. pts. 1, 5, 6, 9, 12, 13, 14, 15, 17, 25, and 52).

[685] FAR 2.101; FAR 25.003.

[686] John Chierichella, Jonathan Aronie, & Andrew Skowronek, *Domestic and Foreign Product Preferences*, in BRIEFING PAPERS No. 00-13 (West Grp. Dec. 2000).

[687] *See supra* Chapter VII for a discussion on the Basis of Award and relevant category of customers.

[688] Price reductions, however, apply only to Schedule items. *See Photon Tech. Int'l v. GSA*, GSBCA No. 14910, 99-2 BCA ¶ 30,456.

[689] In *Information Handling Servs.*, GSBCA No. 7563, 88-2 BCA ¶ 20,789, for example, the GSBCA held that the Government properly reduced the unit price of two items in a MAS contract because the contract contained a Price Reductions Clause and, during the term of the contract, the vendor sold those same items to another federal agency at a reduced price. Under the terms of the then-current Price Reductions Clause, according to the GSBCA, if the vendor sold any contract item to another federal agency at a reduced price, the vendor was required to give notice and similarly reduce the contract price for that item. The GSBCA found it immaterial that the item had been purchased under a separately negotiated contract with another agency because the clause made no distinction between different types of agencies or contracts.

[690] *3M Bus. Prods. Sales, Inc.*, GSBCA No. 4722 *et al.*, 78-2 BCA ¶ 13,362, *aff'd on reconsideration*, 79-1 BCA ¶ 13,567.

[691] Contractors, however, could offer temporary "Government only" price reductions. This temporary "Government only" reduction

allowed the vendor to reduce the price to the Government for short periods of time without having the reduction apply for the remainder of the contract period, as had previously been the case.

[692] 47 Fed. Reg. 50,242, 50,243 (Nov. 5, 1982) (to be codified at 48 C.F.R. Chapter 5).

[693] GSAR 552.238-76 (effective Oct. 19, 1994).

[694] GSAR 552.238-75(c)(1) (Sept. 1999).

[695] GSAR 552.238-75(b) (Sept. 1999).

[696] *Racon, Inc.*, GSBCA No. 3628, 73-1 BCA ¶ 9789.

[697] GSAR 552.238-75(c)(2) (Sept. 1999). As noted previously in Chapter VII, vendors can attempt to negotiate a relationship between the Basis of Award customer and the Government that is absolute rather than proportional. It is essential to memorialize such an agreement in writing.

[698] *Id.* It is useful to note that the dramatic impact of the price reduction in this example may suggest that the vendor negotiated an inappropriate Basis of Award category of customers. *See supra* Chapter VII for more information on selecting an appropriate Basis of Award category of customers.

[699] *See, e.g., Julian Freeman*, ASBCA No. 46675, 94-3 BCA ¶ 27,280, at 135,906-07 ("In general, a BPA is not considered to be a contract because it lacks mutuality of consideration. . . . Under a BPA, neither party actually commits itself nor assumes any duty toward the other.").

[700] *3M Business Prods. Sales, Inc.*, GSBCA No. 4722R *et al.*, 78-2 BCA ¶ 13,362, *aff'd on reconsideration*, 79-1 BCA ¶ 13,567; *see also United States v. Data Translation, Inc.*, 984 F.2d 1256, 1264 (1st Cir. 1992) (discussing contractors application of "Volume Purchase Agreements" providing that "if the year's purchase orders exceed, or fall short of, the amount of the initial commitment, [then the contractor] will adjust the discount accordingly").

[701] Letter from GSA National Furniture Center to Schedule Vendor (Sept. 10, 1996). *See also Invacare Corp.*, VABCA Nos. 6574, 6599, 6600, Oct. 3, 2002, 02-2 BCA ¶ 32,040 (noting VA OIG's decision not to exclude commercial company from Basis of Award because, among other things, the contract "did not contain a penalty provision or provision for monetary adjustment for nonperformance.").

[702] GSAR 552.238-75(d)(3) (Sept. 1999).

[703] Robert S. Brams *et al.*, *Multiple Award Schedule Contracting: A Practical Guide to Surviving its Shortcomings, Ambiguities and Pitfalls*, 19 Pub. Contr. L.J. 441, 472 (1990).

[704] *Id.*

[705] This proposition has been corroborated by GSA. In private conversations with contractors, GSA contracting officers have suggested that GSA would not be bothered if a *small* number of customers idiosyncratically were to receive a better than disclosed discount. It is questionable, however, whether the OIG will adopt a similar reading of the Price Reductions Clause. And, obviously, neither the contracting officer nor the OIG will sit idly by if such "exceptions" start to become the rule. *See 3M Bus. Prods. Sales, Inc.*, GSBCA No. 4722, 78-2 BCA ¶ 13,362, at 65,308 (rejecting contractor's argument that the price reduction was not implicated because "the higher discounts given were sporadic and few in number" but *only* because "[c]onsiderable sums of money were involved").

[706] *See* GSAR Figure 515.4-2, Column 5.

[707] GSAR 552.212-70(a) (Aug. 1997).

[708] GSAR 552.238-75(c)(1)(ii) (Sept. 1999) (emphasis added).

[709] GSAR 552.212-70(a) (Aug. 1997).

[710] *Id.*

[711] *See infra* Chapter XXV for additional details regarding the importance of a functional internal infrastructure.

[712] GSAR 552.238-75(b) (Sept. 1999) (emphasis added).

[713] *Id.* at (f) (emphasis added).

[714] *See* 70 Fed. Reg. 20831 (April 22, 2005).

[715] 70 Fed. Reg. 21729.

[716] The definition is codified in 15 U.S.C. § 632(o).

[717] *See* 15 U.S.C. § 644(e).

[718] *See* 68 Fed. Reg. 59999 (October 20, 2003).

[719] FAR 2.101(b)(2).

[720] Pub. Law No. 108-136.

[721] *See* DFARS 207.170; 69 Fed. Reg. 55986 (September 17, 2004).

[722] *Id.*

XV.

ORDER FULFILLMENT

"The woods are lovely, dark and deep.
But I have promises to keep,
And miles to go before I sleep . . . ."

-Robert Frost

After a brief overview of how the Government places Schedule orders, this chapter examines the practical aspects of managing Schedule contracts as they relate to order fulfillment. In this context, "order fulfillment" encompasses taking and processing orders, negotiating blanket purchase agreements ("BPAs"), submitting invoices, and understanding the GSAR requirements relating to packing and packaging. In practice, many of these issues depend upon a vendor's relationship with its contracting officer. Thus, the information in this chapter should serve as a starting point, not as a comprehensive how-to manual.

A. *Understanding How The Government Places Schedule Orders*

While the MAS Program unquestionably facilitates the placement of Government orders, it does not do away with—nor was the Program intended to do away with—all formalities. Generally speaking, the steps that a Schedule purchaser must take before making a purchase depend upon the value of the supplies or services being purchased.

- For orders that do not exceed the micro-purchase threshold,[723] Schedule purchasers may place orders with any Schedule vendor without performing a best value analysis.[724] Although the FAR does not require agencies to solicit information from a specific number of schedule vendors (except with respect to some DOD purchases), it does advise agencies to "attempt to distribute orders among contractors."[725]

- For orders that exceed the micro-purchase threshold but that are below the contract's maximum order threshold,[726] Schedule purchasers are required to review GSA *Advantage!* and make a best value determination *or* review the price lists of three different Schedule vendors and make a best value determination. FAR 8.405-1 provides that, when making a best value determination, the ordering office may consider (i) past performance, (ii) special features, (iii) trade-in considerations, (iv) probable life of the item, (v) warranty considerations, (vi) maintenance availability, (vi) past performance, (vii) environmental and energy efficiency considerations, and (viii) delivery terms.[727]

- For orders that exceed the maximum order threshold, in addition to undertaking the foregoing activities, Schedule purchasers must review additional Schedule price lists and seek further price reductions "from the schedule contractor(s) considered to offer the best value". If further price reductions are not offered, the Agency still may place the order.[728] Either way, however, the ordering agency must ensure that its selection provides the best value and results in the lowest overall cost alternative.[729]

In each scenario, for purchases over the micro-purchase threshold, the Schedule purchaser must place the order with the vendor offering the best value.[730] The Government Accountability Office ("GAO"), however, will afford GSA substantial latitude in making this determination.[731]

Schedule orders are placed by the acquiring agency's contracting officer.[732] Once the contracting officer has complied with the ordering requirements and has selected the vendor representing the best value for purchases over the micro-purchase threshold, the contracting officer must then actually place the order. Orders may be placed using any of the methods elected by the vendor. Vendors can elect to receive orders either by computer transmission or by fax.[733] If the vendor elects to have orders processed electronically, it will be required to enter into one or more Trading Partner Agreements ("TPAs") with each agency placing orders.[734] TPAs are required to ensure that both parties have a mutual understanding of their rights and responsibilities and agree on the ordering protocol.[735] Ordering agencies may also make orders via the mail; and, if an order is mailed, it is considered issued on the date the order is mailed by the agency.[736] If a vendor is using dealers for marketing, it has the option of allowing dealers to receive orders.[737] Finally, ordering agencies can place orders through GSA *Advantage!*, GSA's on-line ordering system; however, the system is not fully operational and some vendors' supplies and services (and prices) still are not included on-line. For purchases under the micro-purchase threshold, orders may be made orally.

Agencies generally will issue a purchase order using Form 347, the standardized form for ordering supplies and services.[738] However, use of the form is optional; therefore, the agency may choose to issue the order in another format. Regardless of the format, the order must contain the minimum following information:

- Complete shipping and billing addresses
- Contract number and date
- Agency order number

- F.o.b. delivery point
- Discount terms
- Delivery time
- Special item number or national stock number
- Brief, complete description of each item
- Quantity
- Number of units
- Unit price
- Total price of the order
- Points of inspection and acceptance
- Other pertinent data
- Marking requirements
- Preservation, packaging, and packing instructions[739]

Vendors should confirm the accuracy of the order and ensure that the order is clearly identified as a Schedule order prior to entering the vendor's accounting system. Differentiating MAS orders from open market orders for the purpose of paying the IFF is becoming increasingly important as GSA increases its audits in this area. *See* Chapter XIV for further information on this important issue.

B. *Requests for Quotation (RFQs)*

The FAR's requirement that agencies place Schedule orders with the vendor offering the best value (at least where the order exceeds the micro-purchase threshold) does not mean that the agency must conduct a formal evaluation of offers. For example, agencies need not conduct a formal negotiated procurement;[740] issue a solicitation;[741] conduct a competition;[742] conduct a formal evaluation;[743] provide vendors with evaluation criteria on which the Agency will perform its best value analysis;[744] comply with FAR Part 15;[745] issue an RFQ or otherwise request proposals;[746] undertake a price realism analysis;[747] provide advance notice of Agency's selection criteria;[748] seek competition outside the Schedules program;[749] synopsize the requirements;[750] provide vendors any specific minimum amount of time to respond to solicitation, to the extent a solicitation is issued;[751] hold discussions;[752] prepare extensive documentation;[753] or conduct a formal debriefing.[754] Vendors that understand these advantages of the MAS program are better equipped to assist their customers make sensible purchases that do not exceed the bounds of the MAS program.

Nonetheless, agencies frequently will issue an RFQ—and often will conduct a FAR Part 15-like procurement—in order to identify the particular Schedule vendor that will offer the Government the best value for the money. Where an agency takes this approach and undertakes a formal evaluation of offerors, it increases its obligations. Indeed, the GAO will treat such an approach akin to a FAR Part 15 procurement and, in the face of a bid protest, will assess the agency's action as though FAR Part 15 applied to the procurement, even though, under normal circumstances, FAR Part 15 would not apply to a Schedule purchase.[755]

One approach that more and more agencies are taking is to post an RFQ on GSA's new E-Buy web site. E-Buy is GSA's new electronic RFQ web site. According to the FAR, E-Buy "allows ordering activities to post requirements, obtain quotes, and issue orders electronically. The E-Buy system is accessible via www.ebuy.gsa.gov.

C. *Taking Schedule Orders*

When the vendor receives an order (whether following the issuance of an RFQ or not), it should confirm that all of the necessary information is clearly delineated. Vendors should also confirm that the buyer placing an order is an authorized purchaser. If the vendor questions the buyer's authority, it should confirm the order with its GSA contracting officer. Furthermore, vendors also should confirm that the product or service being purchased clearly falls within the scope of the particular Schedule Contract under which it is being purchased.[756] As a result of alleged abused by agencies and contractors, both the GSA Office of Inspector General and the Industrial Operations Analysts now conduct "scope of contract" reviews.

D. _Sole Source Justification and Approval_

While orders placed under the MAS program are exempt from FAR Part 6's competition requirements, agencies do not have unfettered discretion to make sole source awards to their favored contractors. Indeed, the GAO has held that such awards, at least where the value of the award exceeds the micro-purchase threshold, clearly violate the terms of the MAS Program.[757] Under appropriate circumstances, however, agencies may make sole source awards so long as the follow the specific procedures outlined in FAR Part 8 for doing so.

FAR Part 8 provides that agencies may procure requirements on a sole source basis "only if the need to do so is justified in writing and approved at the [appropriate] levels."[758] The written justification must comply with the requirements of FAR 6.303-2, which describes the written justifications that apply to non-Schedule purchases. FAR 8.405-6 goes on to identify five different thresholds for sole source awards and to establish slightly different requirements for each, as follows:

1. For proposed orders exceeding the micro-purchase threshold, but not exceeding the simplified acquisition threshold, the ordering activity contracting officer may solicit from one source, if the ordering activity contracting officer determines that the circumstances deem only one source is reasonably available (_e.g._, urgency, exclusive licensing agreement, industrial mobilization). The contracting officer shall approve the justification unless a higher approval level is established in accordance with agency procedures.

2. For proposed orders exceeding the simplified acquisition threshold, but not exceeding $500,000, the ordering activity contracting officer's certification that the

justification is accurate and complete to the best of the ordering activity contracting officer's knowledge and belief will serve as approval, unless a higher approval level is established in accordance with agency procedures.

3. For a proposed order exceeding $500,000, but not exceeding $10 million, the competition advocate for the procuring activity, designated pursuant to FAR 6.501, or an official described in FAR 6.304(a)(3) or (a)(4) must approve the justification. This authority is not delegable.

4. For a proposed order exceeding $10 million but not exceeding $50 million, the head of the procuring activity or an official described in FAR 6.304(a)(3)(i) or (ii) shall approve the justification. This authority is not delegable.

5. For a proposed order exceeding $50 million, the official described in FAR 6.304(a)(4) shall approve the justification. This authority is not delegable, except as provided in FAR 6.304(a)(4).

Notwithstanding these sole source possibilities, GAO clearly prefers full and open competition to the extent possible.[759]

E. *Payment Generally*

The MAS Program contemplates numerous different payment mechanisms for Schedule purchasers. Purchasers may pay with cash, imprest funds,[760] and Governmentwide commercial purchase cards or through an electronic funds transfer ("EFT").[761] The Government's decision on the method of payment can have important implications for the vendor as each method has different requirements.

The Government's preferred method of payment is through EFT, and most contracts will include FAR 52.232-33 or 52.232-34, requiring the vendor to accept payment by EFT. If this method is used, the vendor must use a financial institution that will receive and process EFT through the Automated Clearing House ("ACH") system or the Fedwire Transfer system. The ACH system is the primary EFT system used by agencies to make payments.[762] Under the provisions of FAR 52.232-33, the vendor is required to register its payment information in the Central Contractor Registration database.

In order to receive EFT payments within ten days after the billing office receives a proper invoice, the vendor must have received and fulfilled purchase orders using Electronic Data Interchange ("EDI").[763] In addition, the vendor must have generated and submitted its invoice in a valid EDI format. These invoices must be submitted using GSA-approved processes and must adhere to implementation conventions provided by GSA. If the vendor does not adhere to these requirements, the payments will revert to the normal thirty-day cycle.[764]

Additionally, the Government may choose to make payments the old-fashioned way—by check. In such a case, the Government will require that the vendor provide an address where the Government can mail checks.[765] If the vendor's remittance address changes, this change must be reflected by an administrative change for the contract to be effective. Merely changing the address on the invoice is insufficient and may result in payments being sent to the old address.[766]

All payments, regardless of means, are subject to the Prompt Payment Act,[767] which requires the Government to render payment within the time specified in the contract or, if there is no time specified, within thirty days of receipt of an invoice from the vendor. The Government is required to pay interest if payment is not made within the period specified. Interest does not accrue for payments in dispute or for defective invoices.

F. *Governmentwide Commercial Purchase Cards*

GSAR 552.232-77 and 552.232-79[768] govern the use of Governmentwide commercial purchase cards.[769] These purchase cards are simply credit cards issued to Government officials to facilitate the purchase of certain supplies or services.[770] Under the applicable regulations, MAS vendors are required to accept the purchase cards for all purchases at or below the micro-purchase threshold (currently $2,500), regardless of whether the orders were taken orally or in writing.[771] The regulations "encourage" vendors to accept the purchase card for purchases over the threshold, but acceptance is not required. In either situation, the Government may not use the purchase card for any purchase that exceeds the particular agency's order limitation.[772] If a vendor will not accept the purchase card for purchases over the micro-purchase threshold, it must notify the ordering agency within 24 hours of receiving the order.[773]

A vendor may not process a transaction for payment through the "credit card clearinghouse"[774] until the purchased supplies have been shipped or services performed.[775] To ensure that the purchase card payment is not processed prior to order completion, the vendor, depending upon its accounting system, may need to create a special procedure to process these payments. The vendor may want to take into account this restriction when making a decision as to whether or not to accept the purchase card for orders over the micro-purchase threshold.[776] Additionally, the vendor immediately must credit the cardholder's account for any defective or faulty items that are returned to the vendor unless the ordering agency requests correction or replacement rather than a refund.[777] Vendors whose standard commercial practices differ from those required by GSAR 552.232-77 should ensure the implementation of separate policies.

G. *Invoicing*

The MAS Program's invoicing requirements are set forth at FAR 52.212-4(g) and GSAR 552.232-74(d).[778] Vendors are required to submit an original invoice and keep a copy of each invoice in the event of an audit. Such invoices should be retained for at least three years following final payment under the contract.[779]

While a basic point, it is worth emphasizing that vendors should take care to ensure that invoices are addressed not only to the proper agency, but to the proper department within the proper agency. Many vendors have found their payments delayed due to improperly addressed invoices.

There is no single form for a proper Schedule invoice. FAR 52.212-4, however, sets forth the information that must be included on an invoice unless contrary direction is provided in the solicitation or resulting contract. FAR 52.212-4(g), among other things, provides that every invoice for the purchase of commercial items shall include the following information:

(1) Name and address of the Contractor;

(2) Invoice date;

(3) Contract number, contract line item number, and if applicable, the order number;

(4) Description, quantity, unit of measure, unit price and extended price of the items delivered;

(5) Shipping number and date of shipment including the bill of lading number and weight of shipment if shipped on Government bill of lading;

(6) Terms of any prompt payment discount offered;

(7) Name and address of the official to whom payment is to be sent; and

(8) Name, title, and phone number of person to be notified in event of defective invoice.

Additionally, if the Prompt Payment Act is incorporated into the contract—as it is in most Schedule contracts—vendors are encouraged to assign each invoice a unique identification number.

Vendors should be vigilant in ensuring that their invoices are accurate and up-to-date. Not only should the invoice capture all the necessary information from the Schedule purchaser and the purchase (including relevant payment terms and conditions), it also accurately should reflect all necessary information about the vendor. For example, if the vendor accepts electronic payments, the vendor must be certain that the invoice accurately reflects all information relating thereto. Changes in such information (such as a change of a bank or bank account) should be incorporated into a revised invoice immediately.

Finally, as with almost every element of the MAS Program, compliance is important and noncompliance is subject to significant penalties. Inaccurate invoices can lead to inaccurate payments that, subsequently, can lead to Price Reductions Clause violations, Price Adjustment Clause violations, or, worse, False Claims Act allegations. Thus, ensuring accuracy in invoicing is a sound business practice on many levels.

H. *Blanket Purchase Agreements*

The FAR explicitly provides that ordering agencies may establish BPAs with MAS vendors in order to facilitate Schedule purchases.[780] A BPA is defined as a

> simplified method of filing anticipated repetitive needs for supplies or services by establishing "charge accounts" with qualified sources of supply . . . . [781]

The 1990s witnessed tremendous growth in the Government's use of BPAs, fueled by an effective GSA marketing campaign. Lisa M. Burke, a senior attorney at Hewlett-Packard Company, recognizing this growth, aptly described the importance of understanding the nature of BPAs as follows:

> With the promise of ease of use and better prices and the lack of restrictive regulatory guidance, BPAs are undeniably appealing to government procurement professionals. With these factors in mind, it is advisable that COTS suppliers along with in-house counsel evaluate and understand fully the nuances of the BPA procurement methodologies and their inherent effects on the company's business policies, procedures and

financial bottom line. This evaluation should
ultimately address the contractor's question "to
BPA or not to BPA?"[782]

BPAs offer Schedule purchasers and vendors a number of
advantages. BPAs provide Schedule vendors an additional avenue
toward enhancing their Government sales. From the Schedule
purchaser's point of view, BPAs typically provide a means of
procuring additional discounts that exceed the vendor's published
Schedule discounts. (Remember, vendors may discount sales to
federal agencies without triggering the Price Reductions Clause.)
BPAs also provide Schedule purchasers with an even more
simplified avenue for making recurring purchases by avoiding
the need to open new accounts and negotiate new prices on more
than one occasion.[783] Orders under a BPA, however, like any
other MAS order, must comply with all MAS ordering
requirements.[784]

Schedule vendors become involved in Government BPAs in
two ways. First, a Schedule purchaser can approach a vendor
seeking to open a single BPA under the umbrella of the vendor's
Schedule contract. Such BPAs generally are used when the agency
easily can define its requirements. Second, several federal
agencies have very large, multiple award BPAs for which Schedule
vendors can compete. In this context, the BPA is like a "mini-MAS
Program" organized under the auspices of the overall MAS
Program.

In either type of BPA, the Schedule purchaser establishes
the agreement directly with the Schedule vendor. Some agencies
use GSA's standard BPA template (available at *http://
www.fss.gsa.gov/schedules/docs/sugbpa.doc*) to memorialize the
BPA terms and conditions. Other agencies employ their own
lengthy written agreements. Either way, BPAs typically address,
among other things, ordering frequency, invoicing, discounts,
and delivery locations and times.[785] In summary fashion,
FAR 13.303-3 provides that the following terms and conditions
must be incorporated into the resulting BPA:

- A description of the agreement, including a statement that the vendor shall furnish the requested supplies or services during a specified period and within a stipulated aggregate amount
- A statement that the Government "is obligated only to the extent of authorized purchases actually made under the BPA"
- A maximum dollar limitation for an individual purchase order issued under the BPA
- A list of individuals authorized to purchase under the BPA
- A requirement that all shipments, with some exceptions, will be accompanied by detailed sales slips
- A statement regarding invoices

As the foregoing list is merely a summary of the FAR's requirements, Schedule vendors considering participating in a BPA should review FAR Parts 8 and 13 in detail.

Agencies order through BPAs in a similar manner to how they order through the Schedule program generally. Where an agency establishes a single BPA, the agency's authorized users "may place the order directly under the established BPA when the need for the supply or service arises."[786] The process is slightly more detailed where an agency has established multiple BPAs. In such a situation, the Agency must ensure that it is receiving the best value from among the BPA holders. (The agency need not open competition to Schedule holders outside of its BPAs so long as the supply or service being acquired falls within the scope of the BPA.) To this end, the agency must (i) forward its requirements (or a statement of work) and evaluation criteria "to an appropriate additional number of BPA holders, as established in the BPA ordering procedures" and (ii) "evaluate the responses received, make a best value determination, and place the order with the BPA holder offering the best value."[787]

BPAs—particularly single BPAs negotiated with high dollar limits and broadly worded statements of work for services—have recently come under heavy criticism from commentators. As noted above, GSA guidance specifically provides that authorized users under a single BPA "may place the order directly under the established BPA when the need for service arises." Additional guidance provides that "[s]ince a best value selection is made when the single BPA is established, the ordering office does not need to make a separate best value selection for each order under the BPA." Read together, these statements constitute clear guidance to contracting officers to utilize BPAs to engage in sole sourse contracting on an unprecedented scale. Contracting officials have been all too willing to act on this guidance, negotiating BPAs, for example, under which orders valued up to one half billion dollars can be noncompetitively awarded. As one commentator put it:

> We would like to see the legal authority for these extraordinary rules. When the Competition in Contracting Act established that the norm for Government procurement was competition, it declared that the Federal Supply Schedule technique met this norm, but that was at a time when the schedule was being used to buy quantities of commercial products. Surely, Congress didn't contemplate these huge procurements of ill-defined services. It boggles the mind that this authority has been stretched this far.[788]

Given the immense popularity of BPAs within the federal infrastructure, it is likely that this "stretch" will continue until some court, administrative board or the Congress finds that the practice has exceeded its elastic limits.

A final word regarding non-governmental BPAs: Schedule vendors should be aware that GSA does not consider the *potential* value of a commercial BPA to be the value of the order for Price Reductions Clause exemption purposes. This issue is discussed in greater detail in Chapter XIV.

I. *Packing/Packaging*

GSAR 552.211-75 sets forth the requirements for packing and packaging supplies purchased by Schedule purchasers. In short, this provision provides that products must be preserved, packed, and packaged in accordance with normal commercial practices as defined by the product specification.[789] This provision further directs vendors to ensure that supplies are packaged in a manner that complies with the "National Motor Freight Classification" that is in effect at the time of shipment. The National Motor Freight Classification system contains a list of general packing definitions and specifications for commonly used packaging[790] and requires, among other things, that items be shipped in uniform containers (except for residual quantities).

On some occasions, ordering agencies require special packaging. When this is the case, vendors should be certain that such requirements are set forth in a written agreement between the vendor and the ordering agency. It is especially important to memorialize in writing any agreement that is not consistent with the terms and conditions of the Schedule contract itself.

The Schedule contract requires that the vendor include a packing list in every shipment. GSAR 552.211-77 identifies the information that must be included on a proper packing list.

If the vendor fails to package products as required, the Government is within its rights to refuse acceptance of the products and return them to the vendor. In the context of sales to a GSA wholesale center, the Government is within its rights to repack the items as required by the contract and bill the vendor the costs of the repacking (including time and materials).[791] Additionally, the Government can cease future purchases from the vendor until the noncompliance is remedied. If the vendor fails to cure its noncompliance, then it can be found to be in breach of contract, which could lead to termination of the delivery order or even to termination of the contract as a whole.

J. *Deliveries*

The terms and conditions of a MAS contract cover all aspects of the delivery process, from price to schedule to the use of the United States Postal Service ("USPS"). The rules governing the delivery of Schedule orders, often overlooked, should be understood and followed.

With respect to delivery costs, vendors are required to incorporate such costs into the advertised price of all Schedule products.[792] Vendors also are required to indicate which products can be delivered on an expedited basis. Information relating to such expedited delivery will be negotiated with GSA during contract negotiation and will be identified in the terms and conditions section of the resulting contract. The vendor also should ensure that such information and the prices relating thereto are included on its Schedule price list.

The MAS rules relating to a vendor's delivery schedule are set forth at GSAR 552.211-78. This clause allows vendors to establish a delivery schedule—which will be incorporated into the vendor's contract and price list—that will be adhered to throughout the life of the contract unless modified by the contracting officer. The vendor may deliver items in a shorter period of time than is set forth in the contract at its discretion without the permission of the contracting officer.

Not surprisingly, the Schedule provides that MAS supplies ordered by the USPS must be delivered by the USPS as long as the supplies meet the USPS' requirements for mailability (*i.e.*, 70 pounds or less and a combined length and girth of not more than 108 inches).[793] This requirement can be waived by the contracting officer.

While the rules and regulations that relate to the delivery of Schedule items rarely form the basis of a Government audit or investigation, compliance is important for a number of reasons. First, purchasing agencies may care very little about most of the terms and conditions of the MAS Program, but they do care about receiving their purchases on time. Thus, compliance is a critical component in a vendor's client relations plan. Second, many agencies maintain records regarding their vendors' delivery performance. Ultimately, this information becomes part of a vendor's past performance data, which may be accessed, reviewed, and used by other agencies in their future purchasing decisions.[794] Third, a vendor's consistent failure to meet its delivery obligations may result in the contracting officer's refusal to award a follow-on contract (or exercise an option) when the time comes.

K. _Risk Of Loss_

FAR 52.212-4(j) provides that, unless the contract specifically provides otherwise, risk of loss passes to the Government upon either:

> (1) Delivery of the supplies to a carrier, if transportation is f.o.b. origin; or
> (2) Delivery of the supplies to the Government at the destination specified in the contract, if transportation is f.o.b. destination.

Vendors determine whether deliveries will be made f.o.b. origin or f.o.b. destination during contract negotiations. The resulting applicable delivery terms are set forth in the vendor's price list. Whatever terms are negotiated, however, the cost of delivery is embedded in the vendor's advertised Schedule prices.

L. _Open Market Orders_

Following the negotiation of a vendor's MAS contract, the vendor prepares a Schedule price list, described in detail in Chapter VIII. Among other things, the Schedule price list identifies those supplies and services that are available for purchase through the vendor's MAS contract. The inclusion of an item or service on a Schedule price list serves as a representation to the Government that such items and services are reasonably priced and comply with all applicable regulations. As a result, Schedule purchasers are relieved of many of the obligations pertaining generally to Government purchases when they order Schedule supplies and services.

For many years, however, Schedule purchasers supplemented their Schedule purchases with non-Schedule supplies and services. Such supplies and services typically are called "open market items."[795] This practice continued for years with GSA's blessing. As long as the purchases fell below a certain threshold (which varied from year to year and from contracting officer to contracting officer), GSA permitted this practice to persist—notwithstanding the fact that the open market items infrequently were the subject of competition—believing that such purchases fell within an exception to the FAR's competition requirements.[796]

Over the last few years, the law regarding the purchase of open market items has changed drastically. While the impact of these changes probably has affected Schedule purchasers more than Schedule vendors, it is important for both sides to understand the current law. For example, a vendor that fails to make an effort to ensure that a purchaser has complied with the applicable competition requirements risks seeing its award overturned in the event of a bid protest.

Since the inception of the MAS Program, GSA has permitted the purchase of open market items in conjunction with Schedule items as long as the open market items were *incidental* to the Schedule purchase.[797] The meaning of "incidental," however, never was clear. Indeed, even GSA lacked a singular definition of the term. Some contracting officers set the threshold at a certain dollar value; others set it at a certain percentage; some maintained that, as long as the value of open market items constituted less than half of the total purchase price, the open market items were "incidental."

In 1997, the United States Court of Federal Claims ("COFC") weighed into the open market debate in *ATA Defense Industries, Inc.*[798] *ATA* involved an Army Schedule purchase of firing range targets. Approximately 35 percent of the value of the Army's purchase order was attributable to open market items. The Army justified its inclusion of the open market items with its Schedule purchase—and, thus, its decision to purchase the open market items without competition—by claiming that only the Schedule vendor could supply the open market items. The protester (a vendor interested in the procurement, but not on the applicable Schedule) argued that the Army had failed to comply with applicable competition requirements with respect to the open market items.

The COFC upheld the bid protest, finding that the Army failed to comply with the applicable competition requirements. The court held that, unless the purchase of the open market items could be classified as "*de minimis*," the law required that these products be procured on a competitive basis.

Many Schedule purchasers—and, in many cases, GSA itself—ignored the court's *ATA* ruling, relying instead on the GAO decision in *ViON Corp.*[799] that affirmed the legality of open market purchases. For the following three years, Schedule vendors and Schedule purchasers operated in an environment of confusing and often contradictory requirements.

This tension came to a head in 1999 with the GAO's decision in *Pyxis Corporation*.[800] *Pyxis* involved an Army MAS procurement for the purchase of "Point of Use" medical equipment. Pyxis, the losing vendor, claimed that the Army erred in awarding to an offeror (Omnipoint) whose price list contained a significant number of open market items. Even though Pyxis failed timely to raise this protest issue, the GAO agreed to decide the matter "in view of the conflict in this area of the law between the Court of Federal Claims' *ATA* decision and our prior decisions."[801]

In light of the COFC's decision in *ATA* that there was no statutory authority for the "incidentals" test enunciated in the GAO's earlier *ViON Corp.* decision, the GAO sustained Pyxis' protest, in part, and overturned the Army's purchasing decision, finding that the Army did not comply with applicable acquisition regulations. Ironically, the GAO pointed to GSA's own published requirement that purchasers must adhere to all applicable procurement regulations in order to support its ruling. Thus, when the value of open market items exceeds the micro-purchase threshold, the purchaser must conduct a best value analysis. In rendering its decision, the GAO overruled its earlier *ViON* decision. Several recent cases have reaffirmed the GAO's *Pyxis* decision.[802]

In short, the current law governing the purchase of open market items is that Schedule purchasers must comply with all applicable competition requirements.[803] Thus, contracting officers must exercise care in reviewing the Schedule offerings of their vendors to ensure that all desired supplies and services appear on the Schedule. Where desired supplies and services do not appear on the Schedule, purchasers have three options. First, they can obviously decide not to purchase the open market items at all. Second, they can prompt the vendor to add the supplies or services to its Schedule. Third, they can purchase the open market items outside of the MAS Program as long as they adhere to all applicable competition requirements. (In valuing the open market items for purposes of determining what competition requirements apply, contracting officers must include the total value of the open market items, including options.[804])

On June 27, 2002, the FAR Council issued a final rule clarifying the procedures to be used for the purchase of open market items.[805] Under the rule, open market items (defined as "items not on the Federal Supply Schedule") may be added to an order only if all regulations concerning publication, competition, and contracting methods (*i.e.*, "all applicable acquisition regulations") have been followed. In addition, the contracting officer must make a determination that the prices for these items are fair and reasonable.[806] Open market or incidental items must be clearly labeled as such on the order.[807] Aside from being a contract requirement, this final point is especially important for vendors who, appropriately, do not pay the Industrial Funding Fee on open market purchases since many auditors and reviewers may view such purchases as "sales under the contract" without clear evidence to the contrary.

Notwithstanding the clarity of the new "open market" rules, agencies and vendors alike continue to push the envelope in this area. Vendors, however, do so at significant risk. First, "out of scope contracting" now is a significant area of audit concern.[808] The Office of Inspector General, the Industrial Operations Analysts, the Government Accountability Office,[809] and even Congress[810] have focused their sights on this particular target. Second, the Defense Contract Audit Agency has announced that it will review open market purchases by Department of Defense agencies as part of its standard incurred cost audits.[811] Third, DOD and the various branches of the military have published specific guidance to their members regarding the use of GSA Schedule contracts in order to prevent out of scope contracting.[812] Fourth, protesters (*i.e.*, disappointed bidders) have become more and more alert to the strictness of the rules in this area and will not hesitate to challenge an agency's award of a MAS order if they believe that the order includes non-Schedule items.[813]

Accordingly, vendors should take care to ensure that the products and services they offer are clearly within the scope of their particular Schedule.[814] Where the answer to this question is not clear, vendors should look to the essential nature of the work being performed.[815] Where the answer still is not clear, they should seek guidance from their contracting officer.[816]

Notes:

[773] *Id.*

[774] The ACH is a nationwide electronic funds transfer system governed by operating rules that "provide for the interbank clearing of electronic payments for participating depository financial institutions." For more information regarding the ACH, *see http://www.nacha.org/About/what_is_ach_.htm.*

[775] GSAR 552.232-77(d) (Mar. 2000).

[776] Currently the micro-purchase threshold is $2,500.

777 GSAR 552.232-77(d) (Mar. 2000).

778 GSAR 552.232-74(d) (Sept. 1999) removes the requirement for vendors to submit an original and three copies of the invoice.

779 Both GSAR 552.215-70 (Feb. 1996) and FAR 52.212-5(d) require records to be kept for three years after final payment.

780 FAR 8.405-3 (2004) provides that BPAs may be established "under any schedule contract to fill repetitive needs for supplies or services." *See, e.g., Labat-Anderson Inc. v. United States*, 50 Fed. Cl. 99 (2001). *See* The Nash & Cibinic Report, ¶ 48, Vol. 15, No. 9 (Sept. 2001), for additional discussion regarding the use and misuse of BPAs under the MAS Program.

781 FAR 13.303-1(a).

782 Lisa M. Burke, *Contractor Strategies: To BPA or Not to BPA?*, Commercial Product and Service Contracting: GSA Schedules and Beyond, 1999 A.B.A. Sec. Pub. Contract L., Com. Prods. & Servs. Comm. Book, at Tab I.

783 BPAs, however, do bring with them some obligations for the agencies that administer them. For example, FAR 8.405-3(d) provides that the ordering activity must review each of its BPAs at least once a year to determine whether (i) the schedule contract, upon which the BPA was established, is still in effect, (ii) the BPA still represents the best value to the agency, and (iii) the estimated quantities/amounts upon which the BPA was established have been exceeded such that additional price reductions can be obtained by the agency.

784 *See* FAR 8.405-3 (2004).

785 FAR 8.405-3(a)(2).

786 FAR8.405-3(b)(1) (2004).

787 FAR 8.405-3(b)(2) (2004). "If the BPA is for hourly rate services, the ordering activity shall develop a statement of work for requirements covered by the BPA. All orders under the BPA shall specify a price for the performance of the tasks identified in the statement of work." FAR 8.405-3(b)(3) (2004).

788 Ralph C. Nash & John Cibinic, *Blanket Purchase Agreements, The Ultimate in Acquisition Reform"*, 18 No. 7 Nash & Cibinic Report ¶ 32, at 111 (July 2004).

789 GSAR 552.211-75 (Feb. 1996).

[790] For more information, visit the National Motor Freight Traffic Association, Inc. web site at *http://www.nmfta.org.*

[791] GSAR 552.211-76 (Feb. 1996).

[792] GSAR 552.211-78 (Feb. 1996).

[793] FSS Clause F-FSS-230 (Jan. 1994).

[794] *See* FSS Procurement Information Bulletin 99-2 (Jan. 3, 1999) and FSS Acquisition Letter FC-95-1 (Feb. 9, 1995).

[795] Such orders also have been called "Incidental Items," "Not Specifically Priced Items," "Non-FSS Items," and "Non-Schedule Items."

[796] *See* Jonathan Aronie, *Open market, insert foot*, FEDERAL COMPUTER WEEK, Aug. 30, 1999, at 17.

[797] *See ViON Corp.*, B-275063.2 *et al.*, Feb. 4, 1997, 97-1 CPD ¶ 53 (GAO held that a Federal Supply Schedule contractor may properly offer an ordering agency a one-time price reduction from its Schedule contract. GAO also held that agency could order incidental items that were not listed on the contractor's MAS contract as long as the cost of the non-Schedule items was small compared to the total cost of the procurement.).

[798] *ATA Defense Indus., Inc. v. United States*, 38 Fed. Cl. 489 (1997).

[799] *See* Jonathan Aronie, *Open market, insert foot*, FEDERAL COMPUTER WEEK, Aug. 30, 1999, at 17.

[800] B-282469 *et al.*, July 15, 1999, 99-2 CPD ¶ 18.

[801] *Id.* at 4.

[802] In *SMS Sys. Maint. Servs., Inc.*, B-284550.2, Aug. 4, 2000, 2000 CPD ¶ 127, the GAO emphasized that agencies must follow all applicable procurement rules and regulations for purchases of incidental items over the micro-purchase threshold of $2,500 and that only incidental items under the micro-purchase threshold may be purchased without further competition. In *Draeger Safety, Inc.*, B-285366 *et al.*, Aug. 23, 2000, 2000 CPD ¶ 139, the GAO held that an agency could not purchase items that were not on Schedule. Here, the agency could not purchase shipboard fire fighting equipment without the comfort belt because, on the Schedule, the equipment came with the comfort belt. The agency has to order the product as it is listed on the Schedule. Here, the company offered the product both with and without the comfort belt. However,

only the belt version was on the Schedule. In *T-L-C Systems*, B-285687.2, Sept. 29, 2000, 2000 CPD ¶ 166, the GAO held that the removal of certain incidental items from an agency order was insufficient to defeat a protest where the agency had demonstrated an intention to obtain such items using sole source methods after deleting them from the order. In *Firearms Training Systems, Inc.*, B-292819.2 *et al.*, April 26, 2004, a case far different from those previously cited, the GAO found the FSS open market rules inapplicable where the agency conducted the procurement using full and open competition. According to the GAO, "Using a task order against the awardee's FSS contract to implement the selection decision at the end of the competition is a matter of administrative convenience; it does not convert this procurement to an FSS buy, or raise the kinds of concerns normally associated with including open market items in an FSS purchase . . . ."

[803] FAR 8.402(f) (2004) ("For administrative convenience, an ordering activity contracting officer may add items not on the Federal Supply Schedule (also referred to as Open Market Items) to a Federal Supply Schedule Blanket Purchase Agreement (BPA) or an individual task or delivery order only if—(1) All applicable acquisition regulations pertaining to the purchase of the items not on the Federal Supply Schedule have been followed . . . .").

[804] *See SMS*, 2000 CPD ¶ 127.

[805] 67 Fed. Reg. 43,514 (June 27, 2002) (to be codified at 48 C.F.R. pt. 8).

[806] 48 C.F.R. 8.401(d)(2).

[807] *48 C.F.R. 8.401(d)(3).* A "best practice" here is for the contractor clearly to label the open market items on its quotation and its invoice.

[808] *See, e.g., Information Ventures*, B-293743, 2004 CPD ¶ 97 (sustaining protest that life sciences data maintenance was outside the scope of the offeror's IT Schedule).

[809] In December 2004, the GAO announced that it was examining the role Schedule vendors should play in ensuring that agencies purchase only Schedule items through Schedule contracts. *See* "Friday Flash," Coalition for Government Procurement (Dec. 23,2004).

810 "In a recent case, Sen. Chuck Grassley (R-Iowa) raised a red flag when it was revealed that an IT contract held by Apogen Technologies Inc. was used to hire nurses. However, this case is not as simple as it would seem." "Editorial," FEDERAL COMPUTER WEEK, August 30, 2004.

811 "Memorandum for Regional Directors, DCAA," 04-PAC-022(R) (April 9, 2004).

812 *See, e.g.*, Office of the Under Secretary of Defense, "Proper Use of Non-DoD Contracts," June 17, 2005; *see also, e.g.*, Army Guidance at www.acq.osd.mil/dpap/specificpolicy/index.htm.

813 *See, e.g., Armed Forces Merchandise Outlet, Inc.*, B-294281, Oct. 12, 2004 (upholding protest because offered product failed to meet precise fabric of similar product available on Schedule).

814 *See Jonathan S. Aronie, That's "Dee" to my friends*, FEDERAL COMPUTER WEEK (July 11, 2005).

815 *Ralph C. Nash & John Cibinic, Blanket Purchase Agreements: The Ultimate in "Acquisition Reform"*, 18 No. 7 NASH & CIBNIC REPORT ¶ 32, at 112 (July 2004).

816 Perhaps responding to pressure from their own Inspectors General, some agencies have taken to requiring vendors to certify that their products are within the scope of their Schedule contract. Such a certification is wholly inconsistent with the terms of the Schedule Contract. As GSA official made clear to industry in an April 2005 briefing, "no contractor should be required to certify that the work is within scope." Notes from Industry Meeting with David Drabkin and Emily Murphy (April 18, 2005).

XVI.

SERVICES

"I had many years that I was not so successful as
a ballplayer, as it is a game of skill."
-Charles Dillon ("Casey") Stengel

I nitially limited to products only, the MAS Program has grown over the years to offer a virtually limitless range of supplies and services. Indeed, currently, services represent about 60 percent of all Schedule offerings.[817] In general, the MAS Program encompasses two categories of services—ancillary services and professional services. After reviewing the still-evolving history of the term "commercial item" to include services, this chapter discusses GSA's current definition of the term and reviews some of the more important regulatory and contractual provisions relating thereto.

A. *Background*

MAS contracts always have been limited to "commercial items." Prior to 1996, GSA interpreted this phrase as excluding commercial services (except for installation and maintenance services incidental to the purchase of a commercial item). In late

1995, however, GSA began awarding MAS contracts consisting exclusively of commercial services offered on an hourly basis. At about this same time, Congress passed the Federal Acquisition Streamlining Act ("FASA"), section 8001 of which made clear that only services "offered and sold competitively, in significant quantities, in the commercial marketplace at established catalog prices or standard rates and under standard commercial terms and conditions" could constitute "commercial items."[818] This change, which soon thereafter was incorporated into the FAR, significantly narrowed the scope of the commercial item definition. Indeed, the narrow definition implemented by FASA exists today:

> "Commercial item" means . . . [s]ervices of a type offered and sold competitively in substantial quantities in the commercial marketplace based on established catalog or market prices for specific tasks performed under standard commercial terms and conditions. This does not include services that are sold based on hourly rates without an established catalog or market price for a specific service performed.[819]

Technically, unless a service is procured explicitly in support of a commercial item (such as installation services or maintenance services),[820] the service must meet the foregoing requirements in order to constitute a "commercial item."

Historically, the FAR provided little definitional assistance as to the meaning of "of a type offered . . . in the commercial marketplace" or "established catalog or market prices." Over the years, however, the courts have provided some useful guidance in this regard. Thus, vendors looking to offer commercial services on Schedule now know that:

- The services need not be *identical* to commercially offered services. Rather, it is sufficient that the services are the same "type" of services that the vendor offers commercially.[821]

- The overall price of the service need not be "established" as long as the components of the overall price are established.[822]

Additionally, the FAR recently was amended to incorporate the following definitions of catalog price and market price:

- "Catalog price" is defined as "a price included in a catalog, price list, schedule, or other form that is regularly maintained by the manufacturer or vendor, is either published or otherwise available for inspection by customers, and states prices at which sales are currently, or were last, made to a significant number of buyers constituting the general public."[823]
- "Market prices" is defined as the "current prices that are established in the course of ordinary trade between buyers and sellers free to bargain and that can be substantiated through competition or from sources independent of the offerors."[824]

While policymakers, lawyers, and others likely will debate the propriety and legality of commercial services for years to come, the trend still seems to be in favor of broadening the interpretation of "commercial services" rather than further narrowing it.

B. _Current Status Of Commercial Services_

Vendors can offer two different categories of commercial services within the context of the MAS Program. First, vendors can offer commercial services that support a commercial product (_i.e._, ancillary services). Such services can be offered as long as the source of the services offers such services to the general public and the Federal Government contemporaneously and under similar terms and conditions.[825] Second, vendors also can offer professional services that are of a type offered and sold competitively in substantial quantities in the commercial marketplace, the prices of which are based on established catalog or market prices for specific tasks performed under standard commercial terms and conditions.[826] Notably, the FAR specifically excludes from the definition of commercial item stand-alone services based on hourly rates without an established catalog or market price for a specific service performed.[827]

Whether a particular service falls within or outside the FAR's commercial item definition, however, is a thorny question—although it used to be thornier than it is now. For quite some time, the Government interpreted the statute under which the current commercial item definition was promulgated (FASA) to prohibit time-and-materials[828] and labor-hour[829] contracts. Analyzing the legality of commercial service contracts in the July 2001 issue of *Federal Contracts Report*, Richard J. Wall and Christopher B. Pockney, of Ernst & Young, described this prohibition as a "sad irony" in that

> one of the principal methods of purchasing
> professional and technical services in the
> commercial marketplace was expressly prohibited
> by regulation, although arguably not by law.[830]

Notwithstanding much criticism from industry[831] and the existence of at least one potentially positive proposal,[832] this irony survived for quite some time.

On November 24, 2003, however, questions concerning the legality of time-and-material and labor-hour Schedule contracts was answered, at least in part, by the United States Congress and the President. The Fiscal Year 2004 Defense Authorization Act (known more commonly as the "Services Acquisition Reform Act") formally authorized the use of time-and-material and labor-hour contracts for commercial items contracts.[833] When the FAR Council implemented Section 1432 (as the provision relating to time-and-material orders is known), however, it specifically noted that it would address the rule as it relates to MAS contractors "as a follow-up to the final rule."[834] Thus, as of the submission of this Second Edition to the publisher, Schedule vendors still are without clear guidance regarding time-and-material orders. Nonetheless, with Congress' formal authorization of GSA's long-standing, formal practice of permitting such orders, the practice continues unabated.

C. _GSA's Current Services Offerings_

The MAS Program currently encompasses, among others, the following professional services Schedules:

- _Engineering Services_, which provide support in areas such as technical and statistical analyses; CAD, CAE, and CAM work; project management; economic/business case analyses; design specifications; and more
- _Management Services_, which provide support in areas such as management, organization, and business improvement services ("MOBIS"); environmental advisory services; and mail management services
- _Marketing and Media Services_, which provide support in areas such as direct mail services, commercial photography services, commercial art and graphic design services, market research, media analysis and related services, press and public relations, web site design and maintenance, trade shows and exhibits, conference and events planning services, miscellaneous business services, and videotape and film production services
- _Financial Services_, which provide support in areas such as auditing services and financial management services, business information services, financial asset services, and GSA SmartPay services
- _Travel and Transportation Services_, which provide support in areas such as domestic express delivery services, Government-wide employee relocation services, and prepayment audit services

- *Information Technology Services*, which provide a wide range of services relating to information technology

While vendors seeking to offer services through the MAS Program obtain, complete, and submit a solicitation just like any other Schedule offeror, GSA has adopted certain additional procedures to govern the interaction between Schedule vendors and Schedule purchasers in the services area.

D. *Clauses Unique To Services Contracts*

Schedule vendors offering services through the MAS Program can expect to see several unique clauses in their solicitations and contracts. Such clauses *may* include, but may not be limited to, the following:

- FAR 52.232-7 (Payments Under Time-and-Material and Labor-Hour Contracts)—*see* below for more information regarding this clause and its application
- FAR 52.222-41 (Service Contract Act of 1965, as Amended)—*see* below for more information regarding this clause and its application
- FAR 52.222-42 (Statement of Equivalent Rates for Federal Hires)—used in conjunction with FAR 52.222-41
- FAR 52.222-43 (Fair Labor Standards Act and Service Contract Act—Price Adjustment (Multiple Year and Option Contracts))—provides for increases in wages for contracts of more than one year
- FAR 52.222-44 (Fair Labor Standards Act and Service Contract—Price Adjustment)—defines the manner in which vendors providing services may effect increases in wages and fringe benefits under Government contracts
- FAR 52.222-46 (Evaluation of Compensation for Professional Employees)—requires the vendor to submit its professional employees compensation package for review by the Government to ensure that wages are realistic

- FAR 52.222-48 (Exemption from Application of Service Contract Act Provisions for Contracts for Maintenance, Calibration, and/or Repair of Certain Information Technology, Scientific and Medical and/or Office and Business Equipment-Contractor Certification)—may exempt contract from Service Contract Act
- FAR 52.237-1 (Site Visit)—requires that certain services be performed in Government facilities
- FAR 52.237-2 (Protection of Government Buildings, Equipment, and Vegetation)—requires that certain services be performed on Government property
- GSAR 552.228-70 (Workers Compensation Laws)—also requires the performance of certain services on Government property

As the appearance of these clauses will vary from solicitation to solicitation and from contract to contract, vendors must review their solicitations and contracts carefully to ensure compliance.

E. *GSA's Ordering Procedures For Services Procurements Involving A Statement Of Work*

FAR 8.402 authorizes GSA to establish special procedures governing orders placed against MAS contracts.[835] Pursuant to this authority, GSA had created special ordering procedures for services requiring a statement of work.[836] As of June 18, 2004, however, these procedures were incorporated into the FAR.[837] Vendors offering services through the MAS Program should become familiar with these ordering procedures.[838]

GSA's ordering procedures for services requiring a statement of work place the responsibility for ensuring that the total firm, fixed-price or ceiling price being offered is fair and reasonable upon the ordering office. To this end, the ordering procedures require that the ordering office undertake the following activities before placing an order for services involving hourly rates.[839] As with the purchase of products, the specific requirements for ordering services depend upon the value of the order.

With respect to very small orders, as with products, "ordering activities may place orders at, or below, the micro-purchase threshold with any Federal Supply Schedule contractor that can meet the agency's needs."[840] The FAR advises agencies, however, to "attempt to distribute orders among contractors."[841]

For orders that exceed the micro-purchase threshold, but are below the maximum order threshold, the FAR requires that the purchasing agency develop a statement of work, which "shall include the work to be performed; location of work; period of performance; deliverable schedule; applicable performance standards; and any special requirements . . . ."[842] The rules also make clear that, "to the maximum extent practicable," the statement of work shall be performance-based.

The agency also must prepare a Request for Quotation ("RFQ") that requests "firm-fixed prices to perform the services identified in the statement of work"[843] and includes the applicable evaluation criteria against which offerors will be assessed.[844] The RFQ must be provided to "at least three schedule contractors that offer services that will meet the agency's needs."[845] Posting the RFQ on GSA's E-Buy system would appear to satisfy this requirement.[846]

For orders exceeding the applicable maximum order threshold, the FAR requires that the agency "provide the RFQ (including the statement of work and evaluation criteria) to additional schedule contractors that offer services that will meet the needs of the ordering activity,"[847] as well as to any contractor that requests a copy.[848] In deciding how many contractors should receive a copy of a given RFQ, the FAR advises the agency to consider, at least, the "complexity, scope and estimated value of the requirement" and the "market search results."[849] Again, posting the RFQ on GSA's E-Buy system would appear to satisfy this requirement as well.[850]

Following the agency's identification of the appropriate number of contractors, the Agency then must "seek price reductions." While the FAR is silent regarding from whom such price reductions must be sought, using the ordering procedures for supplies and services not requiring a statement of work as a guide, the agencies likely must seek price reductions only from those vendors that appear to offer the best value.[851]

Once the acquiring agency receives the quotations, it must evaluate those quotations in strict conformance with the criteria provided to the offerors.[852] It is up to the ordering activity, however, to consider "the level of effort and the mix of labor proposed to perform a specific task being ordered, and for determining that the total price is reasonable."[853] The ordering activity then must "place the order, or establish the BPA, with the schedule contractor that represents the best value," and "provide timely notification to unsuccessful offerors."[854]

F. *Special Procedures For Blanket Purchase Agreements For Recurring Services*

The FAR provides that ordering offices may establish BPAs for recurring services as long as the foregoing special ordering procedures are adhered to and as long as the BPA "addresses[e] the frequency of ordering, invoicing, discounts, requirements (e.g., estimated quantities, work to be performed), delivery locations, and time."[855] Additional procedures for the use of BPAs in the context of professional services contracts are set forth in GSA's ordering procedures.[856]

G. *The Service Contract Act*

The McNamara-O'Hara Service Contract Act of 1965 ("SCA")[857] requires that contractors performing contracts for the United States Government, among other things,

- Pay service employees (of the contractor and subcontractors) prevailing monetary wages and fringe benefits;
- Ensure that working conditions for such employees meet safety and health standards; and

- Notify employees of the compensation due them pursuant to the SCA.[858]

Additionally, the SCA encompasses significant record keeping requirements.[859]

Originally conceived in response to the fear that awarding contracts to the lowest bidder would contribute to the reduction of wages to service employees,[860] the SCA currently has broad application. Unless a statutory or administrative exemption applies, a service contract falls within the scope of the SCA if:

1. The contract involves an amount over $2,500;[861]
2. The "principal purpose" of the contract is to provide services;[862]
3. The work performed under the contract is conducted by "service employees";[863]
4. The activity is conducted inside the United States;[864] and
5. The work does not fall within an exemption to the SCA.[865]

Obviously, many MAS service contracts meet these requirements.

Statutory exemptions under the SCA include contracts for construction, alteration, or repair of buildings or public works; work subject to the provisions of the Walsh-Healey Public Contracts Act; contracts for the shipment of supplies or personnel where published tariffs apply; contracts for the supply of telecommunication services, subject to the provisions of the Communications Act of 1934; contracts for public utility services; employment contracts involving the provision of direct services to a federal agency; and contracts with the United States Postal Service, the primary purpose of which is the operation of postal contract stations.[866] Additionally, the Secretary of Labor is authorized to permit an "administrative exemption" where "necessary and proper in the public interest or to avoid the serious impairment of government business."[867] An administrative exemption must be "in accord with the remedial purpose of [the SCA] to protect prevailing labor standards."[868]

The DOL Wage and Hour Division administers and enforces the wage and hour requirements of the SCA.[869] Penalties for violating the SCA include contract terminations and liability for any resulting costs to the government, withholding of contract payments in sufficient amounts to cover wage and fringe benefit underpayments, legal action to recover the underpayments, and debarment from future contracts for up to three years.[870]

While vendors may appeal determinations of violations, ignorance of the SCA's requirements will not provide a viable defense.[871]

H. *Performance Incentives*

On May 2, 2001, an interim rule was published that established a preference for performance-based contracts or task orders for services.[872] A performance-based contract is one that is "structur[ed] around the purpose of the work to be performed"[873] and sets forth the requirements with "measurable outcomes"[874] that are "set forth in clear, specific and objective terms."[875] Agencies acquiring services, even those procured under MAS contracts, must use performance-based contracts to the maximum extent practicable.[876] Ordering agencies are to follow the order of precedence below:

- A firm, fixed-price performance-based contract or task order
- A performance-based contract or task order that is not firm, fixed-price
- A contract or task order that is not performance-based[877]

Contracting officers are to tie profit or fee incentives to the results achieved by the vendor against specific negotiated targets.[878]

All contracts for services provide for incentives to be negotiated between the vendor and the ordering office under fixed-price contracts or BPAs.[879] The ordering office is required, to the maximum extent practicable, to consider establishing incentives when performance is critical to the agency's mission and such an incentive will motivate the vendor.[880] Incentives must be based on measurable tasks.

I. *Delivery Schedule (Commercial Professional Services)*

This clause, if included in the solicitation/contract, requires that the vendor deliver services in accordance with its standard commercial delivery terms and conditions. For example, if computer repair services are offered to the Government on Schedule, the response time for the Government must be equivalent to the vendor's standard response time. Vendors may negotiate more favorable delivery schedules on individual orders if they desire, and agencies may consider delivery time as an evaluation factor in selecting the offer that represents the "best value."

J. *Services Performed by Subcontractors*

For years contractors have struggled with the question of how to bill the Government for Schedule services performed by a subcontractor. The question takes a number of different forms. For example, if a vendor sells a "Technician" on Schedule for $250 per hour, but subcontracts that work to a subcontractor who charges the vendor $200 per hour for the Technician, does the vendor bill the Government at the $250 Schedule rate or at the $200 subcontract rate? What if the subcontractor has a Schedule contract of its own that identifies the Technician as having a $225 rate? Then what? Unfortunately, these questions come with no easy answer because the Government is of two minds on the subject.

Of one mind is GSA. Consistent with the nature of MAS Contracts generally, GSA advises vendors that "the prime contractor should bill for services (*i.e.*, labor) performed by subcontractors at the prime contractor's GSA Schedule rates, rather than at the subcontractor's rates."[881] Where such services are provided to the Government as part of a team approach (i.e., as part of a Schedule "Contractor Team Arrangement"), then GSA's guidance makes clear that each vendor should invoice the Government at its applicable Schedule rate.[882] According to GSA, "A contractor may only charge the rates/prices that have been awarded under the company's GSA Federal Supply Schedule contract. The same holds true for other team members."[883]

Of a different mind, however, is the Defense Contract Audit Agency, which issued audit guidance to its field auditors in April 2004 focusing precisely on this point.[884] While recognizing GSA's position on the subject, the audit guidance references FAR 52.232-7, the Payments Under Time-and-Material and Labor-Hour Contracts clause, noting that clause

> specifically limits the reimbursement of costs in connection with subcontracts to the amounts paid by the prime contractor, causing uncertainty among auditors and contractors as to what rates should be used to reimburse the prime contractor for the effort of the subcontractor.[885]

DCAA goes on to note that FAR 52.232-7 vests the Government with audit rights that would not be exercisable against a Schedule vendor in the context of a traditional goods (versus services) purchase.

As it happens, DCAA is correct that FAR 52.232-7, which now is incorporated into most Schedule contracts offering services, provides that "[t]he Government will limit reimbursable costs in connection with subcontracts *to the amounts paid for supplies and services* purchased directly for the contract . . . ."[886] DCAA also is correct that the FAR clause, arguably at least, vests DCAA with certain audit rights: "At any time before final payment under this contract the Contracting Officer may request audit of the invoices or vouchers and substantiating material."[887]

So where does this all leave Schedule vendors? In a word, confused. Indeed, even DCAA, in its audit guidance, notes that "the incorporation of the contract clause at FAR 52.232-7 . . . causes confusion over the nature of the Schedule contract and any attendant audit rights."[888] While GSA is working on remedying this area of admitted confusion as of the publication of this Second Edition, vendors are well advised, in the mean time, to seek and obtain clear, written direction from the Schedule contracting officer that labor will be charged at the applicable Schedule rate regardless of whether it is performed by the vendor or a subcontractor. Out of an abundance of caution, vendors also should advise Schedule purchasers, in writing, of the same fact and reference the GSA guidance on which it is relying.

K. *DOD Acquisition of Services*

Pursuant to Section 803 of the Defense Authorization Act for Fiscal Year 2002 ("Section 803")[889], DOD has implemented new procedures to increase competition for all Schedule contract purchases for services.[890] For Schedule orders over $100,000, DOD contracting officers, as well as contracting officers from non-DOD agencies placing orders on behalf of DOD, must issue a fair notice of intent to make a purchase to either

- as many Schedule holders as practicable, consistent with market research appropriate to the circumstances, to reasonably ensure that proposals will be received from at least 3 sources that offer the required work for consideration for award; or
- all schedule holders that offer the required work.[891]

In the event that the contracting officer receives fewer than three proposals, the contract file must be documented to reflect why reasonable efforts would not result in more offers, based on adequate market research.[892] A notice of intent to purchase must include a description of the work the contractor is to perform and the basis upon which selection will be made. These procedures are also applicable to BPAs established against Schedule contracts.[893]

Notes:

[817] Presentation of Carolyn Alston, Assistant Commissioner, Office of Acquisition Management, Federal Supply Service, *Wheel of Service Conference* (Mar. 7, 2001).

[818] House-Senate Conference Committee commentary to Section 8001 of FASA, 41 U.S.C. § 403(12), H.R. Conf. Rep. No. 103-712, at 228-29 (1994), *reprinted in* 1994 U.S.C.C.A.N. 2561, 2658-59.

[819] FAR 2.101 (definition of commercial item, subsection (6)).

[820] *See* FAR 2.101 (definition of commercial item, subsection (5)).

[821] *Aalco Forwarding, Inc.*, B-277241.8 *et al.*, Oct. 21, 1997, 97-2 CPD ¶ 110. As stated by the GAO: "[I]t is apparent that the services used for the movement of household goods of military personnel, *i.e.*, packing, loading, hauling, storage and other accessorial services, and delivery, are not services that are unique or provided only to the government, but are essentially the same moving services provided in the commercial market, in that movers use the same trucks, warehouses, ocean or air carriers, crews, packing materials, and other equipment to perform both DOD's and the commercial market's household goods moving requirements." *Id.* at 11-12.

[822] *Id.*

[823] FAR 2.101.

[824] *Id.*

[825] *Id.*

[826] *Id.*

[827] *Id.*

[828] A time-and-materials contract is, as its name implies, a contract providing for the acquisition of supplies or services on the basis of (i) direct labor hours at specified fixed hourly rates and (ii) materials at cost. Government Contracts Reference Book 516. *See* FAR 16.601.

[829] A labor-hour contract is a type of time-and-materials contract "under which the Government pays a fixed amount for each hour of work performed by specified classes of labor." Government Contracts Reference Book 320. *See* FAR 16.602.

[830] Richard J. Wall & Christopher B. Pockney, *Contracting for Commercial Professional and Technical Services: The Federal Acquisition Streamlining Act's Unfinished Business*, FED. CONTRACTS REP. 76, 80 (July 17, 2001).

[831] *See id.* at 80-81.

[832] 65 Fed. Reg. 83,292 (Dec. 29, 2000) (to be codified at 48 C.F.R. pts. 12 and 16). As of November 12, 2001, the final rule was approved for publication but has not actually been published. Industry and the American Bar Association, however, have criticized this proposal for failing explicitly to authorize the use of time-and-materials and labor-hour contracts to acquire commercial services. *See, e.g.*, Comment letter of the ABA Public Contract Law Section, dated July 25, 2001, regarding FAR Case 2000-13, available on ABA web site at *http://www.abanet.org/contract/federal/regscomm/commercial_012.pdf*.

[833] Section 1432 of the FY 2004 Defense Authorization Act (P.L. 108-136).

[834] 69 Fed. Reg. 34233 (June 18, 2004).

[835] *See also* FSS Clause G-FSS-920 (May 2000).

[836] *See* FSS Procurement Information Bulletin 98-7 (Apr. 13, 1998), at Insert 1.

[837] 69 Fed. Reg. 34231 (June 18, 2004) (FAC 2001-24).

[838] In what was an important case decided February 14, 2001, the court held that GSA's prior services ordering procedures were advisory and not mandatory and that a contracting officer may choose to request a quote from only one vendor *Cybertech Group, Inc. v. United States*, 48 Fed. Cl. 638 (2001). Cybertech Group, Inc. ("CGI"), an incumbent Schedule contractor, filed a protest after award of a delivery order under a MAS contract. CGI had not been sent an RFQ. The court held that "CGI had no right whatsoever to receive an RFQ in the first instance." *Id.* at 645. The court held the wording of the special ordering procedures to be advisory rather than mandatory.[838] As of June 18, 2004, however, the ordering procedures no longer are "advisory."

[839] FAR 8.405-2(a) (2004).

[840] FAR 8.405-2(c)(1) (2004).

841 *Id.*
842 FAR 8.405-2(b) (2004).
843 FAR 8.405-2(c)(2)(iii) (2004).
844 FAR 8.405-2(c) (2004).
845 FAR 8.405-2(c)(2)(ii) (2004).
846 FAR 8.405-2(c).
847 FAR 8.405-2(c)(3)(i) (2004).
848 FAR 8.405-2(c)(4) (2004).
849 FAR 8.405-2(c)(3)(i) (2004).
850 FAR 8.405-2(c) (2004).
851 See FAR 8.405-1(d)(2) (2004).
852 FAR 8.405-2(d) (2004).
853 *Id.*
854 *Id.* The FAR now provides that an unsuccessful offeror is entitled to receive upon request "a brief explanation of the basis for the award decision" where the award was based upon factors other than price along. *Id.*
855 FSS Clause G-FSS-920, at (b). FAR 8.405-3(a)(2).
856 *See* Chapter XV, Section F infra.
857 Pub. L. No. 89-286, 79 Stat. 1035 (1965) (codified as amended at 41 U.S.C. § 351 *et seq.*).
858 29 C.F.R. § 4.104.
859 *See id.* § 4.185.
860 *See, e.g.,* S. REP. NO. 798, at 3-4 (1965), *reprinted in* 1965 U.S.C.C.A.N. 3737, 3738-39.
861 With respect to indefinite-quantity contracts, such as MAS contracts, the Department of Labor regulations provide that the SCA shall apply "unless the contracting officer has definite knowledge in advance that the contract will not exceed $2,500 in any event." 29 C.F.R. § 4.142. Since MAS contracts are not awarded unless GSA believes that the vendor will have more than $25,000 worth of sales (FSS Clause I-FSS-639 (July 2000), this requirement should be met in all cases.
862 The "principal purpose of a particular contract is . . . a question to be determined on the basis of all the facts in each particular case." 29 C.F.R. § 4.111(a). "A procurement that requires tangible items

to be supplied to the Government or the contractor as a part of the service furnished is covered by the Act so long as the facts show that the contract is chiefly for services, and that the furnishing of tangible items is of secondary importance." *Id.* § 4.131(a) (2000). The following example taken directly from the applicable DOL SCA regulations is illustrative: "[A] contract for the maintenance and repair of typewriters . . . may require the contractor to furnish typewriter parts, as the need arises, in performing the contract services. Since this does not change the principal purpose of the contract, which is to furnish the maintenance and repair services through the use of service employees, the contract remains subject to the Act." *Id.* § 4.131(b).

863 The SCA is applicable only where the services are furnished through the use of "service employees" covered under the SCA. The SCA defines a service employee as "any person engaged in the performance of a contract . . . the principal purpose of which is to furnish services . . . other than any person employed in a bona fide executive, administrative, or professional capacity, as those terms are defined in part 541 of title 29." 41 U.S.C. § 357(b); *see also* 29 C.F.R. §§ 4.113, 4.150-4.156. In general, an "executive" employee is an employee primarily engaged in management, an "administrative" employee is an employee primarily engaged in assisting an executive or performing other office work, and a "professional" employee is an employee possessing specialized knowledge of the sort gained through specialized study. 29 C.F.R. pt. 541. Thus, only MAS contracts for services performed by nonprofessional service employees fall within the scope of the SCA.

864 "The Act and the provisions of this part apply to contract services furnished 'in the United States,' including any State of the United States, the District of Columbia, Puerto Rico, the Virgin Islands, Outer Continental Shelf lands as defined in the Outer Continental Shelf Lands Act, American Samoa, Guam, the Commonwealth of the Northern Mariana Islands, Wake Island, and Johnston Island. The definition expressly excludes any other territory under the jurisdiction of the United States and any United States base or possession within a foreign country. Services to be performed

exclusively on a vessel operating in international waters outside the geographic areas named in this paragraph would not be services furnished 'in the United States' within the meaning of the Act." 29 C.F.R. § 4.112(a).

[865] 41 U.S.C. § 351(a).

[866] *Id.* § 356.

[867] *Id.* § 353(b).

[868] *Id.*

[869] "The Department of Labor (and not the contracting agencies) has the primary and final authority and responsibility for administering and interpreting the [SCA], including making determinations of coverage." 29 C.F.R. § 4.101(b); *Woodside Village v. Secretary of Labor*, 611 F.2d 312 (9th Cir. 1980); *Nello L. Teer Co. v. United States*, 348 F.2d 533, 539-40 (Ct. Cl. 1965); *see also* Workplace Standards for Federally Assisted or Funded Contracts, *available at* http://www.dol.gov/asp/programs/handbook/sca.htm.

[870] 29 C.F.R. Part 4.

[871] *See, e.g., National Electro-Coatings, Inc. v. Brock*, 29 Wage & Hour Cas. (BNA) 1272 (N.D. Ohio 1990) (rejecting contractor's claim that it relied upon contracting agency representation as to its exemption from the SCA).

[872] 66 Fed. Reg. 22,082 (May 2, 2001) (to be codified at 48 C.F.R. pts.2 and 37).

[873] *Id.* at 22,083.

[874] *Id.*

[875] *Id.*

[876] *Id.*

[877] *Id.* at 22,083, 22,084.

[878] FAR 16.402-2.

[879] FSS clause I-FSS-60 Performance Incentives (4/00).

[880] *Id.*

[881] Memorandum for Regional Directors, DCAA, 04-PAC-022(R) (April 9, 2004) (hereafter "MRD 04-PAC-022").

[882] *Id.*

[883] GSA Contractor Team Arrangements, Frequently Asked Questions, www.fss.gsa.gov.

884 MRD 04-PAC-022.

885 *Id.* at 1.

886 FAR 52.232-7(b)(4)(ii) (emphasis added).

887 FAR 52.232-7(e).

888 MRD 04-PAC-022 at 2.

889 Pub. L. No. 107-107, 115 Stat. 1012.

890 67 Fed. Reg. 65505 (Oct. 25, 2002).

891 DFARS 208.404-70(c).

892 *Id.*

893 DFARS 208.404-70(d).

XVII.

LEASING

(by William Gormley and Larry Allen)

"Let us all be happy and live within our means,
even if we have to borrow the money to do it with."
-Artemus Ward

Leasing has become an accepted federal acquisition method as procurement rules have become more flexible and greater emphasis has been placed on the use of commercial off-the-shelf items. Once discouraged over concerns that agencies were acquiring unneeded products, leasing today provides agencies access to current technology without the expenditure of significant capital resources. The MAS Program features leases for many different types of products, as well as different types of leases. Schedule vendors offer everything from information technology products and office equipment to medical equipment and furniture.

Those contemplating offering leasing through a Schedule contract, however, need to be aware of some fundamental differences between commercial lease terms and those that the Government can accept. These terms are currently in flux, leaving many schedule vendors to negotiate specific lease provisions at the task order level. Examining the many types of potential leasing arrangements, therefore, determining which are best for your company, and knowing how they compare with those offered by competitors can all be important parts of a company's initial planning. In other words, you need to perform thorough market research to determine if leasing is for your company.

A. *Types Of Leases*

On the surface, leasing programs available through the MAS Program mirror those available commercially. While a few of the most common leasing alternatives are outlined below, there are sure to be many variations from vendor to vendor, depending on what each was able to negotiate with its MAS contracting officer. Even companies on the same Schedule can have differing terms. As with other elements of a Schedule contract, whether and how a vendor offers leasing through its Schedule contract will be based largely on its corporate commercial market experience.

Lease-To-Ownership Program ("LTOP"): This type of lease has been part of the MAS Program for many years. The LTOP is essentially one means through which a federal customer can purchase equipment over time, often using operational funds, instead of with one large up-front capital outlay. The customer pays the cost of the equipment, plus a finance charge for the ability to purchase it over time. The customer owns the equipment at the end of the lease.

Closed-End Leases: This type of lease is similar to many automobile leases. It provides the customer with the use of the equipment over the course of the lease, but at the end of the term the customer does not own it. The customer may either return the equipment to the vendor or purchase the equipment at the end of the lease term. Many companies choose to offer two types of closed-end leases: one with a pre-determined end-of-lease purchase price and one with a "fair market value" purchase price. The rate for this type of lease may be more favorable than that for an LTOP because the customer is not making a firm commitment to purchase the equipment at the initiation of the lease.

Third-Party Leases: The MAS Program allows financing companies to offer third-party leases on some Schedule contracts. These arrangements are most common on the information technology Schedule. Under such agreements, a financing or other similar company offers no specific product to the Government but, rather, simply negotiates leasing rates under various scenarios. Though there is steady business through third-party leasing companies, some companies remain uneasy about having to provide their products to a customer via a leasing company with which they may have no relationship.

Step Leases: Under a Step Lease, the Government and the vendor agree to a standard lease term—12, 36, or 48 months, for example. A Step Lease, though, allows the Government to discontinue the lease agreement at the end of each fiscal year without further penalty. The rate for the first year of a Step Lease, therefore, is typically higher than under other agreements. If the lease continues, subsequent rates are structured based upon a mutually agreed future value at the end of each subsequent fiscal year.

B. *Negotiating Leases*

Negotiating Schedule leasing terms is similar to other Schedule negotiations in that both are based on a company's commercial practices. Instead of negotiating product prices, however, the core of leasing negotiations covers interest rates charged for various types of leases and the differences between Government and commercial lease terms that affect those rates. This section examines three of the most common and important differences to consider.

The GSA contracting officer will seek a vendor's most favorable commercial leasing terms. As with supplies and services, the vendor may or may not decide to offer the Government the best deal it offers any other customer but will have to convince the contracting officer as to why the Government is not entitled to the best terms if something else is offered.

In addition to interest rates, a vendor also will negotiate the *length of the leasing terms* it will offer, *warranties*, and other terms. In rare cases early termination charges may still be negotiated, so long as they do not violate the federal Anti-Deficiency Act, which prevents government agencies from obligating funds for which no appropriation has been received.

Length: Variable lengths may be offered to the Government, with typical terms starting at 12 months and extending to 48. Vendors should take care to remember that the risk of early termination increases with the length of the lease. One benefit of the MAS Program, however, is that agencies may place a multiyear order with a vendor at any time the contract is in effect, up to and including its last day. While these orders are renewable annually unless the agency has multi-year funding, most of the time, customers do renew unless there has been a material change in need. See the next paragraph for exceptions to this, however. A Schedule contract is a truly valuable tool for pursuing Government business.

Early Termination Charges: This is an important part of leasing negotiations for a Schedule vendor. Most companies seek to provide themselves with maximum protection if a customer wants to break its lease early. The Government, though, has certain statutory rights that limit the recovery options available when an agency terminates a lease early. Termination for convenience, termination for non-appropriation, or simple termination for non-renewal are all a part of standard Schedule leasing contracts. A company contemplating offering leasing should closely examine this part of the Schedule solicitation and seek outside help to ensure that its position is protected. Recently, GSA has largely stopped negotiating early termination fees as part of a schedule contract, leaving this discussion up to individual customers at the time a leasing order is placed.

Warranties: The GSA contracting officer will negotiate for a vendor's standard commercial warranty terms or better. GSA will also likely seek some protection from companies offering only third-party leasing. Third-party leasing vendors should carefully review any proposed warranty language.

C. *Important Factors To Consider*

As discussed at the outset of this chapter, there are several important differences between commercial leasing and leasing to the Government. Vendors must be aware of these differences before entering into a leasing agreement with the Government. This section will discuss the most common of these factors and the hurdles they represent.

Termination for Convenience: This is the best-known, and most nettlesome, difference between commercial and Government leases. The Termination for Convenience Clause allows a Government buyer to terminate a contract at any time "for the convenience of the Government." For leasing agreements, this means that a federal agency could decide at any time that it no longer wants the equipment and terminate the lease. While agencies are supposed to use convenience terminations only in cases where there is legitimately no longer a need for the equipment or funding for the equipment is no longer available, there are no formal regulations limiting them to these circumstances.

GSA has taken the position that the Termination for Convenience Clause is a statutory requirement for Schedule contracts. It appears in every Schedule leasing contract. Attempts to limit the use of the clause have met with mixed success. Similarly, attempts by some vendors to include termination penalties, allowing them to collect at least a portion of the fees owed based on the multiple year nature of the lease have been disallowed. GSA has determined that such provisions violate the federal Anti-Deficiency Act.[894]

The Termination for Convenience Clause can be a major stumbling block for companies seeking to lease through an outside third party. Third-party leasing companies are reluctant to finance leases where the lessor may decide in the middle of the term to discontinue the agreement. More than one leasing offer has been delayed while a vendor shops around for a finance company that will accept the Government's terms.

Annual Appropriations: Though leases are multiple year agreements, federal agencies that pay for them through appropriated funds must annually renew their lease at the start of every federal fiscal year. This, again, is a result of the Anti-Deficiency Act, which precludes agencies from obligating funds they have not yet been given. If an agency's appropriation is delayed, there is no money available for it to pay the lease. It can also take several weeks between the time an appropriation bill is signed and a specific office actually receives its money. In some years, it can be more than three months into the new fiscal year before everything is straightened out. Many Schedule vendors have reported that their leasing bills go unpaid during this time and that it can take several more months before a normal billing and payment process resumes. During this time, most vendors choose to continue providing supplies and services, at risk of non-payment, rather than run the risk of having the agency terminate the lease.

Property Taxes: While the Federal Government is exempt from state and local property taxes, vendors are not. This can be an important issue in Schedule leasing. In many commercial lease-to-own transactions, the company or person taking possession of the leased equipment usually takes the title to it at the start of the lease. This is not the case in federal leases. The federal agency will not take the title until the last payment has been made. On closed-end leases, the title may never pass to the Government. Since the mid-1990s, state and local governments looking for additional revenue sources have been questioning their federal counterparts as to who owns various pieces of equipment in their offices. The result of these actions is that Schedule vendors often find a bill in the mail from a state or local government requiring them to pay property tax on a piece of leased equipment.

This can be a difficult circumstance for several reasons. First, some state and local entities may not have this type of property tax. Second, for those that do, not all governments have actively pursued the ownership of property in federal offices. Third, there are widely varying tax rates across state and local governments.

Most companies also do not take into account the possibility that they will get a tax bill from a state government when they are negotiating leasing terms with the Federal Government. Even experienced vendors find it difficult to factor in this cost of doing business because it is a "hit or miss" proposition; and, more importantly, federal contracting officers often refuse to allow a mark-up in rates for this possibility, noting that the Federal Government is exempt from such taxes. As a result, vendors may find their net Schedule leasing revenue reduced.

GSA, however, has provided written guidance contractors use with state and local governments showing that contractors should be exempt from property taxes given the location of their equipment in a federal agency. This guidance may be available from the FSS Office of Acquisition.

Despite these concerns, most companies that have made a commitment to offer leasing continue to participate. They have found it to be a popular acquisition method for their customers and one that they must offer in order to provide a full set of customer service options.

Notes:

[894] Ch. 251, § 7, 16 Stat. 251 (1870) (codified as amended at 31 U.S.C. § 1341 *et seq.*). *See Burroughs Corp.*, B-186313, Dec. 9, 1976, 76-2 CPD ¶ 472.

XVIII.

TERMINATION AND CANCELLATION

"All's well that ends well."

-William Shakespeare,
All's Well That Ends Well

Adding to the uniqueness of Government contracts is the fact that the Government maintains unilateral termination rights. Such rights have no counterpart in the commercial world. They truly are unique to Government contracting, and they exist in almost all Government contracts.[895]

The MAS Program permits the Government to relieve itself of its contractual obligations in a number of ways. First, GSA can terminate a contract for its convenience, referred to as a "termination for convenience." Second, GSA can terminate a contract for default, referred to as a "termination for default" or a "termination for cause." Third, GSA (as well as the vendor) can cancel a Schedule contract, referred to as a "cancellation." Each termination/cancellation provision is governed by a separate set of regulations. This chapter examines the regulations pertaining to each.

A. *Cancellation*

GSAR 552.238-73 provides that either party may cancel a Schedule contract by providing written notice to the other party. There is no limitation on the reasons for which a party may cancel a contract.[896] Cancellation takes effect thirty calendar days after the other party receives notice of the cancellation.

Upon written notification that a vendor wishes to cancel its Schedule contract, the GSA contracting officer will formalize the cancellation by a contract modification, "which incorporates the contractor's letter and indicates the effective date of the cancellation (30 days after written notice)."[897] The GSA contracting officer also will notify the vendor and the vendor's Administrative Contracting Officer, if applicable, and cancel the contract in GSA's Internet on-line contract system. Notwithstanding a cancellation, vendors must complete any outstanding Schedule orders.

B. *Termination For Convenience*

FAR 52.212-4(l) provides that "[t]he Government reserves the right to terminate this contract, or any part hereof, for its sole convenience." Terminations for convenience are governed primarily by three regulations: FAR 52.212-4(l), as incorporated into each MAS contract; FAR 8.405-6, as applicable to each MAS contract; and FAR Part 49, as referenced in FAR 8.405-6(c). Notwithstanding these several sources of governance, however, terminations for convenience are normally pretty straightforward.

In order to terminate a contract for convenience, the GSA contracting officer must provide written notice to the vendor pursuant to FAR 49.102. This notice must inform the vendor of the following:

- That the contract is being terminated for the convenience of the Government

- The effective date of the termination
- The extent of the termination (*i.e.*, whether it is complete or partial)
- Any special instructions regarding the termination
- The steps the vendor should take to minimize the impact of the termination on its personnel

While these notifications technically apply to all terminations, in practice, only the first three items typically are relevant to Schedule vendors.

Upon receiving a notice of termination, the vendor must stop all work under the terminated portion of the Schedule contract and notify any affected subcontractors to stop work as well.[898] In the event the vendor has partially performed any order under the terminated Schedule contract, FAR 52.212-4(l) provides that the vendor "shall be paid a percentage of the contract price reflecting the percentage of the work performed prior to the notice of termination, plus reasonable charges the Contractor can demonstrate to the satisfaction of the Government using its standard record keeping system, have resulted from the termination."

While GSA possesses broad authority to terminate Schedule contracts for convenience, its authority is not limitless. For example, GSA may *not* terminate a contract for convenience in "bad faith." A decision recently issued by the United States Court of Federal Claims, however, seems to expand the Government's termination rights to new levels.

The case, known as *Barram v. Travel Centre*,[899] involved a GSA indefinite-delivery/indefinite quantity ("IDIQ") contract for travel services in New England.[900] GSA's solicitation (i) informed offerors that the awardee would be "a preferred source" for the agencies located in the outlined geographic regions and (ii) estimated the contract revenue—based upon the predecessor contract—at $2.5 million. The solicitation warned offerors, however, that the $2.5 million estimate was "for informational purposes only and [did] not represent any guarantee of sales."[901] The solicitation also warned offerors that the estimate did "not reflect any commitment received by GSA from the Federal agencies."[902] Nonetheless, notwithstanding these two warnings, the solicitation expressly instructed offerors to base their offers upon the Government's estimate of $2.5 million.

Travel Centre submitted its initial proposal on May 24, 1995, its best and final offer ("BAFO") on August 15, 1995, and a revised BAFO on October 10, 1995. GSA awarded the contract to Travel Centre on October 25, 1995. Not once during this entire period, however, did GSA inform Travel Centre that, as early as December 1994, it had learned that the Army (a particularly sizeable customer under the predecessor contract) no longer would be purchasing travel services through the GSA program.

Travel Centre, pursuant to the terms of the contract, had opened an office in Portsmouth, New Hampshire. Shortly thereafter, Travel Centre learned that the Army had dropped out of the GSA program. When expected revenues did not materialize, Travel Centre closed its Portsmouth office and serviced its remaining clients from a nearby location. On June 21, 1996, GSA terminated the Travel Centre contract for default, changing it to a termination for convenience on April 30, 1997.

The Federal Circuit's decision was short and to the point. According to the court, Travel Centre's contract with GSA was an IDIQ contract that guaranteed Travel Centre nothing more than $100. Since Travel Centre netted more than $100 under the contract, GSA met its contractual requirements. End of story.

Notably, the Federal Circuit did not even consider GSA's misrepresentation of the predicted level of service or its superior knowledge that its prescribed basis of estimate was wrong. It simply supported the Government's termination for convenience because Travel Centre had made its $100. More than any other recent decision, this case highlights the breadth (and potential harshness) of the Government's termination authority.

C. *Termination For Default (Or Cause)*

FAR 52.212-4(m) provides that the Government may terminate a Schedule contract, or any part thereof,

> for cause in the event of any default by the Contractor, or if the Contractor fails to comply with any contract terms and conditions, or fails to provide the Government, upon request, with adequate assurances of future performance.

Because a termination for cause carries with it the prospect of negative past performance evaluations in the future, the procedure for effecting a default termination is more regulated than the procedure for terminating a contract for convenience.

First, FAR 8.405-5(b) provides that "[o]nly the schedule contracting officer may terminate for default any or all items covered by the schedule contract."[903] Second, GSA may terminate a contract for default only where the vendor (i) defaults on the contract, (ii) fails to comply with the terms and conditions of the Schedule contract, or (iii) fails adequately to respond to a GSA request for "assurances of future performance." In other words, the Government may not terminate a contract for default simply to relieve itself of its contractual obligations. FAR 52.212-4(m) provides, however, that, if a court or a board determines that GSA improperly terminated a contract for default, such termination will be deemed a termination for convenience.[904]

Third, prior to the issuance of a termination for default, GSA must issue either a "cure notice" or a "show cause notice." The vendor then will have a specified time in which to respond. A cure notice is given to the vendor when the contracting officer determines that the period for cure is not longer than the time remaining in the contract period. Generally, the vendor is given ten days (which can be extended by the contracting officer) to cure the problematic condition. The notice must inform the vendor that a failure to cure within the specified period of time may lead to a termination for default.[905]

If the time remaining in the contract delivery schedule is not sufficient to permit a realistic "cure" (*i.e.*, ten days or more), the contracting officer will issue a show cause notice. Additionally, a show cause notice may be issued after the vendor has failed to correct a condition noted in the cure notice. The show cause notice puts the vendor on alert that, due to its failure to perform as required by the contract, the contracting officer is considering terminating the contract for default. Prior to taking any final action, the contracting officer must assess whether the failure to perform was due to causes beyond the vendor's control. Additionally, the vendor is given the opportunity to present, in writing, any facts or circumstances that led to the vendor's failure to perform. The vendor must respond within ten days of receipt of the notice. GSA will treat a failure to respond as an admission that there were no excusable circumstances.

Fourth, as with a termination for convenience, GSA must provide written notice to the vendor of a termination for default in the event the vendor fails to undertake remedial action.[906] In response, the vendor must cease all activity on the terminated portion of the contract and issue a corresponding stop work order to its subcontractors.

For the most part, these same procedures apply to a termination by an ordering agency. One notable exception is the fact that, if the vendor does not agree with an agency's default determination, the agency must refer the matter to the GSA contracting officer.[907] "In the absence of a decision by the schedule contracting officer . . . excusing the failure, the ordering office may charge the contractor with excess costs resulting from repurchase."[908] FAR 8.405-5 provides detailed rules regarding an ordering agency's repurchase of supplies and/or services as well as excess costs relating thereto.

* * *

In the event of a termination for default—whether by GSA or an ordering agency—the Government maintains the right to reprocure the supplies or services that were to be provided by the defaulting vendor and charge the vendor any excess in the costs of the reprocurement (including administrative costs). Additionally, a termination does *not* extinguish the Government's right to pursue other remedies against the vendor. For example, if GSA terminates a Schedule contract because of a vendor's failure to comply with the Price Reductions Clause, the termination does not preclude GSA from subsequently pursuing a price reduction. Furthermore, a termination for default will be reflected in a vendor's past performance history and, thus, may adversely affect the vendor's ability to secure future contracts.

Notes:

[895] In *United States v. Corliss Steam-Engine Co.*, 91 U.S. 321 (1876), the United States Supreme Court held that the Government's right to terminate a contract for its convenience was incorporated into the contract by operation of law. *See also G.L. Christian & Assocs. v. United States*, 320 F.2d 345 (Ct. Cl. 1963).

[896] *See Commercial Drapery Contractors v. United States*, 133 F.3d 1(D.C. Cir. 1998) (cancellation pursuant to Cancellation Clause upheld as not being a denial of due process).

[897] FSS Acquisition Letter FC-00-5 (Aug. 31, 2000), Supplement 1 (Oct. 10, 2000), at 2.

[898] FAR 52.212-4(l).

[899] 236 F.3d 1316 (Fed. Cir. 2001).

[900] For a thorough discussion of the *Travel Centre* case, *see* John W. Chierichella & Jonathan S. Aronie, *Unwary Rabbits Beware: IDIQ Means Never Having To Say You're Sorry*, GOVERNMENT CONTRACT AUDIT REPORT (Lyman Grp. Feb. 2001), at 20.

[901] *Travel Centre v. Gen. Servs. Admin.*, GSBCA No. 14057, 98-1 BCA ¶ 29,536, at 146,428 (1997).

[902] *Id.*

[903] The purchasing agency may terminate an order. *See, e.g., GF Office Sys.*, AGBCA No. 90-182-1, 90-3 BCA ¶ 23,236 (permitting termination of order due to delinquent performance). *See also Centennial Leasing Corp.*, GSBCA No. 12321, 93-3 BCA ¶ 26,200. Centennial Leasing involved a Navy termination of a delivery order under a MAS contract. The contractor appealed the Navy's final decision to the ASBCA. The ASBCA dismissed for lack of jurisdiction, transferring the matter to the GSBCA. The GSBCA then dismissed, finding that the Navy contracting officer lacked the authority to issue a final decision in the first place.

[904] *See Granco Indus., Inc. v. GSA*, GSBCA No. 14900 *et al.*, 99-2 BCA ¶ 30,568 (termination for default ineffective when items in default were not part of vendor's revised bid accepted by GSA).

[905] The United States Court of Federal Claims held in *Composite Laminates, Inc. v. United States*, 27 Fed. Cl. 310 (1992), that telephone calls, letters, and conversations were relevant to a consideration of the adequacy of a cure notice. *See Pro/Des, Inc. v. GSA*, GSBCA No. 13165 *et al.*, 96-2 BCA ¶ 28,510 (After issuance of several cure notices for non-conforming goods, small business' contract was properly terminated for default.).

[906] FAR 49.102.

[907] FAR 8.406-4, 8.406-6(a)-(b).

[908] FAR 8.406-4)a)(1).

XIX.

DISPUTES

"Agree, for the law is costly."

-Sir William Camden

The Government Contracts Reference Book defines a dispute as "[a] disagreement between the contractor and the contracting officer regarding the rights of the parties under a contract."[909] Typically, such disagreements concern the payment of money to or by the Government or the interpretation of a contract term, but may concern any other issue "arising under or relating to" the contract.[910] In other words, almost all disagreements between a vendor and its contracting officer—with a few limited exceptions[911]—are subject to the Disputes Clause, including breach of contract claims, whether raised by the Government or the vendor.[912]

As with all Government contracts, disputes between a Schedule vendor and the Government are resolved pursuant to the Contract Disputes Act of 1978 ("CDA"),[913] as provided in the MAS Disputes Clause:

> This contract is subject to the Contract Disputes Act of 1978, as amended (41 U.S.C. 601-613).

> Failure of the parties to this contract to reach agreement on any request for equitable adjustment, claim, appeal or action arising under or relating to this contract shall be a dispute to be resolved in accordance with the clause at FAR 52.233-1, Disputes, which is incorporated herein by reference. The Contractor shall proceed diligently with performance of this contract, pending final resolution of any dispute arising under the contract.[914]

FAR 52.233-1 sets forth the specific procedures governing disputes between a vendor and the Government.

The disputes process begins with the submission of a "claim." The FAR defines a "claim" as

> a written demand or written assertion by one of the contracting parties seeking, as a matter of right, the payment of money in a sum certain, the adjustment or interpretation of contract terms, or other relief arising under or relating to this contract.[915]

A claim that seeks the payment of money exceeding $100,000 must be certified by an authorized company official.[916]

A claim by a vendor must be submitted to the cognizant contracting officer (*i.e.*, the GSA contracting officer) in writing within six years after the accrual of the claim.[917] For purposes of the Disputes Clause, a claim "accrues" "on the date when all events, which fix the alleged liability of either the Government or the contractor and permit assertion of the claim, were known or should have been known."[918] A valid claim will include the following information:

- Sufficient detail to permit the contracting officer to issue a meaningful decision[919]

- A sum certain, where applicable and determinable[920]
- A request for a contracting officer decision[921]
- A certification, where the claim is for more than $100,000[922]

For a claim to be valid, the dispute must exist *before* the submission of the claim. In other words, the mere submission of the written claim does *not* constitute the dispute.[923] The party to whom the claim is directed must refuse to take the requested action (in the context of a claim against the Government, the action requested would be a "final decision"). The Government, however, cannot withhold a final decision in order to prevent the accrual of a claim. FAR 52.233-1 sets forth the specific procedure for processing disputes under the MAS Program.[924]

Previously, all unresolved disputes had to be referred to the GSA contracting officer for resolution.[925] GSA defined an "unresolved dispute" as

> [a] dispute between an ordering agency and a schedule contractor regarding payment, performance or contract interpretation that must be referred to the schedule contracting office for resolution under the Disputes clause of the schedule contract.[926]

As an example of an unresolved dispute, GSA contemplated "a situation where an ordering agency assesses liquidated damages for late delivery and withholds payment from the contractor, while the contractor alleges that his failure to deliver was excusable and that he does not owe the liquidated damages."[927]

In mid-2002, however, the FAR Council issued a final rule modifying FAR Part 8. The rule now grants ordering offices the authority to issue final decisions on disputes arising from *the performance of an order*.[928] The rule gives the ordering office the option to issue the final decision or refer the dispute to the GSA contracting officer.[929] Importantly, the ordering office's decision-making authority extends only to performance issues. Issues pertaining to contract terms and conditions still must be referred to the GSA contracting officer for resolution under the Disputes Clause.[930] Likewise, issues relating to a termination where the contractor claims an excusable failure to perform also must be referred to the GSA contracting officer for resolution.[931]

While the publication of the final rule in 2002 generally was well accepted, the rule has raised some concerns within the Schedule contracting community. One such concern flows from the fact that the rule provides that a vendor may appeal any final decision either to the board of contract appeals servicing the agency issuing the final decision—*i.e.*, the ordering agency—or to the United States Court of Federal Claims ("COFC").[932] By drastically increasing the number of quasi-judicial bodies playing a role in the MAS Program, the concern is that the rule will reduce the level of consistency vendors can expect within the Program.

Additionally, as highlighted by the American Bar Association ("ABA") in its comments to the FAR Council's proposed rule,[933] the rule very well could create technical and jurisdictional issues for vendors. For example, the distinction between disputes "relating to performance" and those "relating to terms and conditions" is far from clear. As a result, there could be a proliferation of jurisdictional litigation reminiscent of the not so halcyon days when boards of contract appeals addressed claims "arising under" contracts and the Court of Claims resolved claims "relating to" the contract.

Following a negative decision from a contracting officer in response to a properly filed claim, the vendor has the right to appeal the decision either the Board of Contract Appeals for the agency issuing the final decision (either GSA or the ordering agency) or to the U.S. Court of Federal Claims. Appeals to the Board must be filed within 90 days, a deadline that is strictly enforced.[934]

* * *

Advice From The Trenches

(by John Cornell, Esquire, GSA Office of the General Counsel)

There are precious few people who know what's going on with CDA litigation as it applies to Schedule contracts. For the most part, this is because there is not much litigation arising from Schedule contracts, notwithstanding the billions of dollars worth of supplies and services that flow through these vehicles. I'm writing[935] this memorandum on All Souls' Day, 2001. It appears that the FAR will be amended to allow ordering agencies to issue appealable final decisions on disputes pertaining to performance of an order. This new wrinkle in the FAR, of limited interest to a small number of practitioners, poses three questions: Who is the contracting officer? What is the forum? Why does it matter?

Who Is The Contracting Officer?

Prior to the modification to FAR 8.405-7 proposed in FAR Case 99-614, a vendor took any dispute initially to the contracting officer of the ordering agency and, if this did not yield the desired result, to the GSA Schedule contracting officer. Only the GSA[936] Schedule contracting officer could issue an appealable final decision. This will change, with interesting ramifications. Under FAR Case 99-614, the contracting officer of the ordering agency may issue an appealable final decision pertaining to "disputes arising from performance of the order." Disputes as to the terms and conditions of the Schedule contract will still require a final decision from the GSA Schedule contracting officer. Under the new reading of FAR 8.405-7, the vendor will have to determine whether or not the dispute is arising from the performance of the order (placed by the ordering office) or pertaining to the terms and conditions of the GSA Schedule contract. Depending upon how the dispute is characterized, the vendor must obtain a final decision from the *correct* contracting officer.

What Is The Forum?

One of the quirks of practice under the CDA is choice of forum. A vendor can choose to have its case heard either by the COFC or by the agency board of contract appeals. Prior to FAR Case 99-614, this meant that the board of contract appeals in most instances would be the GSBCA, as only the GSA contracting officer could issue an appealable final decision.[937] After FAR Case 99-614, the question of which board of contract appeals becomes interesting. Between two and three-dozen civilian agencies have Memoranda of Understanding in place to use the GSBCA. Agencies within DOD use the Armed Services Board of Contract Appeals ("ASBCA") (as does the Army Corps of Engineers, NASA, and the Central Intelligence Agency). To use an example, the U.S. Coast Guard is nominally part of the Department of Transportation and, thus would have its appeals heard at the Department of Transportation Board of Contract Appeals ("DOT CAB"). Depending upon whether the issue in dispute is one of performance under the order or a dispute pertaining to the terms and conditions of the Schedule contract, the dispute could be heard at the COFC, the DOT CAB, the ASBCA, or the GSBCA.

Why Does It Matter?

As a matter of substantive law, there is not much difference between the possible dispute resolution forums. There are interesting procedural differences between the divers boards and between the boards and the COFC. There will also be interesting issues as to who will represent the contracting officer. In all disputes before the COFC, the agency will be represented by the DOJ's Commercial Litigation Branch. In disputes before agency boards other than the GSBCA, representation will be provided by the ordering agency. In disputes heard by the GSBCA on final decisions rendered by the GSA Schedule contracting officer, GSA Office of General Counsel will represent the Government, even if the real "client" is the ordering agency.[938] If payment is made from the Permanent Indefinite Judgment Fund either by settlement or by final award from the board or the court, pursuant to 41 U.S.C. § 612, the ordering agency will be required to reimburse the fund.[939] Why this matters, for the most part, will boil down to whether or not the vendor's counsel would rather work with the DOJ attorneys and rules of procedure at the COFC or would, instead, prefer to work with agency counsel and the applicable board of contract appeals.

Notes:

[909] GOVERNMENT CONTRACTS REFERENCE BOOK 197.

[910] FAR 52.233-1(c) (definition of "claim"). "This language encompasses both contract claims covered by remedy granting clauses and claims not covered by specific clauses in the contract." John Cibinic, Jr. & Ralph C. Nash, Jr., ADMINISTRATION OF GOVERNMENT CONTRACTS 1224 (3d ed.1995).

[911] The following matters are not covered by the Disputes Clause under normal circumstances: most tort cases (as long as they do not constitute breach of contract cases) (*see* 28 U.S.C. § 1491; *H.H.O., Inc. v. United States*, 7 Cl. Ct. 703 (1985) (The test for jurisdiction is whether there has been in effect a "tortuous" breach of contract rather than a tort independent of the contract.); *Asfaltos Panamenos, S.A.*, ASBCA No. 39425, 91-1 BCA ¶ 23,315 (For jurisdiction, there must be a direct nexus between the Government's alleged tortuous conduct and its obligations under the contract.)); most allegations of fraud (*see Martin J. Simko Constr. Co. v. United States*, 852 F.2d 540 (Fed. Cir. 1988) (Court held that Congress intended

for fraud claims to be excluded from section 605(a) of the CDA.));
many labor disputes (*see, e.g.*, 41 U.S.C. § 605(a); *Imperator Carpet
& Interiors, Inc.*, GSBCA No. 6167, 81-2 BCA ¶ 15,266 (SCA
violations are outside the authorized purview of the CDA.); *Wickham
Contracting Co.*, GSBCA No. 6579, 82-2 BCA ¶ 15,883 (Claims
for violations of the Contract Work Hours and Safety Standards Act
were dismissed for lack of jurisdiction; the Secretary of Labor, not
the GSBCA, is authorized by statute to adjudicate such violations.)).

[912] *See Essex Electro Eng'rs, Inc. v. United States*, 702 F.2d 998 (Fed.
Cir. 1983) (A dispute concerning costs due to a contractor from the
Government's termination for convenience of a contract is to be
determined under the requirements of the Contract Disputes Act.);
Mega Constr. Co. v. United States, 29 Fed. Cl. 396, 415 (1993)
("The Contract Disputes Act abolished the jurisdictional
requirement of specific relief-granting clause, giving contractors
the right, and the obligation, to bring any and all disputes before a
board or the court as a contract dispute under the all-disputes
clause."); *Tefft, Kelly & Motley, Inc.*, GSBCA No. 6562, 83-1 BCA
¶ 16,177, *reconsideration denied*, 83-1 BCA ¶ 16,279 (Breach of
contract claims fall under the authority of the CDA.).

[913] 41 U.S.C. § 601 *et seq.* FAR 52.212-4(d) provides that commercial
items contracts are governed by the Contract Disputes Act of 1978.

[914] FAR 52.212-4(d).

[915] FAR 52.233-1(c).

[916] FAR 52.233-1(d)(2).

[917] FAR 52.233-1(d)(1). Claims submitted to the ordering agency will
be referred to the GSA contracting officer pursuant to FAR 8.405-7.

[918] FAR 33.201.

[919] *E.g., Metric Constr. Co. v. United States*, 1 Cl. Ct. 383 (1983) (claim
must contain sufficient detail to permit reasoned consideration by
the contracting officer); *Marine Constr. & Dredging, Inc.*, ASBCA
No. 38412, 90-1 BCA ¶ 22,573, at 113,286 (claim "must contain
sufficient detail to notify the contracting officer of the basic factual
allegations upon which the claim is premised").

[920] *E.g., Harris Mgmt. Co.*, ASBCA No. 27291, 84-2 BCA ¶ 17,378;
Logus Mfg. Co., ASBCA No. 26436, 82-2 BCA ¶ 16,025.

[921] *E.g., Mingus Constructors, Inc. v. United States*, 812 F.2d 1387 (Fed. Cir. 1987) (contractor's letter did not constitute claim where contractor failed to request decision).

[922] FAR 52.233-1(d)(2).

[923] *Keystone Coat & Apron Mfg. Corp. v. United States*, 150 Ct. Cl. 277 (1960) (finding no dispute where the contracting officer merely demanded payment of funds rather than requested payment and awaited the contractor's refusal); *United Aero, Inc.*, ASBCA No. 26967, 83-1 BCA ¶ 16,268, at 80,835 ("[A] contracting officer's decision in not a procedurally valid 'final' decision unless there is a dispute to decide.").

[924] For an excellent detailed discussion on the Disputes Clause, *see* Nash & Cibinic, ADMINISTRATION OF GOVERNMENT CONTRACTS 1239 *et seq.*, *supra* note 772.

[925] See prior FAR 8.405-7, which governed MAS contracts, which provided that "[t]he ordering office shall refer all unresolved disputes under orders to the schedule contracting office for action under the Disputes clause of the contract." *See also* GSA Procurement Information Bulletin 99-9 (July 2, 1999); *Grant Communications, Inc. v. Social Sec. Admin.*, GSBCA No. 14862-SSA, 99-1 BCA ¶ 30,281; *Centennial Leasing v. GSA*, GSBCA No. 12321, 93-3 BCA ¶ 26,200; *Digital Equipment Corp.*, GSBCA No. 9618 *et al.*, 90-2 BCA ¶ 22,808 (GAO held that contractor could consolidate all of its counterclaims with various agencies into claims against GSA as the oversight agency of MAS contracts. Contractor would not be forced to counterclaim in a piecemeal fashion.).

[926] GSA Procurement Information Bulletin 99-9 (July 2, 1999).

[927] *Id.*

[928] FAR 8.406-6; *see* 65 Fed. Reg. 79,702, 79,703 (Dec. 19, 2000) (to be codified at 48 C.F.R. pts. 8 and 51) for proposed rule leading to the revision of FAR 8.406-6.

[929] FAR 8.406-6(a).

[930] FAR 8.406-6(b).

[931] *See, e.g., United Partition Systems*, ASBCA 53915 (May 2, 2003) (dismissing appeal because ordering agency had no right to issue final decision).

932 *Id*.

933 Draft ABA comments dated Feb. 20, 2001.

934 *See, e.g., Ray Communications vs. General Services Administration*, GSBCA No. 16056 (Feb. 24, 2003) (dismissing appeal of contractor disputing contracting officer's calculation of monies owed to GSA following contract termination).

935 The usual disclaimers apply -- the opinions expressed in this article are my own and do not reflect the position of my clients or the GSA Office of General Counsel.

936 GSA is not the only agency awarding Schedule contracts. The Department of Veterans Affairs, under delegation from the GSA Administrator has a small Schedules division for medical supplies and pharmaceuticals. Disputes under these contracts would require a final decision from the VA contracting officer to be appealable. Either the COFC or the VA Board of Contract Appeals hears these disputes. This footnote will be the only mention of the VA's role in Schedule contracting in this Advisory.

937 The exception to this general rule, of course, is that, even prior to FAR Case 99-614, an ordering agency could terminate an order for default. These terminations are rare, and appeals from these terminations are even more rare. Under these circumstances the appeal would be heard either by the COFC or the board of contract appeals that services the ordering agency.

938 If the ordering office authors the final decision, pertaining to the performance of the order, and the ordering agency uses the GSBCA as its board of contract appeals, then the Government would be represented by counsel for the ordering agency, even though the dispute is heard at the GSBCA.

939 *See Heritage Reporting Corp.*, B-252754, Oct. 6, 1994.

XX.

ETHICS, COMPLIANCE, AND TRAINING

"Conscience is the inner voice which warns us somebody may be looking."

-Henry Louis Mencken

Y ears ago, the concept of organizational ethical conduct—or "business ethics"—was an ideal not widely endorsed or accepted. Over the past few years, however, a multitude of modern commentators have been promoting the virtues of business ethics.[940] In light of this new attention, it is hardly surprising that so many modern businesses are voluntarily implementing formal internal ethics/compliance programs. After setting forth several reasons why such a program should be implemented by every MAS vendor, this chapter discusses the basic components of an effective program.

A. *Why Adopt An Ethics/Compliance Program?*

The terms and conditions of the MAS Program are numerous, complex, and confusing. Countless regulations and statutes create an atmosphere in which even the most ethical organization can find itself on the receiving end of an audit, investigation, civil action, or prosecution. Against this background, an effective ethics/compliance program can help to prevent problems.

Moreover, the Federal Organizational Sentencing Guidelines (the "Guidelines"), promulgated in 1991, provide that a business organization found guilty of criminal conduct may be entitled to a reduction in its fine if it had in place an effective, functioning ethics/compliance program at the time of the offense.[941] Thus, an ethics/compliance program not only works to help prevent problems from occurring, it can help mitigate the damage caused by problems that do occur. Specifically, the existence of an effective functioning ethics/compliance program

- Is explicitly recognized as a mitigating factor in a criminal sentencing hearing
- Is explicitly recognized as a mitigating factor in a suspension or debarment proceeding
- Frequently is considered by an Inspector General in the course of a federal audit and
- May provide evidence to counter the "state of mind" requirement in a civil False Claims Act action

In each of these situations, the existence of an effective ethics/compliance program can save a MAS vendor substantial grief (and money) over the long term.

B. *How To Create An Effective Ethics/Compliance Program*

Beyond fostering sentencing consistency, the Guidelines serve another function as well. Seven elements set forth in the Guidelines "stand as virtually the only formal guidance by the Federal Government on what constitutes an effective compliance program."[942] It is useful, however, to reshuffle and expand these seven elements to reflect the experiences of contractors since 1991 (the year the Guidelines were adopted).[943] Performing such an exercise results in the following ten critical elements of an effective ethics/compliance program:

1. Management must be committed to the program
2. A senior officer must be assigned overall responsibility
3. The program must be tailored to the particular organization
4. The program must incorporate a comprehensive, yet easy-to-understand Code of Conduct
5. Members of the organization must have access to a working hotline
6. Employees and managers must receive realistic training
7. Compliance must be the key to advancement
8. The program must be monitored and audited by an independent authority
9. A breach of the program must result in appropriate and prompt discipline and
10. The program must be reviewed and updated regularly

Each element is discussed in turn below.

1. Management Commitment

MAS vendors must seek and obtain a commitment from a wide internal business base, including finance personnel, corporate auditors, lawyers, administrative officers, vice presidents, presidents, and CEOs. Management must not only authorize the ethics/compliance program; it must understand, appreciate, and meaningfully endorse the importance of such a program. Without this sort of real management commitment, an ethics/compliance program is doomed to fail.

2. Senior Officer Responsibility

When ethics/compliance responsibility is to be delegated, it must be delegated to an individual who is well respected throughout the organization and who knows the organization inside and out. Further, to ensure that the individual has the resources necessary to accomplish his or her task, the individual should be afforded direct access to senior management and the freedom to investigate allegations of wrongdoing. Both are critical components of an effective ethics/compliance program.

3. Program Tailored To Organization

No single ethics/compliance program will work for every organization. As Linda Trevino and Katherine Nelson write in their book, *Managing Business Ethics*, "[s]tandard cookie cutter ethics programs are likely to be ineffective because organizations don't have cookie cutter ethical problems."[944] For example, what works for a "mom and pop" consulting firm probably will not work for General Electric.

4. Code Of Conduct

Most large American corporations have formal ethics codes.[945] This is encouraging. It probably is a safe bet, however, that the numbers are less encouraging for small businesses. This is unfortunate because small businesses have as much to gain from a written Code of Conduct as do their larger counterparts. Whatever the size of the organization, a comprehensive and easy-to-understand Code of Conduct is an essential element of any effective ethics/compliance program.

Like ethics/compliance programs generally, there is no one code that will work for all organizations. There are, however, several basic criteria that a successful code should satisfy. Specifically,[946] the code should:

- Be written in simple, understandable language
- Be comprehensive
- Include both fundamental principles and the more general goals of the compliance program

- Include examples, and perhaps even questions and answers, in common areas
- Be available for consultation
- Include a hotline number and
- Require an acknowledgement of receipt by all employees

Vendors attempting to design such a code for their organizations would be wise to take a lesson from what probably is the Western world's most famous Code of Conduct—the Ten Commandments. The simplicity and thoroughness of this code provide a useful model for anyone charged with drafting a Code of Conduct for an organization.

5. Working Hotline

Every ethics/compliance program should incorporate a method by which employees confidentially can seek guidance and/or report transgressions of the organization's code without risk of retribution. Typically, this takes the form of a toll-free telephone number dedicated to this purpose. To be successful, a hotline should have an easy to remember number, all calls should be treated as confidential, and employees who chose to identify themselves (something that should *not* be required) must understand that—and have confidence that—they will not be the subject of retaliation.

6. Training

Training is the means by which an organization puts its principles (as reflected in its Code of Ethics) into practice. An effective training program may be conducted by in-house personnel or by outside lawyers or consultants retained specifically for that purpose. While every training program is unique in that it must be tailored to the culture of the organization being trained, an effective training program should encompass at least the following basic components:

- Training sessions should be presented to employees *and* supervisors
- Sessions should be presented by individuals who are knowledgeable *and* respected
- The subject matter and length of each presentation should be tailored to the specific audience (*i.e.*, supervisors probably warrant different training than other employees)
- Attendance should be mandatory
- The program should include written material that each employee can retain for reference and
- The program (and the written materials) should be revised and updated regularly

A training program that does not encompass at least the foregoing components might well be viewed as a sham by any judge or debarment official called upon to review it. Of course, this is not to say that every training program must be mind-numbingly intense, but something more than a brief presentation over lunch once a year probably is required.

7. Compliance As A Key To Advancement

According to Trevino and Nelson, "[r]eward systems are probably the single most important formal influence on people's behavior at work."[947] Even a simple policy designed to ensure that each employee's written evaluation reflects his or her compliance history can go a long way toward achieving this goal.

8. Independent Monitoring And Audit

Government vendors are no strangers to audits. The IRS audits their taxes, the GSA OIG audits their contract performance, and the Customs Service audits their trade practices. Indeed, no less than five separate audit clauses flow out of GSA's MAS contract alone. In this atmosphere, one would think that more vendors would appreciate the usefulness of independent monitoring of internal programs upon the theory that it is better to assess the adequacy of one's own ethics/compliance program than to learn of its inadequacy from the Government.

9. Discipline

Just as compliant behavior should lead to advancement, noncompliant behavior should lead to discipline. One is merely the flip side of the other. An organization that lacks effective discipline sends a strong signal that it does not take its ethics/compliance program seriously. This signal will be picked up clearly both by employees and by a debarment official. Employees (and supervisors) must understand that noncompliant behavior will not be tolerated. Such an understanding comes from witnessing this principle in practice. Noncompliant employees should be disciplined. Such discipline should include—and employees should understand that it includes— termination when appropriate.

10.   Reviews And Updates

For the same reasons that a training program should be reviewed and updated regularly, the ethics/compliance program of which the training program is a component should be reviewed at least as often. A formal, comprehensive review is suggested at least annually, with discrete, less formal reviews conducted more frequently. If an aspect of a program proves ineffective—for example, if high employee turnover renders annual training insufficient—that component can (and should) be modified.

* * *

Most vendors, for obvious reasons, would rather contemplate the rewards of doing business with the Federal Government than the risks. But the risks are there, they are real, and they are significant. Vendors that have been subject to a federal audit, that have met with a debarment official, or that have had an "up close and personal" introduction to the False Claims Act know this to be true. Without much warning, a sunny day can turn cloudy and, when the rain comes, an effective ethics/compliance program may prove to be the best umbrella.

Notes:

[940]   *See generally* Linda K. Trevino & Katherine A. Nelson, MANAGING BUSINESS ETHICS: STRAIGHT TALK ABOUT HOW TO DO IT RIGHT (John Wiley & Sons, Inc. 1995) [hereinafter, "Trevino and Nelson"].

[941]   Hon. Jed S. Rakoff, Linda R. Blumkin & Richard A. Sauber CORPORATE SENTENCING GUIDELINES: COMPLIANCE AND MITIGATION § 1.05[3], at 1-21, 1-22 (L.J. Press 1999).

[942]   John T. Boese, THE NUTS & BOLTS OF AN EFFECTIVE COMPLIANCE/ETHICS PROGRAM, at 6 (presented at the First Annual Blue Cross & Blue Shield Assn. Nat'l Compliance Meeting) (Apr. 6, 1997).

[943]   *Id.* at 10.

[944]   Trevino & Nelson at 196.

[945]   Trevino & Nelson at 205.

[946]   Boese, THE NUTS & BOLTS OF AN EFFECTIVE COMPLIANCE/ETHICS PROGRAM 14-16, *supra* note 802.

[947]   Trevino & Nelson at 146.

XXI.

GOVERNMENT AUDITS AND INVESTIGATIONS

"War hath no fury like a non-combatant."
-Charles Edward Montague

As every Schedule vendor knows (or should know), the highway of opportunity that emerges from the MAS Program is not toll-free. While the Program clearly offers vendors significant financial rewards, it also burdens vendors with significant obligations. Among these obligations are multiple audit clauses, requiring Schedule vendors to open their books (and often their doors) to a host of Government auditors.[948]

A. *The Examination Of Records By GSA (Multiple Award Schedule) Clause*

Every vendor awarded a MAS contract agrees that any duly authorized representative of GSA

> shall have access to and the right to examine any books, documents, papers and records of the Contractor involving transactions related to

this contract for overbillings, billing errors, compliance with the Price Reduction clause and compliance with the Industrial Funding Fee clause of this contract. This authority shall expire 3 years after final payment. The basic contract and each option shall be treated as separate contracts for purposes of applying this clause.[949]

Known formally as the Examination of Records by GSA (Multiple Award Schedule) Clause, this clause affords GSA substantial and long-lasting audit rights. They are substantial because (a) it is the Government's position that they can cover almost any document "related" to the contract, (b) a failure to disclose any information to GSA during the negotiation of the contract can lead to an alleged "overbilling," and (c) almost all sales can be considered "related to" the contract whether or not such sales falls within the vendor's relevant category of customers. They are long-lasting because the Government's audit rights continue until three years after "final payment," which, typically, is defined as "[t]he last payment the Government makes on a contract when the parties believe all obligations under the contract have been closed out."[950] Because Schedule purchasers do not all pay their debts as promptly as vendors would like, it often is difficult to identify the "last payment the Government makes."

B. *Pre-Award Audits*

GSA's standard solicitation affords GSA pre-award audit rights, which GSA employs to review a vendor's sales data in order to ensure that information submitted in its Commercial Sales Practices Format ("CSPF" or "CSP Format") is current, accurate, and complete. While GSA will not conduct this audit in all circumstances, pre-award audits have become more common over the past few years as post-award audits have become less common. Indeed, GSA has stated publicly that pre-award audits will be its primary audit tool.[951]

The Office of Inspector General ("OIG") conducts pre-award audits on behalf of GSA. (*See* Chapter VII, which discusses the information a vendor produces to GSA during pre-award negotiations.) To provide some idea of the number and effect of these audits, from October 1999 to March 2000, the GSA OIG performed pre-award audits on 61 contracts with an estimated value of approximately $279 million.[952] According to the OIG, these audits "contained over $39 million in financial recommendations"—14 percent of the contracts' aggregate volume.[953]

In some sense, however, a pre-award audit is not always a bad thing from a vendor's point of view as it may disclose a potential noncompliance at an early stage that could grow into significant problems if not identified and left unchecked. As an example, consider a company that unintentionally omits from its CSP Format the fact that a certain customer receives a better discount than the Government. If found during a pre-award audit, this omission can be cured before the vendor "damages" the Government. While the absence of damages does not solve all of the vendor's problems, it does solve some of them. If the omission were identified during a post-award audit, however, after performance already has begun and the Government already has been damaged, that could cause a host of new problems, each of which may spawn a host of new consequences.

C. *Post-Award Audits*

The GSA OIG conducts most of its post-award audits pursuant to the Examination of Records Clause. While the OIG undertakes such audits primarily to assess compliance with the Price Reductions Clause and the Industrial Funding Fee Clause, the scope of such an audit, as suggested above, can be and often is much broader.

One thing that the GSA OIG is not supposed to do pursuant to the Examination of Records Clause, however, is conduct a defective pricing-type audit—*i.e.*, review of a vendor's books and records with the intent of determining whether the vendor submitted noncurrent, inaccurate, or incomplete information to the Government during contract negotiations. In practice, however, the GSA OIG frequently finds a way to conduct such an audit under the guise of a Price Reductions Clause audit. Moreover, while the Examination of Records Clause typically found in MAS solicitations does *not* provide for post-award audits of pre-award data submissions, the GSAR allows the Examination of Records Clause to be modified "[w]ith the Senior Procurement Executive's approval" to permit such an audit after a finding that, absent the modification, "there is a likelihood of significant harm to the Government."[954]

In 1999, industry petitioned the Office of Federal Procurement Policy ("OFPP") to eliminate the use of the Examination of Records Clause to conduct post-award audits of pre-award submissions.[955] Notwithstanding the fact that the OFPP declined to accept industry's request, industry's argument was a strong one. The Examination of Records Clause is plainly inconsistent with the recent procurement reforms implemented by Clinger-Cohen. In a report issued contemporaneously with the passage of Clinger-Cohen, the House Committee on National Security made it quite clear that the Act

> eliminated certain rights by the government to audit information to be supplied by commercial suppliers in lieu of certified cost or pricing data. In taking this action, Congress clearly and willfully did not intend that this statutory change permit federal agencies to subsequently determine through agency supplements to the Federal Acquisition Regulation whether and to what extent post award audit access is appropriate on commercial item contracts.[956]

MAS contracts are most certainly "commercial item contracts."

The Department of Veterans Affairs ("VA") has contended that Clinger-Cohen is inapplicable to MAS contracts. This position, however, is contradicted by several facts.

First, GSA itself previously has acknowledged, on more than one occasion, the application of Clinger-Cohen to the MAS Program. In an on-line white paper entitled "Multiple Award Schedule Contracts—A Solution for Buying Commercial Technology," for example, GSA recognized that Clinger-Cohen "touched upon virtually every aspect of the solicitation and award process from synopsis to debriefing."[957]

Second, GSA has incorporated statements into its MAS solicitations affirming the applicability of Clinger-Cohen to the MAS Program. The "Significant Changes" section of the information technology solicitation, for example, states clearly that the solicitation was prepared in accordance with Clinger-Cohen.[958]

Third, and probably most critically, the drafters of Clinger-Cohen themselves have emphasized that it applies to the MAS Program, thereby eliminating the authority of federal agencies to perform post-award audits of MAS contracts:

> The [Clinger-Cohen Act] eliminated the authority of Federal agencies to perform post-award audits of suppliers of commercial items. The clear intent of Congress was that these audits would no longer be performed by Federal agencies. Congress clearly did not intend that this statutory change permit Federal agencies to subsequently determine through agency supplements to the Federal Acquisition Regulation whether and to what extent post award audit access is appropriate on commercial item contracts.
>
> GSA is considering a final rule which would amend the GSA Acquisition Regulation to permit post-award audits of certain commercial item contracts. We believe this is inappropriate and

> contrary to Congress' clear intent. *Therefore, for the purpose of this specific regulation related to GSA's Multiple Award Schedule, we reiterate previously stated congressional intent that the only remaining authority for the government to pursue post-award audits of contractor records regarding the purchase of commercial items is the General Accounting Office.*[959]

In light of the foregoing, one must question the basis for the VA's position that Clinger-Cohen does not apply to the MAS Program.

Despite the murkiness of GSA's statutory authority to perform post-award audits, the agency nonetheless has been criticized for its infrequent use of post-award audits to monitor and enforce accurate pricing of MAS purchases.[960] In response to these criticisms, the GSA published an Advance Notice of Proposed Rulemaking requesting comments on whether post-award audit provisions should be included in FSS contracts.[961] GSA also is working with its Inspector General to examine the issue of post-award audits and to improve the efficacy of the audit process generally.[962] As of this writing, the responses to the notice are under review, and no specific language for a new rule has been issued.

In some sense, however, it is irrelevant whether industry devises a new plan of attack against the Examination of Records Clause. GSA has taken the position that whatever authority it lacks under the Examination of Records Clause, it possesses independently under the Inspector General Act of 1978.[963] Put another way, a vendor should not base its business decisions on its ability to stave off an OIG audit on the language of the Examination of Records Clause.

D. *Pre-Award On-Site Equal Employment Opportunity Compliance Review*

Prior to award, depending on the size of the contract, the Government may conduct a pre-award on-site EEO compliance review. The contracting officer is required to request a pre-award audit prior to awarding contracts of $10 million or more.[964] The purpose of this audit is to ensure that the vendor is in compliance with the requirements of Executive Order 11246 (Equal Employment Opportunity).[965] The audit will encompass a review of the vendor's affirmative action program, records concerning payroll, and personnel as well as other employment records. Interviews with employees and company officers may be conducted.

E. *Government Accountability Office Audit*

The Comptroller General Examination of Records Clause[966] affords the GAO the authority to inspect any "directly pertinent" books or records involving transactions related to the contract. This provision allows audits to be performed for three years after final payment under the contract.[967] During this period, the GAO has the right to examine, audit, and reproduce records covered by the clause.[968] Although the vendor's records may be audited, this clause does not require that the vendor develop or keep records that it would not be required to keep in compliance with a law or would not ordinarily maintain.[969]

F. *Defense Contract Audit Agency Audit*

In April 2004, the Defense Contract Audit Agency issued a Memorandum for Regional Director designed to clarify DCCA's role in auditing GSA Schedule Orders.[970] Among other things, the auditing guidance "provides auditors with a set of procedures to follow" when auditing GSA Schedule Orders. The basis of DCAA's audit authority in this area purportedly flows out of FAR 52.232-7, the "Payment under Time-and-Material and Labor-Hour Contracts" clause, a clause incorporated into many if not most, GSA Schedule Contracts.

The audit guidance suggests that DCAA will be focusing its sights on (1) open market item purchased in conjuction with schedule items, (2) travel costs, and (3) services performed by subcontractors. Of these three areas, the third has caused the most heartburn among industry because, as of the submission of this text to the publisher at least, DCAA's review of the proper rate to charge on subcontracted labor differs significantly from GSA's stated review. In short, DCAA believes that a contractor may not charge an agency more than the amount actually paid by the contractor. In contrast, GSA's stated view has been that subcontracted work should be billed at the Schedule holder's negotiated schedule rate, even if that rate is higher than the rate paid to the subcontractor.

While this debate, no doubt, will resolve itself in time, contactors in the mean time would be wise to come to a mutual understanding with their contracting office regarding payments to subcontractors, and to document that understanding in writing.

G. *Inspection Of Services*

MAS contracts for services typically include the clause at FAR 52.246-4, which gives the Government the right to "inspect and test all services called for by the contract, to the extent practicable at all times and places during the term of the contract."[971] Where such inspections are performed, the vendor is obligated to provide the Government "all reasonable facilities and assistance for the safe and convenient performance of these duties."[972]

H. *Department of Labor Audits*

The DOL conducts audits to ensure compliance with applicable labor laws.[973] Indeed, DOL is required to audit vendors that hold contracts in excess of $10 million. DOL has broad powers under its audit rights. DOL can impose administrative sanctions and penalties and can suspend, cancel, or terminate vendors' contracts. DOL even may suspend or debar a noncompliant vendor. Additionally, DOL may refer issues to the

DOJ, which may institute civil or criminal proceedings against the vendor.

I. *"Contractor Assistance Visits" (A.K.A., "IFF Reviews")*

These euphemistically labeled "visits" actually are compliance reviews conducted by GSA "Industrial Operations Analysts ("IOA")" working under the "Contract Management Division" of the Federal Supply Service. These reviews are designed to ensure that vendors have implemented an acceptable sales tracking system capable of identifying and reporting all MAS sales. The IOAs also will assess whether the vendor has submitted its 72a forms and IFF checks accurately and on time. According to GSA, a CAV review, as it is called, takes approximately 2-5 hours and, unless problems are identified, will occur no more than once per year. Vendors receiving notice of such a review should take time in advance of the IOA's arrival to organize all relevant sales records, gather all prior 72a reports, and ensure that an appropriate individual is capable of explaining (and demonstrating) the company's Schedule sales tracking system.

In 2005, GSA expanded the scope of the IOA reviews to include compliance with the Trade Agreements Act and with Small Business Subcontracting Plans.[974] Additionally, and particularly notable in light of several ongoing federal investigations stemming from the acquisition of interrogation services allegedly under a contractor's IT Schedule Contract for use in Iraq, this expansion also encompasses "out of scope" contracting as well.

Notes:

[948] Portions of this chapter are adapted, with permission, from Jonathan Aronie & John Chierichella, *GSA IG Audits - You Can't Afford to Be Unprepared*, OFF THE SHELF, at Insert (Coalition for Government Procurement, Aug. 1998).

[949] GSAR 552.215-71 (Aug. 1997).

[950] GOVERNMENT CONTRACTS REFERENCE BOOK 247.

[951] 62 Fed. Reg. 44,518 (Aug. 21, 1997) (to be codified at 48 C.F.R. pts. 504, 507, 510, 511, 512, 514, 515, 538, 539, 543, 546, 552, and 570).

[952] GSA OIG SEMIANNUAL REP. TO CONG. (Oct. 1, 1999-Mar, 31, 2000), at 25.

[953] Id.

[954] GSAR 515.209-70(c) (July 2000). The right of access expires two years after award or modification.

[955] GEIA Petition to OFPP Administrator, Review of GSAR MAS Pricing Clauses, June 1, 1999.

[956] H.R. REP. NO. 104-563, at 324 (1996).

[957] See http://pub.fss.gsa.gov/schedules/masca598.cfm.

[958] Solicitation FCIS-JB-980001B.

[959] Letter from Hon. William F. Clinger, Jr., Hon. Floyd D. Spence, and Hon. William S. Cohen to the Director of the Office of Management and Budget (Sept. 18, 1996) (emphasis added).

[960] See, e.g., Government Accountability Office, Contract Management: Opportunities Continue for GSA to Improve Pricing of Multiple Award Schedules Contracts, GAO-05-911T (July 26, 2005).

[961] 70 Fed. Reg. 12167-12168 (March 11, 2005) as amended by 70 Fed. Reg 13005 (March 17, 2005) and 70 Fed. Reg. 19051-19052 (April 12, 2005).

[962] See "GSA—Is the Taxpayer Getting the Best Deal? Hearings before the Senate Committee on Homeland Security and Governmental Affairs Subcommittee on Federal Financial Management, Government Information, and International Security" (July 26, 2005) (statements of Kathleen S. Tighe, Counsel to the Inspector General, United States General Services Administration, and of Emily W. Murphy, Chief Acquisition Officer, United States General Services Administration).

[963] GSA has noted specifically that contractual limitations "[do] not impact the Inspector General's independent authority under the Inspector General Act; nor would it preclude a contractor from voluntarily providing audit access should circumstances so warrant." 62 Fed. Reg. 44,518, 44,520 (Aug. 21, 1997) (to be codified at 48

C.F.R. pts. 504, 507, 510, 511, 512, 514, 515, 538, 539, 543, 546, 552, and 570).

[964] FAR 22.805(a). Paragraphs (a)(4) and (a)(8) of FAR 22.805 set forth the exceptions to this requirement.

[965] Executive Order 11246 required Government contractors and subcontractors to ensure that all employees are not discriminated against because of race, color, religion, sex, or national origin and put into place the structure and format for contractor compliance and sanctions for noncompliance.

[966] FAR 52.212-5(d).

[967] Id.

[968] Id.

[969] FAR 52.212-5(d)(3).

[970] DCAA Memorandum for Regional Director, PAC 730.3.B.0I/2004-08 (April 9, 2004).

[971] FAR 52.246-4(c).

[972] FAR 52.246-4(d).

[973] FAR Part 22.

[974] See "Contractor Assessment Initiative Report Card" (Feb. 15, 2005) that includes, among other questions, "Did the contractor demonstrate compliance with the scope of their contract?" "Did the contractor demonstrate compliance with the Trade Agreements Act," and "[D]id the contractor meet the goals specified in the [Subcontracting Plan] or is the contractor progressing toward meeting the goals specified in the plan?"

XXII.

DEALING WITH THE GSA OFFICE OF INSPECTOR GENERAL

"A little neglect may breed great mischief . . . for want of a nail the shoe was lost; for want of a shoe the horse was lost; and for want of a horse the rider was lost."

-Benjamin Franklin

C reated by the Inspector General Act of 1978 (the "IG Act"),[975] Offices of Inspector General currently exist in most large federal agencies. The GSA OIG was created in October 1978 as one of the twelve original OIGs.[976] Comprising five components (Office of Audits, Office of Investigations, Office of Counsel, Internal Evaluation Staff, and Office of Administration), the GSA OIG is tasked with detecting and preventing waste, fraud, and abuse in GSA's programs and operations.[977] To this end, the OIG conducts investigations, audits, and inspections of internal agency programs as well as contracting parties within those programs, and it does so with a fair amount of success, as this passage from the 2000 GSA OIG Semiannual Report suggests:

> Working with the Department of Justice, we
> obtained over $3.4 million in settlements from
> contractors resolving potential liabilities under
> the False Claims Act . . . . Also, we made 220
> referrals for criminal prosecution, civil litigation,
> and administrative action. Criminal cases
> originating from OIG referrals resulted in 9
> successful prosecutions . . . . [978]

These figures do not reflect the significant administrative settlements entered into between vendors and GSA as a result of OIG audits.

By law, the GSA OIG is required to "provide policy direction for and to conduct, supervise and coordinate audits and investigations relating to the programs and operations" of the agency.[979] The IG Act provides OIGs with broad authority to "make such investigations and reports relating to the administration of the programs and operations of the applicable establishment as are, in the judgment of the Inspector General, necessary or desirable."[980] OIGs are statutorily required to report expeditiously to the Attorney General when, during the course of their duties, they come to have "reasonable grounds to believe there has been a violation of Federal criminal law."[981]

The GSA OIG Office of Audits has chief responsibility for conducting contract reviews in support of GSA contracting officials to ensure fair contract pricing and adherence to contract terms and conditions. As suggested above, the Office of Audits conducts two types of MAS audits—pre-award audits and post-award audits. Pre-award audits are performed before award of a contract and are provided to the contracting officer to assist him or her in evaluating the offeror's proposal and negotiating contract pricing and other terms and conditions. Specifically, pre-award audits examine whether a vendor has provided current, accurate, and complete information regarding its sales and discount pricing practices and policies. Because of recent restrictions placed on MAS post-award audit authority, GSA is currently emphasizing pre-award audits.

As a quasi-law enforcement agency, the OIG comes armed with a variety of law enforcement tools. These tools include, among others, the authority to issue subpoenas requiring the production of information, records, and other documents relevant to the OIG's investigation.[982] Such subpoenas are enforceable in federal court. While OIG subpoenas cannot compel testimony from individuals *per se*,[983] OIG investigators can conduct interviews in aid of investigations and are empowered under the IG Act to administer oaths in connection with those interviews.[984] Moreover, OIG investigators, when working under the direction of a prosecutor, are authorized to serve grand jury subpoenas.

Another weapon in the arsenal of the OIG derives simply from the fact that OIG auditors and investigators are engaged in conducting a federal audit. There is a specific federal criminal statute that addresses the obstruction of a federal audit.[985]

Finally, vendors should be aware that the GSA OIG will refer all cases of nonresponsibility to the cognizant GSA suspension/debarment official. Indeed, the great majority of suspension/debarment referrals are made by the OIG.[986] Likewise, the GSA OIG will refer matters of suspected fraud to the DOJ for investigation pursuant to the civil or criminal False Claims Act. Kathleen S. Tighe, Counsel to the GSA IG, writes:

> The GSA OIG refers fraud cases for civil litigation under the civil False Claims Act to either the Department of Justice (DOJ), Civil Division, Commercial Litigation Branch, or directly to the appropriate United States Attorney's Office (USAO). DOJ directives provide for direct referral of affirmative civil fraud cases by agencies to USAOs when single damages are one million dollars or less.[987]

The manner in which a vendor conducts itself during the audit significantly affects whether the experience is a negative one or an uneventful one (a Government audit rarely is a "positive" experience). The following subsections discuss some of the more important aspects of an OIG audit. While the discussion focuses on an GSA OIG audit, the guidelines are applicable to almost any audit or investigation.

A. _Responding To An OIG Audit_

1. Initial Notice From OIG

Generally, the first notice of a GSA OIG audit that a vendor will receive will be in the form of a letter. Typically, the letter introduces the individual(s) who will be conducting the audit, sets forth the goal(s) of the audit (_i.e._, assess compliance with the Price Reductions Clause and other terms and conditions of the contract), and requests data.

2. Initial Response

Upon receipt of a letter notifying of the OIG's intent to audit, the vendor's law department or outside counsel should be notified. While auditors have broad authority to examine a vendor's books or records, their authority is not limitless. The vendor's law department or counsel will be able to assess whether the OIG is operating within or beyond its authority. In addition, the law department or counsel will be able to initiate a privileged internal dialogue (_i.e._, a dialogue that is protected from disclosure outside the company) aimed at assessing the vendor's potential exposure. Finally, the law department or counsel will be able to serve an important coordination function among the various groups within the company that likely will become involved as the audit proceeds (_i.e._, internal corporate audit, contracts, finance, etc.) as well as to assess the need for external support (_i.e._, outside or specialized counsel, outside auditors, Schedule consultants, etc.).

It is wise to respond to the OIG in a timely fashion with a written acknowledgement of its data request. This letter should also identify the member of the vendor's staff who will act as the official point of contact throughout the life of the audit. The appointment of such an individual benefits both the auditor and the vendor. From the auditor's viewpoint, a single point of contact facilitates the acquisition of requested documents and the identification of individuals who can explain those documents. From the vendor's point of view, a single point of contact ensures that the company learns of—and, perhaps, has the opportunity to respond to—any particular areas of concern to the auditor.

The individual assigned as the single point of contact should have good "people skills" and previous experience in dealing with audits and Government personnel. This person generally should be a senior member of the staff with access to all levels within the company. Generally, the single point of contact is someone from either the contracts or finance department. The single point of contact should ensure that all telephone conversations and meetings are documented. All materials provided to the OIG should be identified in a list.

3. Entrance Conference

An early, amicable meeting between the vendor and the auditor can be extremely useful. First, it can afford a better understanding of the scope of the OIG's document request and of the audit generally. Second, it can serve as a useful opportunity to acquaint the auditor with the company. The vendor may want to take this occasion to explain generally how its business works, as well as the nature of the particular industry in which it conducts business. Additionally, the vendor may take this opportunity to introduce those individuals responsible for administering its Schedule contract. Finally, the vendor may take advantage of the entrance conference to set the ground rules for viewing and copying documents and interviewing its employees, to explain its policy concerning visitor escorts (should the OIG decide to come on-site), and to request an exit conference at the conclusion of the audit and prior to the submission of the auditor's final report to GSA.

4. Notification To Employees

The vendor should notify employees who administer the contract and handle the billing and other financial aspects of the contract as well as employees who charge to the contract that is the subject of the audit. Employees should be briefed as to the nature of the audit, made aware of the single point of contact, and instructed that requests from the auditor are to be directed to the single point of contact. Employees should be instructed to be polite to the auditor; but, in the event the auditor asks an employee a question, the employee is to refer the auditor to the single point of contact. Other employees not directly concerned should be informed of the audit and directed to refer all audit questions to the identified single point of contact.[988]

The foregoing procedures will allow the vendor to monitor the audit and maintain control of the process. It also relieves the potentially uninformed and misinformed employee of the burden of trying to cooperate with the auditor, which can be extremely stressful. Relieving employees of the burden of trying to answer auditor questions that have not been passed through the single point of contact has a benefit other than the employees' peace of mind. First, the vendor will be able to assess the validity of the questions being posed in relation to the audit. Second, it will allow the vendor to direct the auditor to the employee with the knowledge being sought. Third, it prevents new issues from being raised by an incorrect, uneducated, or overly broad answer from an employee. Once such issues are raised, the vendor may well be faced with an entirely new and unwanted interest in its business by the OIG. It is much easier and less costly to prevent such occurrences than to attempt to provide an explanation to the auditor. Once the question has been posed to the point of contact, if appropriate, the employee should be instructed to answer the question truthfully, but concisely.

5. Cooperation With Auditors

Cooperating with the auditor is a good idea on many levels. For one, a failure to cooperate could be viewed as "obstructing" the audit.[989] Cooperation is wise also because it represents the single most effective means of facilitating a GSA audit. To cooperate, however, does not mean to volunteer information that has not been requested. It is one thing to say to an auditor "sure I'll have those documents for you right away." It is quite another thing to say "hey, why don't you go into Marty's office and check out his file cabinets." Auditors conduct many audits each year. They know what they are doing and, based on the amount of money they collect from vendors each year, they do their job quite well. They do not need an overzealous vendor responding to questions that have not been asked.

6. Gathering Data

Once the data requested by the auditor has been coordinated with the single point of contact, it must necessarily be gathered and provided to the auditor, again through the single point of contact. The vendor should be expeditious in providing the auditor with the requested material, but the vendor should not provide more than the auditor has requested. Providing requested invoices associated with the contract, for example, is different from providing the entire contract file, including the requested invoices. Again, the vendor should be neither overzealous nor sloppy about the material it provides.

As discussed in more detail below, a vendor also should conduct a parallel internal investigation. Issues arise unexpectedly and must be addressed in real time. A vendor that is reactive rather than proactive may lose valuable opportunities to direct, or at least guide, the course of the audit and to abort any nascent misunderstanding. Moreover, only through the vendor's internal assessment of its potential exposure can it ensure that it is dedicating appropriate resources to responding to the audit. One note of caution, however. A vendor could be forced to turn over to the OIG papers relating to an internal audit conducted in the regular course of the company's business. This internal investigation, therefore, should be conducted at the request—and under the direction—of the vendor's law department or outside counsel. In this context, internal investigators can go about their activities less hindered by a fear that their work product might fall into the hands of the Government.

7. Providing Documents/ Document Management

Generally, the OIG auditor will request documents in writing and will provide the request to the vendor's appointed single point of contact. Responsibility for the collection of the requested documents should be assigned to a person familiar with the contract—generally, the administrator. Again, the vendor should provide the documents in a timely manner, but it should only supply the documents requested. The vendor should keep a written record of what documents were requested and when they were provided. This record will allow the parallel internal audit to be conducted and may reveal if the audit is taking a particular course. Such information may alert the vendor to a possible issue and allow it to prepare for further OIG requests. Again, for control and information purposes, the auditor should be required to request documents from, and should receive documents from, only the single point of contact. Employees should be instructed to politely refer the auditor to this person should they receive a request for documents.

8. Government Access To Company Personnel

Technically, the audit rights of the Government do not extend to interrogation of vendor personnel, and companies are not required to allow the Government access to their employees in company facilities. However, the OIG can issue a subpoena if it wishes to request documents. Moreover, correctly or not, auditors may view denial of access to employees as a lack of cooperation and reflect that negatively in the audit report. Therefore, many vendors seek to control the Government's access to their personnel rather than to deny access altogether. Many vendors will require that either management or counsel be with an employee during a Government interview or will require that questions be passed through management prior to the employee being approached. This type of control allows the vendor to ensure that the questions being posed are within the scope of the audit and that the Government is directed to the employee who can best answer the inquiry. Generally, allowing unfettered access to vendor personnel is not recommended as the employees may not understand the request and may attempt to provide answers to questions they do not understand. These types of misunderstandings will complicate the audit process and may require great expenditures of time and resources to resolve.

9. Dealing With The Contracting Officer

In order to facilitate the resolution of contract issues, avoid misunderstandings, and ensure contract compliance, many vendors require that the contract administrator be the single point of contract for communications with the contracting officer. Other vendors are not as strict but may require the presence of the contract administrator during communications with the contracting officer. During an audit, communications with the contracting officer should occur via the vendor's contract department. Again, the intent is to facilitate the process and to avoid any miscommunication.

10. Exit Conference

According to the OIG, a vendor is not entitled to an exit conference as a matter of right. In practice, however, many auditors afford vendors at least an informal opportunity to discuss their preliminary findings. If an exit conference is afforded, the vendor should seize the opportunity since it provides a chance to comment upon, and perhaps even modify, the auditor's findings.

Furthermore, an exit conference provides a chance to gather information—information that could prove essential in the vendor's effort to prepare for whatever settlement discussions with GSA that might arise from the OIG audit.

11. Importance Of Reviewing The Draft Audit Report

If the vendor is afforded the opportunity to review the draft audit report, it should immediately accept. Review of the draft report is important as it reveals potential issues and their severity. Depending upon the findings of the report, the vendor should take one of several actions. If the report is generally positive, with only a few minor issues being raised, the vendor may want to work with the auditor to see if the minor issues can be cleared up before the report is submitted. If the report indicates the vendor has more serious issues, however, the vendor may want to clear up any misconceptions or inaccurate conclusions that the auditor may have drawn or respond with mitigating information before the audit report is submitted to GSA. In either event, the vendor's law department should be involved in all interactions with the auditors.

12. Rebutting The Draft Audit Findings

If there are negative audit findings, the vendor should review and prepare a rebuttal to each finding. The written rebuttal should be transmitted to the auditor and to the contracting officer. The preparation of valid reasons as to why the auditor's findings are either incorrect or mitigated is extremely important. There may very well be a flaw in the Government's analysis that can be corrected; documents may have been overlooked; inadequate sampling may have been used; the auditor may not have understood the business and how it operates and may have drawn incorrect conclusions; or there may be mitigating circumstances regarding some of the findings. A proactive response may avert potential negative audit findings.

13. Negotiating A Settlement

If the rebuttals are not pursued or accepted, then the vendor may find itself in the unhappy situation of negotiating a settlement with the Government should the OIG make a negative recommendation to the contracting officer.[990] Once this phase is reached, the goal of the vendor is to limit the exposure of the company. Again, the vendor must be proactive in presenting mitigating evidence.

B. *Avoiding Obstruction Of Justice*

As John T. Boese and Beth McClain note in the American Health Lawyers Association's Best Practices Handbook, "[t]he gathering, reviewing, and production of documents in response to a subpoena or other discovery demand must be handled very carefully to avoid obstruction of justice allegations."[991] This rule applies as much to counsel as to the vendor since the DOJ has brought obstruction of justice charges against attorneys. To avoid the risk of such charges, the Handbook offers the following guidance.

1. Responding To Document Demands

a. Clarify And Document The Scope Of The Demand

Document requests (including subpoenas) are infrequently models of clarity. Thus, to avoid the possibility that the vendor will interpret the demand one way while the auditor interprets it another, the vendor should take care (1) to clarify any ambiguous aspect of the subpoena to ensure that both parties understand and agree upon its scope and (2) to memorialize the resulting shared understanding in writing. Adhering to this practice not only helps avoid an obstruction of justice allegation, it also will go a long way toward avoiding good faith misunderstandings that could snowball into an increasingly unpleasant audit experience. Moreover, according to the Best Practices Handbook,

> CID [Civil Investigative Demands] and IG subpoenas are not self-enforcing, and counsel must therefore thoroughly document all efforts to negotiate a reasonable scope for the discovery demand, which can form the basis of an opposition if the government seeks court enforcement.[992]

In short, putting in the time and effort to clarify and document the scope of an OIG subpoena at the outset of an OIG audit can pay significant dividends.

b. Identify An Independent Custodian

In the context of a document production—whether in the context of civil discovery or an OIG subpoena—a "custodian" is an individual given primary responsibility for the collection, recordation, and production of requested documents. The importance of identifying such an individual and affording him or her a comprehensive briefing cannot be overstated.

In selecting an appropriate candidate for the position of independent custodian, the vendor should ensure that he or she

- Is not a lawyer
- Is honest and ethical
- Generally understands the company's organization and record keeping procedures
- Is not involved in the underlying allegations
- Possesses the authority to gather the necessary documents from the highest levels within the company

Once selected and briefed, the custodian should be given a written appointment so that there will be no question as to his or her responsibilities. Additionally, as discussed below, the custodian should be given thorough written instructions.

c. Ensure Responding Parties Are Comfortable About The Scope Of The Vendor's Response

While, ultimately, it is the custodian's decision whether a given document is within or outside the scope of the subpoena, it is important to coordinate difficult decisions in this regard with counsel. Indeed, the Best Practices Handbook calls such cooperation "essential."[993] In virtually every subpoena, questions of this sort will arise, and the failure to achieve consensus among those responding thereto can lead to significant problems.

d. Provide Written Instructions To The Custodian And To The Individuals Conducting The Search

The custodian and every individual involved in searching for responsive documents must be given written instructions that are clear, straightforward, and comprehensive. Such instructions also should incorporate any agreements reached with the Government. Oral instructions are *insufficient*. Experienced counsel typically will have form instructions that can be modified to most situations.

e. Provide Written Instructions To All Relevant Staff That No Relevant Documents Are To Be Destroyed

While the issuance of a subpoena does not necessarily suspend the functioning of a vendor's document destruction policy, it does require vendors to exercise significantly amplified vigilance with respect to what documents are destroyed and what documents are retained. Destroying a relevant document (including electronic documents such as databases and e-mails) in the course of a federal audit can lead to significant penalties—including criminal penalties if the destruction is found to have been intentional. To avoid such negative consequences, vendors must (1) notify all employees that potentially relevant documents must not be destroyed even if they otherwise would be destroyed pursuant to the vendor's normal policies and procedures and (2) carefully monitor the destruction of all documents.

Among other things, written instructions to the custodian of documents should include (1) a clear description of the relevant documents, (2) a statement regarding the relevant time period of such documents, (3) a statement making clear that no relevant documents may be destroyed, (4) a time period for the initial collection effort, and (5) the telephone number of the vendor's attorney in case questions arise. Written instructions to document searchers should include, among other things, (1) a statement regarding the importance of the search, (2) a statement making clear that no relevant documents may be destroyed, (3) instructions regarding what the searcher should do with the documents that he or she locates, and (4) instructions regarding how the searcher should document his or her search if the search turns up no relevant documents.

Finally, all employees should be instructed that no documents should be turned over to the Government until they have been reviewed for attorney-client privileged material by a qualified individual and processed through the appointed single point of contact.

f. Establish Objective Evidence Of Documents Produced

In the legal profession, the term "Bates number" denotes a sequential number placed upon each page of a document being produced to an opposing party during litigation or an investigation. The purpose of the Bates number is twofold: First, it helps the producing party (the vendor) keep accurate records of the material turned over to the Government; and, second, it facilitates the parties' discussion of those documents.

Before any document is turned over to the Government, the document should be copied, Bates stamped, and recorded so that there never is a dispute regarding what material was produced to the Government. Additionally, as an extra precaution, vendors should reference the Bates number range of the documents being produced in the transmittal letter of every production.

2. Communicating With Employees

As with producing documents, communicating with employees during the course of a federal audit or investigation presents risks that vendors must take steps to avoid. Such risks typically occur early in an OIG audit when the OIG auditors express an interest in interviewing one or more of the vendor's employees. In such a situation, there are certain matters that can be communicated to employees and certain matters that *cannot* be communicated to employees. The Best Practices Handbook segregate these matters into three categories: things counsel should say, things counsel can say, and things counsel cannot say.[994]

- Defense counsel *should* advise the potential witness that:

    o The witness must tell the truth
    o Any statement may be used against the witness for criminal prosecution or other purposes

- Defense counsel *may* advise the potential witness of the following:

    o Absent a grand jury subpoena, an OIG testimonial subpoena, or a False Claims Act CID, the witness has the right to decide:

        ■ Whether he or she wants to be interviewed

- The time and place of the interview
- Who will be present at the interview
- Whether the interview is recorded

  ○ The witness has the right to discontinue the interview if he or she believes the agent is abusive or is treating him or her improperly.
  ○ The witness can request a copy of the agent's notes or tape recording.
  ○ Under some circumstances, the employee may retain separate counsel at company expense and the company may recommend a particular lawyer. Care should be taken in explaining the right to reimbursement for legal fees under the vendor's bylaws, SEC rules, and state corporation laws so that it is clear that payment of legal fees is not a financial incentive for testifying in a particular way. It should be made clear to the employee that the lawyers' fees are available regardless of the substance of the testimony.
  ○ That the vendor may wish to have company counsel present during the interview or to debrief the witness on the substance of the interview.

- Defense counsel *should not*:

  ○ Instruct a witness not to cooperate or not to talk to the agent
  ○ Instruct an employee or witness whom the lawyer does not personally represent to exercise his Fifth Amendment right to refuse to answer questions
  ○ Suggest that the witness or employee give misleading or false answers

Additionally, counsel typically—and rightly—may advise witnesses (1) to take their time, (2) to remember that they are making a record, (3) to be unfailingly and consistently polite, (4) not to answer questions that they do not understand, (5) to admit that they do not remember something when they do not remember it, (6) not to guess or speculate unless instructed to do so by the interviewer, (7) to be clear about the factual basis of the testimony, (8) not to volunteer information not specifically requested by the interviewer, (9) to take the proceeding seriously, and (10) not to be afraid to raise questions with counsel whenever necessary during the interview.

Finally, the following rules typically are taken as gospel by anyone briefing or debriefing an employee who will meet or has met with a federal investigator:

(1) Conduct the interview with a second, uninterested party present.

(2) Begin the interview with a written statement setting forth (a) the reason for the interview, (b) the importance of telling the truth, (c) whom the interviewer (typically a lawyer) represents, and (d) the potential uses of the interviewer's notes. According to the Best Practices Handbook, "[t]his written statement should be read verbatim so that there is no question regarding the content of counsel's statement to the employee."[995]

(3) Avoid suggesting "correct" testimony.

Adhering to the foregoing rules will go a long way toward avoiding any allegation of an obstruction of justice. As with all other aspects of federal audits and investigations, vendors are well advised to consult their attorneys early and often. Indeed, most vendors retain counsel (or designate in-house counsel) throughout the entire audit/investigation period.

C. *Voluntary Disclosures*

In the context of reporting contract violations to the Government, there are three types of vendors: those that disclose the violation before the Government discovers it; those that disclose the violation as soon as the Government discovers it; and those that deny the violation, notwithstanding the fact that the Government discovered it. This discussion focuses on vendors that fall into the first category—disclosure *before* discovery.

The act of disclosing a violation to the Government before it is discovered by the Government is known as a "voluntary disclosure." Some agencies—the DOD comes most readily to mind—maintain a formal voluntary disclosure program, replete with policies, procedures, and reduced penalties.[996] Other agencies, while they encourage voluntary disclosures, maintain no formal program and deal with such disclosure on a case-by-case basis. GSA falls into this later category.

Because GSA lacks a formal DOD-type voluntary disclosure program—and, thus, the relative consistency and predictability that comes with it—a vendor making a voluntary disclosure to GSA does so at its own risk. As counsel to the GSA OIG has written, due to GSA's lack of a formal voluntary disclosure program:

> It cannot make formal assurances regarding criminal prosecution or debarment and suspension and has treated the voluntary disclosures made to date on a case-by-case basis.[997]

While these words should give a vendor pause, they should not be read to suggest that a voluntary disclosure is necessarily a bad idea. Indeed, a voluntary disclosure offers vendors several significant benefits:

- Under the civil False Claims Act, a voluntary disclosure can reduce a vendor's liability from three times the amount of actual damages to two times the amount of actual damages.[998]
- Under the FAR's suspension/debarment rules, a suspension/debarring official will consider a vendor's voluntary disclosure as an indicator of present responsibility.[999]

- Under the criminal sentencing guidelines, a voluntary disclosure is a factor that can lead to a reduced sentence.[1000]

Moreover, the risk of *not* making a voluntary disclosure can be quite high. Once a vendor is on notice that it has violated its contract or an applicable regulation or statute, all sorts of new risks can arise if the vendor fails to disclose the violation to the Government. For example, the Government could argue that subsequent sales constitute a "knowing" violation of the False Claims Act.

Notwithstanding the several potential benefits of a voluntary disclosure, however, such an undertaking can be risky. For example, in all likelihood, a voluntary disclosure will prompt a full-scale audit. Additionally, if the OIG identifies knowing misconduct on the part of the vendor (*i.e.*, fraud), then the OIG will refer the matter to its investigative branch or the DOJ. In light of these risks, some vendors choose to await the occurrence of a routine GSA audit before making any disclosure at all. While this may be a legitimate business decision, it is a risky one as the vendor's financial exposure (as well as its susceptibility to civil and/or criminal liability) may expand over time. The Coalition for Government Procurement advises the readers of its self-audit manual that "[c]ontractors should carefully weigh the risks before choosing this option."[1001] Indeed, most vendors should go a step further and involve an attorney in any such risk assessment. Counsel will be able to help assess evidence of knowing misconduct, identify opportunities to mitigate potential damages, and prevent the release of privileged or otherwise protected data.

If a vendor decides to make a voluntary disclosure, it should ensure that the disclosure is current, accurate, and complete, yet no broader than necessary. In its useful guide to performing a MAS self-audit, the Coalition for Government Procurement suggests that a voluntary disclosure presentation set forth the following information:

- A clear description of the violation being disclosed
- The vendor's strongest argument demonstrating that the violation does not constitute fraud
- An offer to refund or settle any amount owed to the Government
- A plan detailing corrective action taken to prevent future compliance problems[1002]

In addition to these items, a vendor probably also should offer GSA the opportunity to meet with its contract personnel to learn more about the problem and the vendor's proposed solution.

Along with the foregoing items, in all likelihood the GSA OIG will have certain additional expectations of a vendor making a voluntary disclosure, including the following:

(1) The vendor will be expected to cooperate fully with any resulting audit or investigation;
(2) The vendor will afford the OIG access to all relevant documents and employees;
(3) If an internal evaluation is performed, the vendor will be expected to produce a copy of the resulting internal report to the OIG; and
(4) If the vendor has calculated an amount that it believes is owed to the Government, the vendor must immediately pay that amount to the Government with an agreement that that payment shall not constitute a waiver of any future Government rights or claims.[1003]

These expectations further illustrate the importance of involving counsel in any voluntary disclosure decision-making process.

* * *

Advice From The Trenches—
The Auditor's Perspective

(by John Walsh—GSA OIG)

MAS audits are complicated processes and rarely are two audits alike. However, here are some tips from the perspective of the auditor on how best to approach the audit process.

Do provide timely and complete information. This will always result in reduced audit steps and testing and, accordingly, reduce the performance time of the audit. All companies want the auditors gone as quickly as possible and this is the best method to achieve that goal.

Do obtain a complete understanding of requests made by the auditor. It is always better to get this information before doing any work because this will save time in having to redo the work provided. Many times the auditor may not have an extensive knowledge of a contractor's accounting and/or computer systems and, as a result, may request information in a cumbersome manner. In addition, in these situations, an auditor may request more information than what may be needed. Simply giving the auditor what he asks for usually results in additional work because the auditor may find out what he asked for is not sufficient to support an audit conclusion. This will only lead to a request for additional information. There are many reasons why a contractor may just give the auditor the specific information he asks for and these reasons range from not wanting to upset the auditor to being frustrated with the audit process. It is always better to find out as much information as you can about the request before providing the information. Keep in mind that some auditors do not want to tell contractors specifically what they will be using the information for out of fear that the contractor will try to manipulate the data. While this can (but very rarely does) happen, an auditor must perform tests to verify the integrity of the data received, and contractor assistance in the area of data verification should alleviate audit concerns related to the data provided by the contractor.

Do allow complete access to any personnel with whom the auditor needs to speak. The contractor has the right to participate in the interviews and should always remember that the audit is not an investigation. Although many people are not enthused about talking to an auditor, if an auditor believes that he is not being allowed to talk to key people in the area upon which the audit is focusing, he will request additional information and audit performance time.

Do try to give the auditor wide access to computer data. Many companies are reluctant to do this on principle alone. This results in increased manpower and manual work on both the part of the company and the auditor. Try to put aside the natural fear of giving an auditor access to the computer system, and the result will be a more efficient and economic audit that is completed in a shorter period of time.

Do ask questions. The more familiar you are with the process, the more prepared you will be to address any issues that arise. Keep in mind that the auditor is precluded from discussing specific audit results with the contractor. However, the auditor should discuss any major issues with the contractor to ensure that the auditor has a full understanding of the factors that might impact the audit findings. From this information, the contractor should be able to plug in the amounts and arrive at the specific audit findings. In addition, the auditor should address any concerns of the contractor, including the privacy issues related to proprietary data.

Do understand the auditor's role. The auditor is working for the contracting officer and has no authority to direct the administration of the contract or to negotiate a settlement. But also remember reality. The contracting officers sometimes rely heavily upon the auditor and the practical effect of this is that, if the auditor is not convinced, the contracting officer may not be. Also, the contracting officer does have a certain trepidation toward the auditor and, in most cases, does not want to upset the OIG.

Do try to settle the audit as quickly as possible. The only situation in which you should not do this is if you believe the audit is completely incorrect. No settlement should be approached in that situation. However, if there is validity to the audit findings, settling early is almost always better than settling later. One theory holds that the longer an issue is dragged out, the better the chance of everything going away. This certainly has happened; however, this is the exception rather than the rule. Issues that drag on for years often encounter a change in personnel that results in multiple reviews of the same information and, possibly, even new audits being performed. In addition, the longer an audit is open, the greater the chance of additional issues being uncovered. Generally speaking, the longer an audit drags on, the more good money is spent achieving a resolution that could have been achieved early in the process.

Some things to watch out for or avoid in the area of MAS audits are:

Don't be antagonistic or attempt to impede the progress of the audit. While this may seem like a good psychological approach to minimizing the audit findings and the time spent by the auditor on the project, the practical effect is almost always the opposite. Auditing guidelines are clear that, in these types of situations, additional audit steps and testing are required. In addition, many OIGs do have subpoena authority and providing information through a subpoena is always more costly and time consuming than providing the information freely during an audit.

Don't intentionally provide incorrect or misleading information to the auditor. If the auditor believes this has happened, the auditor will be required to bring in an investigator and this could lead to involvement of the DOJ. This is the worst possible scenario. Having DOJ involved will not only increase the cost and time of the audit in an exponential fashion, but it will also basically remove the contracting officer's ability to settle the matter. In addition, the involvement of DOJ will introduce the element of at least civil penalties and fines that will be required for DOJ to settle the case.

Don't allow an auditor to be unreasonable. While it may seem that all audits are unreasonable, try to separate negative audit perceptions from actual misconduct on the part of the auditor. If you believe that your company is being mistreated, contact both the contracting officer and the supervisor of the auditor.

Don't try to save money by devoting inadequate resources to assist in completion of the audit. Normally, money spent up front in a audit is money well invested.

Don't ignore an audit or the purpose of an audit. Contractors will sometimes blindly provide information and then, when they receive a letter from a contracting officer requesting a refund, they will be totally unprepared. Close monitoring of an audit is always in the contractor's best interest. An auditor is not sent out to find error, and every audit has the possibility of coming out in the contractor's favor. However, always be aware that the auditor may be computing a refund due to the Government.

Notes:

[975] Pub. L. No. 95-452, 92 Stat. 1101, and amendments, including Inspector General Act Amendments of 1988, Pub. L. No. 100-504, 102 Stat. 2515 (codified as amended in scattered sections of 5 U.S.C. and 5 U.S.C. app. 3).

[976] For an overview of the role of the GSA OIG in the MAS Program from the Government's perspective, see Kathleen S. Tighe, *The Role of the GSA Inspector General in Federal Supply Schedule Negotiation and Administration*, COMMERCIAL PRODUCT AND SERVICE CONTRACTING: GSA SCHEDULES AND BEYOND (A.B.A., June 29, 1999).

[977] Like GSA, the Department of Veterans Affairs also has an active OIG. While this chapter focuses on the GSA OIG, the information contained herein applies equally to the VA OIG.

[978] GSA OIG Semiannual Rep. to Cong. (Oct. 1, 1999-Mar. 31, 2000), at Foreword.

[979] 5 U.S.C. app. 3, § 4(a)(1).

[980] *Id.* § 6(a)(2).

[981] *Id.* § 4(d).

[982] OIG subpoenas are authorized in the Inspector General Act of 1978, 5 U.S.C. app. 3 § 6(a)(4). The United States Court of Appeals for the Third Circuit, in *United States v. Westinghouse Elec. Co.,* 788 F.2d 164 (3d Cir. 1986), confirmed the DOD OIG's authority to subpoena a vendor's own internal audit reports. Vendors that perform internal audits should become familiar with this case.

[983] *See, e.g., United States v. Iannone,* 610 F.2d 943 (D.C. Cir. 1979).

[984] 5 U.S.C. app. 3, § 6(a)(5).

[985] *See* 18 U.S.C. § 1516(a), which provides that "[w]hoever, with intent to deceive or defraud the United States, endeavors to influence, obstruct, or impede a Federal auditor in the performance of official duties" shall be fined, imprisoned, or both. *See also* John Chierichella & James J. Graham, *Three New Criminal Statutes from the 100th Congress,* Contract Management, at 14 (Feb. 1989).

[986] Tighe, *supra* note 832, at 12.

[987] Tighe, *supra* note 832, at 8, citing to 28 C.F.R. Part O, Subpart Y, Appendix, Directive 14-95 (Apr. 6, 1995).

[988] Additionally, out of an abundance of caution, companies would be wise to advise employees against idle hallway and restroom chatter.

[989] 18 U.S.C. § 1516.

[990] The OIG may only "advise" regarding the disposition of a matter. 5 U.S.C. app. § 4(a)(5).

[991] Best Practices Handbook in Advising Clients on Fraud & Abuse Issues (Am. Health Lawyers Assn. June 1999), at 72.

[992] *Id.*

[993] *Id.* at 73-75.

[994] *Id.* at 73-74.

[995] *Id.* at 74.

[996] *See, e.g.,* Harvey G. Sherzer, Scott Arnold & David Francis, A Complete Guide to the Department of Defense Voluntary Disclosure Program (George Washington Univ. Law School 1996);

DEPARTMENT OF DEFENSE VOLUNTARY DISCLOSURE PROGRAM: A DESCRIPTION OF THE PROCESS (A.B.A. 1994).

[997] Tighe, *supra* note 832, at 9.

[998] 31 U.S.C. § 3729(a).

[999] FAR 9.406-1(a).

[1000] *See* U.S. SENTENCING GUIDELINES MANUAL § 3E1.1 (1998).

[1001] Coalition's MAS Self-Audit Manual at 65.

[1002] Coalition's MAS Self-Audit Manual at 64.

[1003] Tighe, *supra* note 832, at 9.

XXIII.

MULTIPLE AWARD SCHEDULE VENDORS AND THE CIVIL FALSE CLAIMS ACT

By John T. Boese
Fried, Frank, Harris, Shriver & Jacobson LLP

"Oh what a tangled web we weave,
When first we practice to deceive!"

-Sir Walter Scott

Since far-reaching amendments broadened its scope in 1986, the False Claims Act ("FCA")[1004] has become the Government's weapon of choice in combating fraud, waste, and abuse. The popularity of the FCA is due to several factors. First, the misconduct actionable under the FCA is broad. Second, the intent requirement of the FCA (deliberate ignorance or reckless disregard) is relatively relaxed. Third, the flexibility of the FCA is well known to plaintiffs' lawyers. And fourth, the potential recoveries under the FCA are huge.

"Recoveries under the FCA are climbing every year . . . to the point where the FCA has joined the ranks of securities class actions and [Racketeer Influenced and Corrupt Practices Act] suits as a primary source of income to the plaintiffs' bar."[1005]

Recoveries under the civil FCA's unique *qui tam* provisions since 1986 are more than $8 billion, and the Justice Department reports that total recoveries since 1986 exceed $12 billion, making the FCA an indisputably powerful weapon in the Government's fight against fraud. Unfortunately, while some of this income is derived from objectively valid cases, much of it is derived from companies settling cases brought by disgruntled employees out of fear of trusting such cases to the whims of juries.

The civil FCA has been applied to virtually every sector of the American economy. Although the primary targets of FCA suits have, in the past, been defense contractors and health care providers, FCA actions are filed with increasing frequency against companies that sell standard commercial products to the Federal Government (many of whom do not consider themselves to be "Government contractors") and to other enterprises that may appear to have little or no connection to federal programs. Contractors, federal grantees, pharmaceutical suppliers, financing institutions, bulk mailers, and importers have all been targets of recent FCA lawsuits.

General statements regarding the risk of significant liability, however, do not do justice to the FCA's scope. The following illustrative settlements should serve to make the point:

- In 1991, Carlisle Memory Products paid more than $2 million to settle FCA charges that it overbilled its MAS customers.
- In 1991, Data General paid more than $1 million to settle FCA charges that it violated the MAS Price Reductions Clause.
- In 1992, Motorola paid the Government $15.1 million to settle FCA claims that it sold MAS customers refurbished products instead of new products.
- In 1994, Novell paid $1.7 million to settle similar charges.
- In 1994, Tandem paid $300,000 to settle an FCA allegation that it sold its MAS customers used parts instead of new parts.

- In 1996, Superior Surgical Manufacturing Company, Inc. paid $6.2 million to settle FCA allegations that it failed to provide current, accurate, and complete discount and pricing information to GSA and the VA.
- In 1997, Canon USA paid $6 million to settle FCA claims that it concealed its lowest prices and discount practices from GSA.
- In 1997, GTSI paid $400,000 to settle FCA allegations that it failed to pass along manufacturer rebates to its MAS customers.
- In 1997, Krueger Int. paid $5.1 million following a voluntary disclosure to settled FCA allegations that it violated the Price Reductions Clause.
- In 1997, Trendway paid $1.25 million to settle FCA allegations that it failed to offer GSA the same discount it offered its commercial customers.
- In 1998, InvaCare Corporation paid $2.6 million to settle FCA allegations that it violated the Buy America Act and failed to disclose accurate pricing data to the VA.
- In 1999, an Ingersoll-Rand subsidiary paid $3 million to settle FCA allegations that it failed to provide accurate pricing information to GSA.
- In 1999, Case paid $1.9 million following a GSA OIG audit to settle FCA allegations that it violated the Price Reductions Clause.
- In 2000, Toshiba paid $23 million to settle a class action lawsuit and FCA allegations that it sold defective laptop computers to the Government.
- In 2001, Johnson & Johnson Medical, Inc. paid $3.9 million to resolve claims that it failed to provide accurate pricing information to the VA.
- In 2001, Lifescan, Inc. paid $15 million under a voluntary disclosure to resolve potential FCA liability for failing to notify the Department of Veterans Affairs ("VA") of reductions in commercial contract prices to amounts below those paid by the Government.

- In 2001, Moore Medical Corp. agreed to pay $5.2 million to resolve FCA claims that it failed to abide by the pricing requirements of its VA Schedule contract.
- In 2001, Presidio Corp. paid $273,000 to settled allegations that it violated the Price Reductions Clause.
- In 2003, American Management Systems paid $15 million to resolve allegations that it misrepresented anticipated costs, its ability to deliver software products, and the personnel who would be assigned to a software project.
- In 2004, Polaroid paid $3.2 million to resolve allegations that it provided false pricing information to GSA and failed to report certain discounts given to non-federal customers.
- In 2004, Snap-on Industrial paid $10 million to resolve allegations that it violated its Price Reductions Clause.
- In 2005, Office Max, Office Depot, and Staples paid $9.8 million, $4.75 million and $7.4 million respectively to resolve allegations that they sold products on schedule in violation of the Trade Agreements Act.

The list reads like a Who's Who of MAS contracting.

Add to the potential for massive recoveries the fact that, under the *qui tam* provisions of the FCA, a private citizen (known as a "relator" or, more informally, as a whistleblower) can bring suit against a defendant on behalf of the United States and stand to collect up to 30 percent of the total recovery, and one begins to understand why it is imperative that commercial vendors understand how the FCA works.

While an in-depth analysis of the civil FCA is beyond the scope of the discussion in this chapter, some fundamentals are necessary.[1006]

A. *Liability*

Liability under the FCA is statutory and is based upon proof of a violation of one or more of the seven subsections of the FCA found at 31 U.S.C. § 3729(a)(1) through (a)(7). The primary violations are:

- Submitting, or causing another to submit, a false claim (31 U.S.C. § 3729(a)(1))
- Submitting, or causing another to submit, a false statement in support of a false claim (31 U.S.C. § 3729(a)(2))
- Conspiring to submit a false claim (31 U.S.C. § 3729(a)(3))
- Making or using a false record or statement to avoid payment of, or to decrease, an obligation to the United States (a "reverse false claim") (31 U.S.C. § 3729(a)(7))

The other three liability provisions found in §§ 3729(a)(4), (5), and (6) are not frequently invoked in FCA litigation.

1. False Claim

Subsections 3729(a)(1) through (a)(3) of the FCA require the submission of a "false claim." The elements of a false claim are as follows:

- A claim
- That is false
- Submitted to the U.S. Government
- With sufficient knowledge/intent

Courts are split over the necessity of proving a fifth element, damage to the Federal Treasury.[1007] Each element of a "false claim" must exist for a violation of Sections 3729(a)(1), (a)(2), or (a)(3) to occur.

a. What Constitutes A "Claim?"

In the simplistic sense, a claim is a request for payment (*e.g.*, an invoice). Courts considering the nature of a claim have held that a mere bid is not a "claim" under the FCA because it is simply an offer of performance, and not a request or demand for payment of money.[1008] Similarly, an application is not a claim within the meaning of the FCA,[1009] even when it is accompanied by a request for money.[1010] However, under case law and the 1986 amendments, a "claim" need not be submitted directly to the Federal Government in order to violate the FCA.

b. When Is A Claim "False?"

The two most actively litigated and disputed elements of any FCA case involve whether or not the claim is "false" and, if "false," whether the claim was submitted with sufficient "knowledge" of its falsity. These two issues are occasionally confused or treated as overlapping by some courts, but a distinction between them is critical.

If the "falsity" of a claim is not apparent on its face, it is often necessary to examine the applicable laws, regulations, and/or contractual terms. Some courts have held that facially valid claims are "false" if the defendant violated applicable regulations, particularly if the defendant falsely certified compliance with those regulations. Some of the most hotly litigated cases arising under the FCA today involve allegedly false "implied" certifications of compliance with applicable regulations or contract terms. The implied certification cases are discussed briefly in Section E, below.

c. When Is A "False Claim" Submitted "Knowingly?"

Before the FCA was amended in 1986, it was necessary to prove that the defendant acted with specific intent to defraud. That knowledge standard was reduced in 1986, when Congress added explicit language to Section 3729(b) defining the terms "knowing" and "knowingly." A person is deemed to have acted knowingly under the FCA if he or she:

(1) Has actual knowledge of the information,

(2) Acts in deliberate ignorance of the truth or falsity of the information, or

(3) Acts in reckless disregard of the truth or falsity of the information.

No proof of specific intent to defraud is required. However, a merely negligent or mistaken interpretation of federal regulations or a federal contract does not trigger liability under the FCA.[1011] Rather, reckless disregard is the lowest element that is required for liability. "Reckless disregard" and "deliberate ignorance" are not defined in the FCA, but the D.C. Circuit has held that "reckless disregard" is comparable to "an extreme form of ordinary negligence."[1012] A conspiracy claim under 31 U.S.C. § 3729(a)(3) must, however, allege a specific intent to defraud, as discussed below.

2. False Statement

The second most common basis of liability under the FCA is a false statement made in support of a false claim. Under 31 U.S.C. § 3729(a)(2), the Government or the *qui tam* relator must prove that a false statement was made in support of a false claim. The plaintiff, thus, must prove three factors in addition to those that must be proven under Section 3729(a)(1):

a. That the statement was actually made,
b. That the statement was false, and
c. That the statement was material to the Government's funding decisions or decision to pay that claim.

The materiality requirement is discussed in greater detail below.

3. Conspiracy

The third most common basis for liability, the conspiracy provision under 31 U.S.C. § 3729(a)(3), is different from the two provisions discussed above. Unlike the other liability provisions of the FCA, Section 3729(a)(3) omits the term "knowingly" and uses the term "defraud," which indicates that specific intent to defraud must be demonstrated.[1013] Thus, the Government or *qui tam* relator must prove that an agreement to submit a false claim actually existed and that the defendant specifically knew that the claim was false (reckless disregard or deliberate ignorance is not sufficient).

4. Reverse False Claims

The newest basis for liability under the FCA, the so-called "reverse false claims" provision, was adopted in 1986. This section was added to resolve a conflict in the case law as to whether false statements to the Government were actionable under the pre-1986 FCA if there was no affirmative claim for payment to the Government.[1014] To recover under Section 3729(a)(7), the Government or *qui tam* relator must prove at a minimum:

a. That an obligation existed to pay money to the United States;
b. That a record or statement was made;
c. That the record or statement was false;
d. That the defendant "knew" (under Section 3729(c)) that the record or statement was false;
e. That the record or statement was intended to, and did, avoid, conceal, or decrease the obligation; and
f. That this caused some direct financial impact on the Federal Treasury.

Originally, the typical reverse false claims case involved natural resource royalty contracts. Contractors that falsely understated the quantity or quality of resources removed from federal lands to avoid paying the appropriate royalty to the Government were the original targets of the reverse FCA provisions. This type of reverse false claims case continues to yield significant recoveries under the FCA today. However, the reverse false claims provision of the FCA has been applied by *qui tam* relators in aggressive and expansive ways since 1986, a phenomenon that is discussed in greater detail below.

B. *Damages And Penalties*

If it is proven by the preponderance of the evidence[1015] that the defendant violated one or more of the seven subsections of Section 3729(a), the FCA provides that the court shall assess three "times the amount of damages which the Government sustains because of the act of that person . . . ."[1016] In addition to those damages, the court must also assess a civil penalty "of not less than $5,000 and not more than $10,000 for each false claim."[1017] This penalty amount was adjusted for inflation under the Federal Civil Monetary Penalties Inflation Adjustment Act of 1990[1018] and the Debt Collection Improvement Act of 1996[1019] to between $5,500 and $11,000 for conduct occurring after September 29, 1999.[1020]

In *Vermont Agency of Natural Resources v. United States ex rel. Stevens*,[1021] the Supreme Court observed that the FCA's treble damages provisions are "essentially punitive in nature." In a more recent Supreme Court decision, *Cook County v. United States ex rel. Chandler*,[1022] the Court held that FCA damages have both punitive *and* compensatory elements. The Court's characterization of FCA damages as punitive has significant implications for many FCA defendants. For example, in *United States v. Mackby*,[1023] the Ninth Circuit Court of Appeals held that, because FCA damages and penalties have a punitive purpose, courts must consider whether a judgment imposed under the FCA violates the Excessive Fines Clause of the Eighth Amendment. Additionally, the characterization of FCA damages and penalties as "punitive" raises important due process considerations and issues regarding the propriety of imposing punitive damages on corporate principals for the unauthorized acts of their agents.[1024]

1. Calculating Damages

Damages are generally calculated under the FCA as the difference between what the Government actually paid and what the Government either received or should have paid if the claim or statement had not been false. In some situations, this is a simple calculation, but in most FCA cases, determining damages can be quite difficult. In cases based upon substandard products, for example, any loss to the Government is difficult to determine.[1025]

a. False Claims Act Damages In The MAS Context

Damages calculations can become even more complex in MAS cases. In cases based on allegedly false certifications of regulatory or statutory compliance (*see* Section E, below), the Government and relators often allege that defendants' "false" certifications allowed them to sell products to the Government that they otherwise would not have been entitled to sell. Under this theory, it is argued that damages equal the total amount paid for the noncompliant products.

In MAS FCA cases based on purportedly defective pricing disclosures, it is alleged that the defendant failed to disclose the lowest prices, special terms, or discounts that are offered to commercial customers. In such cases, the Government alleges that damages should be based on the difference between the amount the Government actually paid for an item and the lowest price paid by a commercial customer.

However, for the Government to obtain this measure of damages under the FCA, the Government must prove that the parties actually would have agreed to this price if the discount disclosure had been truthful. Alleged defective pricing cases litigated under the FCA differ from those filed under the Truth in Negotiations Act ("TINA"). Under TINA cases, a rebuttable presumption exists that the Government's damages are directly related to the dollar amount by which the pricing information submitted to the Government was inaccurate.[1026]

Thus, in TINA cases, a presumption exists that an undisclosed $100 discount caused the Government to incur $100 in damages. No such presumption exists under the FCA, however, and the *Government* must prove in MAS cases based on alleged failure to disclose discounts that, if the Government had insisted on receiving that price, the supplier would have agreed to enter into a contract with the Government on those terms.[1027]

It may well be that a supplier is willing to offer deep discounts to commercial purchasers on a limited basis but would be unwilling to sell large quantities at the same discounted price to the Government. This may occur, for example, where only a small number of deeply-discounted products will be sold to the commercial purchasers and a profitable aftermarket will help offset the unprofitable sale of the discounted products. It does not necessarily follow, however, that the same supplier would be willing to sell large quantities of the same product at the same deep discount to the Government, especially where the aftermarket may not be profitable enough to offset the discounts.

b. Availability Of Consequential Damages Under The FCA

When Congress amended the FCA in 1986, initial drafts of the amendments provided for the recovery of double damages and consequential damages.[1028] However, the final language of the amendments omitted consequential damages, and damages were increased from double to treble. Legislative history[1029] and Supreme Court precedent[1030] demonstrate that Congress intentionally omitted consequential damages and deemed the increased damages multiplier to be a rough method of obtaining adequate compensation for the Government.

The Southern District of Ohio, in *United States ex rel. Roby v. Boeing Company*,[1031] considered the availability of consequential damages under the FCA and properly concluded that consequentials are not recoverable under the FCA. However, the court held that "direct" and "incidental" damages are recoverable and that damages must be awarded that will make the Government whole,[1032] and this ruling was affirmed by a deeply divided panel of the Sixth Circuit Court of Appeals.[1033]

The panel majority held in *Roby* that the Government was entitled to damages that equaled the difference between the market value of the product that the Government received (which the majority held was zero, because the product, a helicopter, crashed and was destroyed), and the market value of the product for which the Government had contracted (a properly re-furbished helicopter). The majority noted that although it was not holding that the defendant was entitled to replacement costs, replacement costs might be the measure of damages if it was not possible to determine the actual market value of the bargained-for refurbished helicopter.[1034] This decision ignores the clear Congressional understanding that these were the types of damages that were not recoverable and that the Government is presumed to be made whole through the treble damages multiplier. The decision is highly questionable and should not be followed.

2. Calculating Penalties

Generally, each false invoice or voucher submitted to the Government is considered a separate violation of the FCA and gives rise to liability for one penalty. Some courts have concluded that they lack discretion to reduce the FCA's penalty below the minimum allowed under the statute and that a civil penalty is to be assessed for each false claim.[1035] However, other courts have reduced or eliminated FCA penalties, noting that the Excessive Fines Clause requires "proportionality" between the damages suffered and the penalties imposed under the FCA.[1036] Until recently, this latter group was in the minority, but the growing recognition that FCA penalties are punitive is likely to lead to more universal application of the Excessive Fines Clause in FCA cases.

C. *Qui Tam Enforcement*

Although the DOJ is the primary enforcer of the civil FCA, the FCA contains unique *"qui tam"*[1037] provisions that permit private citizen "whistleblowers" to litigate alleged FCA violations on behalf of the Federal Government.[1038] Although there are important procedural differences between an FCA suit brought by the Federal Government and a *qui tam* false claims action, the underlying issues of liability and damages that are summarized above remain the same in both types of suits.

Some of the important features of *qui tam* litigation under the FCA include the following:

- *Qui tam* suits must be filed under seal to allow the Federal Government an opportunity to investigate the allegations and determine whether it wants to intervene in the suit. The relator must also file a "written disclosure of substantially all material evidence and information the person possesses."[1039] Although the FCA provides for a sixty-day seal period, extensions are typically granted. A defendant may be investigated for several years with the *qui tam* case under seal and not be aware that the suit is pending. Because many relators are employees of the defendant, they often have access to confidential records and information that may be used against the defendant in the *qui tam* suit.

- If the Government declines intervention in the *qui tam* suit, the relator may proceed to litigate the case on its own;[1040] if the Government intervenes, the action is conducted by the Government.[1041]

- When the action is conducted by the Government, *qui tam* relators are usually entitled to between 15 and 25 percent of any "recovery" obtained as a result of the suit.[1042] If the Government declines intervention and the relator litigates the action on his own, the statute provides for a relator's share of not less than 25 and not more than 30 percent.[1043]

- If the Government declines intervention but pursues an "alternate remedy" (*i.e.*, fines available under an administrative regime), the relator may be entitled to a share of that recovery.[1044]
- A relator's recovery may be reduced under the FCA if the relator planned and initiated the fraud;[1045] however, a relator convicted of criminal conduct related to the FCA allegations must be dismissed from the litigation and is not entitled to any share of the recovery.[1046]
  Successful relators may also recover attorneys' fees and costs.[1047]
- Prevailing defendants may recover attorneys' fees and costs from a *qui tam* relator if the relator's claim "was clearly frivolous, clearly vexatious, or brought primarily for purposes of harassment."[1048] Fees and costs may be recovered from the Government only under limited circumstances under 28 U.S.C. § 2412(d).

D. *Whistleblower Retaliation*

Section 3730(h) of the FCA provides a remedy for employees who are retaliated against by their employers because of lawful actions taken "in furtherance of" an action under the FCA. Most courts considering the issue have held that it is not necessary that a *qui tam* suit actually be initiated in order to recover under Section 3730(h).[1049] However, debates within a company about preferred methods of conducting business and an employee's mere "saber rattling" are not protected under the FCA.[1050]

Whistleblowers who can prove retaliation under Section 3730(h) may recover "all relief necessary to make the employee whole." Specifically, the FCA provides for recovery of:

- Reinstatement
- Two times the amount of back pay
- Compensation for "special damages," including litigation costs and reasonable attorneys' fees

E. *Marshalling A Defense*

1. Taking Advantage Of An Ambiguous Regulation or Contract Provision

As *qui tam* relators continue to press for expansive application of the False Claims Act, an increasing number of FCA cases are based on alleged regulatory or contract violations. When the underlying regulations or contract terms are ambiguous and subject to more than one legitimate interpretation, such suits are commonly defended on two primary grounds: 1) the claim submitted was not "false," because the contractor was operating under a permissible interpretation of the ambiguous regulation or contract provision,[1051] and 2) the contractor did not "knowingly" submit a false claim, because it believed that its interpretation was correct.

Courts often lack precision in their analysis of these two issues, and may not specify whether an FCA claim fails on the grounds that it was not false, or if the plaintiff failed to establish that the contractor acted with the requisite intent. Courts that focus primarily on the intent issue typically hold that even when it is later determined that the claim was submitted in violation of a material regulatory requirement or contract term, the defendant's good faith belief that it was operating under a correct interpretation of the regulation negates even the low reckless disregard FCA intent standard. Thus, "[w]here there are legitimate grounds for disagreement over the scope of a contractual or regulatory provision, and the claimant's actions are in good faith, the claimant cannot be said to have knowingly presented a false claim."[1052]

One of the best-reasoned decisions issued in an FCA case based on an allegedly improper interpretation of an ambiguous contract involved allegedly "defective pricing" by an MAS contractor. In *United States v. Data Translation, Inc.*[1053] the Government alleged that Data Translation was literally required to reveal every discount ever offered to any other customer, and Data Translation conceded that it had not done so. In a decision authored by Judge (now Justice) Breyer, the court found that the Government's discount provisions were, if read literally, "virtually unintelligible," but did appear to require this type of exhaustive disclosure.[1054] However, the court concluded that the Government's interpretation of the contract was so broad that no reasonable person could have believed that the Government really required the type of disclosure demanded by the contract.[1055]

The court's decision was based in part on the trial testimony of a GSA expert, who testified that the MAS questionnaire was so broad that it was unlikely that any supplier ever answered it with complete truthfulness.[1056] The court affirmed a directed verdict in favor of Data Translation as to the Government's "defective pricing" allegations, after concluding that the Government's discount disclosure forms were hopelessly ambiguous and that Data Translation could not have reasonably believed that the Government expected the type of disclosure that was required under the literal terms of the contract.[1057]

2. The *Sikorsky* Case: No Collective Knowledge And No Intent To Submit A False Claim

United States v. United Technologies Corp., Sikorsky Aircraft Division[1058] is the first published decision to date dealing with an attempt by the Government to apply the "collective knowledge doctrine" to an FCA case. Under the collective knowledge theory of liability, it is argued that a corporation can possess "knowledge" of a fraud—even if no single employee knows about the alleged fraud—if the fraud would be apparent when the knowledge of several employees is combined. Thus, under the collective knowledge theory of liability, if Stellar Corporation Employee A knows that the Government can be billed only for Acme widgets, and Stellar Corporation Employee B knows that the corporation is billing the Government for Zenith widgets, this knowledge could be combined—in theory—to yield a "knowing" submission by Stellar Corporation of a false claim for the Zenith widgets.

However, the Government's attempt to apply this theory in *Sikorsky* was soundly rejected by the court. The Government alleged that Sikorsky provided false cost or pricing data during its negotiations with the Government and that it falsely certified the completeness and accuracy of its pricing information. While MAS vendors typically need not provide certified cost or pricing data, the scope of the Price Adjustment Clause makes this case particularly relevant to MAS vendors.

In *Sikorsky*, the defendant admitted that it failed to disclose certain pricing information and that this failure constituted a violation of TINA.[1059] However, the court concluded that the omission of this information "was the result of a failure in Sikorsky's in-house transmission of information rather than a deliberate misrepresentation."[1060] The court further concluded that the individual responsible for gathering this information "did not intentionally avoid learning" the information or act with "reckless indifference to the true state of the . . . prices."[1061]

The Government claimed that the application of the collective corporate knowledge doctrine was well settled in similar cases and argued that it was only necessary to demonstrate that one employee at Sikorsky had actual knowledge of the accurate pricing information and that another knew of the company's obligation to report this information accurately. The Government also asserted that language in a Certificate of Current Cost or Pricing Data signed by a Sikorsky employee expressly provided that:

> The responsibility of the contractor is not limited by the personal knowledge of the contractor's negotiator if the contractor had information reasonably available at the time of agreement, showing that the negotiated price is not based on accurate, complete and current data.[1062]

The court rejected both arguments, disputing first the applicability of the collective knowledge doctrine to Sikorsky's potential liability under the FCA. The court also concluded that the Government did not prove that the individual signing the certification had any knowledge that the representations in the certification were false. Holding that the Government failed to prove that Sikorsky knowingly made false claims or statements to get a claim paid or approved, the court refused to apply the collective knowledge doctrine to the facts of the case before it and concluded that, at best, the defendant's actions involved mere negligence or inadvertent mistake and were, therefore, not subject to liability under the FCA.

3. Materiality And False Certifications

An increasing number of civil FCA cases are premised on the submission to the Government of allegedly false certifications of compliance with various statutes and regulations.[1063] In the context of the MAS Program, for example, a vendor must certify compliance with the Trade Agreements Act, the small disadvantaged business rules, and other MAS provisions. A number of recent cases litigated under the false certification theory, however, have failed because the courts determined that the certifications, even if false, were not *material* to the Government's determination to pay the claim or otherwise provide funding to the defendant.

a. The Materiality Requirement

Most courts considering the issue have held that materiality is an element of FCA liability.[1064] In *United States ex rel. Harrison v. Westinghouse Savannah River Co.*,[1065] the Fourth Circuit Court of Appeals stated that:

> Liability under each of the provisions of the False Claims Act is subject to the further, judicially-imposed, requirement that the false statement or claim be material. Materiality depends on "whether the false statement has a natural tendency to influence agency action or is capable of influencing agency action."[1066]

Another court has held that an alleged falsity is "material" if it is "an essential, important, or pertinent part of the claim."[1067]

Thus, if a certification is indeed false, courts must also turn to the question of whether the falsity actually caused the Government to provide a benefit or triggered a loss to the Government. In the *Harrison* case, for example, the court held that this requirement in "false certification cases is essentially a heightened materiality requirement: The Government must have conditioned payment of the claim upon certification of compliance with the provision of the statute, regulation, or contract at issue."[1068]

False certification cases may arise in the GSA MAS contracting setting where contractors are required to provide current, accurate, and complete information regarding discounts and special terms that are available to commercial customers. In *United States ex rel. Brown v. Merant Inc.*, [1069] for example, a former employee alleged that the defendant falsified its GSA commercial sales disclosures, and that by failing to reveal discounts given to commercial customers, the defendant allegedly caused the Government to pay inflated prices. However, the court found no evidence that the alleged disclosure failures actually caused the Government to be overcharged, and summary judgment was granted in favor of the MAS contractor.[1070]

Similar discount and marketing data must be submitted to the VA in connection with its MAS Program. In FCA suits based on allegedly false certifications regarding discounts offered to commercial customers, it is alleged that the failure to provide accurate pricing and discount information renders subsequent payment requests "false" under the FCA.

b. "Implied" False Certifications As A Basis For Liability Under The FCA

A few courts have permitted FCA cases to move forward, even in the absence of an express certification of compliance, based on the theory that the defendant *implicitly* certified its compliance with a statute or regulation. Under this theory, claims for payment made in violation of that "implicit" certification are false.[1071] However, a number of decisions have questioned the validity of this theory[1072] or have limited its application to "those exceptional circumstances where the claimant's adherence to the relevant statutory or regulatory mandates lies at the core of its agreement with the Government, or, in more practical terms, where the Government would have refused to pay had it been aware of the claimant's non-compliance."[1073]

Unfortunately, a growing number of courts have allowed FCA cases to go forward under the false implied certification theory, and some of these cases have resulted in the payment of significant judgments or settlements by the defendants.[1074] In *United States ex rel. Augustine v. Century Health Services*,[1075] for example, a panel of the Sixth Circuit affirmed a bench verdict holding defendants liable for allegedly making false implied certifications of ongoing regulatory compliance. The *Augustine* case involved express certifications of compliance that were apparently technically accurate when made, but defendants then engaged in transactions that, according to the Government, rendered those express certifications false.[1076] Both the appellate and the trial court relied in part on uncontroverted evidence that the defendants were required to file amended cost reports if their use of the funds did not comport with Government regulations, and held that "liability can attach if the claimant violates its continuing duty to comply with the regulations on which payment is conditioned."[1077]

The Tenth Circuit Court of Appeals also affirmed a jury verdict based on some form of certification theory in *Shaw v. AAA Engineering & Drafting, Inc.*[1078] The contractor in *Shaw* (AAA) provided photography services to the Air Force and was paid a fixed monthly fee, but sought an equitable adjustment, claiming that it was providing roughly 30 percent more services than the Air Force had estimated would be required under the contract. Ultimately, AAA sought an equitable adjustment of nearly $250,000 and certified that the claim was supported by current, accurate, and complete data. The Government paid a $78,000 settlement. The contractor accepted the payment but appealed to the ASBCA, arguing the settlement was insufficient.[1079]

An employee filed a *qui tam* FCA suit against AAA. Evidence was presented at trial that work orders supporting the equitable adjustment claim were altered and falsely inflated and that the defendant knowingly failed to comply with certain contract terms. The jury imposed liability on AAA for three false claims and for actual damages of $4,900. The Court of Appeals affirmed the verdict as to the FCA claims, holding that the allegedly false work orders could be the basis for liability under the FCA and that the evidence supported the conclusion that the work orders were false statements made recklessly or deliberately in order to get a false claim (the equitable adjustment) paid.[1080]

The court also held that monthly invoices submitted when the contractor was knowingly not complying with contract terms can be the basis of FCA liability. The court concluded that an FCA claim can be premised on a false implied certification of contractual compliance.[1081] The court also concluded that the relator "presented ample evidence that AAA knowingly failed to [comply with the contract] but nevertheless invoiced for and accepted full payment under the contract."[1082] The court emphasized, however, that FCA liability for an implied certification of contractual compliance "requires that the contractor knew, or recklessly disregarded a risk, that its implied certification of compliance was false."[1083] While the court analyzed the issue as an "implied certification" case, the court apparently did not need to do so. The underlying claims submitted to the Government were found by the jury to be false. This is not a case where the claims are correctly billed for services or supplies actually provided but some other regulation is allegedly violated.

Moreover, the *Shaw* and *Augustine* decisions represent a significant departure from the more restrictive view of the implied certification theory. As the D.C. Circuit Court of Appeals held in *United States ex rel. Siewick v. Jamieson Science and Engineering, Inc.*,[1084] a decision that was issued shortly after *Shaw*, the implied certification theory is a "non-starter," "doomed by the rule . . . that a false certification of compliance with a statute or regulation cannot serve as the basis for a *qui tam* action under the FCA unless payment is conditioned on that certification."[1085]

4. False Estimates As A Basis For Liability Under The FCA

At least two courts have permitted FCA claims to proceed based on allegedly false estimates. In *United States ex rel. Harrison v. Westinghouse Savannah River Co.*,[1086] the Fourth Circuit held that the relator had stated a claim when he alleged that the defendant knowingly made statements to the Government that contained false estimates of the likely duration and cost of a subcontract.[1087] The court acknowledged that expressions of opinion are not actionable as fraud and that figures that are clearly identified as estimates might diminish the materiality of their influence.[1088] However, the court concluded that "an opinion or estimate carries with it 'an implied assertion, not only that the speaker knows no facts which would preclude such an opinion, but that he does know facts which justify it.'"[1089] This decision was subsequently followed in *United States v. United Technologies Corp.*[1090]

F. *Reverse False Claims*

As noted above, the reverse false claims provision, Section 3729(a)(7), was added to the FCA when the FCA was amended in 1986. It imposes liability for the use of a false record to decrease or avoid an existing "obligation" to the United States. Since 1986, an increasing number of FCA suits have been filed under Section 3729(a)(7), alleging liability based on the failure to report statutory or regulatory violations—violations that could give rise to potential Government fines.[1091] Government contractors can be accused of violating Section (a)(7), for example, in performance-based or specification-based FCA cases where there is a warranty provision in the contract.[1092] Relators have also argued that false certifications by MAS contractors regarding compliance with various laws and regulations were made to avoid paying liquidated damages to the Government, thus giving rise to alleged reverse false claims liability. With a few early and unfortunate exceptions,[1093] decisions published in the last few years have properly limited the scope of reverse false claims liability to current, existing obligations.

One of the earliest appellate decisions on the reverse false claims provision issue came from the Eighth Circuit, in *United States v. Quick International Courier*.[1094] In *Quick*, the defendant was accused of violating Section 3729(a)(7) when it shipped bulk mail offshore and re-mailed it to the United States, enjoying less expensive international postage rates in the process. The Government argued that the defendant improperly reduced its "obligation" to pay full postage rates. The Court of Appeals rejected this argument, concluding that, at most, the defendant was subject to a potential fine or penalty. For liability to arise under Section 3729(a)(7), "a defendant must have had a present duty to pay money or property that was created by a statute, regulation, contract, judgment, or acknowledgment of indebtedness."[1095]

In *United States ex rel. American Textile Manufacturers Institute v. Limited, Inc.*,[1096] the Sixth Circuit reached a similar conclusion, where the defendant was alleged to have concealed violations of certain Customs laws. The Sixth Circuit panel held that "a plaintiff may not state a reverse false claim unless the pertinent obligation attached *before* the defendant made or used [a] false record or statement."[1097] The court held that contingent obligations to the Government do not give rise to liability under Section 3729(a)(7): "A defendant does not execute a reverse false claim by engaging in behavior that might or might not result in the creation of an obligation to pay or transmit money or property to the government."[1098] Contingent obligations were defined by the court as "those that will arise only after the exercise of discretion by government actors . . . ."[1099]

* * *

In the preface to the first edition of *Civil False Claims and Qui Tam Actions*, Mr. Boese comments that "[i]t is unclear whether the False Claims Act represents the cutting edge of a revolutionary new means of protecting the interests of the United States, or just an anachronistic, and unfair, way of 'shaking down' careless government contractors and grantees in some of today's most highly-regulated transactions."[1100] Either way, the importance of understanding the scope of the FCA cannot be overstated. The costs involved in defending against a FCA allegation alone can be extraordinary.[1101]

Notes:

[1004] Ch. 67, 12 Stat. 698 (1863) (codified as amended at 31 U.S.C. §§ 3729-33.). The False Claims Act is a Civil War-era statute, originally signed into law by President Lincoln because of fraud committed against the Government by war profiteers. Litigation has exploded under the FCA since Congress reduced barriers to filing suit and enhanced recoveries available under the FCA in 1986. *See* Dep't of Justice Fiscal Year 2003 *Qui Tam* FCA Statistics, available at *http://www.ffhsj.com/quitam/fcastats.htm.*

[1005] *See* John T. Boese, CIVIL FALSE CLAIMS AND QUI TAM ACTIONS, (Aspen Publishers, 2d ed. Supp. 2004-1), at xvii.

[1006] *See* Boese, CIVIL FALSE CLAIMS AND QUI TAM ACTIONS, for a more detailed discussion of the history and scope of the FCA.

[1007] *See, e.g., United States ex rel. Hutchins v. Wilentz, Goldman & Spitzer*, 253 F.3d 176, 184 (3d Cir. 2001) (FCA does not apply to claims that "do not or would not cause financial loss to the Government"); *United States ex rel. Hopper v. Anton*, 91 F.3d 1261 (9th Cir. 1996) (regulatory violation does not support FCA claim unless funding is conditioned upon regulatory compliance); *United States ex rel. Berge v. Board of Trustees of the Univ. of Ala.*, 104 F.3d 1453 (4th Cir. 1997) (overturning a jury verdict in favor of the *qui tam* relator because the alleged false statement was deemed not material to the Government's decision approving research grants); *Daff v. United States*, 31 Fed. Cl. 682, 695 (1994), *aff'd*, 78 F.3d

1566 (1996). *But see Varljen v. Cleveland Gear Co., Inc.*, 250 F.3d 426, 431 (6th Cir. 2001); *United States ex rel. Atkinson v. Pennsylvania Shipbuilding Co.*, No. 94-7316, 2000 U.S. Dist. LEXIS 12081, at *26 n.12 (E.D. Pa. Aug. 24, 2000) ("loss causation" must be demonstrated to recover damages, but is not necessary to state a claim for a violation of the FCA, because penalties can be imposed even in the absence of damages); *United States ex rel. Thompson v. Columbia/HCA Healthcare*, 20 F. Supp. 2d 1017 (S.D. Tex. 1998); *Tyger Constr. Co. v. United States*, 28 Fed. Cl. 35 (1993); *United States ex rel. Stinson, Lyons, Gerlin & Bustamante v. Provident Life & Accident Ins. Co.*, 721 F. Supp. 1247, 1258-59 (S.D. Fla. 1989); *United States v. Board of Educ. of Union City*, 697 F. Supp. 167, 179 (D.N.J. 1988); *Blusal Meats, Inc. v. United States*, 638 F. Supp. 824, 827 (S.D.N.Y. 1986), *aff'd*, 817 F.2d 1007 (2d Cir. 1987). *See also United States ex rel. Harrison v. Westinghouse Savannah River Co.*, 176 F.3d 776 (4th Cir. 1999) (discussed in greater detail *infra*).

[1008] *United States. v. Farina*, 153 F. Supp. 819 (D.N.J. 1957).

[1009] *Dookeran v. Mercy Hosp.*, 281 F.3d 105 (3d Cir. 2002); *United States ex rel. Cooper v. Gentiva Health Servs., Inc.*, No. 01-508, 2003 WL 22495607, at *7 n.9 (W.D. Pa. Nov. 4, 2003).

[1010] *United States. v. McNinch*, 356 U.S. 595 (1958).

[1011] S. REP. No. 99-345, at 20-21, *reprinted in* 1986 U.S.C.C.A.N. 5266, 5285-86. *See also United States ex rel. Rueter v. Sparks*, 939 F. Supp. 636 (C.D. Ill. 1996), *aff'd*, 111 F.3d 133 (7th Cir. 1997) (finding mere negligence, rather than reckless disregard or deliberate indifference, where a contractor's improper payroll records were not cited by Department of Labor auditors in an earlier audit). *See also* John T. Boese & Shannon L. Haralson, *Mistakes Are Not Fraud*, LEGAL TIMES, June 17, 1996, at S34.

[1012] *United States v. Krizek*, 111 F.3d 934, 942 (D.C. Cir. 1997).

[1013] *See United States ex rel. Johnson v. Shell Oil Co.*, 183 F.R.D. 204, 208 (E.D. Tex. 1998). Readers should note that the author of this chapter represented one of the defendants in this matter.

[1014] *Compare United States v. Marple Cmty. Record, Inc.*, 335 F. Supp. 95 (E.D. Pa. 1971) (no reverse FCA liability), *with United States*

v. *Lawson*, 522 F. Supp. 746 (D.N.J. 1981) (reverse false claim actionable before 1986).

[1015] 31 U.S.C. § 3731(c).

[1016] *Id.* § 3729(a).

[1017] *Id.* Damages must also be proven by the preponderance of the evidence.

[1018] Pub. L. No. 101-410, 104 Stat. 890 (1990).

[1019] Pub. L. No. 104-134, ch. 10, § 31001, 110 Stat. 1321-1358 (codified in scattered sections of 5 U.S.C., 26 U.S.C., 28 U.S.C., 31 U.S.C., and 42 U.S.C.).

[1020] 64 Fed. Reg. 47,099-48,104, Part 85, § 85.3 (Aug. 30, 1999) (to be codified at 8 C.F.R. pts. 270, 274a, and 280 and 28 C.F.R. pts. 20, 22, 36, 71, 76, and 85). Agencies are required to adjust penalties for inflation every four years, and under the Government Accountability Office's interpretation of the Inflation Adjustment Act, the Justice Department should have announced its next increase by August 30, 2003. *See* Gen. Acct. Off., GAO-03-409, *Agencies Unable to Fully Adjust Penalties for Inflation Under Current Law* (Mar. 2003), at 13. However, no additional adjustments were announced by the time this chapter went to press, and it is likely that because of the low inflation rates between 1999 and 2003, no increase was permitted under the Inflation Adjustment Act's rounding rules. *See id.* at App. II, Table 8 (indicating that a $5,500 penalty will require a 9.1 percentage increase in inflation in order to trigger the next $1,000 adjustment, and that an $11,000 penalty will require a 22.8 percentage increase in inflation before the penalty is increased by $5,000, to $16,000).

[1021] 529 U.S. 765, 784-85 (2000).

[1022] 538 U.S. 119, 123 S. Ct. 1239, 1246 (2003).

[1023] 243 F.3d 1159 (9th Cir.), *op. withdrawn, substitute op., remanded,* 261 F.3d 821 (9th Cir. 2001). Other decisions in which courts have applied Excessive Fines principles to FCA awards include *Petersen v. Weinberger*, 508 F.2d 45, 55 (5th Cir. 1975); *United States ex rel. Smith v. Gilbert Realty Co., Inc.*, 840 F. Supp. 71, 73-74 (E.D. Mich. 1993); *United States v. Advanced Tool Co.*, 902 F. Supp. 1011, 1018 (W.D. Mo. 1995), *aff'd*, 86 F.3d 1159 (8th

Cir. 1996); *United States v. Cabrera-Diaz*, 106 F. Supp. 2d 234 (D.P.R. 2000). *Cf. Hays v. Hoffman*, 325 F.3d 982, 992 (8th Cir. 2003) (vacating most of an FCA judgment on other grounds, but agreeing that FCA damages are punitive and therefore subject to Eighth Amendment limitations), *cert. denied*, 124 S. Ct. 277 (U.S. Oct. 6, 2003).

[1024] These issues, though of great importance to any MAS contractor facing potential liability under the FCA, are beyond the scope of this chapter. For more detailed discussion of the punitive aspects of FCA damages and penalties, *see* Boese, CIVIL FALSE CLAIMS AND QUI TAM ACTIONS.

[1025] *See United States v. Advance Tool Co.*, 902 F. Supp. 1011 (W.D. Mo. 1995), *aff'd*, 86 F.3d 1159 (8th Cir. 1996).

[1026] 10 U.S.C. § 2306a(e).

[1027] *Cf. Universal Restoration Inc. v. United States*, 798 F.2d 1400, 1406 (Fed. Cir. 1986) (contractor successfully rebutted TINA claims by demonstrating that it would not have accepted less than a 115 percent markup for overhead and that there would have been no contract if the Government had insisted on a smaller markup).

[1028] *See* S. REP. NO. 99-345, at 19 (1986), *reprinted in* 1986 U.S.C.C.A.N. 5266, 5284; *see also* 132 CONG. REC. H6480 (Sept. 9, 1986) (statement of Rep. Fish).

[1029] *See* Boese, CIVIL FALSE CLAIMS AND QUI TAM ACTIONS, 3-57 n.150.

[1030] *See Cook County*, 123 S. Ct. at 1247 n.9 (noting that "[t]he treble damages provision was … adopted by Congress as a substitute for consequential damages.").

[1031] 79 F. Supp. 2d 877 (S.D. Ohio 1999), *summary judgment denied*, 100 F. Supp. 2d 619 (S.D. Ohio 2000).

[1032] *Id.* at 895.

[1033] *United States ex rel. Roby v. Boeing Co.*, 302 F.3d 637, 648-49 (6th Cir. 2002), *cert. denied*, 123 S. Ct. 2641 (U.S. 2003).

[1034] *Id.* at 648 n.9.

[1035] *United States v. Bornstein*, 423 U.S. 303 (1976); *Brown v. United States*, 524 F.2d 693 (Ct. Cl. 1975).

[1036] *See, e.g., Weinberger*, 508 F.2d at 55; *Cabrera-Diaz*, 106 F. Supp. 2d 234; *Advanced Tool Co.*, 902 F. Supp. at 1018; *Gilbert Realty*, 840

F. Supp. at 73-74. *Cf. Mackby*, 243 F.3d 1159 (remanding an FCA judgment to the district court for a determination as to whether the FCA damages and penalties imposed violated the Excessive Fines Clause) and *Hays, supra* note 20.

[1037] The term "*qui tam*" is derived from the Latin phrase "*qui tam pro domino rege quam pro se ipso in hac parte sequitur*," which translates to "he who pursues this action on our Lord the King's behalf as well as his own." *Qui tam* actions were relatively rare in modern American law but were a common form of action under English common law, stretching back as far as the thirteenth century.

[1038] 31 U.S.C. § 3730(b)(1). *Qui tam* enforcement of the FCA survived one of the more serious constitutional challenges to be brought before the Supreme Court, ensuring, for now at least, the continued importance of the FCA to virtually any organization doing business with or regulated by the Federal Government. *See Vermont Agency of Natural Res. v. United States*, 529 U.S. 765 (2000) (holding that *qui tam* relators have standing to sue on behalf of the Federal Government).

[1039] 31 U.S.C. § 3730(b)(2).

[1040] *Id.* § 3730(b)(4)(B).

[1041] *Id.* § 3730(b)(4)(A).

[1042] *Id.* § 3730(d)(1).

[1043] *Id.* § 3730(d)(2).

[1044] *Id.* § 3730(c)(5).

[1045] *Id.* § 3730(d)(3).

[1046] *Id.*

[1047] *Id.* § 3730(d)(1).

[1048] *Id.* § 3730(d)(4).

[1049] *See, e.g., United States ex rel. Eberhardt v. Integrated Design & Constr., Inc*, 167 F.3d 861 (4th Cir. 1999).

[1050] *Luckey v. Baxter Healthcare Corp.*, 183 F.3d 730, 733 (7th Cir. 1999).

[1051] *United States ex rel. Augustine v. Century Health Servs., Inc.*, 136 F. Supp. 2d 876, 880 (M.D. Tenn. 2000) ("[C]ourts have held that errors based upon flawed reasoning and differences in interpretation of disputed legal questions are not false under the FCA."), *aff'd,*

289 F.3d 409 (6th Cir. 2002) (citing *United States ex rel. Lamers v. City of Green Bay*, 168 F.3d 1013, 1018 (7th Cir. 1999).

[1052] *United States v. Southland Mgmt. Corp.*, 326 F.3d 669, 684 (5th Cir. 2003) (en banc) (Jones, J. concurring). *See also United States ex rel. Hagood v. Sonoma County Water Agency*, 929 F.2d 1416, 1421 (9th Cir. 1991) ("To take advantage of a disputed legal question . . . is to be neither deliberately ignorant nor recklessly disregardful.").

[1053] 984 F.2d 1256 (1st Cir. 1992). For another published decision involving FCA claims based on the alleged failure to disclose discounts to the Government, *see X Corp. v. John Doe*, 816 F. Supp. 1086 (E.D. Va. 1993).

[1054] *Data Translation*, 984 F.2d at 1260.

[1055] *Id.* at 1261.

[1056] *Id.* at 1262.

[1057] *Id.* at 1265.

[1058] 51 F. Supp. 2d 167 (D. Conn. 1999).

[1059] *Id.* at 197.

[1060] *Id.* at 183.

[1061] *Id.*

[1062] *Id.* at 197.

[1063] *See, e.g., United States ex rel. Thompson v. Columbia/HCA Healthcare Corp.*, 125 F.3d 899, 902 (5th Cir. 1997) (allegedly false certifications of compliance with Medicare laws); *United States v. Job Resources for the Disabled*, No. 97 C 3904, 2000 U.S. Dist. LEXIS 6343 (N.D. Ill. May 9, 2000); *United States ex rel. Fallon v. Accudyne Corp.*, 880 F. Supp. 636, 638 (W.D. Wis. 1995) (allegedly false certifications of compliance with Fair Housing Act non-discrimination and affirmative action requirements); *Ab-Tech Constr., Inc. v. United States*, 31 Fed. Cl. 429 (1994), *aff'd*, 57 F.3d 1084 (Fed. Cir. 1995) (allegedly false certifications of compliance with Small Business Administration minority contracting requirements).

[1064] *See, e.g., United States ex rel. Durcholz v. FKW, Inc.*, 189 F.3d 542 (7th Cir. 1999); *United States ex rel. Harrison v. Westinghouse Savannah River Co.*, 176 F.3d 776 (4th Cir. 1999); *United States ex rel. Bennett v. Genetics & IVF Inst.*, No. 98-2119, 1999 U.S. App. LEXIS 27911 (4th Cir. Oct. 28, 1999) (unpublished decision); *United States ex rel. Lamers v. City of Green Bay*, 168 F.3d 1013 (7th Cir. 1999). *See also Southland Mgmt. Corp.*, 326 F.3d at 679 (Jones, J. concurring) ("[T]here should no longer be any doubt that materiality is an element of a civil False Claims Act case. Our past precedent and every circuit that has addressed the issue have so concluded. This conclusion is strengthened in a case involving allegedly false certifications contained in official payment vouchers, because, for FCA liability to arise, a false certification must be a "false statement" made "to get" a false claim paid. The express connection of a false statement with "getting" a false claim paid is tantamount to requiring that the false statement be material to the payment decision."). *But see United States ex rel. Roby v. Boeing*, 184 F.R.D. 107 (S.D. Ohio. 1998) (relying on precedent rejecting materiality requirement in a criminal false statements case).

[1065] 176 F.3d 776 (4th Cir. 1999).

[1066] *Id.* at 785 (citation omitted).

[1067] *See Tyger Constr. Co.*, 28 Fed. Cl. at 55 (holding that the FCA covers only those statements that are material).

[1068] *Harrison*, 176 F.3d at 793. *See also United States ex rel. Costner v. United States*, 317 F.3d 883, 887 (8th Cir. 2003); *United States ex rel. Mikes v. Straus*, 274 F.3d 687, 700 (2d Cir. 2001); *United States ex rel. Thompson v. Columbia/HCA Healthcare Corp.*, 125 F.3d 899, 902 (5th Cir. 1997).

[1069] No. 99-6481, 2002 U.S. Dist. LEXIS 5474 (E.D. Pa. Mar. 29, 2002).

[1070] *Id.* at *15-16.

[1071] *See, e.g., Ab-Tech Constr.*, 31 Fed. Cl. at 434; *United States ex rel. Pogue v. American Healthcorp*, 914 F. Supp. 1507, 1509 (M.D. Tenn. 1996); *United States ex rel. Aranda v. Cmty. Psychiatric Ctrs. Of Okla., Inc.*, 945 F. Supp. 1485 (W.D. Okla. 1996).

[1072] *See United States ex rel. Willard v. Humana Health Plan of Tex., Inc.*, 336 F.3d 375, 382 (5th Cir. 2003); *Harrison*, 176 F.3d at 787; *United States ex rel. Gay v. Lincoln Tech. Inst., Inc.*, No. Civ.A. 301 CV505K, 2003 WL 22474586, at *3 (N.D. Tex. Sept. 3, 2003); *United States ex rel. Swan v. Covenant Care, Inc.*, No.

CIVS99-1891 DFL JFM, 2003 WL 22037752, at *1 n.3, *7 (E.D. Cal. Aug. 5, 2002).

[1073] *United States ex rel. Mikes v. Straus*, 84 F. Supp. 2d 427, 435 (S.D.N.Y. 1999), *aff'd*, 274 F.3d 687 (2d Cir. 2001). *See also Luckey v. Baxter Healthcare Corp.*, 2 F. Supp. 2d 1034, 1045 (N.D. Ill. 1998), *aff'd*, 183 F.3d 730 (7th Cir. 1999); *City of Green Bay*, 168 F.3d at 1019; and *Anton*, 91 F.3d 1261.

[1074] *See, e.g., United States ex rel. Barrett v. Columbia/HCA Healthcare Corp.*, 251 F. Supp. 2d 28 (D.D.C. 2003); *United States ex rel. Pogue v. Diabetes Treatment Ctrs. of Am., Inc.*, 238 F. Supp. 2d 258 (D.D.C. 2002).

[1075] 289 F.3d 409 (6th Cir. 2002).

[1076] *Id.* at 412, 414-15.

[1077] *Id.* at 415.

[1078] 213 F.3d 519 (10th Cir. 2000).

[1079] *Id.* at 526 n.6. This appeal was recently dismissed by the ASBCA, which held that AAA was collaterally estopped by the Tenth Circuit's ruling in *Shaw*. *See Appeals of AAA Eng'g & Drafting, Inc.*, ASBCA No. 47940 *et al.*, 01-1 BCA ¶ 31,256.

[1080] *Shaw*, 213 F.3d at 530-31.

[1081] *Id.* at 532.

[1082] *Id.* at 533.

[1083] *Id.*

[1084] 214 F.3d 1372 (D.C. Cir. 2000).

[1085] *Id.* at 1376. *See also United States ex rel. Totten v. Bombardier Corp.*, 139 F. Supp. 2d 50, 52 n.1 (D.D.C. 2001) ("Requesting payment for noncompliant products which satisfy neither their contracts nor . . . regulations is not a violation of the False Claims Act. Only the false certification of compliance, where certification is a prerequisite to obtaining payment, would suffice.").

[1086] 176 F.3d 776 (4th Cir. 1999).

[1087] *Id.* at 792.

[1088] *Id.*

[1089] *Id.*, citing W. Page Keeton, et al., PROSSER & KEETON ON THE LAW OF TORTS § 109, at 760 (5th ed. 1984).

[1090] No. C-3-99-093, 2003 WL 1191727, at *2 (S.D. Ohio Mar. 6, 2003).

[1091] *See, e.g., United States ex rel. Sequoia Orange Co. v. Sunland Packing House Co.*, 912 F. Supp. 1325 (E.D. Cal. 1995), *aff'd*, 151 F.3d 1139 (9th Cir. 1998); *United States ex rel. Stevens v. McGinnis, Inc.*, No. C-93-442, 1994 U.S. Dist. LEXIS 20953, at *10 (S.D. Ohio Oct. 26, 1994); *Pickens v. Kanawha River Towing*, 916 F. Supp. 702 (S.D. Ohio 1996).

[1092] *See, e.g., United States ex rel. Jordan v. Northrop Grumman Corp.*, No. 95-2985-ABC (C.D. Cal. Jan. 8, 1998), where it was alleged that defendant failed to disclose the noncompliance of products supplied under a Government contract in order to avoid providing warranty services under the contract.

[1093] *See, e.g., McGinnis*, U.S. Dist. LEXIS 20953.

[1094] 131 F.3d 770 (8th Cir. 1997).

[1095] *Id.* at 773.

[1096] 190 F.3d 729 (6th Cir. 1999), *cert. denied*, 529 U.S. 1054 (2000). The author of this chapter was one of the counsel for defendants in this matter.

[1097] *Id.* at 734 (emphasis in original).

[1098] *Id.* at 738.

[1099] *Id. See also United States v. Pemco Aeroplex*, 195 F.3d 1234 (11th Cir. 1999) (affirming the principle that only existing legal obligations can give rise to reverse false claims liability, but finding that such obligations existed as to the defendant).

[1100] Boese, CIVIL FALSE CLAIMS AND QUI TAM ACTIONS, Preface to First Edition at xx.

[1101] *See, e.g.*, John T. Boese, John W. Chierichella, & Richard A. Sauber, *The Civil False Claims Act: More Relevant Than You May Think*, DIRECTOR'S MONTHLY (Oct. 2000), at 13.

XXIV.

OTHER ADVERSE DEVELOPMENTS

*"What upsets me is not that you lied to me, but
that from now on I can no longer believe you."*
                                                    -Nietzsche

As the chapters regarding the False Claims Act and Office of Inspector General audits ought to have made clear, a MAS contract is a double-edged sword, a powerful weapon in terms of revenue production, but also one quite capable of cutting the hand that holds it. This chapter examines a few of these other potential "cuts." While most MAS vendors, fortunately, never will see blood, it is essential to understand the possibilities.

A. *Suspension And Debarment*

Suspension and debarment are two of the most deadly arrows in the Government's quiver. Typically (but wrongly) referred to as one action (*i.e.*, a "suspension/debarment"), suspension and debarment actually constitute two separate, and sequential, Government actions. A suspension is a temporary matter that, in the right (or wrong) circumstances, can lead to a debarment. The purpose of each, however, is similar. Both suspensions and debarments are invoked to preclude contractors that are not "responsible" vendors from continuing to contract with the Government. Neither is (supposedly) designed to punish a contractor for *past* actions.[1102] The consequences of each are essentially similar. Both prohibit agencies from soliciting offers from, awarding contracts to, or permitting subcontracting with suspended or debarred contractors.[1103] They also prohibit agencies from placing additional orders under previously awarded Schedule contracts in the absence of a written determination of a compelling reason for doing so.[1104] Additionally, in many cases, a suspension or debarment prevents a contractor from contracting with state governments (due to reciprocity rules discussed below).

1. Suspension

A suspension is an action taken by the head of an agency

> [t]o disqualify a contractor temporarily from Government contracting and Government-approved subcontracting.[1105]

A suspension can arise out of any of the following activities:

(1) Commission of fraud or criminal offense in connection with obtaining, attempting to obtain, or performing a public contract or subcontract;

(2) Violation of federal or state antitrust statutes relating to the submission of offers;

(3) Commission of embezzlement, theft, forgery, bribery, falsification or destruction of records, making false statements, tax evasion, or receiving of stolen property;

(4) Commission of any other offense indicating a lack of business integrity or business honesty that seriously and directly affects the present responsibility of a Government contractor or subcontractor;

(5) Violations of the Drug-Free Workplace Act of 1988;
(6) Intentionally affixing a label bearing a "Made in America" inscription (or any inscription having the same meaning) to a product sold in or shipped to the United States when the product was not made in the United States; or
(7) Commission of an unfair trade practice.[1106]

Unless otherwise narrowed, a suspension applies to the vendor's entire business—not merely the division involved in the challenged activity.[1107]

Due to the potentially severe consequences of a suspension, Government agencies may impose a suspension only upon "the basis of adequate evidence" when "it has been determined that immediate action is necessary to protect the Government's interest."[1108] Importantly, the existence of "adequate evidence" does not *compel* a suspension. The FAR instructs agencies to consider the seriousness of the offense.[1109] The FAR also permits, but does not require, agencies to consider the following mitigating factors.[1110]

(1) Whether the contractor had effective standards of conduct and internal controls or implemented such standards prior to the investigation of the activity cited for debarment;
(2) Whether the contractor cooperated fully with Government agencies during the investigation and any court or administrative action;
(3) Whether the contractor has taken appropriate disciplinary action against the individuals responsible for the activity;
(4) Whether the contractor has implemented or agreed to implement remedial measures;
(5) Whether the contractor has conducted a full investigation and made the results available to the debarring official;
(6) Whether the contractor has paid or agreed to pay all criminal, civil, and administrative liability associated with the incident(s);

(7) Whether the contractor has instituted or agreed to institute new or revised controls and/or procedures;

(8) Whether the contractor has had adequate time to eliminate the circumstances within the organization that led to the debarment proceedings;

(9) Whether the contractor's management comprehends the seriousness of the situation and has implemented programs to prevent recurrence; and

(10) Whether the contractor brought the debarring activity to the attention of the Government in a timely manner.[1111]

Following an agency's initial decision to suspend a vendor, the vendor will receive written notice of the pending suspension and of the alleged irregularities that prompted the suspension. While this notice may not be comprehensive, it must be sufficient to put the vendor "on notice without disclosing the Government's evidence."[1112] Subsequent to official notice, the vendor has thirty days to respond and provide information "that raises a genuine dispute over the material facts."[1113]

Following the vendor's formal response to the agency—and any proceedings conducted at the discretion of the agency to resolve undisputed facts—the agency may modify the suspension, terminate the suspension, or leave it in force.[1114] (A suspension that is later modified or terminated will be without prejudice to the subsequent suspension or debarment of the vendor.[1115]) Unless the agency explicitly initiates further legal proceedings against the vendor, a suspension may last no longer than eighteen months.[1116] If further legal proceedings are initiated, a suspension may continue until the proceedings are completed.

2. Debarment

Unlike a suspension, a debarment action is not taken by an agency head, but rather by an authorized "debarment official."[1117] Often referred to as a "death penalty" for a Government contractor, debarment is essentially an order to exclude a contractor from Government contracting and Government-approved subcontracting for a reasonable, specified period.[1118]

The same actions that may form the basis for a suspension also form the basis for a debarment with a few notable additions. Vendors may be debarred for:

(i) Violation of the terms of a Government contract or subcontract so serious as to justify debarment, such as—

    (A) Willful failure to perform in accordance with the terms of one or more contracts; or

    (B) A history of failure to perform, or of unsatisfactory performance of, one or more contracts.[1119]

Vendors also may be debarred for a violation of the Drug-Free Workplace Act, an intentional mislabeling of products as "Made in America," the commission of unfair trade practices, and a failure to comply with "Immigration and Nationality Act employment provisions, based upon a determination by the Attorney General of the United States."[1120]

Before debarring a vendor, the debarment official (typically the GSA Debarment Official in the context of MAS vendors) must determine whether the debarment is "in the Government's interest."[1121] As with a suspension, a finding of adequate cause for a debarment does not *require* a debarment. The debarring official "should" consider both the "seriousness of the contractor's acts or omissions and any remedial measures or mitigating factors."[1122] Recall that, in the context of a suspension, the suspending agency "may, but is not required to, consider" mitigating factors.[1123] In both cases, however, the mitigating factors to be considered are the same.

Unless a debarment is limited to a specific element of a vendor's organization, a debarment affects every element of the vendor's organization.[1124] Moreover, a debarment is Governmentwide, that is, it forecloses contracting opportunities with *every* Federal Government agency unless a specific agency offers a compelling reason for a waiver.[1125] In the absence of such a waiver, federal agencies may not solicit offers from, award contracts to, or consent to subcontracts with a debarred vendor.[1126]

The period for debarment generally does not exceed three years.[1127]

Unlike a civil or criminal prosecution conducted by the DOJ, which GSA has no authority to compromise, GSA does have the authority to settle a matter that otherwise could lead to a debarment. For example, several years ago, following a six-month suspension, Harris Corporation entered into a settlement with GSA under which it avoided a debarment by paying $1 million and implementing an extensive internal compliance program.[1128] The internal compliance program required, among other things, reassignment of corporate responsibilities, verification of future pricing information by independent outside accountants, legal review by Harris corporate counsel, and a training program on Government contract requirements.[1129]

3. Collateral State Debarment

Like the Federal Government, several states have developed suspension/debarment provisions of their own over the years. Some of these states consider a federal debarment to be *per se* evidence of irresponsibility and, consequently, grounds for a collateral state debarment.[1130] Several of these states specifically reference the GSA List of Excluded Parties as a primary trigger for a state debarment. As a result, a vendor that is debarred or suspended at the federal level has a significant likelihood of finding itself debarred at the state level as well.[1131] This is particularly true when federal funding is being used for projects.

4. List Of Excluded Parties

GSA maintains a "List of Parties Excluded from Federal Procurement and Nonprocurement Programs," which is accessible by or available to all agencies and contractors. As its name suggests, this list identifies those companies that are either suspended or debarred from contracting with the Federal Government.[1132] The FAR directs contracting officers to review this list prior to award of any federal contract.[1133] Likewise, MAS vendors must review this list prior to entering into subcontracts.[1134]

In addition to reviewing the GSA List of Excluded Parties, MAS vendors must certify that they are not debarred or proposed for debarment. (*See* Chapter IX for a more detailed discussion regarding this certification.) Failure to furnish this certification to GSA with a proposal will result in rejection of the proposal as nonresponsive.[1135]

5. Avoiding Suspension And Debarment

Because suspensions and debarments are questions of *current and future* responsibility, the most effective steps a vendor can take to protect against such an event involve, not surprisingly, actions that demonstrate responsibility. To this end, the following six rules easily can be derived simply by rephrasing the list of mitigating factors identified in the FAR:

- Maintain effective standards of conduct and an effective internal control system
- Take appropriate disciplinary action against individuals responsible for wrongdoing
- Implement remedial measures following the discovery of wrongdoing
- Review internal control procedures regularly and revise as necessary
- Implement an ethics training program
- Develop an internal program that illustrates management's commitment to compliance

The past experiences of MAS vendors aptly demonstrate the wisdom of the foregoing rules. Several years ago, for example, as discussed above, Harris Corporation avoided a potential debarment by agreeing to pay GSA $1 million and to implement "an extensive program of management and outside controls."[1136] The program included legal reviews, account reviews, and a training component, among other elements. Similarly, in 1983, Tektronix Inc. paid $5 million to settle a False Claims Act case. In addition to this payment, Tektronix committed to implement significant new internal safeguards.[1137]

The foregoing rules, however, provide no guarantee for avoiding a suspension or debarment. Because of this fact, and because the financial effect of a suspension or debarment can be truly devastating, vendors are well advised to involve legal counsel in any matter that could lead to a suspension or debarment. As *The Practitioner's Guide to Suspension and Debarment* notes:

> The exercise of these government protective measures, which can be serious, if not cataclysmic, for a contractor or participant, frequently raises legal issues. Even in the absence of a legal question, however, the [lawyer] can often provide valuable practical advice for clients facing the prospect of suspension or debarment . . . . [1138]

As federal use of suspensions and debarments continues to increase, the importance of this advice cannot be overstated.

* * *

Obviously, the foregoing discussion only touches the surface of the complex world of suspension and debarment. For a thorough treatment of the subject, we highly recommend the American Bar Association's Section of Public Contract Law's *Practitioner's Guide to Suspension and Debarment*. This monograph covers history, procedures, collateral effects, and, perhaps most importantly, avoidance techniques.

B. *Search Warrants*

In the context of the MAS Program, the Federal Government typically obtains the information it needs through its various contractual and audit powers. The contracting officer has a contractual right to request certain documents. The GSA OIG can issue a subpoena to obtain what it seeks. The Government Accountability Office ("GAO") has a regulatory right to review documents relating to contract performance. The DOJ uses civil discovery, OIG subpoenas, or Civil Investigative Demands to obtain documents. While all of these document-gathering tools are serious matters, each typically is employed by the Government in a civil (*i.e.*, non-criminal) context.

A search warrant, on the other hand, is a court order authorizing law enforcement officials to search (and remove) specific property for evidence *of a crime*. While very few MAS vendors ever find themselves the subject of a search warrant, the possibility exists in the context of any Government contract. Thus, MAS vendors, like all Government contractors, should know what steps to take if ever faced with Government agents—or any law enforcement personnel—attempting to execute a search warrant. The following steps (directed at the individual upon whom the warrant is served) have proven their worth over the years:

1. Contact the company's law department as soon as possible. Additionally, if asked to identify an individual to accompany the agents executing the warrant, take a company witness with you.

2. Politely inform the agents that the company does not consent to the search, but do not impede or obstruct the agents conducting the search *at any time.*

3. Politely request identification of the agent serving the warrant and all of the agents with him or her. (You have

the right to do this.) Also, ask the agent in charge whether each person is authorized to participate in the search. Record the name and affiliation (*e.g.*, FBI, GSA, DOD) of the person in charge. Ask each agent to sign in before entering the facility if that is company policy.

4. Ask the agent executing the warrant to produce a copy of the warrant and any related papers.

5. Review the warrant and ask the agent in charge whether you can have time to obtain advice with respect to the appropriate course of conduct. (Again, if the answer is no, do not obstruct the search.) Try to learn the nature of the investigation that prompted the search from the agent in charge. For example, ask what crimes are suspected and whether the company (as opposed to an individual) is the subject of the investigation. Additionally, pay attention to these elements of the warrant:

   - The premises covered
   - The specific documents and/or files covered
   - The allegations that are the subject of the warrant
   - The date the warrant was issued
   - If the search is being conducted after normal business hours, whether the warrant authorizes an after-hours search

6. Ask the agent in charge whether he or she is willing to postpone the search until after business hours (with appropriate safeguards against the destruction of evidence).

7. As soon as possible, instruct someone to contact the following individuals (the law department already should have been notified):

   - Each individual named in the warrant whose office is to be searched. Advise these individuals of the pending search and caution them *not* to remove, modify, or destroy anything

- Company headquarters
- Internal public relations department (in order to prepare for the press inquiries that inevitably follow a federal search and seizure)

8. Do not consent to an expansion of the search beyond the limits set forth in the warrant. Politely insist that the agents abide by the terms of the warrant. (Again, if the agents are insistent on expanding the scope of the search, do not obstruct their efforts. The attorney on the scene likely will contact the cognizant federal supervisory agent or Assistant United States Attorney.)

9. Assign someone to monitor each agent or group of agents. This individual should not get in the way of the agents, but should take notes as to where they search, what they remove, and anyone to whom they speak. If an agent objects to this activity, consult the agent in charge. Importantly, employees are *not* obligated to answer any substantive questions and *should not do so* before consulting counsel. To reduce the risk that agents will try to question employees, many companies have a policy of sending all non-essential personnel home upon the issuance of a warrant. If any employee does talk to the agents conducting the search, have at least one other company witness present at all times. And remember, all conversations with federal agents are "on the record."

10. Without obstructing the search, try to assess whether any of the documents covered by the warrant might be protected by the attorney-client privilege (*e.g.*, a document prepared by a company lawyer or written to a company lawyer). If you determine that privileged documents do fall within the scope of the warrant:

- Identify the privileged documents and their location to the agent in charge. Politely insist that the agent follow appropriate procedures to protect the privilege.

- Tell the agent in charge that you object to the seizure of privileged documents. Offer to segregate and preserve all privileged documents until the company's attorney can meet with the Government's attorney.
- If, notwithstanding these actions, the agent insists on removing the privileged documents, request that they be segregated and kept under seal until the court decides the issue. Maintain a copy or list of the documents seized.

11. At the conclusion of the search, ask for an inventory of all property seized. Additionally, preserve all notes that have been taken by company personnel regarding the documents seized, the locations from which the documents were taken, and conversations with or objections and requests lodged with the agents. Ask permission to keep a copy of all documents seized (including electronic media). Finally, if any of the seized documents are essential to day-to-day business, ask the agent in charge to grant you access to the documents after they have been removed.

In short, contact your law department immediately, take good notes, and cooperate, but do not consent.

C. _Subpoenas_

As discussed previously, a subpoena can find its way into the hands of a Schedule vendor through a number of channels. The GSA OIG and the VA OIG,[1139] the GAO,[1140] and a grand jury[1141] all can issue subpoenas. Whatever the channel, a subpoena must be taken seriously. Legal counsel should be contacted immediately and, in most cases, should coordinate the vendor's compliance efforts. In this context, counsel, among other things, will review the subpoena, attempt to establish a working relationship with the issuing agency, assess the viability of any legal objections, and oversee the vendor's efforts to comply with the terms of the subpoena in a timely fashion. The subsection entitled "Responding to Document Demands" in Chapter XXII discusses the steps that a vendor should employ when faced with a Government document request. These steps apply with additional force in the context of a subpoena.

D. *Other Applicable Statutes*

While countless other statutes are tangentially related to the MAS Program—*e.g.*, workplace safety statutes, environmental statutes, labor statutes—the following four statutes relate specifically to fraud and can be used to bring additional pressure to bear against MAS vendors (and, for that matter, any Government contractor) when necessary.

The *False Statements Act* (typically referred to as "1001"—a reference to its statutory citation, 18 U.S.C. § 1001) provides as follows:

> [W]hoever, in any matter within the jurisdiction [of any department or agency] of the United States knowingly and willfully falsifies, conceals, or covers up by any trick, scheme, or device a material fact, makes any materially false, fictitious or fraudulent statement or representation, or makes or uses any false writing or document knowing the same to contain any materially false, fictitious or fraudulent statement or entry, shall be fined under this title or imprisoned not more than five years, or both.[1142]

Unlike the False Claims Act, the False Statements Act requires no financial demand to have been made on the public fisc. As a result, an individual or company may violate the False Statements Act even where a contract ultimately is not awarded.

The *Program Fraud Civil Remedies Act* ("PFCRA")[1143] provides for double damages and penalties of up to $5,000 per claim for persons who submit false claims to the Government. The PFCRA also provides for a separate civil penalty ($5,000 per statement) for the submission of a false statement unrelated to a claim for payment. Designed for matters smaller than a typical False Claims Act case, the PFCRA covers false claims worth less than $150,000.[1144] The PFCRA provides for a federal investigation, a review, and a hearing before an Administrative Law Judge.[1145]

The _Major Fraud Act of 1988_ was intended to provide the Government with an additional criminal statute to employ in its fight against procurement fraud.[1146] This act provides for fines of $1,000,000 and/or not more than ten years' imprisonment for procurement fraud. These penalties are imposed upon persons who knowingly execute or attempt to execute a scheme to defraud the United States or obtain money or property by false representations for contracts of $1,000,000 or more.[1147] The fine may be as large as $5,000,000 if the gross loss to the Government or gain to the defendant is $500,000 or more or involved a "conscious or reckless of serious personal injury."[1148] Like the False Claims Act, the Major Fraud Act includes a _qui tam_ component, which encourages—and rewards—whistleblowers.[1149]

The _Mail and Wire Fraud Act_[1150] provides for fines and imprisonment of not more than five years for using the postal system, the telephone system, or electronic commerce to execute a fraudulent scheme. Since almost all MAS vendors rely upon one of these forms of communication either to take orders or fulfill orders, this statute, while infrequently employed, is frequently "in play."[1151] Penalties include a fine and/or imprisonment of up to five years.[1152]

* * *

While any of the foregoing statutes are intimidating on their own, the Government frequently combines statutes to bring additional pressure to bear upon suspected offenders. In this regard, the account of Nashua Corporation is telling. In 1984, Nashua pleaded guilty in federal court to making false statements to GSA officials in relation to a commercial price list. Nashua was given the maximum criminal penalty of $20,000 applicable to corporations. Prior to pleading guilty, however, Nashua paid the Government $1.5 million to settle a variety of civil claims relating to its alleged noncompliance with the terms and conditions of its MAS contract.

Notes:

[1102] The FAR requires that such sanctions should be imposed "only in the public interest for the Government's protection" and not to punish the contractor. FAR 9.402(b).

[1103] *See* FAR 9.405(a). Awards may be made to a debarred/suspended contractor if the agency head determines there are compelling reasons for the action.

[1104] FAR 9.405-1(a).

[1105] GOVERNMENT CONTRACTS REFERENCE BOOK 501.

[1106] FAR 9.406-2.

[1107] FAR 9.407-1(c).

[1108] FAR 9.407-1(b)(1).

[1109] FAR 9.407-1(b)(2).

[1110] FAR 9.407-1(b)(2), referring the contractor to FAR 9.406-1(a).

[1111] FAR 9.406-1(a).

[1112] FAR 9.407-3(c).

[1113] FAR 9.407-3(c)(5).

[1114] FAR 9.407-3(d)(1)-(3).

[1115] FAR 9.407-3(d)(3).

[1116] FAR 9.407-4(b) (2001) (twelve months plus a six-month extension, if approved).

[1117] Within GSA, the debarment official (who also is the suspension official) is the Associate Administrator for Acquisition Policy.

[1118] GOVERNMENT CONTRACTS REFERENCE BOOK 158.

[1119] FAR 9.406-2(b)(1)(i)(A), (B).

[1120] FAR 9.406-2(b)(1)(ii)-(iv) and (b)(2).

[1121] FAR 9.406-1(a).

[1122] *Id.*

[1123] FAR 9.407-1(b)(2).

[1124] FAR 9.406-1(b).

[1125] FAR 9.406-1(e).

[1126] FAR 9.405(a). Under FAR 9.405-1(b), a suspended or debarred contractor may not "place orders under optional use Federal Supply Schedule contracts, blanket purchase agreements, or basic ordering agreements . . . ."

[1127] FAR 9.406-4.

[1128] *The GSA Schedule*, Federal Publications Seminars LLC (2000), at 170.

[1129] *Id*. In addition to Harris, Digital Corporation paid $3.2 million and Tektronix, Inc. paid $5 million in 1993 to settle False Claims Act cases. Both companies avoided a debarment. *Id*. at 170.

[1130] *See* THE PRACTITIONER'S GUIDE TO SUSPENSION & DEBARMENT, Comm. on Debarment & Suspension, Sec. of Pub. Contract Law (A.B.A. 2d ed. 1996), at 37-38.

[1131] *See* policies for California's CMAS Program, Ohio's Administrative Rules, Utah's Procurement Code, and Florida Professional Consultant Qualifications.

[1132] FAR 9.404. The list may be accessed at *http://epls.arnet.gov.*

[1133] FAR 9.405(d)(1).

[1134] FAR 9.405-2. Subcontracts may be allowed if the agency head or designee states in writing that there is a compelling reason where the contracting officer's consent is required (FAR 9.405-2(a)) or if the prime contractor follows procedures listed at FAR 9.405-2(b) for subcontracts not requiring such approval.

[1135] FAR 9.408(b).

[1136] *See Lanier Agrees to Pay GSA $1 Million*, Washington Post, Mar. 3, 1984, at D8.

[1137] *Id*.

[1138] THE PRACTITIONER'S GUIDE TO SUSPENSION & DEBARMENT Preface, *supra* note 982.

[1139] 5 U.S.C. App. 3, § 6(a)(4).

[1140] The General Accounting Office Act of 1980 gives the GAO the authority to subpoena documents to which it has access by law or agreement (*i.e.*, under the Examination of Records Clause).

[1141] Fed. R. Crim. P. 17; Fed. R. Civ. P. 45. As a practical matter, federal prosecutors decide whether a grand jury issues a subpoena. *See, e.g., In re Grand Jury Proceedings (Schofield)*, 486 F.2d 85, 90 (3d Cir. 1973).

[1142] 18 U.S.C. § 1001(a)(1), (3).

[1143] 31 U.S.C. §§ 3801-3812.

[1144] *Id.* § 3803(c)(1)(2).

[1145] *Id.* § 3803.

[1146] Pub. L. No. 100-700, 102 Stat. 4631 (codified as amended at 18 U.S.C. § 1031).

[1147] 18 U.S.C. § 1031(a).

[1148] *Id.* § 1031(b).

[1149] The legislative history of the 1989 amendments to the Major Fraud Act equate its whistleblower provisions with the *qui tam* provisions of the False Claims Act. Pub. L. No. 101-123, 1989 U.S.C.C.A.N. (103 Stat. 759) 593, 594.

[1150] 18 U.S.C. § 1341 *et seq.*

[1151] Additionally, a vendor that violates the Mail and Wire Fraud Act also may find itself in violation of the Racketeer Influenced Corrupt Organizations Act. 18 U.S.C. § 1961 *et seq.*

[1152] 18 U.S.C. § 1341.

XXV.

PREVENTING PROBLEMS
BEFORE THEY OCCUR

"Penny wise, pound foolish."

-Robert Burton

While a vendor cannot prevent an audit, investigation, or False Claims Act lawsuit, it can take action well in advance that can help to mitigate the negative effects of such an experience if and when it occurs. Clearly, the most straightforward path toward this goal is through strict contract compliance. Plain and simple. Compliance alone, however, typically is not enough and even the most scrupulous Schedule vendor can find itself expending significant resources in response to charges that could have been avoided (or at least mitigated) with proper advance planning. Adopting the following six steps can help save significant time, resources, and money.

A. *Negotiate The Contract Carefully*

While the boilerplate terms and conditions of a Schedule contract generally are not negotiable, other key provisions are. A vendor's "relevant category of customers" and its "discount relationship," for example, clearly are negotiable. Likewise, a vendor may attempt to negotiate the value of the maximum order threshold applicable to its Schedule contract. Vendors that take care to negotiate terms that they are able—and willing—to live up to will be rewarded in the end. On the other hand, vendors that fail to take advantage of legitimate negotiation opportunities often find themselves paying for that oversight.

B. *Hire, Retain, And Train Competent Employees*

A vendor that entrusts the administration of its Schedule contract to well-trained, competent individuals will find that the retention of such individuals pays unexpected dividends. An employee who is able to explain, honestly, accurately, and in plain English, the vendor's record keeping system, invoicing policies, and industrial funding fee reporting procedures (to name just three areas of concern to the Office of Inspector General ("OIG")) will do wonders to accelerate the pace of an audit. (As a general rule, a short audit is a good audit.)

C. *Adopt And Adhere To Written Policies And Procedures*

Well-settled, well-written, and well-understood policies and procedures are a must for any Schedule vendor—not only as a means of ensuring contract compliance, but also as a signal to an auditor that the vendor runs a "clean shop." The absence of such policies and procedures will almost guarantee that an auditor will take a particularly hard look at the vendor's actual practices. Likewise, sloppily drafted policies and procedures will prompt a similar auditor response.

The existence of well-written policies, however, is only the beginning. Such policies must be publicized to all cognizant company personnel; they must be incorporated into a regular training program; and, importantly, they must be reviewed and revised as regulations and/or internal company practices change. Policies that are outdated and incompatible with actual company practices present as great a risk as—and, in some ways, a greater risk than—failing to have policies in the first place.

D. _Keep Adequate And Organized Records_

The importance of adequate record keeping is unquestionable. A system that incorporates clear policies, efficient procedures, adequate document retention, and proper oversight not only will help ensure compliance with the contract's various reporting requirements, but also will permit the vendor to respond quickly and adequately to an auditor's requests for data.

E. _Develop An Ethics/Compliance Plan_

While few major companies are without a formal ethics/ compliance plan, many small companies do not feel the need for even a simple written Code of Conduct. To put it bluntly, these companies are being imprudent. An ethics/compliance plan that incorporates time-honored components (several excellent articles have been written setting forth these standard components) and to which the management of the company is committed will enhance a vendor's ability to comply with the terms and conditions of its Schedule contract. In addition, such a plan is further evidence to an auditor that he or she is investigating an honest company. Moreover, should an OIG audit take an unfortunate turn, the existence of an ethics/compliance plan may be viewed as a mitigating factor by a suspension or debarring official.

F. _Conduct Internal Reviews_

While not without its exceptions, a useful rule of thumb in contracting with the Federal Government is that it is better for a vendor to identify its shortcomings on its own than to have the Government identify those shortcomings for it. The most effective means of putting this rule into practice is by conducting an internal review.

Internal reviews come in many shapes and sizes. Some are broadly constituted while others are narrowly tailored. Some are performed by in-house personnel while others are conducted by outside lawyers. Some go on for months while others begin and end within a week. Whatever their shape or size, all have a common purpose: to look inside the company's closets and see what ghosts are lurking there.

Before conducting an internal review, however, a vendor *must* be ready to react to whatever ghosts it finds. Whatever exposure a vendor faces as a result of failing to comply with the terms and conditions of its MAS contracts expands geometrically the moment those failures become known. Thus, identifying an internal problem without then taking the necessary steps to remedy that problem is, in legal terms, a "really bad move."

Once a vendor makes the decision to open its closets and take a peek inside, the next step is to decide whether to venture in alone or engage a professional, *i.e.*, a lawyer or a consultant. There are advantages and disadvantages to each. Performing a self-audit is usually the most cost effective as long as the individual(s) responsible for the audit are well trained and competent. In all but the smallest companies, however, a self-audit probably is not the best approach. It may save money initially, but the risks are significant. First, many auditors for commercially oriented enterprises are not trained in the complexities of Government contracts. Second, company personnel typically react more openly and honestly to outside attorneys or consultants. Third, and perhaps most importantly, the information produced during the course of a non-law department managed self-audit is *not* protected by the attorney-client privilege or the attorney work product doctrine. Thus, all such information potentially will have to be turned over to the Government in the course of a federal audit or investigation.[1153]

This is not to say, however, that a self-audit is never a good idea. For a small company without the financial means to bring in outside counsel, or for a company of any size seeking to conduct a basic pre-award audit or to review only a very limited slice of its organization, a self-audit just might be the right thing. In such cases, the Coalition for Government Procurement publishes a terrific self-audit manual that should be on the bookshelf of any vendor contemplating a self-audit. In most cases, a vendor's in-house attorney will know whether or not a self-audit will suffice.

An important caution, however. If a vendor chooses to go the self-audit route, legal counsel should be brought in immediately if the self-audit discloses potential "knowing" wrongdoing. The Coalition for Government Procurement describes it this way:

> If the self audit has discovered any evidence of transactions or disclosures that involved potential wrongdoing, such as any "knowledge" or intent on the part of the company or any employee of the company to supply the government with fraudulent information, *the contractor should immediately contact experienced counsel to explore possible legal defenses to a likely civil or criminal investigation.*[1154]

As any vendor that has gone through a federal audit or investigation will acknowledge, the Coalition's emphasis in this regard is not overstated.

One step beyond a self-audit is an internal review performed by a consultant. Many consultants are quite experienced in conducting such reviews of MAS vendors. Many, however, are not. Appendix I lists the names of some consultants with whom we have had positive past experiences. Vendors must keep in mind, though, that consultants are *not* lawyers; and, thus, their work product, if not generated for or under the direction of counsel, is not protected by the attorney-client privilege or the attorney work product doctrine.

Finally, many cases call for the involvement of legal counsel. Whether in the context of a vendor that suspects that it has ghosts in its closets or a vendor that wants to be absolutely sure that its closets are clean, larger MAS vendors frequently involve legal counsel experienced in performing internal investigations. While more expensive in the short term than a self-audit or an audit performed by an outside consultant, many vendors believe that the protections offered by an experienced law firm are worth the extra expense. Specifically:

- An experienced attorney can advise a vendor's management with respect to the decisions it faces—and the business and legal risks inherent in each—in the event a problem is uncovered during the course of the review.
- An attorney's work product, interview notes, findings, and correspondence with, and recommendations to, management generally are protected from disclosure to the Government by the attorney-client privilege and the attorney work product doctrine.[1155]
- The existence of an internal investigation conducted by an experienced law firm may be used by a suspension/debarment official as evidence of a responsible vendor.

While many law firms will be willing to conduct an internal investigation on behalf of a MAS vendor, a suitable law firm must have experience conducting *procurement-related* investigations. An in-house law department will be able to identify such a firm.

* * *

While the foregoing principles will not guarantee that any GSA audit proceeds swiftly and painlessly, they will better the odds for the vendor that takes them to heart (and, more importantly, puts them to use) prior to the commencement of performance or, at a minimum, well in advance of the OIG's arrival on its doorstep.

Notes:

[1153] *See United States v. Westinghouse Elec. Co.*, 788 F.2d 164 (3d Cir. 1986) (holding that OIG subpoena extended to a contractor's internal audit reports).

[1154] MULTIPLE AWARD SCHEDULE SELF AUDIT MANUAL: A PRACTICAL WORKBOOK FOR GUIDANCE IN CONDUCTING CORPORATE INTERNAL AUDITS 64-65 (Coalition for Gov't Procurement, rev. 1999) (emphasis in original).

[1155] *See, e.g., In re Grand Jury Subpoena*, 599 F.2d 504, 510-11 (2d Cir. 1979) (holding that, to fall within the attorney-client privilege, an internal audit report must be for legal rather than managerial purposes).

XXVI.

MISCELLANEOUS MATTERS

"O mother
what have I left out
O mother
what have I forgotten . . . ."

-Allen Ginsburg, *Kaddish*

A. *Freedom Of Information Act (FOIA) Considerations*

M any MAS vendors believe that the information they submit to the Government will be seen only by authorized Government officials. Unfortunately, this is not always the case. Indeed, much of the information vendors submit to the Government is not protected at all. The primary reason for this lack of protection is the existence of the Freedom of Information Act,[1156] commonly referred to as "FOIA."

Since 1966, FOIA has afforded any person the right to obtain records created or held by a federal agency, subject to nine exemptions.[1157] Initially conceived to promote openness in governmental affairs, FOIA has grown into a powerful weapon for the acquisition of legal business intelligence. Companies (both within and outside the MAS Program) regularly employ FOIA to learn more about their competitors. Like many elements of Government contracting, however, FOIA is a double-edged sword that can be used by a competitor against a vendor just as well as it can be used by the vendor against the competitor. In this light, understanding how FOIA works serves a dual purpose. It can help a vendor learn more about its competitors while, at the same time, protect its own proprietary information to the maximum extent possible.

Ironically, because its language is so broad, the heart of FOIA is in its exceptions. While FOIA presumes that a document in the hands of the Government is releasable to the public, it includes several powerful "exemptions" that permit certain classes of documents to be kept from the public's inquiring eyes. From the perspective of a MAS vendor, the most important of these exemptions is Exemption 4, which protects "trade secrets and commercial or financial information obtained from a person [that is] privileged or confidential."[1158]

Documents falling within the scope of Exemption 4 typically comprise confidential commercial or financial information, such as business sales statistics, research data, technical designs, overhead and operating costs, and information on a company's financial condition.[1159] The full scope of Exemption 4, however, is unresolved.[1160] Different agencies take different positions regarding the releasability of documents. GSA, for example, has stated that it will release all pricing information concerning a contract in the face of a FOIA request.[1161] Other agencies embrace FOIA less warmly. DOJ and DOD go so far as to authorize the release of much contractor information *without* notification to the contractor.[1162] These policies, however, are being challenged in court as discussed later in this chapter.

Regardless of the agency involved, the courts have developed a two-pronged test for determining whether information is "confidential" within the meaning of Exemption 4.[1163] In order to be exempt from public disclosure under Exemption 4, the entity seeking protection must demonstrate that disclosure of the information sought is likely (1) "to impair the Government's ability to obtain necessary information in the future" or (2) "to cause substantial harm to the competitive position of the person from whom the information was obtained."[1164] This two-pronged test was reaffirmed in 1992 by the D.C. Circuit.[1165]

As a general rule, information that is submitted voluntarily to the Government will be afforded greater protection under the first prong of Exemption 4 than information submitted involuntarily.[1166] It is unresolved, however, whether information submitted to the Government in response to a Government solicitation is considered voluntary or involuntary.[1167] Most likely, courts will consider such information to have been submitted *in*voluntarily.[1168]

In *Mallinckrodt Inc. v. West*, a FOIA decision of particular interest to MAS vendors, the U.S. District Court for the District of Columbia, on June 22, 2000, found that the Department of Veterans Affairs ("VA") was prohibited from disclosing the rebates and incentives offered a particular Schedule vendor because the information was shielded from disclosure under Exemption 4. The VA had made a decision to disclose the vendor's rebate and incentive information to a competitor. The court overturned this decision after finding that the information had been submitted to the Government "involuntarily."[1169]

Finally, on September 7, 2001, the District Court for the District of Columbia dealt a severe blow to the DOJ's Office of Information and Privacy policy, which required the release of contract unit prices without notification to the contractor. In deciding a combination of reverse FOIA cases, the court overturned GSA's decision to release detailed pricing information in response to a FOIA request.[1170] In addition, the court held that agencies may not release unit pricing information in response to a FOIA request if the information is confidential or trade secret information under Exemption 4.[1171] The court ruled that changes to FAR Part 15 did not change the nature of confidential information or the way its release should be handled. In reaching this conclusion the court relied upon the District of Columbia Circuit's prior ruling against the Government on the issue of releasing contract unit prices without notification.[1172]

Regardless of the legal complexities that will continue to surround the issue of FOIA, vendors should be aware that the information they consider confidential may not be afforded protection by GSA. Because of this uncertainty, vendors would be well advised to take the following steps to afford their proprietary data the maximum protection possible:

- Disclose proprietary information to the Government only where necessary.
- Label all documents submitted to the Government (including routine contractual correspondence) that contain proprietary information as follows:

"PROPRIETARY AND CONFIDENTIAL NOT SUBJECT TO RELEASE UNDER FOIA SUBJECT TO THE TRADE SECRETS ACT"

This legend alone does not bring a document within an exemption to FOIA, but it does prompt the official reviewing the information in response to a FOIA request to pay close attention to the material.[1173]

- Restrict access to proprietary information to individuals with a "need to know." This not only will help protect information generally, but it also is a specific question that courts ask when assessing whether information truly is proprietary.
- Respond professionally, firmly, and *quickly* to any Government notice that a third party has requested access to your proprietary information. If release of the information sought would damage the vendor's interest, then legal counsel should be involved in drafting the response to the agency.

While these steps will not preclude the release of proprietary information, they will (1) reduce the likelihood of an inadvertent release and (2) place the vendor in a stronger position to argue in favor of precluding release if the situation arises.

B. *The Trade Secrets Act*

Some of the information a vendor submits to the Government in the course of contract negotiation or contract compliance may be protected from disclosure by the terms of the Trade Secrets Act.[1174] The Trade Secrets Act ensures the confidentiality of all sorts of information (including financial, business, scientific, technical, economic, and engineering information), regardless of the medium in which it is memorialized, so long as:

> (A) The owner [of the information] has taken reasonable measures to keep such information secret; and
> (B) The information derives independent economic value, actual or potential, from not being generally known to, and not being readily ascertainable through proper means by, the public . . . . [1175]

Any organization or individual (even a Government official) who knowingly discloses a vendor's trade secret information to an unauthorized party may be subject to criminal penalties, including fines and, at least for the individual(s) involved, jail time.[1176] Information releasable under FOIA is *not* protected by the Trade Secrets Act.[1177] Conversely, it has been held that the Trade Secrets Act prohibits the release of any information falling within Exemption 4 to the FOIA.[1178]

C. *Reverse Auctions*

In a clear sign of the times, the MAS Program recently ventured into the world of "on-line reverse auctions." Indeed, on-line reverse auctions continue to gain increasing popularity as a method for Government agencies to obtain the most competitive prices.

In a reverse auction, the Government issues a solicitation and then, during a finite time frame, accepts bids via the Internet.

Each offeror's bid price is displayed for all to see. Offerors are permitted—indeed they are encouraged—to revise their bids as they see their competitors' lower bids displayed. This revision process continues until the end of the pre-announced time period. The lowest bid submitted by that time is awarded the contract. Obviously, this process varies significantly from the normal way the Government purchases supplies and services.

Beyond the obvious, the reverse auction approach to Government procurement differs from the traditional approach in that the Government is a bystander throughout most of the process. A third party handles the actual receipt and posting of offers and, in some cases, even "qualifies" the prospective bidders.

The private sector has been experimenting with this form of buying with significant success. A few states have given it a whirl, also with success. Pennsylvania, for example, claims to have saved $8.5 million through the use of on-line auctions.[1179] GSA announced its plans to enter the reverse auction marketplace in March 2000. In May 2000, GSA added reverse auctions to its list of services available through the MAS Program. More recently, GSA's Federal Technology Service launched an e-portal at *http://www.buyers.gov*, which describes itself as "the Government Business and Auction exchange." The web site offers federal agencies assistance in reverse auctions and other electronic purchasing techniques.

For all its benefits, however, the reverse auction phenomenon is not without its shortcomings. Many vendors object to having their bids disclosed to their competitors, fearing that such a disclosure would reveal too much about the vendors.[1180] There also has been some question as to the legality of reverse auctions. Prior to 1997, the FAR explicitly prohibited reverse auctions.[1181] But, in 1997, the prohibition was deleted, and the FAR now is silent on the subject. Finally, there also has been some concern expressed that reverse auctions, while economically efficient, will result in a reduction in the quality of the supplies and services procured by the Government.[1182]

D. *Corporate Contracts (Consolidated Contracts)*

In June of 2000, Schedule vendors holding multiple Schedule contracts were given the option of entering into a single "Corporate Contract."[1183] Corporate Contracting allowed vendors to offer their entire product line through a single Schedule. While GSA touted Corporate Contracting as a cost-effective gateway to the federal marketplace for vendors[1184] and a means to reduce the market research burdens of user agencies,[1185] the program was not widely used.

The original rule permitted Schedule holders to migrate to a Corporate Contract at their option.[1186] In the event of a migration, GSA would cancel each of the vendor's current Schedule contracts after the migration and, simultaneously, issue a single new Corporate Contract.[1187] (Corporate Contracts did not affect small business set-asides.[1188])

In October 2003, GSA announced an effort to reform the Corporate Contracting Program because, in the words of the Assistant Commissioner of GSA's Federal Supply Service, the program had "not lived up to expectations."[1189] At the time of the submission of this manuscript to the publisher, details regarding the modified program were still in short supply.

E. *Bankruptcy*

In the unfortunate event of a bankruptcy, a vendor must fulfill certain obligations. First, the vendor must notify its contracting officer of the bankruptcy proceedings so that the contracting officer can take steps to protect the Government's interests.[1190] For example, upon receiving such notification, the contracting officer must notify the appropriate Acquisition Center director, certain personnel from the GSA Office of Finance, and the cognizant Administrative Contracting Officer ("ACO").[1191] From the Government's point of view, prompt notification to the ACO is particularly important as the ACO administers the industrial funding fee ("IFF") and vendors in a precarious financial position may have missed one or more IFF payments. Once the ACO is apprised of the bankruptcy, it is the ACO's responsibility to ensure that GSA legal counsel is notified and a "Proof of Claim" is filed in a timely manner. A Proof of Claim is required to ensure that the Government's claim is valid and to receive notices regarding the bankruptcy proceedings. [1192] If the ACO is notified of the bankruptcy directly by the vendor, he or she immediately should notify the contracting officer and legal counsel.

A contracting officer who has reason to suspect that a vendor is failing financially should refer to FAR Subpart 42.9 and GSAR Subpart 542.9 for guidance.

Notes:

[1156] 5 U.S.C. § 552.

[1157] Department of Justice Freedom of Information Act Guide, May 2000, *available at http://www.ojp.usdoj.gov/foia.htm.*

[1158] 5 U.S.C. § 552(b)(4).

[1159] *See, e.g., Judicial Watch, Inc. v. Export-Import Bank,* 108 F. Supp. 2d 19, 24 (D.D.C. 2000) (describing Exemption 4).

[1160] For a more complete discussion of the issue and its history, *see* Jonathan S. Aronie, John W. Chierichella & James J. McCullough, *When is Information Confidential?*, CONTRACT MANAGEMENT (Nov. 2000), at 56. The ongoing tug-of-war between the Government and the courts over FOIA's Exemption 4 leaves contracts professionals in a bind.

[1161] Four suits were filed in April-May 2000 by Worldcom, Sprint, AT&T, and Bell Atlantic in response to a decision by GSA to release contractor unit pricing under multiyear contracts without prior notice to the affected contractors.

[1162] *See Unit Price FOIA Officers Conference,* U.S. Department of Justice, Office of Information and Privacy Memorandum (Feb. 24, 2000); and *DOD Policy Concerning Release of Unit Prices Under the FOIA,* DOD Memorandum 00-CORR-025, Directorate for Freedom of Information and Security Review (Wash., D.C.: DOD, Mar. 3, 2000).

[1163] *National Parks & Conservation Ass'n v. Morton,* 498 F.2d 765 (D.C. Cir. 1974).

[1164] *Id.* at 770.

[1165] *Critical Mass Energy Project v. Nuclear Regulatory Comm'n*, 975 F.2d 871 (D.C. Cir. 1992). Note also that information provided to the Government *voluntarily* often is entitled to greater protection. *See also Mallinckrodt Inc. v. West*, 140 F. Supp. 2d 1 (D.D.C. 2000) (Mem. Op.), *available at* 2000 U.S. Dist. LEXIS 11008). *See* FFHSJ Government Contract Alertä News Brief No. 00-7-6, portions of which are reproduced in this section, *available at http:// www.ffhsj.com/govtcon/ffgalert/Index.html.*

[1166] *Critical Mass*, 975 F.2d at 872 (lower threshold to qualify for Exemption 4 protection for information submitted voluntarily).

[1167] *See* Aronie, Chierichella & McCullough, *supra* note 1012.

[1168] *See Mallinckrodt*, 2000 U.S. Dist. LEXIS 11008, at *11 ("[I]t is beyond dispute that unit pricing data is required to be submitted in order to compete for a government contract and would therefore be disclosable . . . .").

[1169] *See Critical Mass*, 975 F.2d at 872. Financial or commercial information provided to the Government on a voluntary basis is exempt from disclosure under Exemption 4 "if it is of a kind that the provider would not customarily make available to the public."

[1170] *MCI Worldcom, Inc. v. GSA*, No. 00-914 (Mem. Op.) (D.D.C. Sept. 7, 2001).

[1171] Portions of this discussion are taken from FFHSJ Government Contracts Alertä News Brief No. 01-9-5.

[1172] *McDonnell Douglas Corp. v. NASA*, 180 F.3d 303, 305 (D.C. Cir. 1999) (If information falls within Exemption 4, the Government is precluded from releasing it under the Trade Secrets Act.). Five years later, the District of Columbia Circuit reached the same conclusion with regard to the disclosure of unit prices and option prices in *McDonnell Douglas Corp. v. Air Force*, 375 F.3d 1182 (D.C. Cir. 2004).

[1173] Rather than labeling every page of a document as being proprietary and confidential, vendors should consider labeling the first page of the document and then only those particular pages that contain proprietary information in order to avoid a "boy who cried wolf" scenario in the eyes of the Government FOIA officer.

[1174] 18 U.S.C. § 1831 *et seq.*

[1175] *Id.* § 1839(3)(A), (B).

[1176] *Id.* § 1832.

[1177] *Id.* § 1838.

[1178] *See McDonnell Douglas*, 180 F.3d at 305; *CNA Fin. Corp. v. Donovan*, 830 F.2d 1132, 1151 (D.C. Cir. 1987) (The Scope of the Trade Secrets Act is "at least co-extensive with that of Exemption 4 of FOIA.")

[1179] William Matthews, *Bold New Bid*, FEDERAL COMPUTER WEEK 30 (Apr. 17, 2000).

[1180] *Id.* at 28.

[1181] *Id.*

[1182] *Id.*

[1183] *See* Solicitation No. FCO-00-CORP-0000C.

[1184] *Id.*

[1185] *See* Procurement Information Bulletin 98-14 (July 22, 1998).

[1186] Vendors cannot hold both a Corporate Contract and an individual MAS contract at the same time. *See* Solicitation FCO-00-CORP-0000C.

[1187] GSA Procurement Information Bulletin 98-14 (July 22, 1998) and GSA Procurement Information Bulletin 98-20 (Sept. 28, 1998) provide instructions to contracting officers on effecting the merger or transition of contracts. Vendors' Corporate Contracts become effective and their existing contracts will be canceled on the first day of the first month of the next established standard sales quarter (*i.e.*, January, April, July, October).

[1188] GSA Procurement Information Bulletin 98-20 (Sept. 28, 1998).

[1189] "GSA to Change Corporate Schedule Program," FEDERAL COMPUTER WEEK, Oct. 29, 2003 (quoting Mr. Neal Fox).

[1190] FAR 52.242-13.

[1191] *See* GSA Procurement Information Bulletin 99-16 (Nov. 19, 1999) for other parties to be notified and directives to be followed.

[1192] *Id.*

XXVII.

RESEARCH SURVIVAL GUIDE FOR THE NON-GOVERNMENT CONTRACTS PRACTITIONER

(by G. Diane Sandford and Cynthia B. Curling, Fried Frank Harris Shriver & Jacobson)

"When you steal from one author, it's plagiarism;
if you steal from many, it's research."
-Wilson Mizner

The words "maze of federal regulations" are often heard in the context of Government contracting, and for good reason. Federal contracts are extremely complex because of the interrelationship of general and individual agency regulations and the nuances introduced by agency publications and decisions. Think of this as the quick and dirty guide to that maze. Using the information in this chapter, you will be able to find and update general and agency-specific federal regulations as well as find decisions.

This guide highlights essential research resources and seeks to provide an understanding of some of the more arcane terminology involved. While this chapter should enable you to answer basic questions, we highly recommend seeking the advice of an expert for complex issues. This guide also refers you to basic sources for more information, such as consultants, associations, and publications. (The Vendor Resource Guide at the conclusion of this book provides additional research resources.)

A. *General Federal Regulations—The Federal Acquisition Regulation*

The Federal Acquisition Regulation ("FAR") constitutes the primary body of law with which a vendor must comply whenever it contracts with agencies from the federal executive branch. It is supplemented by additional regulations from individual agencies, but never superseded by them. Until the 1980s, regulations covering federal contracts were relatively scattered, and the FAR was put into effect to bring some order to the chaos. As with other agency regulations, changes to the FAR are officially published in print as proposed and then as final regulations in the *Federal Register*. For a compiled version of the FAR that incorporates changes from the *Register*, use the *Code of Federal Regulations* ("*CFR*"). The *CFR* is the official Government publication in which final regulations are codified by subject over time. Within the *CFR*, the FAR can be found at Title 48, chapter 1. The FAR is also available through commercial publishers such as Commerce Clearing House, via fee-based on-line services such as Lexis and Westlaw, and through many free web sites such as *http://www.arnet.gov*. For further information, see the Vendor Resource Guide.

Be aware that the compiled print editions *and* electronic versions will probably need updating and that the *Federal Register* (in print or electronic format) is the best place to go to be absolutely sure that you have the most recent changes. However, some updates may appear on an agency web site prior to official publication in the *Federal Register*. Changes to the FAR are also announced in *Federal Acquisition Circulars* ("*FACs*") shortly after they become available in the *Federal Register*. Recent *FACs* are available at *http://www.arnet.gov/far/*.

B. *Updating The Federal Acquisition Regulation*

There are several methods to ensure that a section of the FAR is current. One inexpensive and efficient way is to use the FAR home page at *http://www.arnet.gov/far*. That site will give you a fairly current version of the FAR, as well as access to the most recent updates in the *FACs*. Though the FAR is marked "current" and includes amendments from the *FACs* effective as of a particular date, more recent *FACs* may have updated your section. To check, you can use either the *FACs* as published in looseleaf format or in the *Federal Register*—both are available from the FAR home page. The better option of the two, however, is the *Federal Register* format. Both contain the same information, but dates in the looseleaf format may be confusing. The *Federal Register* format clearly shows the issue number of each *FAC* and the date of its release. To see dates in the looseleaf format, you must open the *FAC* in question. Once you are in the body of the document (in either format), you will be able to see when the text from the update becomes effective.

> *Note:* Do not be deceived by the issue numbers of the *FACs*. The issues look as if they are numbered by year, but they are *not*. For example, it is tempting to assume that *FAC* 97-26 would be the twenty-sixth release during the year 1997. Instead, it is actually dated May 16, 2001. You *must* open the *FAC* to see the date of the issue unless you are using the *Federal Register* format.

A bonus of the FAR home page is that, in addition to the regulations and updates, it also lists proposed changes, archived versions, GSA forms, an index, an appendix, and more. Together, these extra features make the FAR home page the first place to visit when you have a question about the regulations.

A second option is to use a fee-based service such as Lexis or Westlaw. The *CFR* on both Lexis and Westlaw is updated more often than its print counterpart, though it may still not be completely current. On Westlaw, a line at the top of the document will indicate the currency of the text. If a section has been amended after that time (possibly a month or more), there will be a "jump marker" that links to the amendment. On Lexis, the *CFR* sections are updated slightly more often than on Westlaw, but you may still need to check for amendments. In Lexis, you must search the *Federal Register* from the date of the last revision of your section to find updates. If you do not have an account on Lexis or Westlaw yourself, to be absolutely current you may want to consult with an expert who does or consider a limited access account yourself. Both services have extensive collections of these and many other current Government contracts materials as well as older documents.

A third option is to subscribe to an updated print service covering the FAR. The U.S. Government Printing Office offers a FAR subscription that is updated by *FACs*, though as mentioned above, by the time the *FACs* are issued, the actual changes will have already been published in the *Federal Register*. Alternatively, the GSA offers an e-mail update service that will inform you of new *FACs*, proposed rules, public meetings, and other FAR-related issues of interest. Sign up for that e-mail service at *http://www.arnet.gov/far/mailframe.html*.

A more current and comprehensive, but also more expensive option, is offered by Commerce Clearing House ("CCH"). The *Government Contracts Report* on CD-ROM (updated monthly) and the web (updated more frequently, often within days of changes) contains up-to-date regulatory texts, news, analysis, related cases, and more. Most of the CCH materials on Government contracting are also available on-line through Lexis. Unfortunately, print versions of the FAR are not updated as frequently. For instance, CCH issues paperbound versions of the FAR only twice each year.

If you are working with a limited budget, you may prefer to update using the official print or web-based versions of the *CFR*, the *List of Sections Affected* (*LSA*), and the *Federal Register*. These resources will be available in print at any major law library. Web versions are available as follows:

> CFR—*http://www.access.gpo.gov/nara/cfr/index.html*
> LSA—*http://www.access.gpo.gov/nara/lsa/aboutlsa.html*
> Federal Register—*http://www.access.gpo.gov/su_docs/ aces/aces140.html*

The process for updating each format is similar since the web versions are only as current as their print counterparts. Using the web does, however, give you two advantages. It is more generally accessible, and it is searchable, though search capability is rudimentary. The instructions below pertain to updating print regulations, but can also be used for Internet updating. Simply keep in mind that the dates referred to on the cover pages of the print publications will be listed on the main pages of the web versions.

To update a regulation or to find proposed changes:

1. Find the text of the regulation in the *CFR*; note the revision date on the cover of the volume.
2. Check the most recent pamphlet entitled *LSA: List of CFR Sections Affected*. This is usually available with any full print set of the *CFR*. Entries in the *LSA* are organized by *CFR* part and refer to *Federal Register* pages. Compare the date on your *CFR* volume to the date listed on the *LSA* title page. [This will tell you the currency of the *List of Sections Affected*.]
3. Check the list of "*CFR* Parts Affected" for months not covered by step 2 to find out about any more recent changes. This list appears at the end of the *Federal Register* every day and is cumulative for that month. The last day of the month, therefore, will contain the complete list of changes for the entire month.
4. If the last day of the month has not yet passed, you must also check the list of "*CFR* Parts Affected" at the end of

the last issue of the *Federal Register* available for the current month.

5. Using the citations found in the above steps, if any, check the *Federal Register* at the cited pages to see the text of the changes.

As mentioned above, regulatory issues can be extremely complex. Once you have obtained a current copy of the regulation, you may still have questions. If so, we recommend that you contact an expert for further advice.

C. *Superseded Regulations*

Government contracting questions concerning contracts awarded prior to the date the FAR became effective (April 1, 1984) must be researched in one of several superseded regulations:

- 1948-80—Armed Services Procurement Regulation ("ASPR")
- 1980-84—Defense Acquisition Regulation ("DAR")
- 1949-84—Federal Procurement Regulations ("FPR")
- 1965-96—Federal Information Resources Management Regulation ("FIRMR")

Unfortunately, older versions of regulations are not readily available in print or on the web. Instead, superseded regulation research will probably necessitate a trip to a large library or access to a fee-based information service.

D. *Agency Specific Regulations*

In addition to the general federal materials, there are many agency specific materials that bear on Government contracts.

FAR Supplements are additional regulations promulgated by individual agencies that supplement the FAR but that are specific to the procurement issues of that agency. They can not supersede or re-state the FAR, only add to it. The supplements are available in Title 48 of the CFR, chapters 2 through 57 and may be relevant to a Schedule procurement as long as they do not conflict with the terms of the MAS Program.

The major supplements are the Defense FAR Supplement (DFARS), available at Title 48 of the CFR, chapter 2; the National Aeronautics and Space Administration FAR Supplement ("NFS"), available at Title 48 of the CFR, chapter 18; and the GSA FAR Supplement ("GSAM"), available at Title 48 of the CFR, chapter 5. A complete list of the remaining supplements is available with web links to their texts at *http://www.law.gwu.edu/ burns/research/gcrg/gcrg.htm* in *The Practitioners' Research Guide: Researching Government Contracts Law on the Internet.*

E. *Other Regulatory Issues*

Supplies manufactured under Government contracts are sometimes exported from the United States. Contractors dealing with the export of certain supplies and technology must comply with U.S. export control laws and their implementing regulations. Two principal laws govern the export of American products, technology, and services: (1) the Export Administration Act of 1979 ("EAA") and (2) the Arms Export Control Act of 1976 ("AECA").

- The EAA, administered by the Department of Commerce and implemented through the Export Administration Regulations, focuses on items that have both civilian and limited military applications. The AECA, administered by the Department of State and implemented through the International Traffic in Arms Regulation, deals with items that are determined to be inherently military in nature.
- The U.S. Customs Office of Regulations and Rulings is responsible for providing informed compliance information

to members of the trade community. Primary among its many functions is provision of policy and technical support concerning the application of laws, regulations, and procedures administered by Customs. These include rulings and guidelines relating to the classification and value of merchandise, entry, licensing, intellectual property rights, restricted merchandise, and disclosure law. Customs rulings and regulations are available on the web along with many other Customs-related materials at *http://www.customs.ustreas.gov/impoexpo/ impoexpo.htm*. Customs Administration Rulings (Headquarter Series and New York Series) are available in Lexis and Westlaw. If you have more than a very basic exporting or importing question, we recommend that you consult a legal expert.

F. *Other Important Federal Materials*

In addition to regulations, you must also be aware of publications from federal administrative agencies concerned in the contract process such as the GSA.

The GSA produces a variety of publications that bear on Government contracting. These are typical for administrative agencies and include:

- Schedules—The source for the latest GSA Schedules contract award information is the GSA Schedules E-Library at *http://www.fsa.gsa.gov/schedules/*. The GSA also provides a contractor's guide to the Schedules at *http://www.fss.gsa.gov/vendorguide/*.
- Solicitations—These are details of contracts up for bids and requests for proposals. They are published, along with solicitations from other agencies, in *Commerce Business Daily*, a GPO publication available at *http:// cbdnet.access.gpo.gov/* and in FedBizOpps available at *http://www.FedBizOpps.gov*.

- Manuals—The *General Services Administration Acquisition Manual* ("*GSAM*") incorporates the *General Services Administration Acquisition Regulation* ("*GSAR*") as well as internal agency acquisition policy. The *GSAM* and its updates are available online at *http://www.arnet.gov/GSAM/gsam.html*.
- Policy papers—Policy papers are documents that interpret current regulations or bear on the development of future regulations. An index to GSA's policy, guidelines, regulations, and best practices is available at *http://www.gsa.gov/Portal/main.jsp?catcode=1-4-0-0-0-0*.

Sometimes policy papers or other internal agency documents can best be obtained with a Freedom of Information Act ("FOIA") request. For the GSA, two such examples are:

- FSS Acquisition Letters—Letters issued from the General Services Administration's Federal Supply Service, by the Assistant Commissioner, Office of Acquisition. FSS Acquisition Letters provide guidance on various policies and provide information on new solicitation/contract clauses and implementation requirements.
- Procurement Information Bulletins ("PIBs")—These bulletins announce important policy changes to internal procurement personnel. They are issued from the GSA's Federal Supply Service, by the Director of the FSS Acquisition Management Center. PIBs provide information and guidance to contracting officers concerning the MAS Program, covering such topics as the clauses to be included in a solicitation and contract, disputes, pricing, etc.

Unfortunately, to acquire the above or similar internal documents, interested parties must send a FOIA request with specifics on the information needed to the agency or sub-agency Freedom of Information Act Officer. For the GSA, requests would be addressed to:

GSA Freedom of Information Act Officer
Information Collection
Management Branch (CAIR)
General Services Administration
1800 F Street, N.W.
Washington, DC 20405

The requestor is generally responsible for paying any copying, research, or delivery costs incurred by the agency.

For more information, see the Vendor Resource Guide.

G. *Statutes*

If you would like further information on statutes relating to Government contracts, an annotated list is available at *http://www.law.gwu.edu/burns/research/gcrg/gcrg.htm* and in *The Practitioners' Research Guide: Researching Government Contracts Law on the Internet*.

* * *

Current awareness tools are another essential element in understanding the contracting process and are a great resource for early warning of pending changes not only to statutes, but also to regulations and to information on the latest case law. The web-based CCH service referred to above offers an e-mail alert feature, as do both Lexis and Westlaw. However, there are several web-based current awareness resources available for free. Fried Frank offers detailed information on recent news in the *Government Contracts Alert* at *http://www.ffhsj.com/govtcon/ffgalert/index.html* and via e-mail. The *Alert* is issued monthly with more frequent special alerts as necessary. Other law firms also offer monthly or quarterly overviews of Government contract news and issues online and in print newsletters. Other current awareness materials are identified in the Vendor Resource Guide.

XXVIII.

APPENDICES

APPENDIX I[1193]

VENDOR RESOURCE GUIDE

"Oh, I get by with a little help from my friends . . . ."
-John Lennon and Paul McCartney

COMMERCIAL SCHEDULE CONSULTANTS

There is no dearth of consultants willing to help guide vendors through the complex world of the MAS Program. We have identified in this Guide several consulting firms with which we have had positive experiences.

Ernst & Young
Washington, DC
202.327.6260
http://www.eygcs.com
Ernst & Young's Government Contract Services helps businesses understand and implement Federal Government laws and regulations on contract costing, pricing, financing, and administration. EY/GCS offers a full range of services developed from the extensive industry knowledge of its professional team—

from training and proposal assistance, to claims and litigation support. EY/GCS applies the full breadth of practical experience gained from its large international client base to create proven solutions that help companies meet their business goals. EY/GCS is well recognized for its thoughtful leadership, especially in the areas of commercial item acquisition and MAS contracting, and was pleased to contribute to this book through Richard J. Wall of the Washington, DC office.

The Washington Management Group
Washington, DC
202.833.1120
http://www.washmg.com

Founded in 1977, the Washington Management Group, based in Washington, DC, offers its clients assistance with a complete range of MAS contracting issues, including follow-up marketing and procurement-related public policy. Recently, former FSS Assistant Commissioner William Gormley joined Washington Management Group as a Senior Vice President in charge of consulting operations. Mr. Gormley, the Washington Management Group, and its sister industry organization, the Coalition for Government Procurement, have contributed significantly to the publication of this book.

Neal Fox Consulting
Washington, DC
703.644.4252

Founded in 2005, Neal Fox Consulting provides consulting services to companies seeking to contract with GSA, or any other federal agency. Neal Fox is the former Assistant Commissioner for Commercial Acquisition at the General Services Administration, where he managed the GSA Schedules, GWAC, and SmartPay programs. He has over 29 years of GSA and Department of Defense procurement experience. All consulting is done personally by Mr. Fox, so you will receive the advice directly from him.

Contracts Unlimited Incorporated
Brambleton, VA
703.327.3812
http://www.contractsunlimitedinc.com
Contracts Unlimited has been helping companies obtain and administer federal contracts, including GSA Schedule Contracts, for more than 20 years. The firm works with both large and small businesses in the context of DOD and civilian contracts. The firm also prepares subcontracts, license agreements, helps secure the protection of intellectual property, and performs compliance reviews.

FedLinx, Inc.
Greensboro, NC
336.379.0442
http://www.fedlinx.com
FedLinx, Inc. specializes in providing Government contracting assistance. With over 60 years of combined State and Federal Government experience, this firm offers a comprehensive approach to support services in contract administration, GSA schedules, VA schedules, GSA *Advantage!* upload, and compliance audits.

GSA Schedules Incorporated
Bowie, Maryland
301.805.1300
http://www.gsa-schedules.com
For more than a quarter century, GSA Schedules, Inc. has helped a multitude of leading manufacturers and integrators enter the Government marketplace. The firm assists companies from the earliest stages of GSA Schedule Contract preparation, to submission and negotiation, implementation, and sales and marketing. The president of the firm is a key member of the advisory council with the GSA Quality Partnership "Alliance Coalition" at the General Products Acquisition Center, a frequent presenter at GSA and industry expositions, and an active member of the Security Industry Association (SIA).

The Lyman Group
Washington, DC
202.833.1954
http://www.lymangroup.com

The Lyman Group provides Government contract advisory services in the areas of accounting, costs, pricing, and administration of contracts. The firm also publishes the Government Contract Audit Report, a newsletter that tracks, reports, and analyzes developments in Government contract accounting, auditing, pricing, and finance.

Parker, Chaney & Anderson
Manassas, VA
703.369.7098
http://www.parkeranderson.com

Parker, Chaney & Anderson specializes in Government marketing and relations. This firm's services include market research and trend analysis, pricing and competitive analysis, regulatory advice and assistance, and bid proposals and strategies.

MARKETING AND COMMUNICATIONS

While several of the GSA Schedule consultants listed above are quite knowledgeable in the areas of marketing and selling to the federal Government, the companies in this section focus their operations particularly in this area.

Ricci Communications
Alexandria, VA
703-519-7162, ext. 103
http://www.riccicom.com

For more than a decade, Ricci Communications has successfully developed national, regional and local marketing communications and media outreach campaigns to educate consumers and professionals. The firm's substantial experience, knowledge and contacts within both the commercial and government markets provide clients with practical, integrated approaches to achieve their business development objectives. Ricci Communications understands the nuances of targeted efforts with results-oriented messaging and emphasizes the proper mix of creativity, practicality and consistency. The firm is a full service firm offering in-house strategic planning, public relations, graphic and interactive design, copy writing and event planning.

PROPOSAL WRITING

While the GSA Schedule consultants listed above have significant experience preparing MAS proposals, the companies listed here market themselves exclusively as proposal preparation experts.

Organizational Communications, Inc.
Reston, VA
703.689.9600

OCI is a full-service proposal consultant firm providing all services needed to prepare contract proposals. OCI has led or assisted in preparing proposals for contracts worth over $50 billion with a win rate of 83%. A large consultant database helps the company respond rapidly to customer needs.

OTHER CONSULTANTS

ConXsis Group
Fort Worth, Texas
817.348.0060

The ConXsis Group, Inc. is a professional services firm specializing in environmental, business, and technology consulting solutions. Services include business planning/analysis, strategic marketing planning, proposals and presentations, Federal Government contract administration, QA program development and training, economic/financial assessments, small business consulting, and government contracting.

BGV Strategies
El Paso, Texas
915.581.0081

BGV's principals, associates and affiliated consultants have significant experience as accountants, business consultants, lawyers and senior executive officers for companies ranging from Fortune 500 companies to start-ups. BGV was developed with the inherent multidisciplinary strengths to help its clients in this environment. The firm's structure promotes internal interaction that gets past departmental boundaries that limit creativity and results. BGV has the cultural diversity and multinational work experience to assist companies and individuals doing business in United States, Mexico, Central and South America, and Western Europe.

INDUSTRY AND PROFESSIONAL ASSOCIATIONS

There are as many industry associations as there are industries. We have listed several of the more relevant associations below. In addition to these associations, a simple Internet search will lead you to an association for practically every industry imaginable.

Coalition for Government Procurement

Washington, DC

202.331.0975

http://www.coalgovpro.org

Every vendor involved in the MAS Program should at least be aware of the Coalition for Government Procurement. Founded in 1979, the Coalition is a multi-industry trade association that represents over 300 companies selling commercial supplies and services to the Federal Government. Collectively, Coalition members account for nearly half of all commercial supplies and services purchases made by the Federal Government each year.

National Contract Management Association

Vienna, VA (with regional offices nationwide)

800.344.8096

http://www.ncmahq.org

The NCMA is the "preeminent source of professional development for contract managers." The organization not only serves as a useful resource for identifying qualified contract management staff, it also hosts seminars relating to Government contracting (and MAS contracting in particular) and publishes a monthly magazine that frequently runs articles relating to MAS contracting. Beyond its central office in Vienna, Virginia, the NCMA staffs regional offices across the United States, all of which can be contacted through the national web site.

The Commercial Products and Services Committee of the ABA's Public Contracts Section

Washington, DC

http://www.abanet.org/contract/home.html

This ABA Committee seeks to improve the functioning of public procurement by contributing to developments in procurement legislation and regulations; by objectively and fairly evaluating such developments; by communicating the Committee's evaluations, critiques, and concerns to policy makers and Government officials; and by sharing these communications with Section members and the public.

Government Electronics and Information Technology Association (GEIA)

Arlington, VA

703.907.7566

http://www.geia.org/

The GEIA represents the "high tech" industry doing business with the Government. In 1999, GEIA challenged the Price Adjustment Clause that has been the bane of MAS vendors for years. GEIA continues to be a strong voice for reform in the MAS Program.

National Defense Industrial Association (NDIA)

Arlington, VA

703.522.1820

http://www.ndia.org/

The NDIA is a non-partisan, non-profit organization with a membership that includes close to 900 companies and over 22,000 individuals. NDIA has a specific interest in Government policies and practices concerning the Government's acquisition of supplies and services, including research and development, procurement, and logistics support. NDIA's members provide a wide variety of supplies and services to the Government and include some of the nation's largest defense contractors.

Association of Proposal Management Professionals

Washington, DC (with regional offices nationwide)

http://www.apmp.org/home.html

This association is committed to the advancement of the arts, sciences, and technology of proposal management.

National Association of Purchasing Management

Tempe, AZ

800.888.6276

http://www.napm.org/

This association exists to educate, develop, and advance the purchasing and supply management profession. NAPM is a communication link with more than 48,000 purchasing and supply management professionals. This association provides opportunities for expansion of professional skills and knowledge.

National Institute of Governmental Purchasing (NIGP)

Herndon, VA

800.367.6447

http://www.nigp.org/

The NIGP's stated mission is to provide its membership with education, research, technical assistance, and networking opportunities in public purchasing, while promoting excellence, enhancing effectiveness, and increasing public trust.

GENERAL SERVICES ADMINISTRATION DIRECTORY

Locating the right Government office within the maze of the federal bureaucracy often can be a daunting task. Below we have set forth several Government offices that might be of particular interest to Schedule vendors: As of the submission of this Second Edition to the publisher, the GSA was finalizing the ongoing reorganization of the Federal Technology Service (FTS) and the Federal Supply Service (FSS) into the Federal Acquisition Service (FAS). Some of the information below may have changed subsequent to the publishing of this book:

General Services Administration (GSA)
Washington, DC
202.501.0705
http://www.gsa.gov/

GSA Federal Supply Service
Washington, DC
800.488.3111
http://www.fss.gsa.gov/

General Products Acquisition Center
819 Taylor Street Room 6A24
Fort Worth, TX 76102
Phone: 817.978.4545
Fax: 817.978.2776
E-mail: *marketing.gpc@gsa.gov*

National Furniture Center
1901 South Bell Street, Suie 403
Arlington, VA 22202
Phone: 703.605.9300
Fax: 703.305.7934

Customer Service
Office Supplies and Paper Products
Phone: 877.472.3777
E-Mail: *GSA.Advantage@gsa.gov*

Scientific Equipment
14A02 819 Taylor Street Fort Worth, TX 76102
Phone: 817.978.0662
Fax: 817.978.3749

Management Services
2757 400 15th SW
Auburn, WA 98001-6599
Phone: 800.241.7246
Fax: 253.931.7544
E-mail: *warren.hayashi@gsa.gov*

Center for Facilities Maintenance and Hardware Marketing Team
1500 E. Bannister Road Room SBE 16-1
Kansas City, MO 64131
Phone: 816.926.6760
Fax: 816.926.1661
E-mail: *HSSMarketing@gsa.gov*

General Services Administration
Federal Supply Service
Services Acquisition Center (FCX)
1901 South Bell Street
Crystal Mall #4, Suite 503
Arlington, VA 22202
Fax: 703.305.5094

Professional Engineering Service
1941 Jefferson Davis Highway
Room 507
Arlington, VA 22202
Phone: 703.605.2838
Fax: 703.305.5094
E-mail: *Jeffrey.manthos@gsa.gov*

Advertising and Integrated Market Solutions
1941 Jefferson Davis Highway Room 503
Arlington, VA 22202
Phone: 703.605.2827
Fax: 703.305.6144
E-mail: *janis.freeman@gsa.gov*

Financial and Business Solutions
Suite 503
1901 S. Bell St.
Arlington, VA 22202-0000
Phone: 703.605.2820
Fax: 703.305.6144
E-mail: *transportation.programs@gsa.gov*

Vendor Support Center
2011 Crystal Park Drive
Crystal Park 1, Suie 920
Arlington, VA 22202
Phone: 703.305-6235
Toll Free: 877.495.4849
Fax: 703.305.7944
Email: vendor.support@gsa.gov

USEFUL GOVERNMENT WEB SITES

The U.S. Federal Government Agencies Directory, located at *http://www.lib.lsu.edu/gov/fedgov/html,* provides an excellent listing of federal agencies on the Internet. Additionally, one can access the "U.S. Federal Resources" section of the **Findlaw.com** Internet site or the Federal Government's recently launched **FirstGov.com** site. Both sites offer a comprehensive and well-organized database of Government agencies. For easy reference, we have set forth a selected list of useful Government web sites below.

- **Acquisition Reform Network (ARNet) Library** *(http://www.arnet.gov/)*

    Provides links to procurement resources relating to solicitations, awards, contract administration, procurement laws and regulations, and federal contracting forms.

- **Federal Acquisition Jumpstation (NASA)** *(http://nais.nasa.gov/fedproc/home.html)*

    "Designed to provide the business community a central starting point to quickly access federal procurement documents," this federal site provides a lengthy list of federal acquisitions that go well beyond GSA's MAS Program.

- **FedBizOpps** *(http://www.fedbizopps.gov/)*

    Formerly the Electronic Posting System Homepage, this site contains all Federal Government solicitations including MAS solicitations. The site also allows you to sign up to receive e-mail notification of solicitations. The site has a help line at either FBO.support@GSA.gov or toll-free at 877.472.3779.

- **FedLaw** *(www.thecre.com/fedlaw/default.htm)*

    According to GSA, "FedLaw was developed to see if legal resources on the Internet could be a useful and cost-effective research tool for Federal lawyers and other Federal employees. Fedlaw has assembled references of use to people doing Federal legal research and which can be accessed directly through 'point and click' hypertext connections."

- **Thomas** (*http://Thomas.loc.gov*)
  Administered by the Library of Congress, the Thomas web site provides what is perhaps the best resource for researching legislative issues—whether or not they relate to the MAS Program.

- **GPO Access** (*http://www.access.gpo.gov*)
  Administered by the Government Printing Office, the GPO Access web site provides links to, among other things, the Federal Register, the Code of Federal Regulations, and the United States Code. Each resource is searchable.

- **Government Accountability Office** (*http://www.gao.gov/main.html*)
  The GAO web site offers GAO decisions on bid protests and GAO reports.

- **GSA Web Sites and On-Line Resources**
  - GSA *Advantage!*, the on-line shopping site for MAS contracts *http://www.gsaadvantage.gov/advgsa/main_pages/start_page.jsp*
  - GSA Schedules e-Library www.gsa.eLibrary.GSA.Gov/Elibmain/ELibHome
  - Schedule Sales Query *http://ssq.fss.gsa.gov/*

- **United States Court of Federal Claims** (*www.uscfc.uscounts.gov/*)
  The COFC web site provides decisions and orders of the court and also provides a link to the Department of

Commerce's Office of General Counsel, which provides a useful synopsis of proposed and final regulations and cases relating to public contracts law.

- **Office of Federal Procurement Policy (OFPP)**
  http://www.whitehouse.gov/omb/procurement/index.html

- **Department of Veterans Affairs/FSS Program**
  http://www.va.gov/

- **Small Business Administration (SBA)**
  http://www.sba.gov/
  - **Office of Government Contracting (OGC)**
    http://www.sba.gov/GC/
  - **Size Standards**
    http://www.sba.gov/size/
  - **Regional Small Business Centers**
    http://www.sba.gov/services/
  - **Small Business Development Centers**
    http://www.sba.gov/SBDC/index.html
  - **Local SBA offices**
    http://www.sba.gov/regions/states.html
  - **SBA Pro-*Net***
    http://pro-net.sba.gov/
  - **Small Disadvantaged Businesses Link**
    http://www.sba.gov/sdb/
  - **Women-Owned Businesses Link**
    http://www.sba.gov/womeninbusiness/
  - **Veterans Business Development**
    http://www.sba.gov/VETS/

USEFUL COMMERCIAL ELECTRONIC RESOURCES

- Sheppard Mullin Richter & Hampton (*http://www.sheppard mullin.com*). This web site provides a wealth of information on a number of legal topics.
- The Washington Management Group (*http://www.washmg.com*). This web site offers useful links to several important MAS related Internet sites.
- Coalition for Government Procurement (*http://www.coalgovpro.org*). Among other things, the Coalition's web site offers concise descriptions of the various policy issues facing the Government procurement community as well as on-line request forms to obtain the minutes of the meetings of the Coalition's various industry-specific committees.
- The National Contract Management Association (*http://www.ncmahq.org*). The NCMA's web site offers a wealth of information of interest to contract management professionals.
- Government Executive.Com (*http://www.govexec.com*). Directed at Government readers, this web site offers a host of useful articles, special reports, and Internet links.
- Fedmarket.com (*http://www.fedmarket.com*). This web site offers free news, advice, and "how-to" articles. It also provides links to a wealth of training resources relating to the MAS Program.
- Federal Computer Week (*http://www.fcw.com*). This web site offers timely news articles of interest to IT vendors and purchasers.
- CCH Government Contracting Resources (*http://business.cch.com/ govContracts/default.ASP*). In addition to offering a wide range of books and periodicals, the CCH's web site provides news summaries of interest to Government contractors.
- American Bar Association, Section of Public Contract Law (*http://www.abanet.org/contract/home.html*). In addition to offering a wide range of books and periodicals relating to Government contracting, the Public Contract Law Section's

web site provides information regarding the Section's various committees, such as the Commercial Products and Services Committee.

- George Washington University Law School provides an outstanding, on-line Government Contracts Resources Guide (*http://www.law.gwu.edu/default.htm*).

- LexisNexis™ (*http://www.lexis.com*). One of the leading on-line, fee-for-service research providers, the LexisNexis™ services provide access to a massive database of legislative (*e.g.*, statutes, legislative histories, GAO decisions), executive (*e.g.*, agency regulations and decisions), and judicial (*e.g.*, case law) resources relating to Government contracting.

RESOURCES FOR IDENTIFYING SMALL, MINORITY, AND WOMEN-OWNED BUSINESSES

(Source: General Services Administration,
Office of Enterprise Development)

National Directories

- **National Directory of Women-Owned Businesses**—Business Research Services, Inc., 4201 Connecticut Avenue, N.W., Suite 610, Washington, DC 20008, telephone 202.364.6473.
- **National Directory of Minority-Owned Business Firms**—Business Research Services, Inc., 4201 Connecticut Avenue, N.W., Suite 610, Washington, DC 20008, telephone 202.364.6473.
- **Smoke Signals**—A publication of Native American businesses. For information, contact Tom Godwin, telephone 303.777.1121, fax 303.777.5214, e-mail CSI@henge.com.
- **The Business Women's Network Directory**—The Business Women's Network, 1146 19th Street, N.W., 3rd Floor, Washington, DC 20036, telephone 800.48.WOMEN; web site *http://www.tpag.com/bwn.html*.
- **National Center Directory of American Indian-Owned Businesses**—National Center for American Indian Enterprise Development, 953 East Juanita Avenue, Mesa, AZ 85204, telephone 602.546.1298.

Databases

- **Small Business Administration's (SBA) PRO-*Net***—SBA's new database that allows Federal contracting officers and others to search for small companies that can fill their needs. It also serves as a marketing and research tool for participating small businesses. The PRO-*Net* database can be accessed via the Internet at *http://www.pro-net.sba.gov* and currently includes electronic profiles of nearly 171,000 small businesses, including all SBA 8(a) firms and women-owned firms in the State of Maryland.

- **Minority Business Development Agency (MBDA) Phoenix Database**—Minority businesses register on this database which hotlinks to an opportunities database that matches the registered company. Web site *http://www.mbda.gov/*. Call 202.482.3262 for more information.
- **GSA's Office of Enterprise Development Vendor Profile Database**—A nationwide database that is able to locate small and women-owned businesses that have expressed an interest in contracting with GSA; searches can be done using Standard Industrial Classification (SIC) codes and geographic regions. Call 202.501.1021 for application form.
- **U.S. Hispanic Chamber of Commerce**—Web site *http:// www.ushcc.com*.
- **SBA's Women's Business Centers**—Telephone 202.205.6673 (with local offices nationwide), web site *http://www.onlinewbc.org*.
- **African American Directory**—Web site *http://www.unite-us.com*. A nationwide directory of African-American owned businesses. Searches by type of business. Provides basic contact information on companies.
- **Small Business Depot.com**—Matches small business profiles with corporate and Government contracting requests. Its free Internet Small Business University helps firms identify, win, and better manage new business. Small Business Depot, 1099 Wall Street West, Suite 354, Lyndhurst, NJ 07071, telephone 201.635.9700, web site *http://www.SBDepot.com*.

Publications

- **Black Congressional Monitor**—Reports on legislative actions of the Congressional Black Caucus and on legislative, regulatory, and executive branch initiatives from the Federal Government that impact the African-American community.

Published twice monthly by Len Mor Publications, POB 75035, Washington, DC 20013, telephone 202.488.8879, fax 202.554.3116.

- **Eastwest Report**—Reports to members of the U.S. Pan Asian American Chamber of Commerce on activities of the organization. U.S. Pan Asian American Chamber of Commerce, 1329 18th Street, NW, Washington, DC 20036.

- **Minority Business Journal**—Shedding new light on minority business, published bimonthly by the Minority Business Journal, Inc., Post Office Box 3543, Pittsburgh, PA 15230, telephone 412.682.4386.

- **Set Aside Alert**—A newsletter on minority Federal contracting. Published by Washington Business Information, Inc.; 300 North Washington Street, Suite 200, Falls Church, VA 22046, telephone 703.538.7600, fax 703.538.7676.

- **Federal Acquisition Report**—Covers news and events in federal acquisition. Published monthly by Holbrook & Kellogg, 8230 Leesburg Pike, Suite 530, Vienna, VA 22182, telephone 703.790.9595, fax 703.506.1948.

- **The Savant**—The Service Core of Retired Executives publishes this periodical monthly as a news source for champions of small business. Write the National SCORE Office, 409 3rd Street, S.W., 4th Floor, Washington, DC 20024, or call 1.800.634.0245 for subscription information.

- **Small Business Resource Guide**—Braddock Communications, Inc., 11501 Sunset Hills Road, Reston, VA 20190-4704, telephone 703.471.6543.

- **Washington Business Journal's Book of Lists**—American City Business Journals, Inc., 2000 14th Street North, Suite 500, Arlington, VA 22201-2566, telephone 703.875.2231.

- **Minorities In Business Insider**—Published twice monthly by CD Publications, 8204 Fenton Street, Silver Spring, MD 20910, telephone 301.588.6380; call 800.666.6380 for subscription assistance.

- **Commerce Business Daily**—Published by the Department of Commerce, the CBD is available on line through the Internet at *http://www.govcon.com.*

- **Government Computer News**—The national newspaper of Government computing and communications; published weekly. Mail subscriptions to Post-Newsweek Business Information, Inc., c/o Cahners Publishing Company, 8773 S. Ridgeline Boulevard., Highlands Ranch, CO 80126 (if possible include your mailing label), telephone 303.470.4445; fax 303.470.4280; e-mail cahners.subs@denver.cahners.com.
- **INPUT** *Buyers' Guides*—Over 100 buyers' guides and research reports on the information technology software and services industry to help decision makers apply technology to their specific business needs. Published by INPUT, 1881 Landings Drive, Mountain View, CA 94043-0848; for information, e-mail mgronick@input.com or nberthaut@input.com or call 703.847.6870.

Trade and Professional Associations

- **American Business Women International**—P.O. Box 1137, Palm Desert, CA 92261, telephone 800.606.ABWI (800.606.2294), web site *http://www.abwi.org*.
- **American Business Women's Association**—9100 Ward Parkway, P.O. Box 8728, Kansas City, MO 64114-0728, telephone 800.361.4991, fax 816.361.4991, web site *http://www.abwahq.org*.
- **American Society of Women Accountants**—1595 Spring Hill Road, Suite 330, Vienna, VA 22182, telephone 800.326.2163, fax 703.506.3266, web site *http://www.awsa.org*.
- **American Subcontracting Association**—1004 Duke Street, Alexandria, VA 22314, telephone 703.684.3450.
- **Asian Women in Business**—One West 34th Street, Suite 200, New York, NY 10001, telephone 212.868.1368, fax 212.868.1373, web site *http://www.awib.org*.
- **Association for Women in Computing**—41 Sutter Street, Suite 1006, San Francisco, CA 94104, telephone 415.905.4663, fax 415.391.1709, web site *http://www.awc-hq.org*.
- **Association of Black Women Entrepreneurs**—P.O. Box 49368, Los Angeles, CA 90049, telephone 213.624.8639, fax 310.472.4927.

- **Business Women's Advantage**—921 Gregory Lane, Schaumburg, IL 60193, telephone 847.895.7427, fax 847.584.4292.
- **Business Women Leadership Foundation**—1700 K Street, N.W., Suite 1005, Washington, DC 20006, telephone 202.822.5010, fax 202.293.1508.
- **Chambers of Commerce**—See local telephone directories for U.S., Hispanic, African-American, Pan Asian American, Women, Native-American, and Asian-Pacific Chambers.
- **Diversity Information Resources**—2105 Central Avenue, NE., Minneapolis, MN 55418, telephone 612.781.6819, fax 612.781.0109, web site *http://diversityinforesources.com*.
- **Hispanic Business Professional Women Association**—2204 18th Street, N.W., Washington, DC 20009, telephone 202.234.0598.
- **Hispanic Women's Corporation**—4545 North 36th Street, Suite 207, Phoenix, AZ 85018-5474, telephone 888.388.4HWC, fax 602.954.7563, web site *http://www.hispanicwomen.org*.
- **International Women's Forum**—1621 Connecticut Avenue, N.W., Suite 300, Washington, DC 20009, telephone 202.775.8917, fax 202.429.0271, web site *http://www.iwforum.org*.
- **Latin American Management Association**—419 New Jersey Avenue, S.E., Washington, DC 20003, telephone 202.546.3803, fax 202.546.3807, web site *http://lama-usa.com*.
- **Minority Business Enterprise Legal Defense and Education Fund (MBELDEF)**—900 2nd Street, N.E., Suite 8, Washington, DC 20002, telephone 202.289.1700, fax 202.289.1701.
- **National Association of Minority Contractors**—666 11th Street, N.W., Suite 520, Washington, DC 20001 (with local offices nationwide), telephone 202.347.8259, fax 202.628.1876, web site *http://www.namconline.org*.
- **National Association of Women Business Owners**—1594 Spring Hill Road, Suite 330, Vienna, VA 22182, telephone 800.55.NAWBO, fax 703.506.5266, web site *http://nawbo.org*.

- National Association of Women in Chamber of Commerce, P.O. Box 4552, Grand Junction, CO 81502-4552, telephone 970.242.0075.
- National Association of Women in Construction—327 South Adams Street, Fort Worth, TX 76108, telephone 817.877.5551, fax 817.877.0324, web site *http://wwwnawic.org.*
- National Association of Women's Business Advocates—100 West Randolph Street, Suite 3-400, Chicago, IL 60067, telephone 312.814.7176, fax 312.814.5247.
- National Association of Women's Yellow Pages—8420 Delmar Street, Suite 501, St. Louis, MO 63124, telephone 800.869.1203, fax 314.567.7849, web site *http:/// www.womensyellowpages.org.*
- National Business League—115 E. Marshall Street, Richmond, VA 23219, telephone 804.649.7473, fax 804.649.7474, web site *http://thenbl.com.*
- National Center for American Indian Enterprise Development—953 East Juanita Avenue, Mesa, AZ 85204, telephone 602.545.1298, fax 605.545.4208.
- National Chamber of Commerce for Women—10 Waterside Plaza, Suite 6H, New York, NY 10010, telephone 212.685.3454.
- National Education Center for Women in Business—Seton Hill College, Seton Hill Drive, Greensburg, PA 15601-1599, telephone 724.830.4625, fax 724.834.7131.
- National Federation of Black Women Business Owners— 1500 Massachusetts Avenue, N.W., Suite 34, Washington, DC 20005, phone 202.833.3450, fax 202.331.7822.
- National Foundation for Women Business Owners (NFWBO)—1411 K Street, N.W., Suite 1350, Washington, DC 20005-3407, telephone 202.638.3060, fax 202.638.3064, web site *http://nfwbo.org.*
- National Minority Business Council—25 West 45th Street, Suite 1007, New York, NY 10036, telephone 212.997.4753, fax 212.997.5102, web site *http://nmbc.org.*

- **National Minority Supplier Development Council, Inc.**—1040 Avenue of the Americas, Second Floor, New York, NY 10018, telephone 212.944.2430, fax 212.719.9611, web site *http://nmsdcus.org*.
- **National Small Business United**—1156 15th Street, N.W., Suite 1100, Washington, DC 20005, telephone 202.293.8830, web site *http://nsbu.org*.
- **National Urban League**—120 Wall Street, New York, NY 10005, web site *http://nul.org*.
- **National Women's Automotive Association**—3250 W. Big Beaver Road, Suite 300, Troy, MI 48084, telephone 248.646.5250, fax 248.646.6721.
- **Organization of Women in International Trade**—P.O. Box 65962, Washington, DC 20035 (with offices nationwide), telephone 202.785.9482, web site *http://owit.org*.
- **Professional Women in Business**—24328 S. Vermont Avenue, Suite 244, Harbor City, CA 90710, telephone 310.534.3719, fax 310.534.3749.
- **Professional Women in Construction**—315 East 56th Street, New York, NY 10022, telephone 212.486.7745, fax 212.486.0228., web site *http://www.pwcusa.org*.
- **Women Construction Owners and Executives, USA**—712 Silliman Street, San Francisco, CA 94134, telephone 510.636.1077, fax 510.636-1858, web site *http://wcoeusa.com*.
- **Women Incorporated**—8522 National Boulevard, Suite 107, Culver City, CA 90232, telephone 800.930.3993, fax 310.815.0985, web site *http://womeninc.org*.
- **Women's Business Enterprise National Council**—409 3rd Street, S.W., Suite 210, Washington, DC 20024, telephone 202.205.3850, fax 202.205.6825, web site *http://nwbc.gov*.

Federal Resources

- **White House Office of Women's Initiatives & Outreach**—Telephone 202.456.7300, fax 202.456.7111.

- **SCORE**—The Service Corps of Retired Executives is a 13,000-member volunteer association sponsored by SBA to provide in-depth counseling and training to small business clients in virtually every area of business management. To locate the SCORE office nearest you call 1.800.634.0245 or mail inquiries to National SCORE Office, 409 3rd Street, SW., 6th Floor, Washington, DC 20024, web site *http://score.org*.
- **Women's Business Center, Inc.**—1000 Connecticut Avenue, N.W, Washington, DC 20036, telephone 202.785.4110, web site *http://womensbusinesscenter.org*.
- **Small Business Development Centers**—See local telephone directories for these SBA offices that are spread throughout the country or web site *http://sba.gov/SBDC/mission.html*.
- **Anacostia Economic Development Corporation**—2019 Martin L. King, Jr. Avenue, S.E., Washington, DC 20020, telephone 202.889.5100.
- **Procurement Technical Assistance Centers**—These Department of Defense centers are located in numerous universities throughout the country. They are called PTAC's (centers) or PTAP's (programs) in different places. See web site *http://rcacwv.com/ptac.htm*.
- **Center for Urban Progress**—Office of Latino Affairs, 2000 14th Street, N.W., Suite 330N, Washington, DC 20009, telephone 202.671.2828.
- **Minority-Owned Business Technology Transfer Consortium**—4834 1/2 16th Street, N.W., Washington, DC 20011, telephone 202.722.7601, fax 202.722.7604, web site *http://mbttc.org*.
- **National Association for Black Veterans**—330 W. Wells Street, Milwaukee, WI 53208, telephone 800.842.4597, web site *http://nabvets.com*.
- **Veterans Business Outreach Center**—TEP Consulting, Inc., 858 Dogwood Court, Suite 245. Herndon, VA 20172-0245 (with local offices nationwide), telephone 703.707.0931, fax 703.707.0985.

- **Washington Area 8(a) Academy**—2600 6th Street, N.W., Washington, DC 20059, telephone 202.806.1533.
- **Washington Emerging Technologies Center, Inc.**—1400 20th Street, N.W., Suite 513, Washington, DC 20036, telephone 202.887.6709.

Notes:

[1193] The companies and associations listed in this section have no affiliation with Sheppard, Mullin, Richter & Hampton. They are listed here as a convenience to the reader. The descriptions of each company come primarily from the company's own web site or other marketing material.

APPENDIX II

MULTIPLE AWARD SCHEDULES

GSA Multiple Award Schedules
(*http://www.gsalibrary.gsa.gov/elib/Schedules.jsp*)

Schedule	Description
00CORP	The Consolidated Schedule
00JWOD	NIB/NISH Products
03FAC	Facilities and Maintenance Management
23 V	Vehicular Multiple Award Schedule (VMAS)
26 I	TIRES, PNEUMATIC (NEW), FOR PASSENGER, LIGHT TRUCK, MEDIUM TRUCK, AND BUS, AND RETREAD SERVICES
36	The Office, Imaging and Document Solution
48	Transportation, Delivery And Relocation Solutions
51 V	HARDWARE SUPERSTORE
56	Buildings And Building Materials/Industrial Services And Supplies
58 I	Professional Audio/Video, Telecommunication and Security Solutions
599	Travel Services Solutions

621 I	Professional And Allied Healthcare Staffing Services
621 II	Medical Laboratory Testing and Analysis Services
621 III	Home Infusion Therapy Services, PSC Q999—Other Medical Services
621 V	Teleradiology Services
65 I B	PHARMACEUTICALS AND DRUGS
65 II A	MEDICAL EQUIPMENT AND SUPPLIES
65 II C	DENTAL EQUIPMENT AND SUPPLIES
65 II F	PATIENT MOBILITY DEVICES (INCLUDING WHEELCHAIRS, SCOOTERS, WALKERS)
65 V A	X-RAY EQUIPMENT AND SUPPLIES (INCLUDING MEDICAL AND DENTAL X-RAY FILM)
65 VII	IN VITRO DIAGNOSTICS, REAGENTS, TEST KITS AND TEST SETS
66 II J	Test And Measurement Equipment, Aviation Instruments and Equipment, Aircraft Components, Maintaining and Repairing Services, and Unmanned Scientific Vehicles
66 II N	Chemistry, Biochemistry And Clinical, General Purpose Laboratory Instruments, Laboratory Instruments, Laboratory Furnishings and Accessories, and Related Services
66 II Q	Geophysical, Environmental Analysis Equipment and Services
66 III	CLINICAL ANALYZERS, LABORATORY, COST-PER-TEST
67	Photographic Equipment—Cameras, Photographic Printers and Related Supplies & Services (Digital and Film-Based)
69	TRAINING AIDS & DEVICES, INSTRUCTOR LED TRAINING; COURSE DEVELOPMENT; TEST ADMINISTRATION—Programmed learning devices
70	GENERAL PURPOSE COMMERCIAL INFORMATION TECHNOLOGY EQUIPMENT, SOFTWARE, AND SERVICES
71 I	OFFICE FURNITURE

71 II	HOUSEHOLD AND QUARTERS FURNITURE
77 II H	PACKAGED FURNITURE
77 II K	COMPREHENSIVE FURNITURE MANAGEMENT SERVICES
71 III	SPECIAL USE FURNITURE
71 III E	MISCELLANEOUS FURNITURE
72 I A	FLOOR COVERINGS
72 II	FURNISHINGS
73	Food Service, Hospitality, Cleaning Equipment and Supplies, Chemicals and Services
736	Temporary Admininstrative And Professional Staffing (TAPS)
738 I	MARKETING, MEDIA AND PUBLIC INFORMATION SERVICES
738 II	LANGUAGE SERVICES
738 X	HUMAN RESOURCES MANAGEMENT AND EEO SERVICES
75	OFFICE PRODUCTS/SUPPLIES AND SERVICES AND NEW PRODUCTS/TECHNOLOGY Schedule 75 now includes Videotapes, Audiotapes, Tape Cartridges, Diskettes/Optical Disks, Disk Packs, Disk Cartridges, Anti-Glare Screens, Cleaning Equipment & Supplies, Ergonomic Devices, Next Day Desktop Delivery of Office Supplies, and Restroom Products such as Roll Toilet Tissue Dispensers, Toilet Tissue, Paper Towels, Toilet Seat Covers, Facial Tissues, and Soaps for Restroom Dispensers
751	Leasing of Automobiles and Light Trucks
76	PUBLICATION MEDIA
81 I B	SHIPPING, PACKAGING AND PACKING SUPPLIES
84	TOTAL SOLUTIONS FOR LAW ENFORCEMENT, SECURITY, FACILITIES MANAGEMENT, FIRE, RESCUE, CLOTHING, MARINE CRAFT AND EMERGENCY/DISASTER RESPONS
871	PROFESSIONAL ENGINEERING SERVICES

871 II	ENERGY MANAGEMENT SERVICES
872	AUDITING SERVICES AND FINANCIAL MANAGEMENT SERVICES
873	LABORATORY TESTING AND ANALYSIS SERVICES
874	MANAGEMENT, ORGANIZATION, AND BUSINESS IMPROVEMENT SERVICES (MOBIS)
874 V	LOGISTICS WORLDWIDE (LOGWORLD)
899	ENVIRONMENTAL SERVICES

APPENDIX III

AUTHORIZED SCHEDULE PURCHASERS

According to GSA, the following "executive agencies" are eligible to purchase from MAS vendors under the MAS Program. This list includes only the "major Federal activities and their subordinate entities" about which inquiries have been received by GSA:

African Development Foundation
Agency for International Development
Agriculture, Department of
Air Force, Department of
American Battle Monuments Commission
Armed Forces Retirement Home
Army Corp of Engineers
Army, Department of
Bonneville Power Administration
Bureau of Land Management
Central Intelligence Agency
Christopher Columbus Fellowship Foundation
Commerce, Department of
Commission on Civil Rights
Commission on Fine Arts
Commodity Credit Corporation

Commodity Futures Trading Commission
Consumer Products Safety Commission
Corporation for National Community Service
Defense, Department of
Defense agencies and Joint Service Schools
Defense Nuclear Facilities Safety Board
Education, Department of
Energy, Department of
Environmental Protection Agency
Equal Employment Opportunity Commission
Executive Office of the President
Export-Import Bank of U.S.
Farm Credit Administration
Federal Communications Commission
Federal Election Commission
Federal Maritime Commission
Federal Trade Commission
Forest Service, U.S.
General Services Administration
Government National Mortgage Association
Harry S. Truman Scholarship Foundation
Health and Human Services, Department of
Housing and Urban Development, Department of
Institute of Museum and Library Sciences
Interagency Council on the Homeless
Inter-American Foundation
Interior, Department of the
International Boundary and Water Commission, United States Section
Justice, Department of
Kennedy Center
Labor, Department of
Madison, James, Memorial Fellowship Foundation
Merit Systems Protection Board
Morris K. Udall Foundation
National Aeronautics and Space Administration
National Archives and Records Administration

National Credit Union Administration (not individual credit unions)
National Council on the Handicapped
National Endowment for the Arts
National Endowment for the Humanities
National Labor Relations Board
National Science Foundation
National Transportation Safety Board
Navy, Department of
Nuclear Regulatory Commission
Nuclear Waste Technical Review Board
Occupational Safety and Health Review Commission
Office of Federal Housing Enterprise Oversight
Office of Personnel Management
Office of Special Counsel
Panama Canal Commission
Peace Corps
Pension Benefit Guaranty Corporation
Postal Rate Commission
Presidio Trust
Railroad Retirement Board
St. Elizabeths Hospital
Securities and Exchange Commission
Selective Service System
Small Business Administration
Smithsonian Institution
State, Department of
Tennessee Valley Authority
Trade and Development Agency
Transportation, Department of
Treasury, Department of
U.S. Arms Control and Disarmament Agency
U.S. Information Agency
U.S. International Development Cooperation Agency
U.S. International Trade Commission
U.S. Postal Service
Veterans Affairs, Department of

In addition to the foregoing executive agencies, the following entities have been determined to be eligible to use the MAS Program. According to GSA, this list is not all-inclusive and GSA will rule upon eligibility on a case-by-case basis in response to requests received.

Administrative Conference of the U.S.
Administrative Office of the U.S. Courts
Advisory Commission on Intergovernmental Relations
Advisory Committee on Federal Pay
American Printing House for the Blind
American Samoa
Architect of the Capitol
Architectural and Transportation Barriers Compliance Board
Bank for Cooperatives
Certain non-appropriated fund activities (generally, not for resale)
Coast Guard Auxiliary (through the U.S. Coast Guard)
Committee for Purchase from the Blind and other Severely Handicapped
Contractors and subcontractors—cost reimbursement (as authorized by the applicable agency's contracting official)
Contractors and subcontractors—fixed price (security equipment only when so authorized by the applicable agency's contracting official)
Courts, Federal (not court reporters)
Delaware River Basin Commission
District of Columbia
Farm Credit Banks
Federal Deposit Insurance Corporation
Federal Home Loan Banks
Federal Intermediate Credit Bank
Federal Land Bank
Federal Reserve Board of Governors
Firefighters, Non-Federal (as authorized by the Forest Service, U.S. Department of Agriculture)
Gallaudet University

Government Printing Office
Guam
Harry S. Truman Scholarship Foundation
House of Representatives, U.S.
Howard University (including hospital)
Japan-United States Friendship Commission
Land Grant Institutions (as cost reimbursement contractors)
Legal Services Corporation (not its grantees)
Library of Congress
Marine Mammal Commission
Medicare Payment Advisory Commission
National Bank for Cooperatives (CoBank)
National Capital Planning Commission
National Gallery of Art
National Guard Activities (only through U.S. Property and Fiscal
    Officers)
National Technical Institute for the Deaf
Navajo and Hopi Indian Relocation Commission
Neighborhood Reinvestment Corporation
Northern Mariana Islands, Commonwealth
Senate, U.S.
Stennis, John C., Center for Public Service Training and Development
Susquehanna River Basin Commission
U.S. Institute of Peace
U.S. Representative, Office of Joint Economic Commission
Virgin Islands (including Virgin Islands Port Authority)
Washington Metropolitan Area Transit Authority (METRO)

Finally, the following entities also have been determined to be eligible to purchase through the MAS Program. Like the foregoing lists, this list also is not all-inclusive. Additionally, according to GSA, certain entities may be eligible to use only specific GSA sources and/or services and GSA will rule upon the eligibility of activities on a case-by-case basis in response to requests received.

African Development Fund
American Red Cross

Asian Development Bank
Caribbean Organization
Counterpart Foundation, Inc.
Customs Cooperation Council
European Space Research Organization
Food and Agriculture Organization of the United Nations
Great Lakes Fishery Commission
Inter-American Defense Board
Inter-American Development Bank
Inter-American Institute of Agriculture Sciences
Inter-American Investment Corporation
Inter-American Statistical Institute
Inter-American Tropical Tuna Commission
Intergovernmental Maritime Consultive Organization
Intergovernmental Committee for European Migration
International Atomic Energy Agency
International Bank of Reconstruction and Development (WORLD BANK)
International Boundary Commission-United States and Canada
International Boundary and Water Commission-United States and Mexico
International Center for Settlement of Investment Disputes
International Civil Aviation Organization
International Coffee Organization
International Cotton Advisory Committee
International Development Association
International Fertilizer Development Center
International Finance Corporation
International Hydrographic Bureau
International Institute for Cotton
International Joint Commission-United States and Canada
International Labor Organization
International Maritime Satellite Organization
International Monetary Fund
International Pacific Halibut Commission
International Pacific Salmon Fisheries Commission-Canada

International Secretariat for Volunteer Services
International Telecommunications Satellite Organization
International Telecommunications Union
International Wheat Council
Lake Ontario Claims Tribunal
Multinational Force and Observers
Multinational Investment Guarantee Agency (MIGA)
North American Treaty Organization (NATO)
Organization of African Unity
Organization of American States
Organization for Economic Cooperation and Development
Pan American Health Organization
Radio Technical Commission for Aeronautics
South Pacific Commission
United International Bureau for the Protection of Intellectual
    Property
United Nations
United Nations Educational, Scientific, and Cultural Organization
Universal Postal Union
World Health Organization
World Intellectual Property Organization
World Meteorological Organization
World Tourism Organization

APPENDIX IV

SELECTED BIBLIOGRAPHY

Notwithstanding the proliferation of electronic newsletters, discussions groups, and web sites, many useful resources still exist in good old-fashioned paper form. Among these, we have found the following periodicals and books particularly useful:

JOURNALS AND PERIODICALS

- **Briefing Papers**
  West Group
  > For more than thirty years, this periodical has been a source of legal guidance on Government contracting. It is published monthly (with an additional "Procurement Review" issue in January). This periodical analyzes current procurement issues in an easy-to-read style. You can subscribe through *http:// west.thomson.com/store/ default.asp*. The annual subscription price is about $1,000.

- **Contract Management ("CM")**
  National Contract Management Association
  > According to the NCMA, CM is "presented from both government and industry viewpoints. *CM* articles keep

readers on top of late-breaking developments. Editorial 'departments' present opinion pieces, information for beginners and for legal scholars, information for small businesses, as well as rich and varied feature material." Subscriptions rates are free for members in the United States. You can subscribe on-line at *http:// www.ncmahq.org*.

- **Federal Contracts Report**
  The Bureau of National Affairs, Inc.
  This weekly publication "offers timely, in-depth reports on legislation, federal regulations and policies, auditing, research and development, and other major developments affecting procurement issues and government contracts." The annual subscription price is $1,453. You can subscribe by calling BNA at 800.372.1033.

- **Government Contract Audit Report**
  The Lyman Group
  This report tracks, reports, and analyzes developments in Government contract accounting, auditing, pricing, and finance, including issues relating to the MAS Program. It is published monthly, except in January and August, and is available on an annual subscription basis for $349 (U.S.). You can subscribe by calling 202.833.1954 or by logging on to *http://www.lymangroup.com*.

- **Government Contractor, The**
  West Group
  According to the West Group, "*The Government Contractor* will guide you through the mountains of procurement information, statutes, regulations, legal decisions that pile up daily." Additionally, a subscription to *The Government Contractor* brings with it free attendance at the annual Government Contracts Year in Review Conference. In our opinion, this publication, which has an annual

subscription price of $1,523, will be of primary interest to lawyers. You can subscribe by logging on to *http://www.westgroup.com/store*.

- **Nash & Cibinic Report**
  Kaiser Publications
  Authored by Professors Ralph Nash and John Cibinic, this monthly newsletter is known for its thought-provoking analysis of critical, current, and controversial federal procurement issues. You can subscribe through *http://www.westgroup.com/store*. The annual subscription price is about $1,000.

- **Off The Shelf**
  Coalition for Government Procurement
  Off the Shelf probably is the most MAS-focused publication available. Subscriptions are free to members of the Coalition for Government Procurement and clients of the Washington Management Group. Contact the Coalition for Government Procurement at *http://www.coalgovpro.org* for subscription information.

- **Public Contracts Law Journal**
  The American Bar Association
  The PCLJ regularly publishes articles that present scholarly and pragmatic analysis and insight into issues affecting public contract and grant law. It is the only law journal dedicated exclusively to public contract and grant law and related areas of practice. The Journal's Editorial Board's goal is for each issue to contain high-quality articles that are topical and provocative and that reflect the many views of its diverse membership. Current issues sell for $15 per copy. You can subscribe through the George Washington University Law School web site at *http://www.law.gwu.edu/pclj/publication/subscribe.htm*.

BOOKS

- **Administration of Government Contracts**
  John Cibinic and Ralph Nash
  The George Washington University

  While the scope of this book goes well beyond the MAS Program, it is the most comprehensive treatment of the issues involved in administering Government contracts generally. The book can be ordered through the CCH web site (*http://onlinestore.cch.com*) for $90.

- **Civil False Claims and Qui Tam Actions**
  John T. Boese
  Aspen Publishers

  This treatise is quoted frequently by judges and attorneys. Whether you are a vendor or a lawyer, if you or your clients contract with the Federal Government, you should ensure that this treatise is in your library. You can order the book from the publisher (*http://www.aspenpub.com*) for $175.

- **The Government Contracts Reference Book: A Comprehensive Guide to the Language of Procurement**
  Ralph Nash, Steven Schooner, and Karen O'Brien
  The George Washington University and CCH

  Written as a dictionary, this book serves as an excellent tool for understanding the often arcane language associated with Government procurement.

- **Multiple Award Schedule Self-Audit Manual**
  The Coalition for Government Procurement

  In addition to a good discussion of the steps involved in conducting an internal MAS self-audit, this useful three-ring binder includes worksheets and appendices reproducing important regulations, statutes, and other documents. The Manual is available through the Coalition for Government Procurement for purchase. Contact the Coalition at *http://www.coalgovpro.org* for more information.

- **The Practitioner's Guide to Suspension and Debarment (2d ed.) John T. Boese (ed.) American Bar Association, Committee on Debarment and Suspension**

  According to the ABA, this monograph, "contains emerging trends in the law and historical overview, plus practical techniques to avoid or challenge these actions when imposed. Expands the treatment of the collateral consequences, both in federal and state programs, and the new reciprocity between procurement (contracts) and nonprocurement (benefits) suspension and debarment." You can order the monograph from the ABA (*http://www.abanet.org*) for $45 for non-members.

APPENDIX V

ACRONYMS

ABA	American Bar Association
ACH	Automated Clearing House
ACO	Administrative Contracting Officer
ADA	Americans with Disabilities Act
ADRA	Administrative Dispute Resolution Act
AECA	Arms Export Control Act
APA	Administrative Procedures Act
ARWG	Acquisition Reform Working Group
ASBCA	Armed Services Board of Contract Appeals
ASPR	Armed Services Procurement Regulation
BAA	Buy American Act
BAFO	best and final offer
BPA	blanket purchase agreement
CCH	Commerce Clearing House
CDA	Contract Disputes Act
CFR	Code of Federal Regulations
CICA	Competition in Contracting Act
CID	Civil Investigative Demand
COFC	United States Court of Federal Claims
CSP Format	Commercial Sales Practices Format
DAC	Defense Acquisition Circular

DAR	Defense Acquisition Regulation
DFARS	Defense FAR Supplement
DOJ	Department of Justice
DOL	Department of Labor
DOT CAB	Department of Transportation Board of Contract Appeals
DSMD form	Discount Schedule and Marketing Data form
EAA	Export Administration Act
EAJA	Equal Access to Justice Act
EDI	Electronic Data Interchange
EEO	Equal Employment Opportunity
EFT	electronic funds transfer
EIT	electronic and information technology
FAA	Federal Aviation Administration
FAC	Federal Acquisition Circular
FAR	Federal Acquisition Regulation
FAS	Federal Acquisition Service
FASA	Federal Acquisition Streamlining Act
FCA	False Claims Act
FEMP	Federal Energy Management Program
FIRMR	Federal Information Resources Management Regulations
FOIA	Freedom of Information Act
FPASA	Federal Property and Administrative Services Act
FPR	Federal Procurement Regulations
FSS	Federal Supply Service
FTS	Federal Technology Service
GAO	Government Accountability Office
GEIA	Government Electronics and Information Technology Association
GSA	General Services Administration
GSAM	General Services Administration Acquisition Manual
GSAR	General Services Administration Acquisition Regulation
GSBCA	General Services Administration Board of Contract Appeals

HTS	Harmonized Tariff Schedule
IDIQ	indefinite-delivery/indefinite-quantity
IFF	industrial funding fee
IG	Inspector General
LTOP	Lease-To-Ownership Program
MAS	Multiple Award Schedule
NAICS	North American Industry Classification System
NASA	National Aeronautics and Space Administration
NFS	National Aeronautics and Space Administration FAR Supplement
OAP	Office of Acquisition Policy
OCI	organizational conflict of interest
OEM	original equipment manufacturer
OFCCP	Office of Federal Contract Compliance Programs
OFPP	Office of Federal Procurement Policy
OIG	Office of Inspector General
PIB	Procurement Information Bulletin
PBS	Public Buildings Service
PFCRA	Program Fraud Civil Remedies Act
PI	preliminary injunction
RCFC	Rules of the Court of Federal Claims
RFQ	Request for Quotation
ROI	return on investment
SBA	Small Business Administration
SCA	Service Contract Act
SDB	small disadvantaged business
SF	Standard Form
SIN	Special Item Number
TAA	Trade Agreements Act
TIN	Taxpayer Identification Number
TINA	Truth in Negotiations Act
TPA	Trading Partner Agreement
TRO	temporary restraining order
USPS	United States Postal Service
USTR	U.S. Trade Representative
VA	Department of Veterans Affairs

VAAR	VA Acquisition Regulation
VHCA	Veterans Health Care Act
VSC	Vendor Support Center
WOSB	Women-Owned Small Business

XXIX.

INDEX

(Some index terms may be found within the endnotes referenced on the stated page.)

A

O

Obstruction of justice 484
Office of Federal Procurement Policy 140
Office of Inspector General 9, 31, 34, 64, 71, 87, 91, 92, 124, 134, 169,
    185, 200, 373, 389, 404, 465, 532, 550, 624
Office Of Inspector General 81
Open Market 400, 407
Order fulfillment 383
Organizational conflicts of interest 337
Organizational Sentencing Guidelines 455

P

Packing/packaging 398
Parker, Chaney & Anderson 254, 582
Participating dealers 109
Past Performance Evaluation Report 131
Payment 390
Payments to influence federal transactions certification 213
Performance incentives 419
Perry, Anne 266
Pharmaceuticals 186, 195
Policies and procedures 550
Price Adjustment Clause 106, 107, 124, 133, 134, 139, 140, 141, 142,
    146, 166, 215, 326, 332, 333, 375, 394, 516, 586
Price analysis 153, 167
Price list 131
Price Reductions Clause 52, 69, 82, 91, 92, 93, 94, 95, 98, 100, 103,
    104, 107, 133, 134, 136, 138, 145, 146, 148, 157, 158, 161, 162,
    172, 173, 175, 176, 177, 181, 183, 186, 187, 188, 190, 192, 326,
    332, 354-382, 394, 395, 397, 442, 465, 466, 477, 501, 502, 503
Pricing 150
Procurement Information Bulletins 79, 575
Procurement Integrity 342
Program Fraud Civil Remedies Act 544

T

W

X

Printed in the United States
119434LV00002B/205/A

9 781425 709235